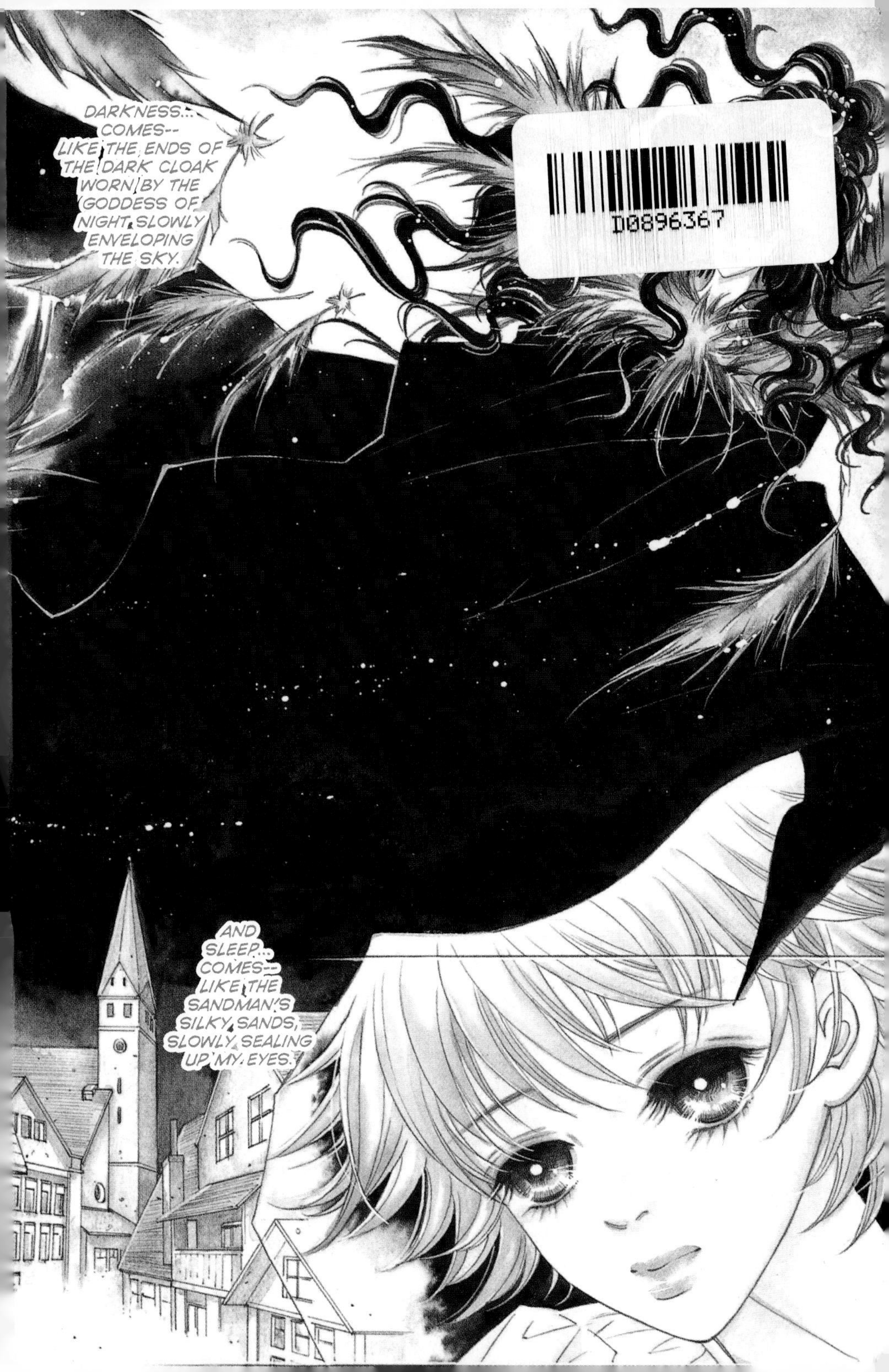
DARKNESS... COMES-- LIKE THE ENDS OF THE DARK CLOAK WORN BY THE GODDESS OF NIGHT, SLOWLY ENVELOPING THE SKY.
D0896367
AND SLEEP... COMES-- LIKE THE SANDMAN'S SILKY SANDS, SLOWLY SEALING UP MY EYES.

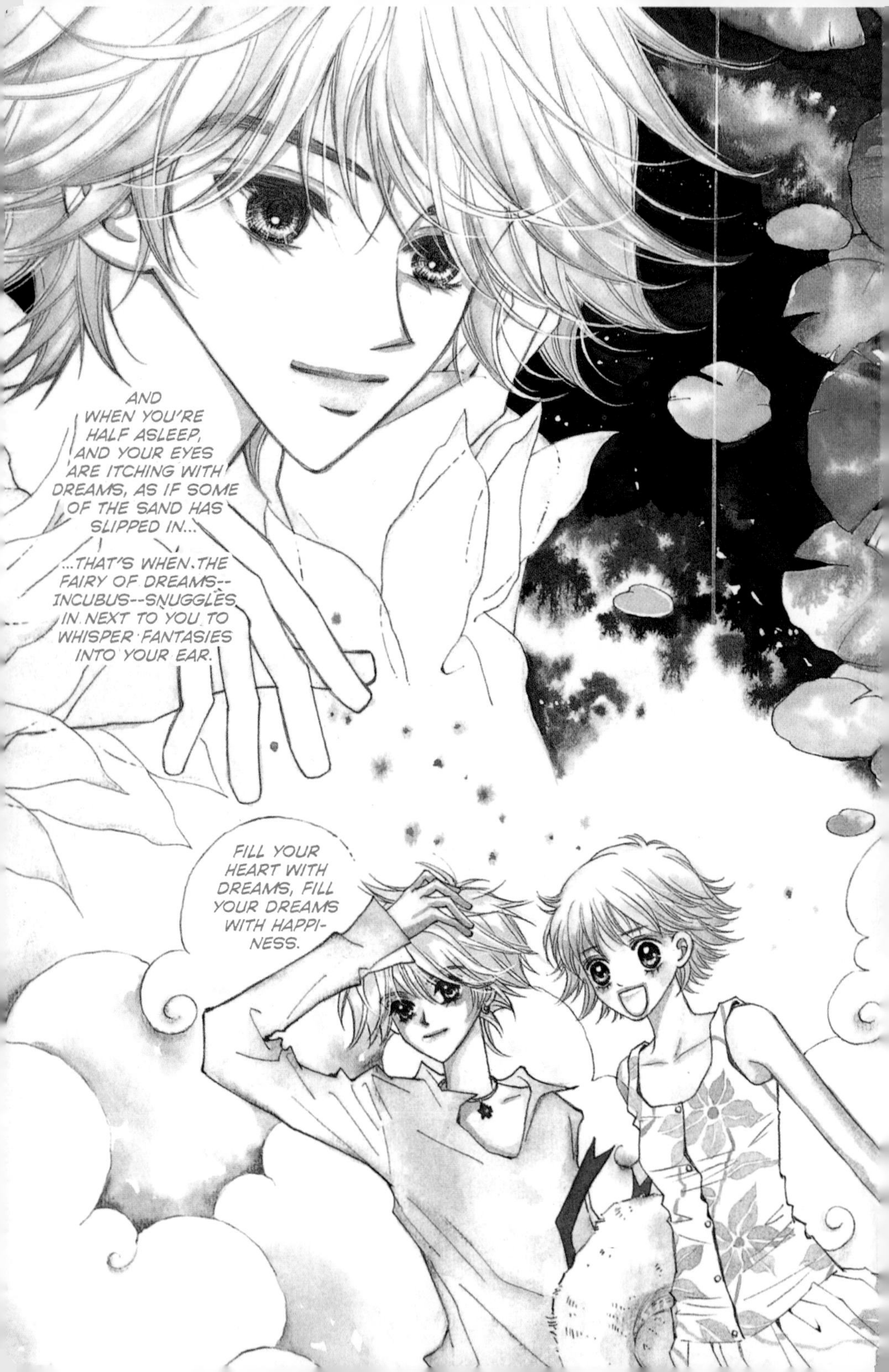
AND WHEN YOU'RE HALF ASLEEP, AND YOUR EYES ARE ITCHING WITH DREAMS, AS IF SOME OF THE SAND HAS SLIPPED IN...
...THAT'S WHEN THE FAIRY OF DREAMS--INCUBUS--SNUGGLES IN NEXT TO YOU TO WHISPER FANTASIES INTO YOUR EAR.
FILL YOUR HEART WITH DREAMS, FILL YOUR DREAMS WITH HAPPI-NESS.

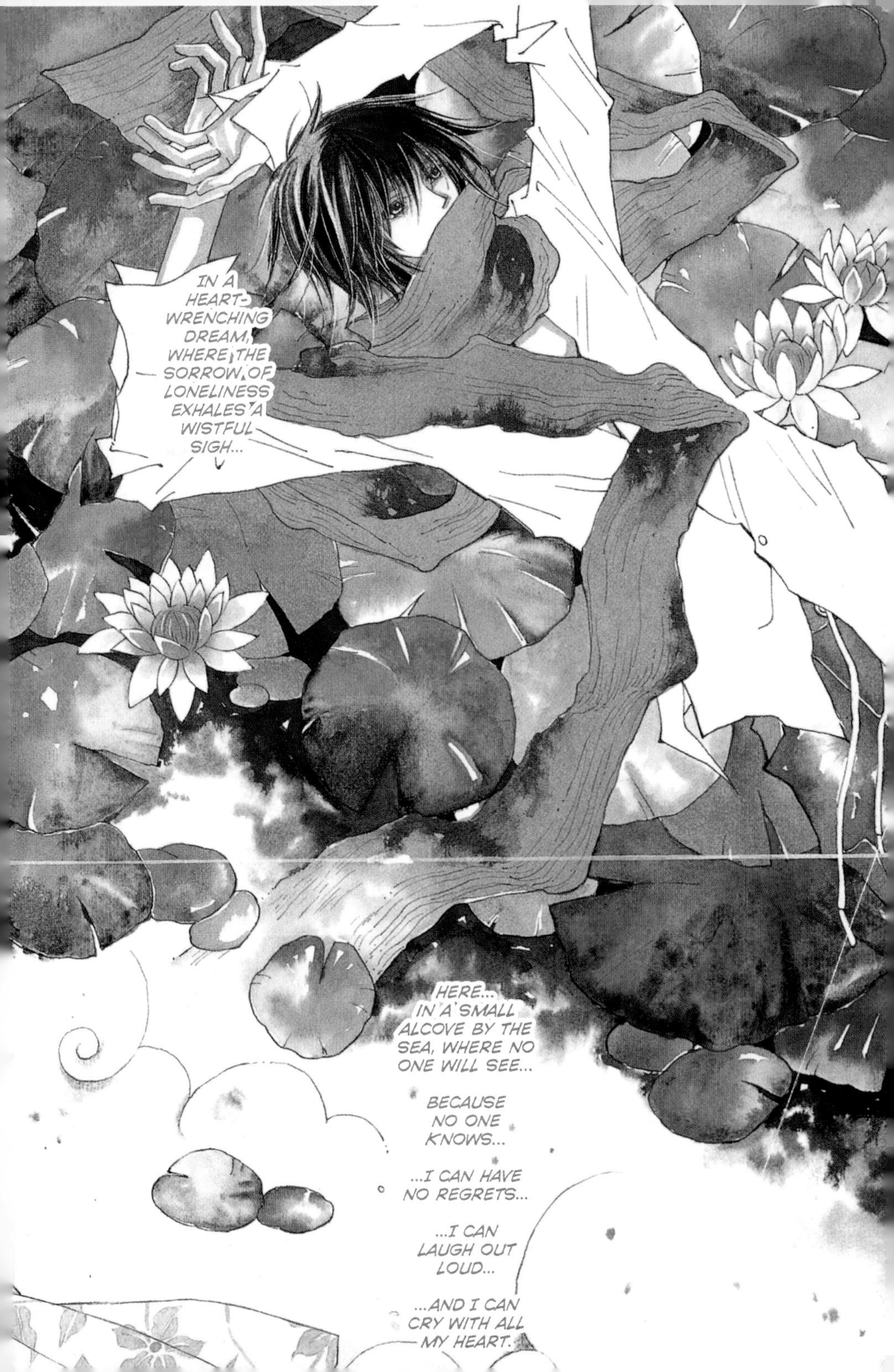
IN A HEART-WRENCHING DREAM, WHERE THE SORROW OF LONELINESS EXHALES A WISTFUL SIGH...
HERE... IN A SMALL ALCOVE BY THE SEA, WHERE NO ONE WILL SEE...
BECAUSE NO ONE KNOWS...
...I CAN HAVE NO REGRETS...
...I CAN LAUGH OUT LOUD...
...AND I CAN CRY WITH ALL MY HEART.

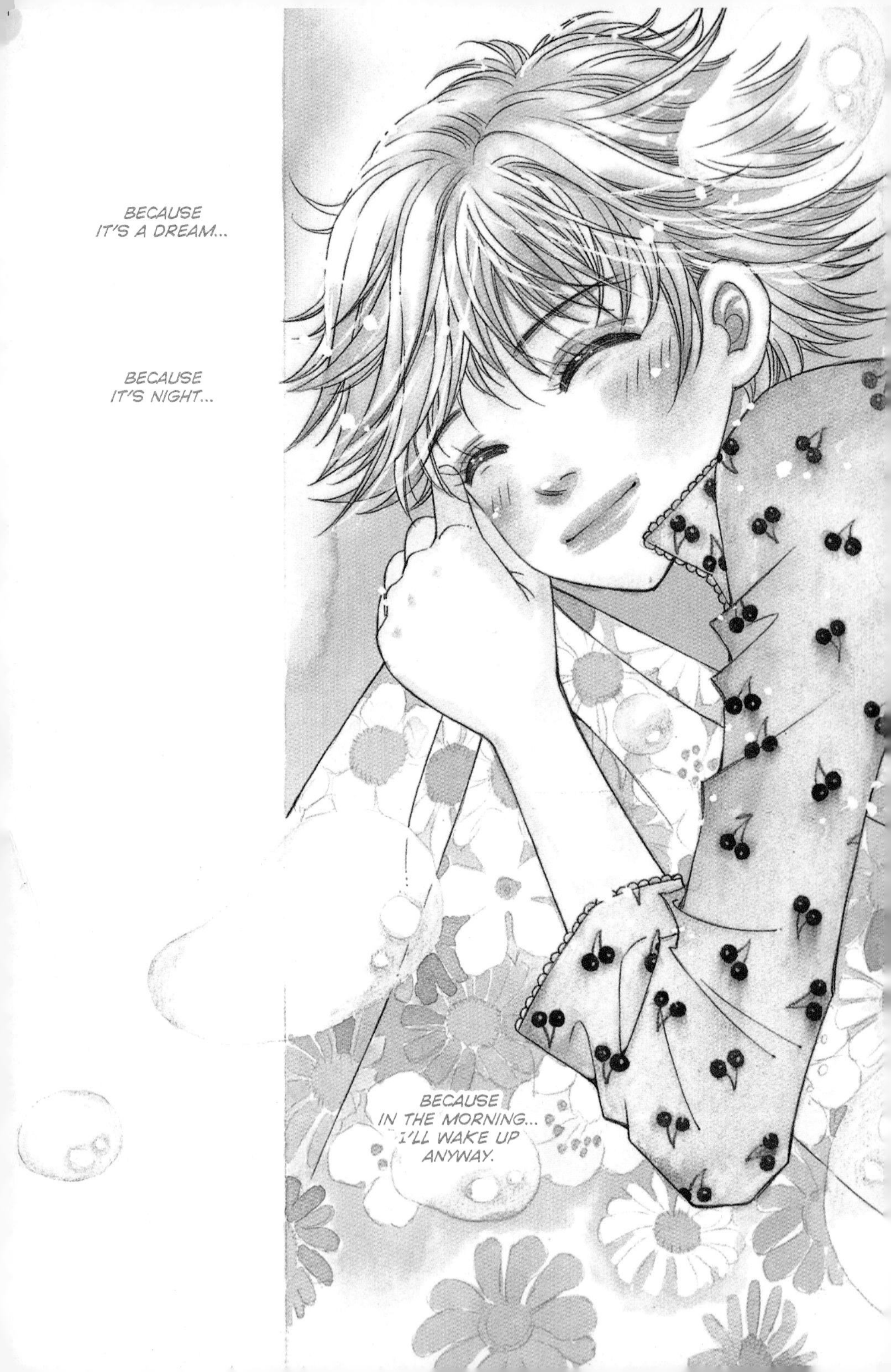
BECAUSE IT'S A DREAM...
BECAUSE IT'S NIGHT...
BECAUSE IN THE MORNING... I'LL WAKE UP ANYWAY.

CHOCOLAT

vol. 5

Shin JiSang · Geo

Yen
Press

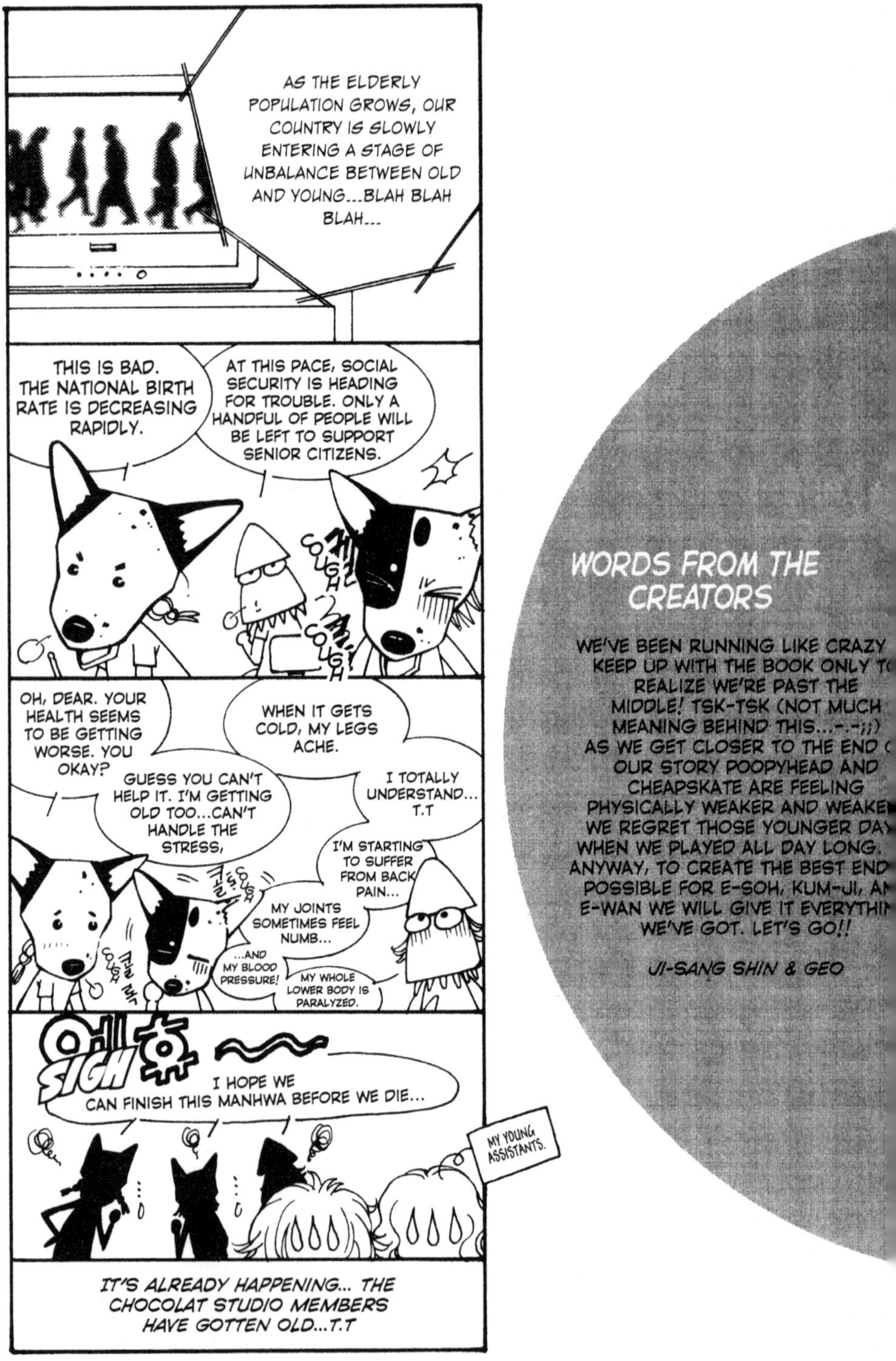
AS THE ELDERLY POPULATION GROWS, OUR COUNTRY IS SLOWLY ENTERING A STAGE OF UNBALANCE BETWEEN OLD AND YOUNG...BLAH BLAH BLAH...
THIS IS BAD. THE NATIONAL BIRTH RATE IS DECREASING RAPIDLY.
AT THIS PACE, SOCIAL SECURITY IS HEADING FOR TROUBLE. ONLY A HANDFUL OF PEOPLE WILL BE LEFT TO SUPPORT SENIOR CITIZENS.
COUGH
COUGH
OH, DEAR. YOUR HEALTH SEEMS TO BE GETTING WORSE. YOU OKAY?
WHEN IT GETS COLD, MY LEGS ACHE.
GUESS YOU CAN'T HELP IT. I'M GETTING OLD TOO...CAN'T HANDLE THE STRESS,
I TOTALLY UNDERSTAND... T.T
I'M STARTING TO SUFFER FROM BACK PAIN...
COUGH
MY JOINTS SOMETIMES FEEL NUMB...
...AND MY BLOOD PRESSURE!
MY WHOLE LOWER BODY IS PARALYZED.
COUGH
SIGH
I HOPE WE CAN FINISH THIS MANHWA BEFORE WE DIE...
MY YOUNG ASSISTANTS.
IT'S ALREADY HAPPENING... THE CHOCOLAT STUDIO MEMBERS HAVE GOTTEN OLD...T.T

WORDS FROM THE CREATORS

WE'VE BEEN RUNNING LIKE CRAZY KEEP UP WITH THE BOOK ONLY T REALIZE WE'RE PAST THE MIDDLE! TSK-TSK (NOT MUCH MEANING BEHIND THIS...-.-;;) AS WE GET CLOSER TO THE END OUR STORY POOPYHEAD AND CHEAPSKATE ARE FEELING PHYSICALLY WEAKER AND WEAKE WE REGRET THOSE YOUNGER DAY WHEN WE PLAYED ALL DAY LONG. ANYWAY, TO CREATE THE BEST END POSSIBLE FOR E-SOH, KUM-JI, A E-WAN WE WILL GIVE IT EVERYTHI WE'VE GOT. LET'S GO!!

JI-SANG SHIN & GEO

A QUICK Q&A WITH JI-SANG SHIN AND GEO

HOW DO YOU DO YOUR RESEARCH FOR <CHOCOLAT>?

THROUGH PERSONAL EXPERIENCES, FAN SITES, AND TV SHOWS, ETC. (WE WATCH ENTERTAINMENT SHOWS AND MUSIC SHOWS ALL THE TIME BECAUSE WE LOVE THEM.)

HOW DO YOU COME UP WITH A STORY FOR <CHOCOLAT> EACH MONTH?

WHEN THE DUE DATE GETS CLOSE, AH-TA MOM GLARES AT CHE-CHE MOM. ▶ AH-TA MOM SCOLDS CHE-CHE MOM. ▶ AH-TA MOM GETS ANGRY AT CHE-CHE MOM. ▶ THEN A STORY FALLS FROM SKY.

WHAT HAS BEEN THE HAPPIEST AND THE HARDEST THING ABOUT WORKING ON <CHOCOLAT>?

JI-SANG SHIN: I WAS SO HAPPY TO MEET THIS ONE FAN WHO CAME TO SEOUL TO SEE US ALL THE WAY FROM PUSAN. ^o^

OUR EDITOR IS DIFFICULT TO DEAL WITH WHEN OUR WORK IS LATE...

GEO: I'M ALWAYS HAPPY, BUT I ALSO HAVE A HARD TIME ALL THE TIME.

WHAT ARE YOUR HOBBIES?

JI-SANG SHIN: COOKING, EATING, AND DOING NOTHING AT HOME.

GEO: BOTHERING JI-SANG AS SHE ENJOYS HER HOBBIES.

WHAT THINGS HAVE CHANGED SINCE YOU STARTED WORKING ON <CHOCOLAT>?

JI-SANG SHIN: THE DEADLINE OF <CHOCOLAT> IS THE CENTER OF MY LIFE EVERY MONTH. (SADLY, I HAVE NO OTHER PLANS OR LIFE.)

GEO: I GROW OLD SO FAST AND GET EXTREMELY LAZY.

ANY FINAL WORDS TO YOUR READERS?

YOU'LL READ <CHOCOLAT> UNTIL THE LAST VOLUME, RIGHT?

YOU KNOW HOW THANKFUL WE ARE THAT YOU LOVE <CHOCOLAT>, RIGHT?

YOU'LL STAY HAPPY, WON'T YOU?

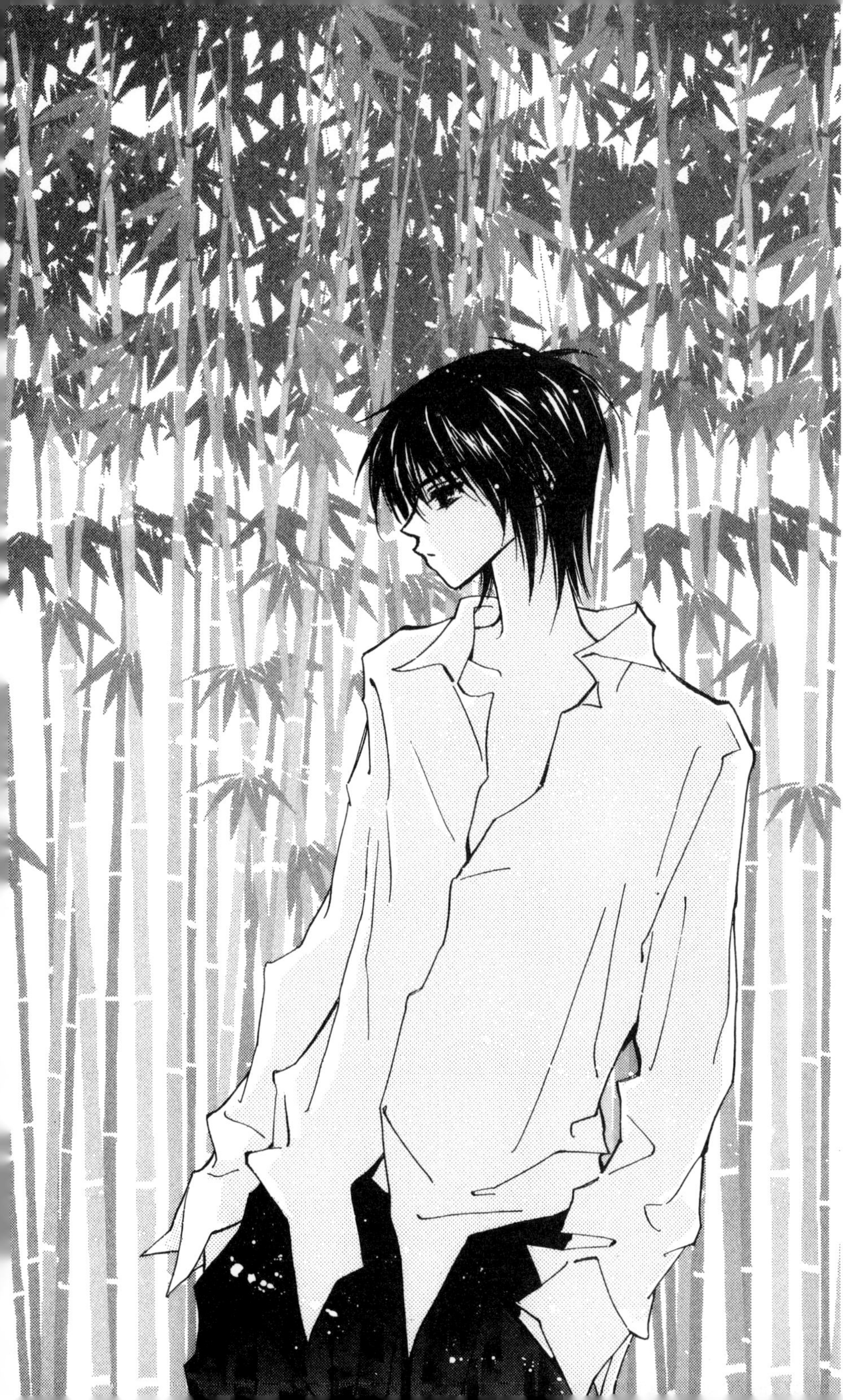

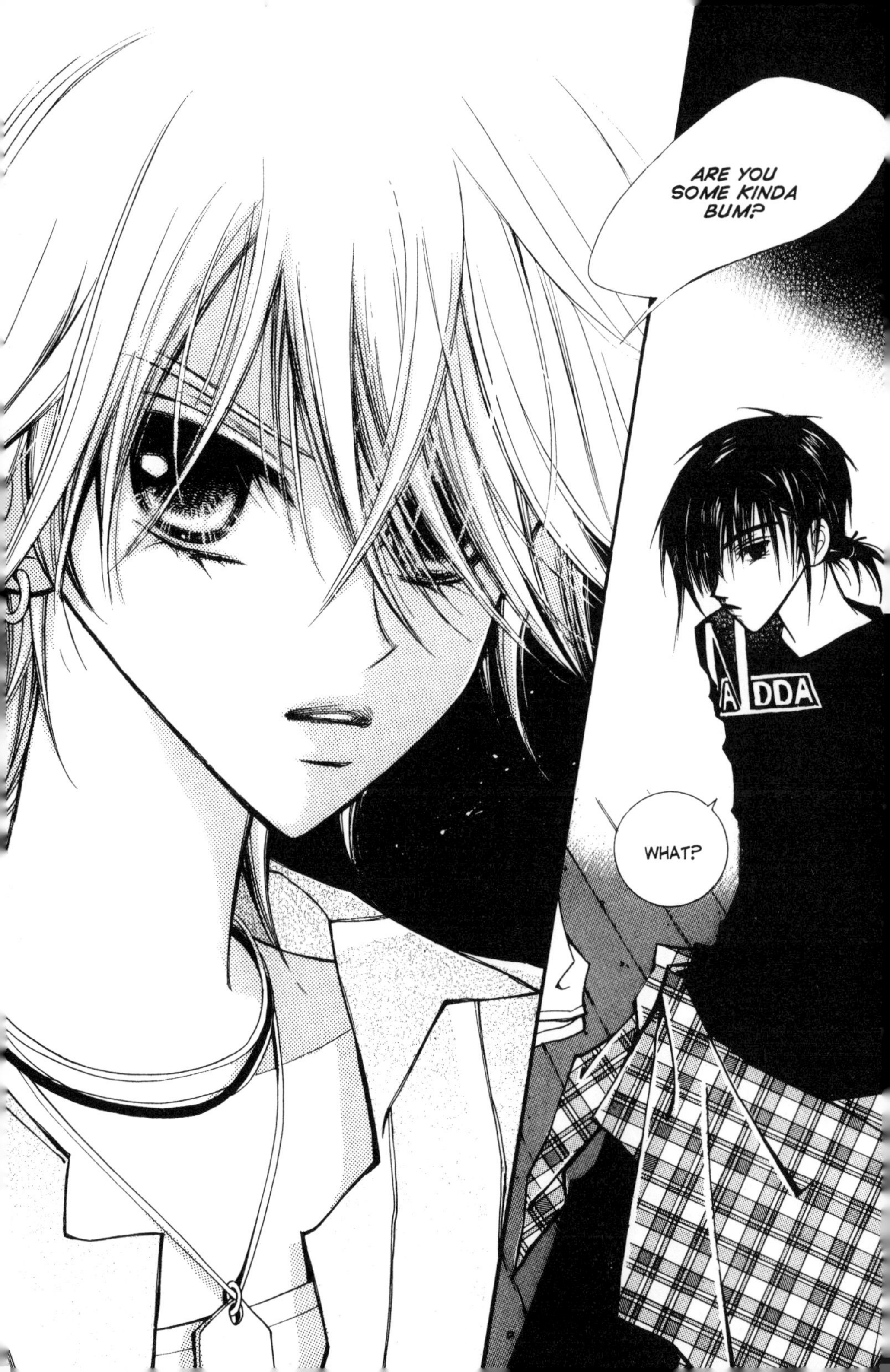
ARE YOU SOME KINDA BUM?
WHAT?
ADDA

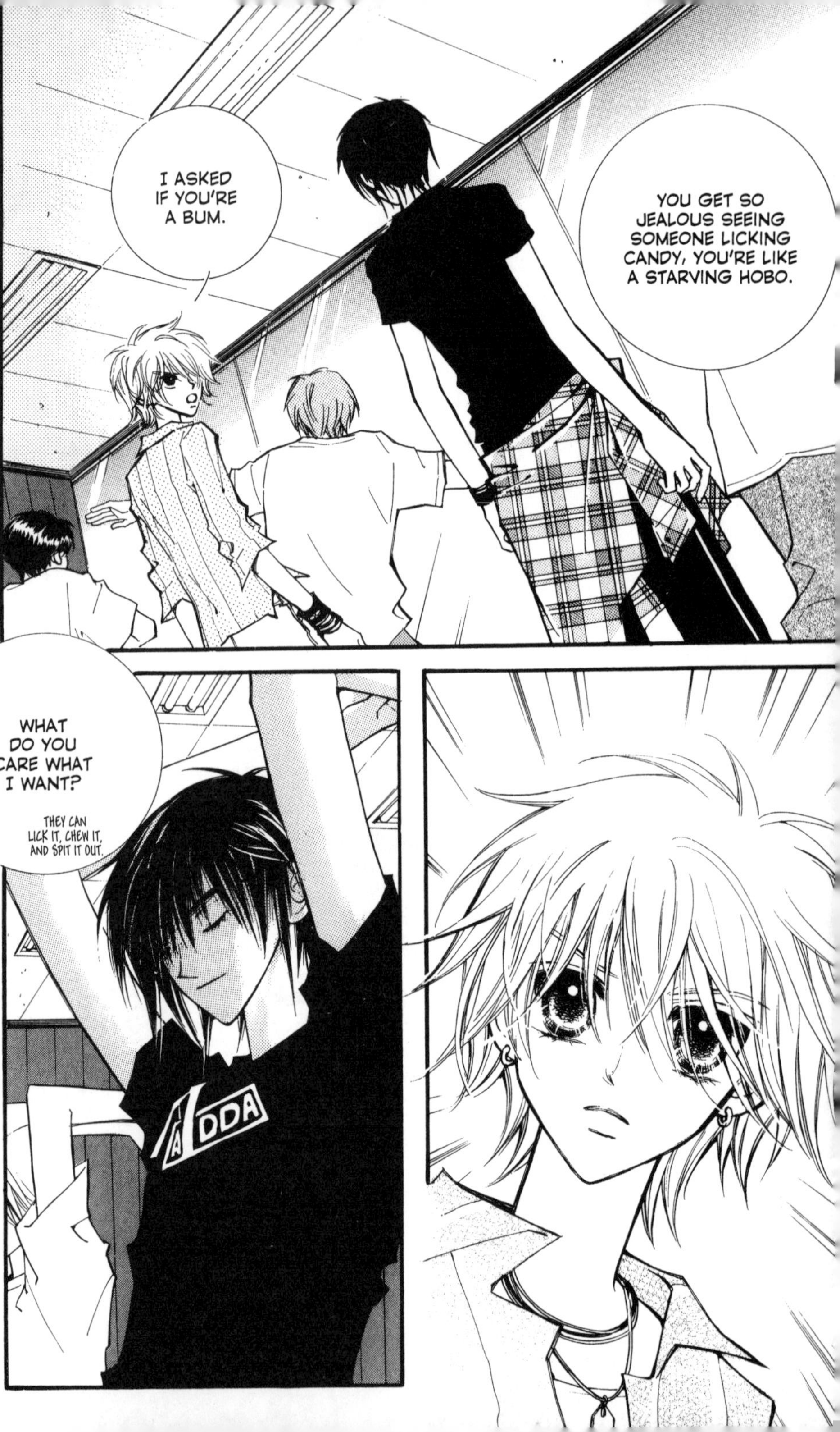
I ASKED IF YOU'RE A BUM.
YOU GET SO JEALOUS SEEING SOMEONE LICKING CANDY, YOU'RE LIKE A STARVING HOBO.
WHAT DO YOU CARE WHAT I WANT?
THEY CAN LICK IT, CHEW IT, AND SPIT IT OUT.

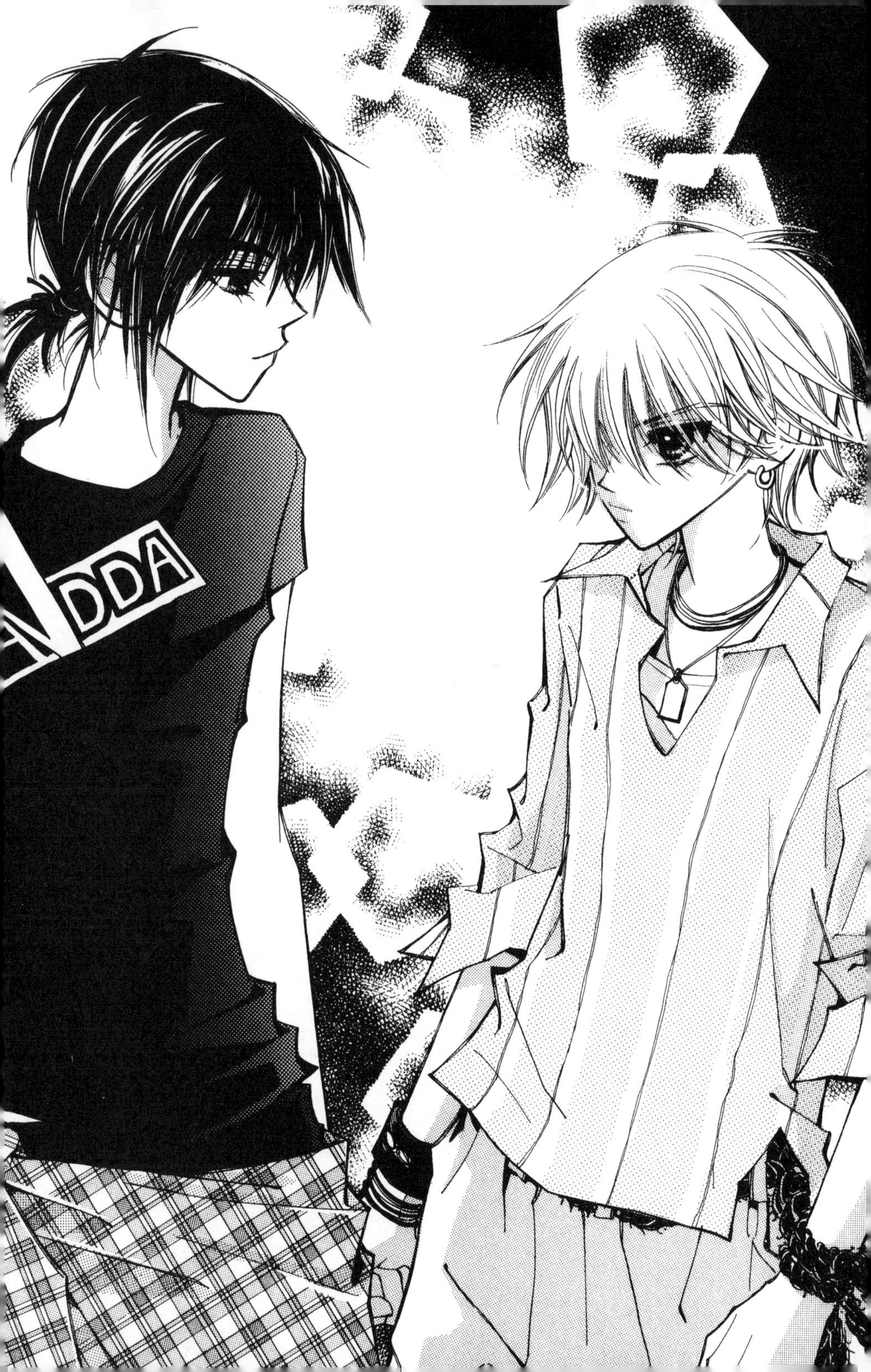
DDA

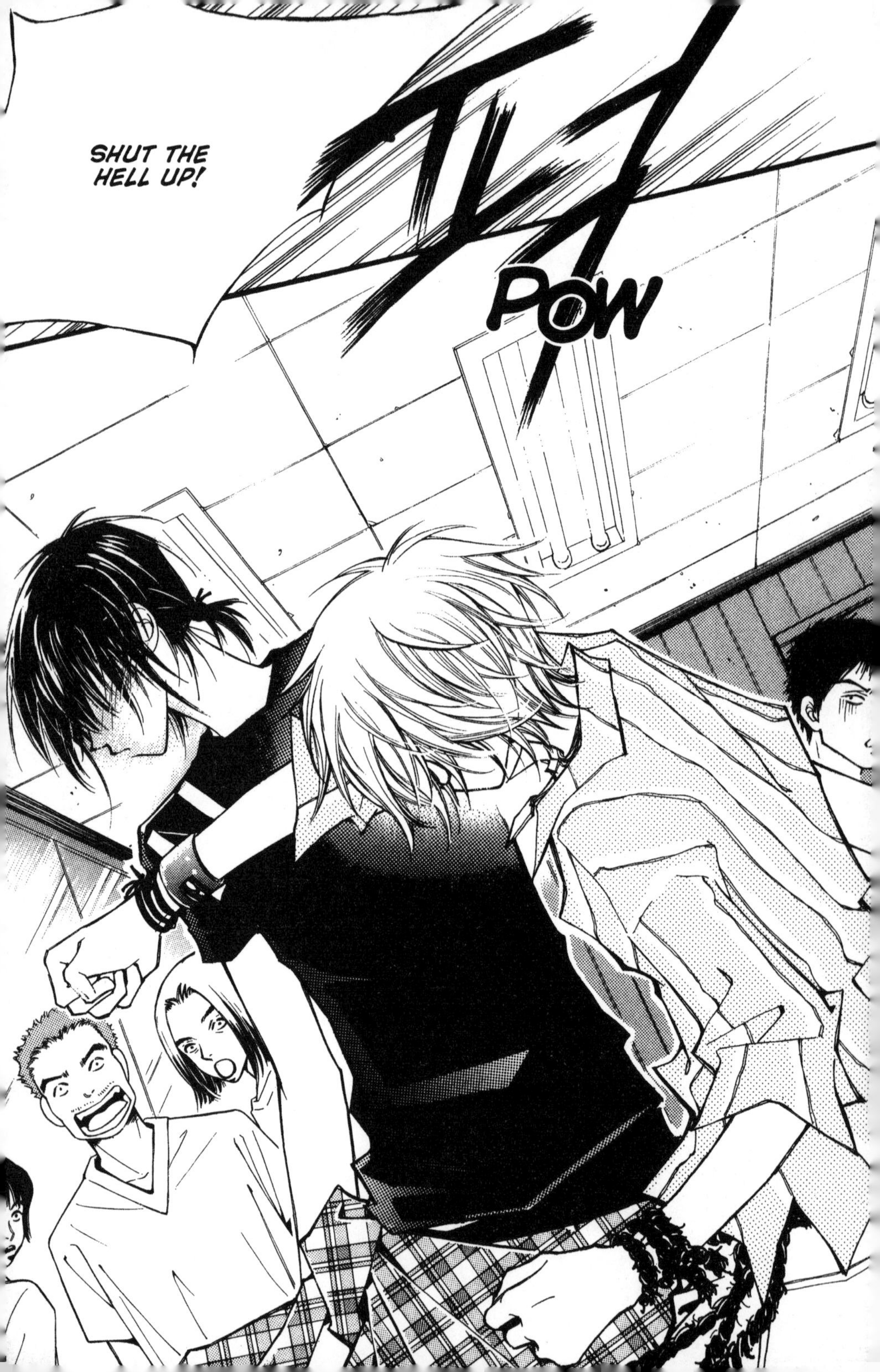
SHUT THE HELL UP!
POW

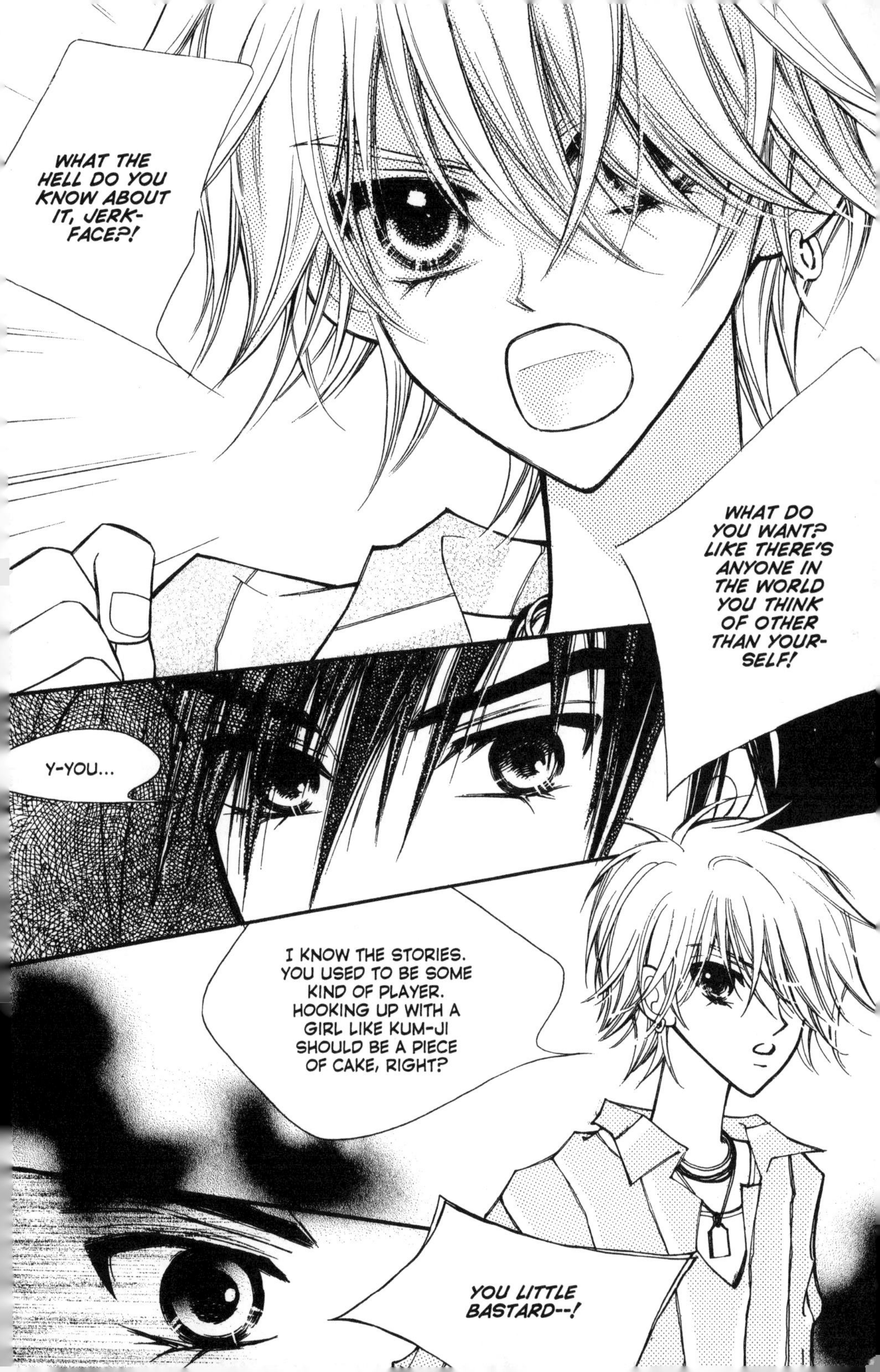
WHAT THE HELL DO YOU KNOW ABOUT IT, JERK-FACE?!
WHAT DO YOU WANT? LIKE THERE'S ANYONE IN THE WORLD YOU THINK OF OTHER THAN YOUR-SELF!
Y-YOU...
I KNOW THE STORIES. YOU USED TO BE SOME KIND OF PLAYER. HOOKING UP WITH A GIRL LIKE KUM-JI SHOULD BE A PIECE OF CAKE, RIGHT?
YOU LITTLE BASTARD--!

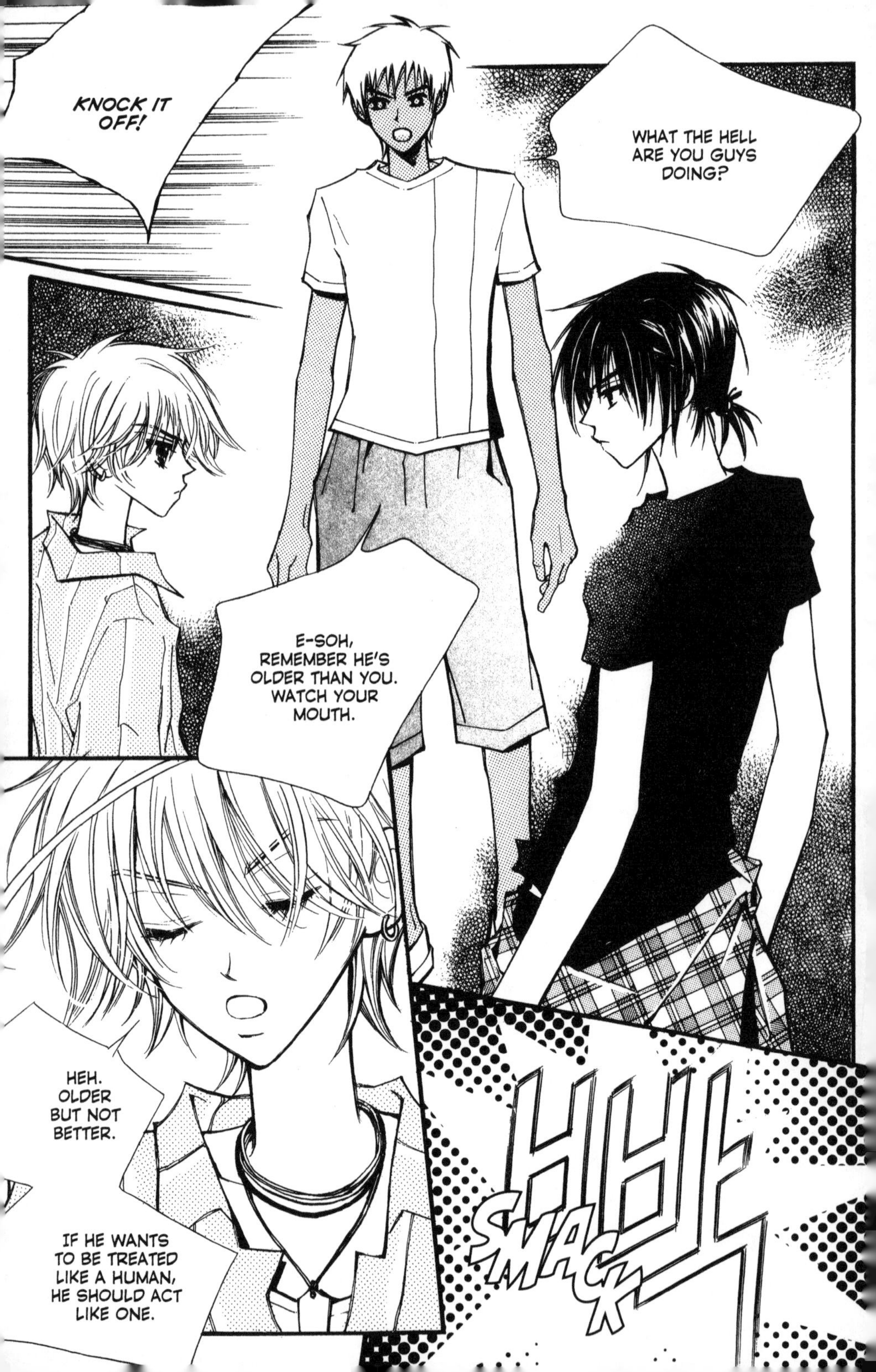
KNOCK IT OFF!
WHAT THE HELL ARE YOU GUYS DOING?
E-SOH, REMEMBER HE'S OLDER THAN YOU. WATCH YOUR MOUTH.
HEH. OLDER BUT NOT BETTER.
IF HE WANTS TO BE TREATED LIKE A HUMAN, HE SHOULD ACT LIKE ONE.
SMACK

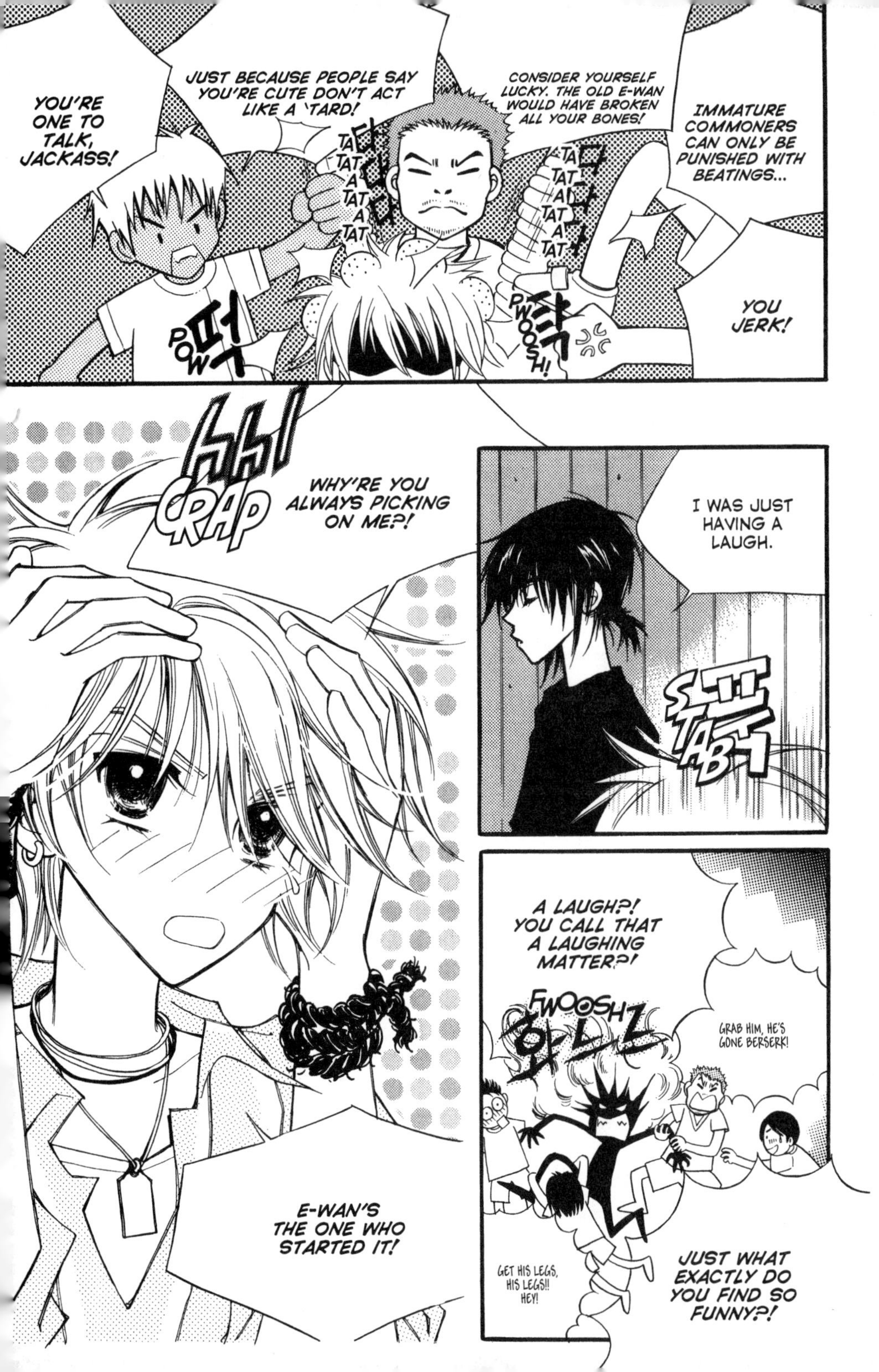

YOU'RE ONE TO TALK, JACKASS!
JUST BECAUSE PEOPLE SAY YOU'RE CUTE DON'T ACT LIKE A 'TARD!
TA TAT A TAT A TAT
POW
CONSIDER YOURSELF LUCKY. THE OLD E-WAN WOULD HAVE BROKEN ALL YOUR BONES!
TA TAT A TAT A TAT
PWOOSH!
IMMATURE COMMONERS CAN ONLY BE PUNISHED WITH BEATINGS...
YOU JERK!
CRAP
WHY'RE YOU ALWAYS PICKING ON ME?!
E-WAN'S THE ONE WHO STARTED IT!
I WAS JUST HAVING A LAUGH.
A LAUGH?! YOU CALL THAT A LAUGHING MATTER?!
FWOOSH
GRAB HIM, HE'S GONE BERSERK!
GET HIS LEGS, HIS LEGS!! HEY!
JUST WHAT EXACTLY DO YOU FIND SO FUNNY?!

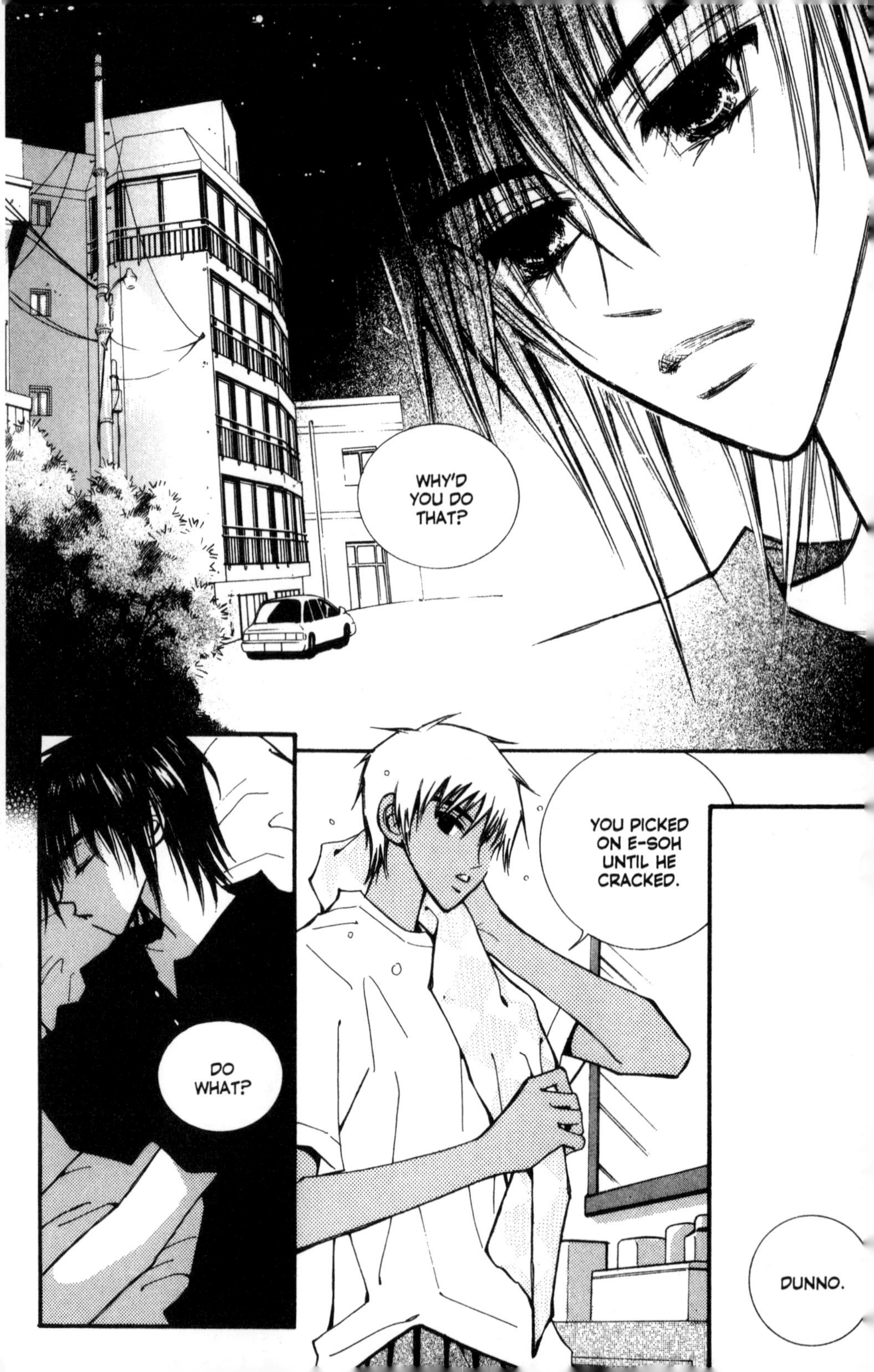
WHY'D YOU DO THAT?
DO WHAT?
YOU PICKED ON E-SOH UNTIL HE CRACKED.
DUNNO.

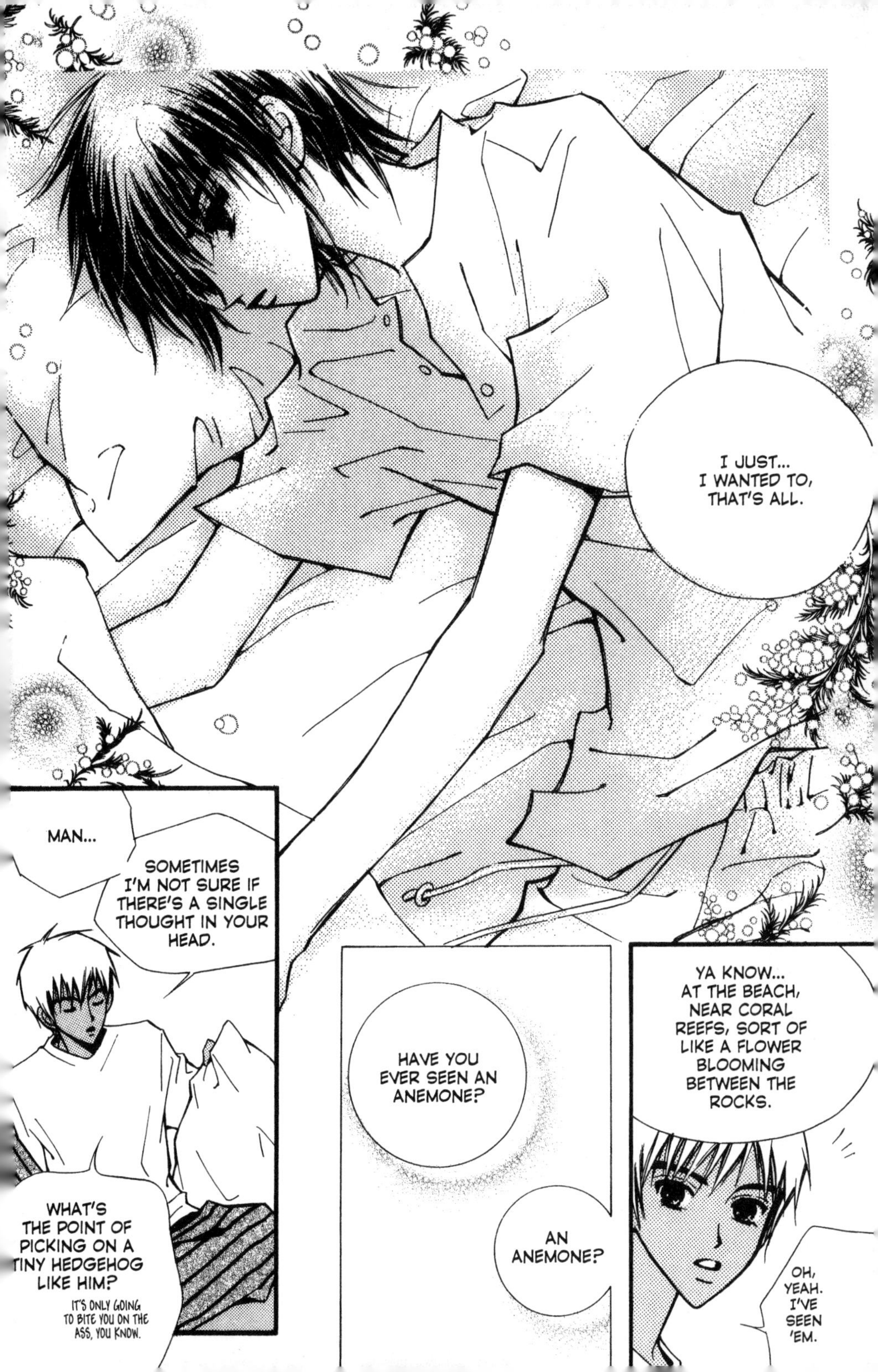
I JUST... I WANTED TO, THAT'S ALL.
MAN...
SOMETIMES I'M NOT SURE IF THERE'S A SINGLE THOUGHT IN YOUR HEAD.
WHAT'S THE POINT OF PICKING ON A TINY HEDGEHOG LIKE HIM?
IT'S ONLY GOING TO BITE YOU ON THE ASS, YOU KNOW.
HAVE YOU EVER SEEN AN ANEMONE?
AN ANEMONE?
YA KNOW... AT THE BEACH, NEAR CORAL REEFS, SORT OF LIKE A FLOWER BLOOMING BETWEEN THE ROCKS.
OH, YEAH. I'VE SEEN 'EM.

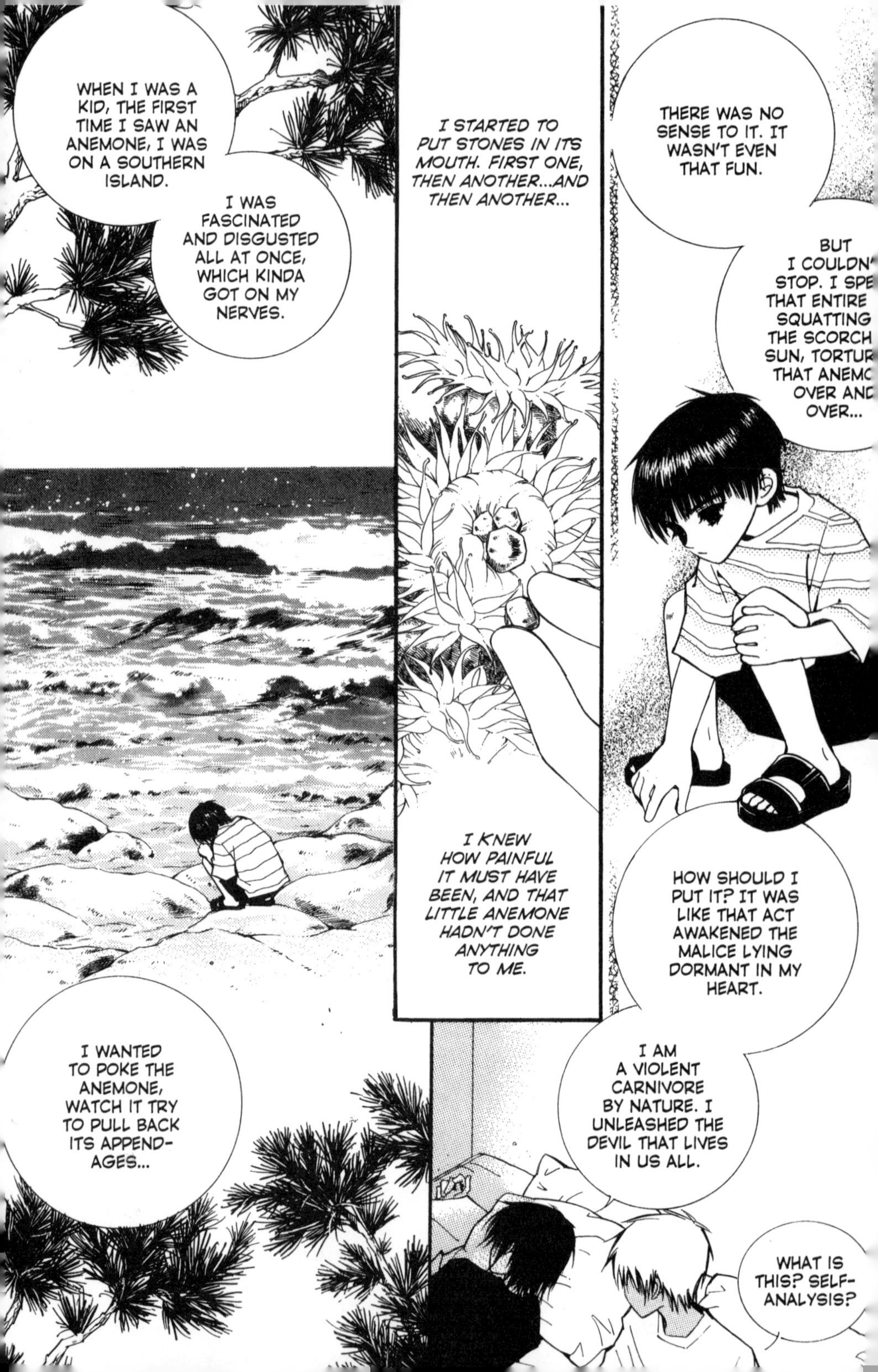
WHEN I WAS A KID, THE FIRST TIME I SAW AN ANEMONE, I WAS ON A SOUTHERN ISLAND.
I WAS FASCINATED AND DISGUSTED ALL AT ONCE, WHICH KINDA GOT ON MY NERVES.
I WANTED TO POKE THE ANEMONE, WATCH IT TRY TO PULL BACK ITS APPEND-AGES...
I STARTED TO PUT STONES IN ITS MOUTH. FIRST ONE, THEN ANOTHER...AND THEN ANOTHER...
I KNEW HOW PAINFUL IT MUST HAVE BEEN, AND THAT LITTLE ANEMONE HADN'T DONE ANYTHING TO ME.
THERE WAS NO SENSE TO IT. IT WASN'T EVEN THAT FUN.
BUT I COULDN' STOP. I SPE THAT ENTIRE SQUATTING THE SCORCH SUN, TORTUR THAT ANEMO OVER AND OVER...
HOW SHOULD I PUT IT? IT WAS LIKE THAT ACT AWAKENED THE MALICE LYING DORMANT IN MY HEART.
I AM A VIOLENT CARNIVORE BY NATURE. I UNLEASHED THE DEVIL THAT LIVES IN US ALL.
WHAT IS THIS? SELF-ANALYSIS?

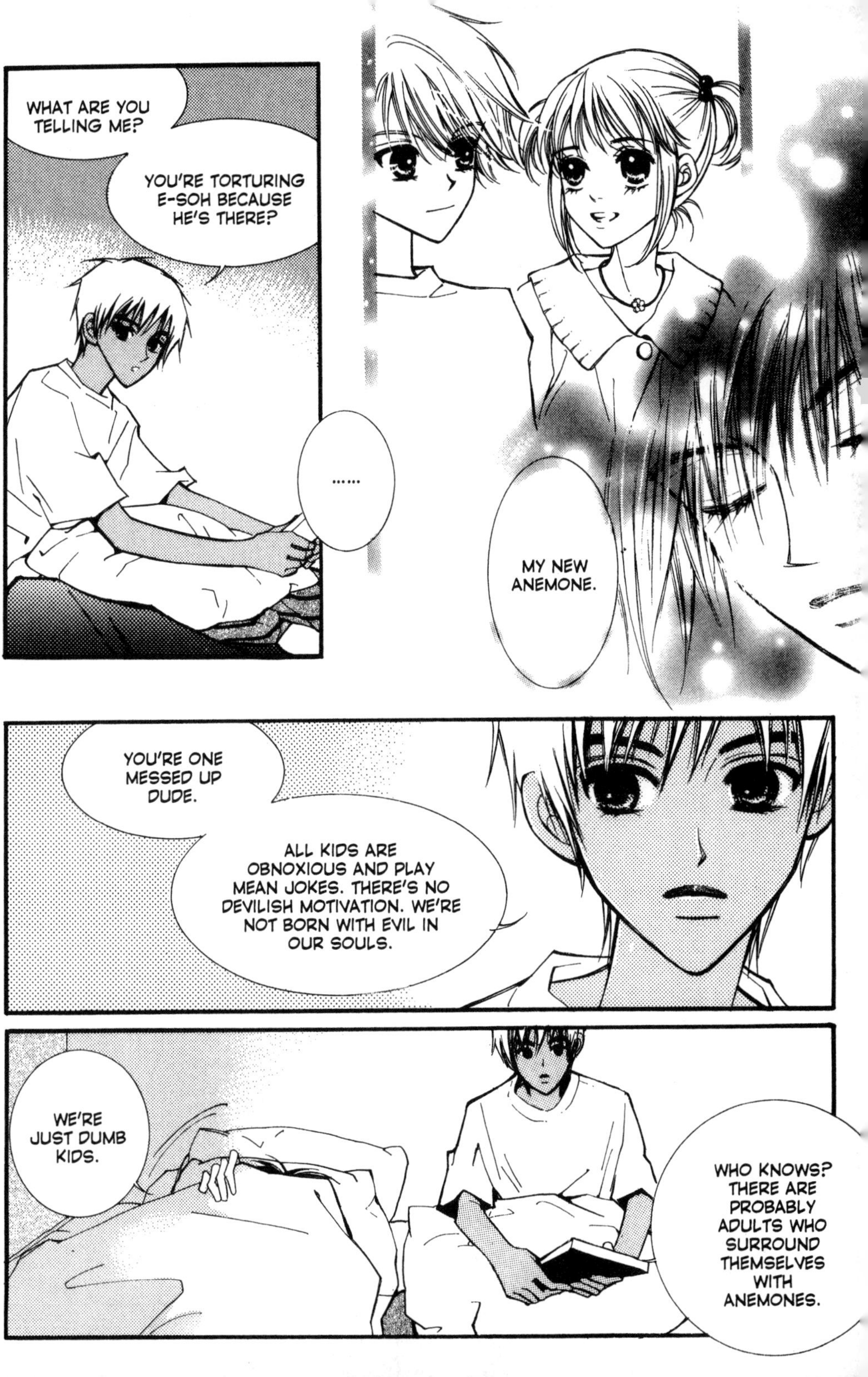
WHAT ARE YOU TELLING ME?
YOU'RE TORTURING E-SOH BECAUSE HE'S THERE?
......
MY NEW ANEMONE.
YOU'RE ONE MESSED UP DUDE.
ALL KIDS ARE OBNOXIOUS AND PLAY MEAN JOKES. THERE'S NO DEVILISH MOTIVATION. WE'RE NOT BORN WITH EVIL IN OUR SOULS.
WE'RE JUST DUMB KIDS.
WHO KNOWS? THERE ARE PROBABLY ADULTS WHO SURROUND THEMSELVES WITH ANEMONES.

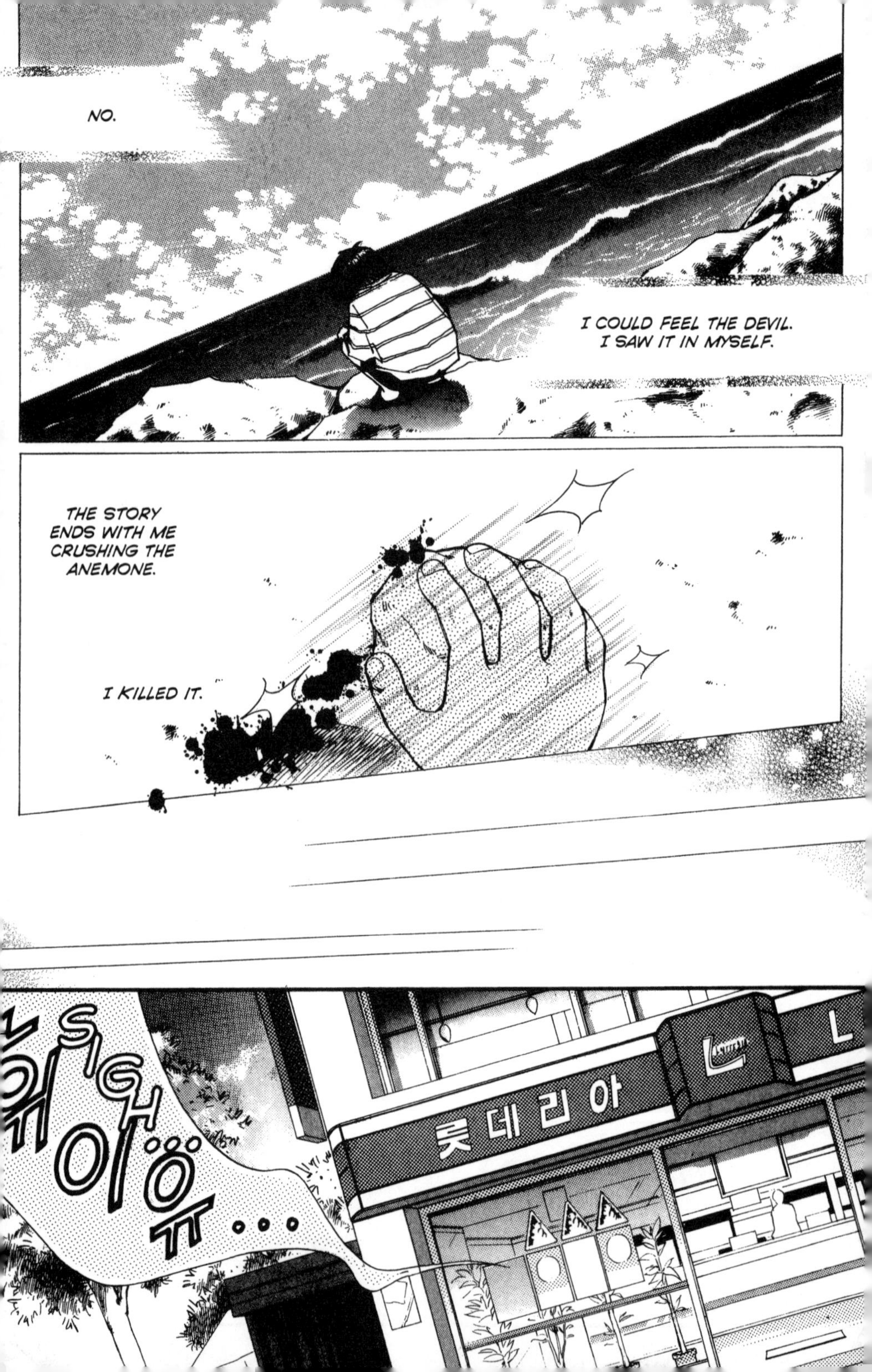
NO.
I COULD FEEL THE DEVIL.
I SAW IT IN MYSELF.
THE STORY ENDS WITH ME CRUSHING THE ANEMONE.
I KILLED IT.
SIGH...
롯데리아
L

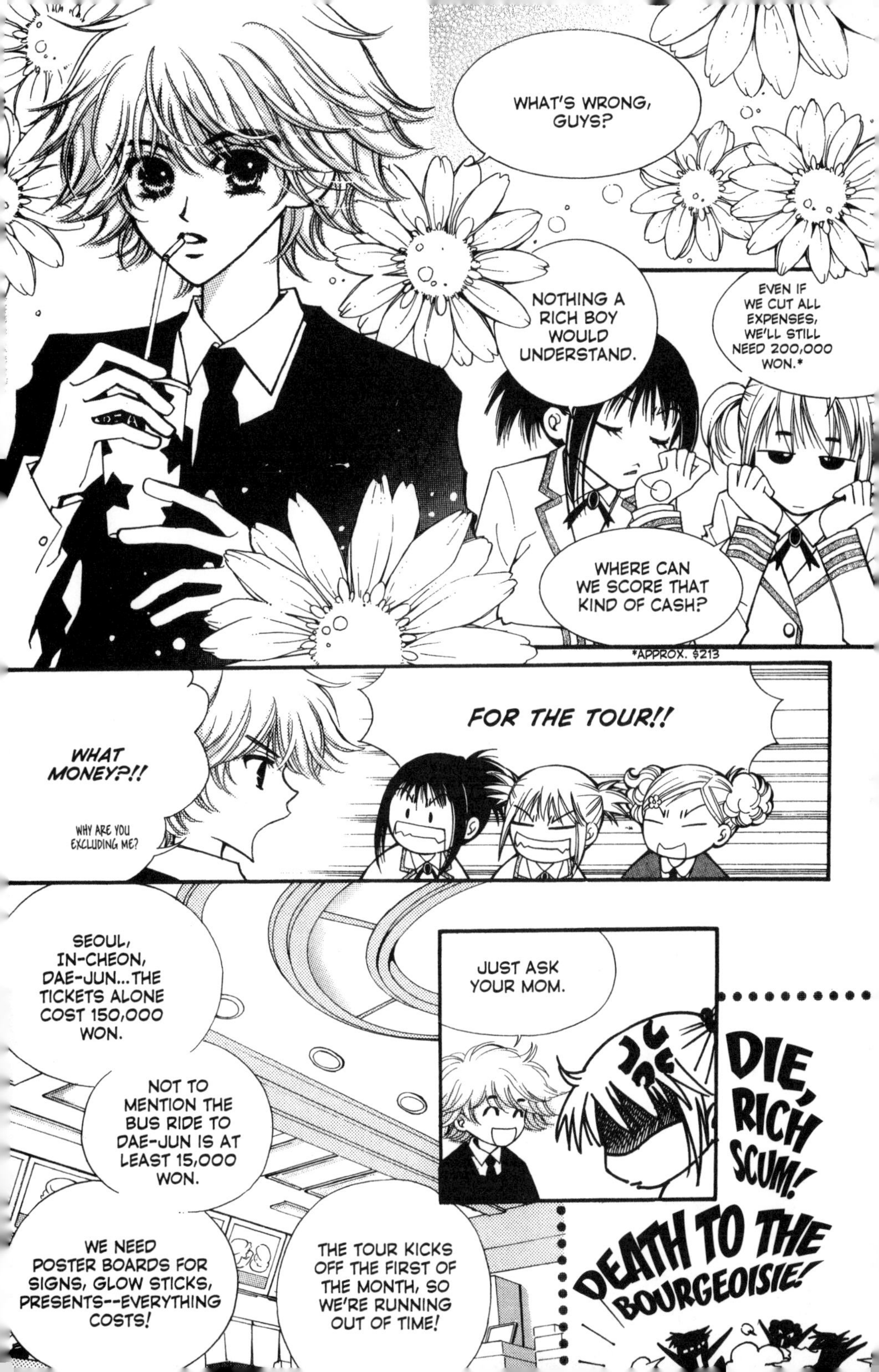
WHAT'S WRONG, GUYS?
NOTHING A RICH BOY WOULD UNDERSTAND.
EVEN IF WE CUT ALL EXPENSES, WE'LL STILL NEED 200,000 WON.*
WHERE CAN WE SCORE THAT KIND OF CASH?
*APPROX. $213
WHAT MONEY?!!
WHY ARE YOU EXCLUDING ME?
FOR THE TOUR!!
SEOUL, IN-CHEON, DAE-JUN...THE TICKETS ALONE COST 150,000 WON.
NOT TO MENTION THE BUS RIDE TO DAE-JUN IS AT LEAST 15,000 WON.
WE NEED POSTER BOARDS FOR SIGNS, GLOW STICKS, PRESENTS--EVERYTHING COSTS!
THE TOUR KICKS OFF THE FIRST OF THE MONTH, SO WE'RE RUNNING OUT OF TIME!
JUST ASK YOUR MOM.
DIE, RICH SCUM!
DEATH TO THE BOURGEOISIE!

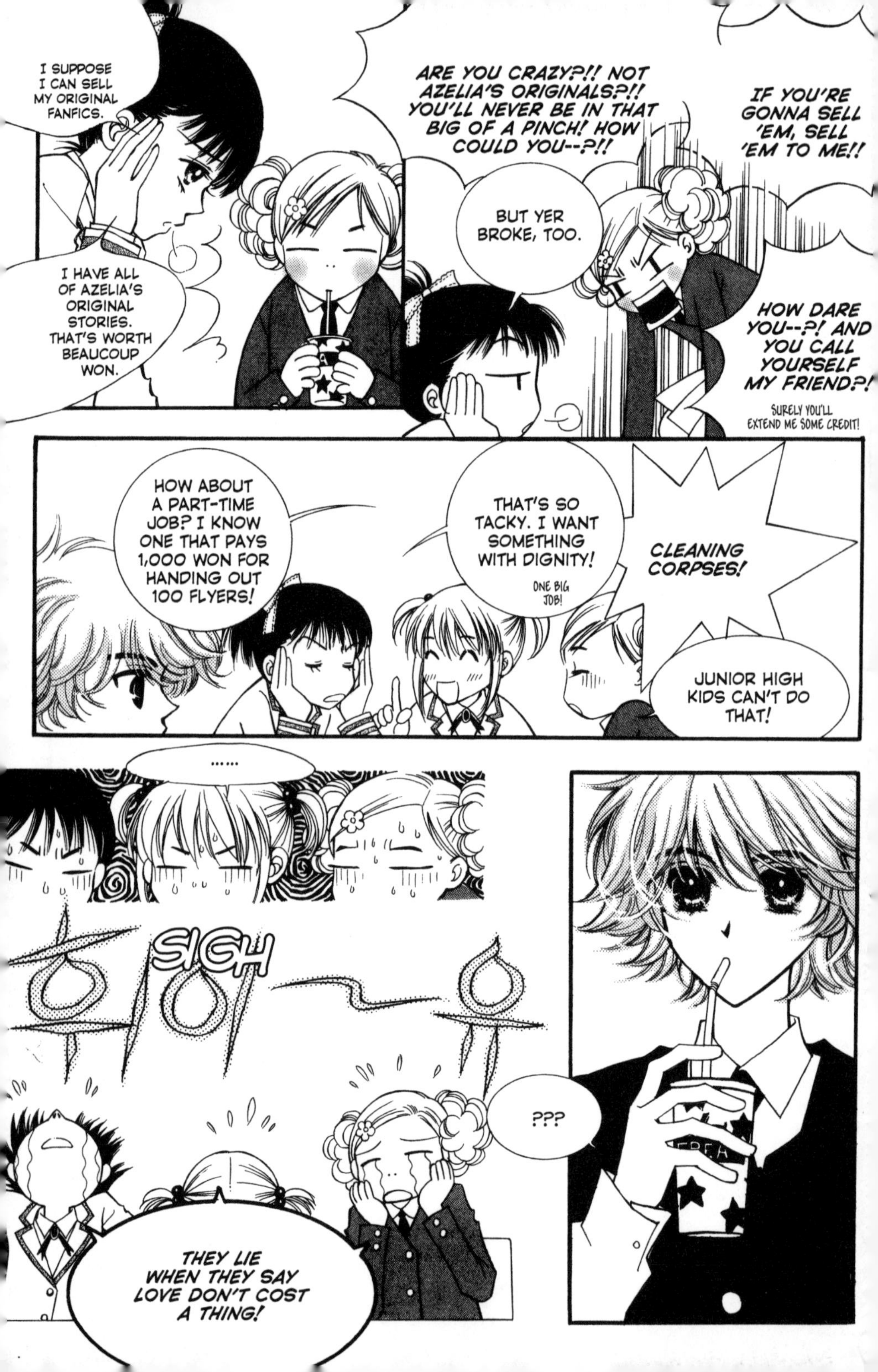
I SUPPOSE I CAN SELL MY ORIGINAL FANFICS.
I HAVE ALL OF AZELIA'S ORIGINAL STORIES. THAT'S WORTH BEAUCOUP WON.
ARE YOU CRAZY?!! NOT AZELIA'S ORIGINALS?!! YOU'LL NEVER BE IN THAT BIG OF A PINCH! HOW COULD YOU--?!!
IF YOU'RE GONNA SELL 'EM, SELL 'EM TO ME!!
BUT YER BROKE, TOO.
HOW DARE YOU--?! AND YOU CALL YOURSELF MY FRIEND?!
SURELY YOU'LL EXTEND ME SOME CREDIT!
HOW ABOUT A PART-TIME JOB? I KNOW ONE THAT PAYS 1,000 WON FOR HANDING OUT 100 FLYERS!
THAT'S SO TACKY. I WANT SOMETHING WITH DIGNITY!
ONE BIG JOB!
CLEANING CORPSES!
JUNIOR HIGH KIDS CAN'T DO THAT!
......
SIGH
???
THEY LIE WHEN THEY SAY LOVE DON'T COST A THING!

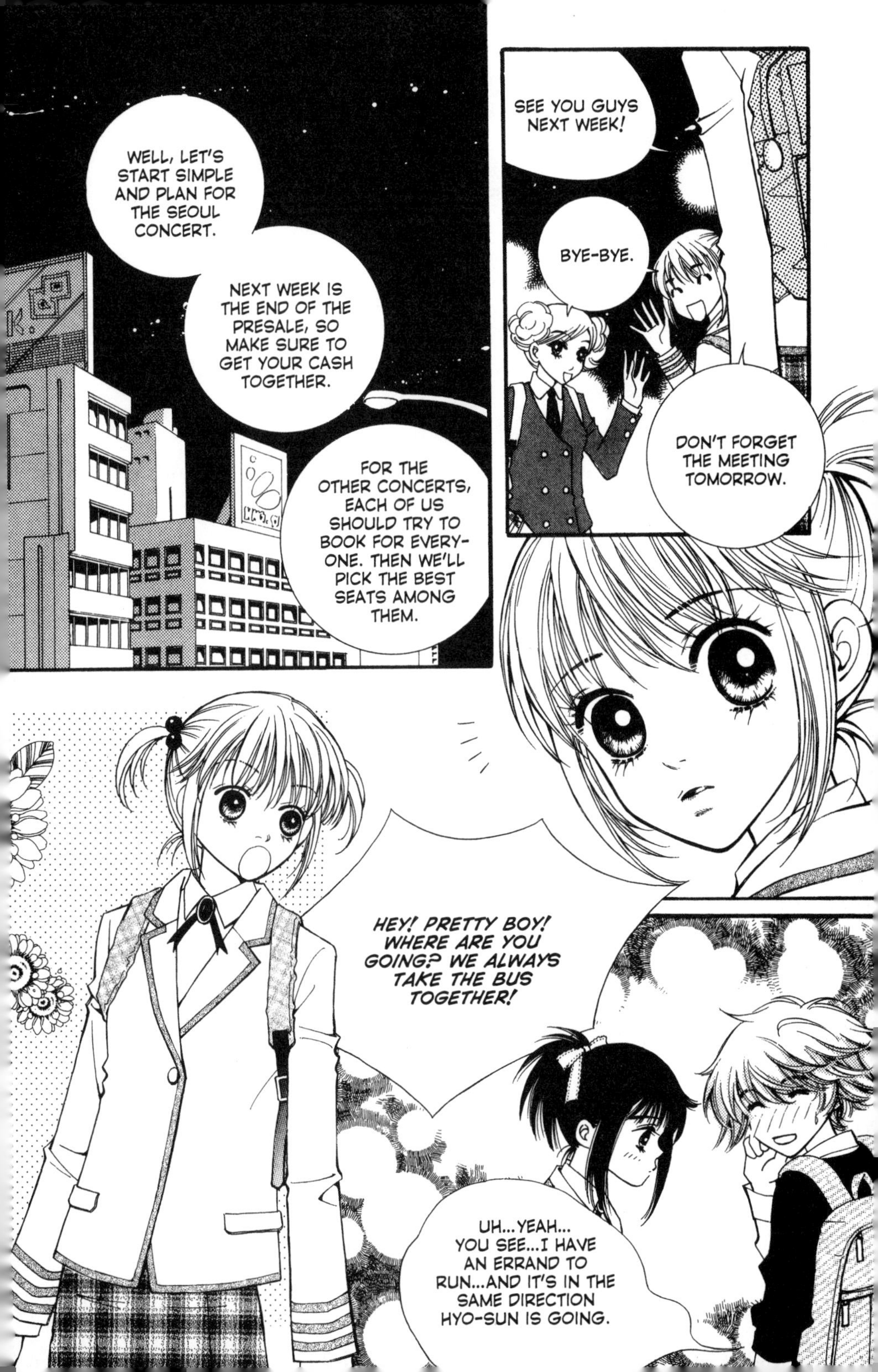
WELL, LET'S START SIMPLE AND PLAN FOR THE SEOUL CONCERT.
NEXT WEEK IS THE END OF THE PRESALE, SO MAKE SURE TO GET YOUR CASH TOGETHER.
FOR THE OTHER CONCERTS, EACH OF US SHOULD TRY TO BOOK FOR EVERY-ONE. THEN WE'LL PICK THE BEST SEATS AMONG THEM.
SEE YOU GUYS NEXT WEEK!
BYE-BYE.
DON'T FORGET THE MEETING TOMORROW.
HEY! PRETTY BOY! WHERE ARE YOU GOING? WE ALWAYS TAKE THE BUS TOGETHER!
UH...YEAH... YOU SEE...I HAVE AN ERRAND TO RUN...AND IT'S IN THE SAME DIRECTION HYO-SUN IS GOING.

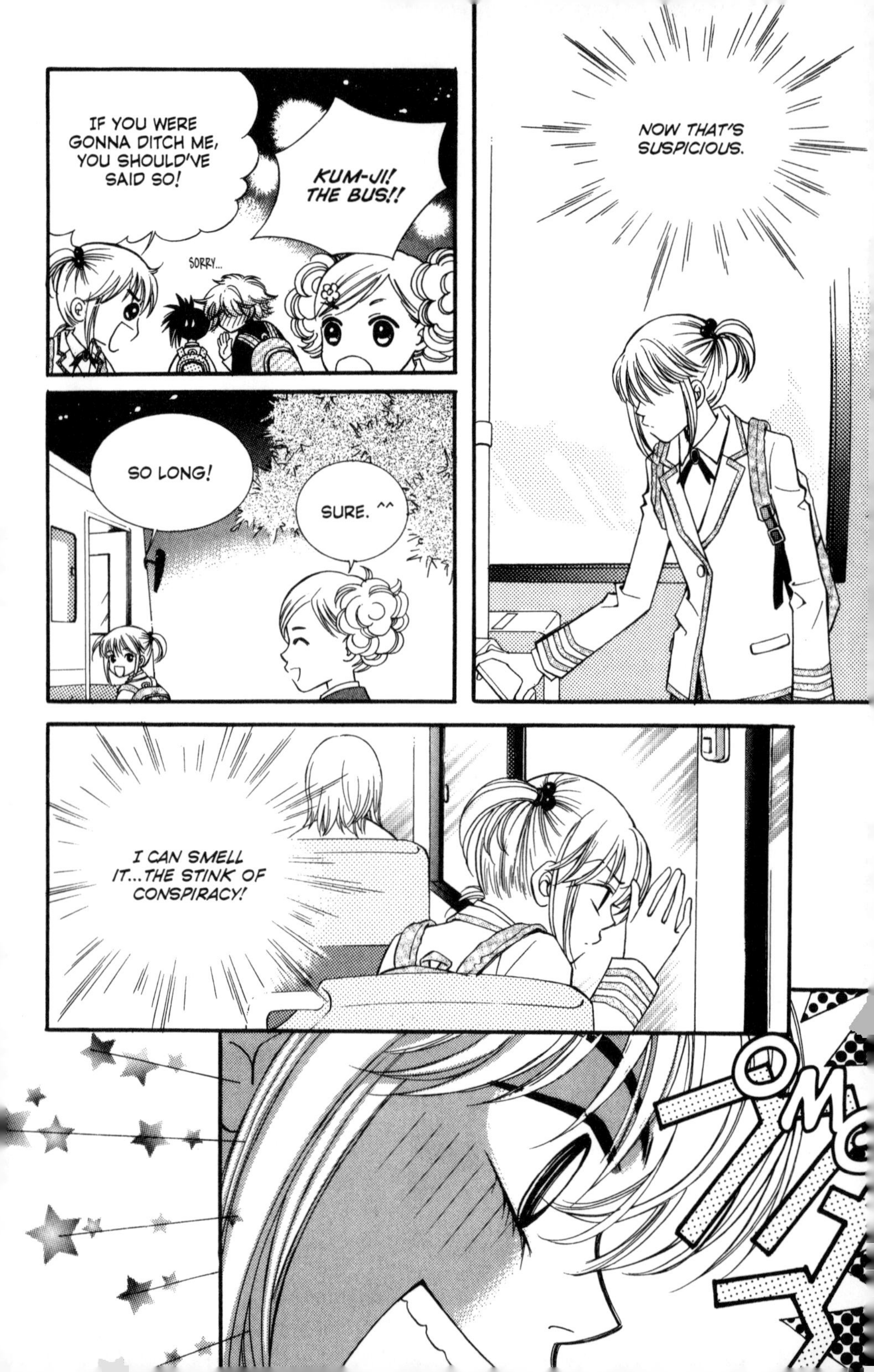
IF YOU WERE GONNA DITCH ME, YOU SHOULD'VE SAID SO!
SORRY...
KUM-JI! THE BUS!!
SO LONG!
SURE. ^^
NOW THAT'S SUSPICIOUS.
I CAN SMELL IT...THE STINK OF CONSPIRACY!

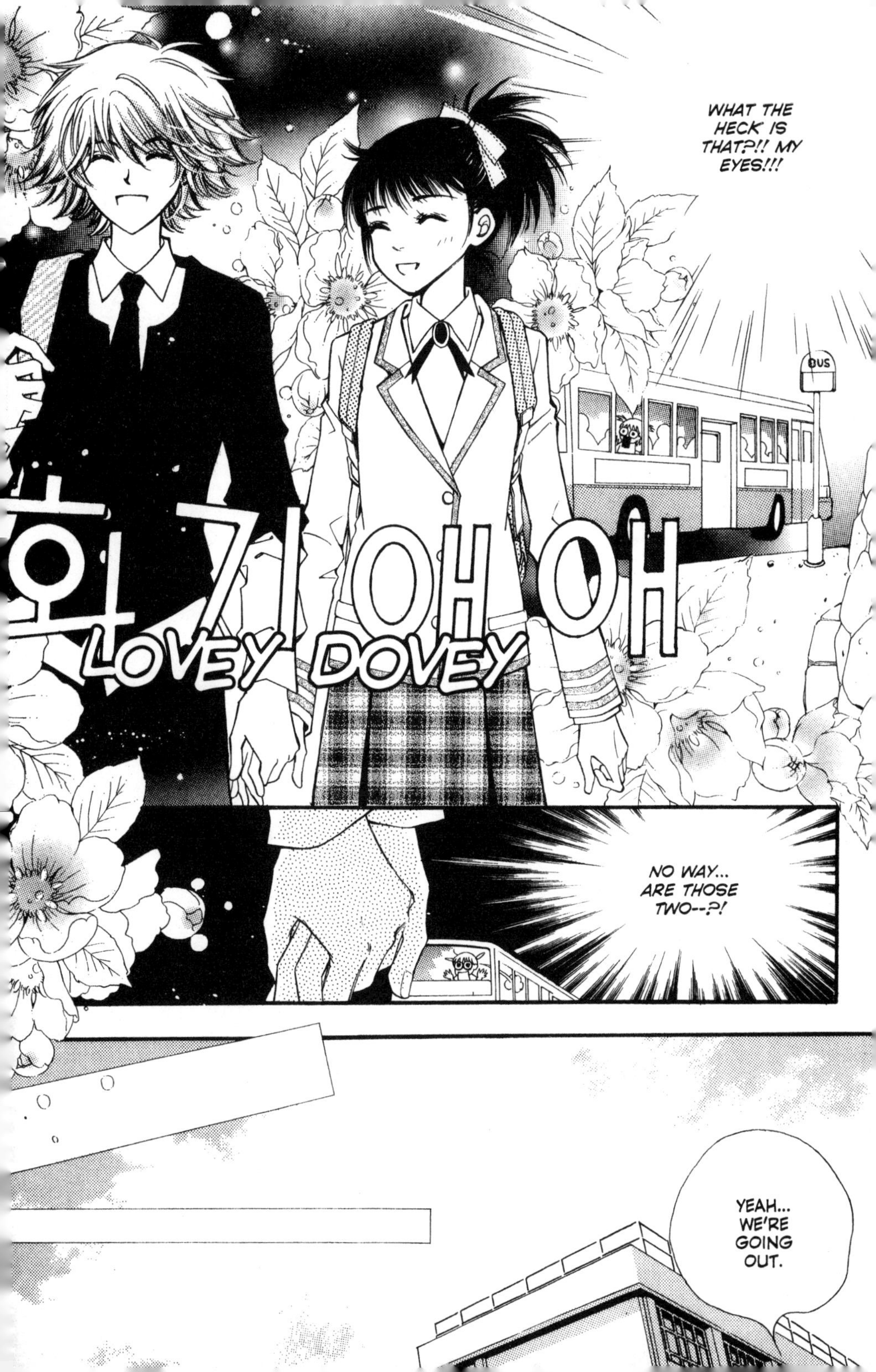
WHAT THE HECK IS THAT?!! MY EYES!!!
BUS
화기애애
LOVEY DOVEY
NO WAY... ARE THOSE TWO--?!
YEAH... WE'RE GOING OUT.

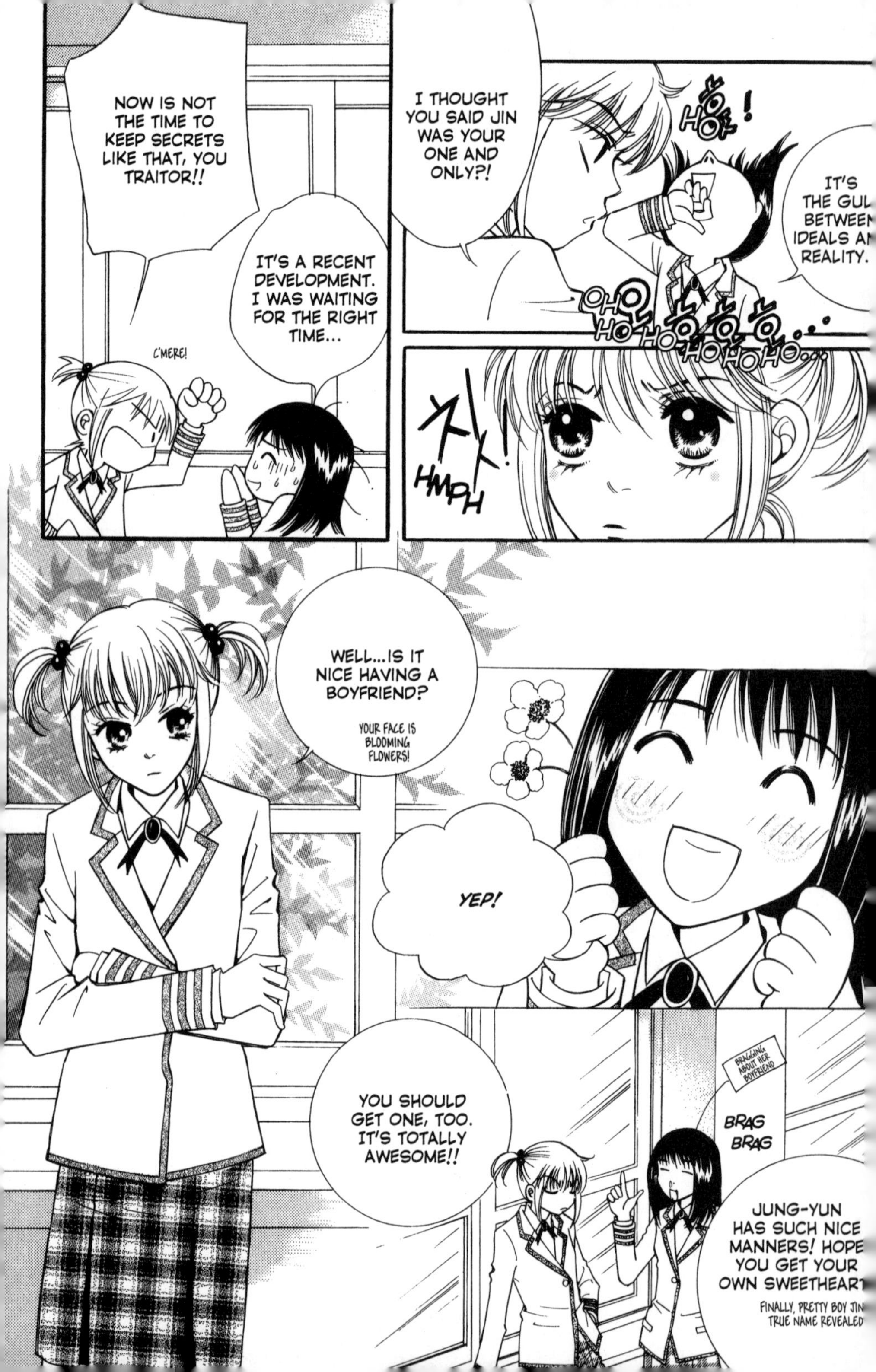
NOW IS NOT THE TIME TO KEEP SECRETS LIKE THAT, YOU TRAITOR!!
IT'S A RECENT DEVELOPMENT. I WAS WAITING FOR THE RIGHT TIME...
C'MERE!
I THOUGHT YOU SAID JIN WAS YOUR ONE AND ONLY?!
HOK!
IT'S THE GUL BETWEEN IDEALS AN REALITY.
HO HO HO HO HO...
HMPH
WELL...IS IT NICE HAVING A BOYFRIEND?
YOUR FACE IS BLOOMING FLOWERS!
YEP!
YOU SHOULD GET ONE, TOO. IT'S TOTALLY AWESOME!!
BRAGGING ABOUT HER BOYFRIEND
BRAG BRAG
JUNG-YUN HAS SUCH NICE MANNERS! HOPE YOU GET YOUR OWN SWEETHEART
FINALLY, PRETTY BOY JIN TRUE NAME REVEALED

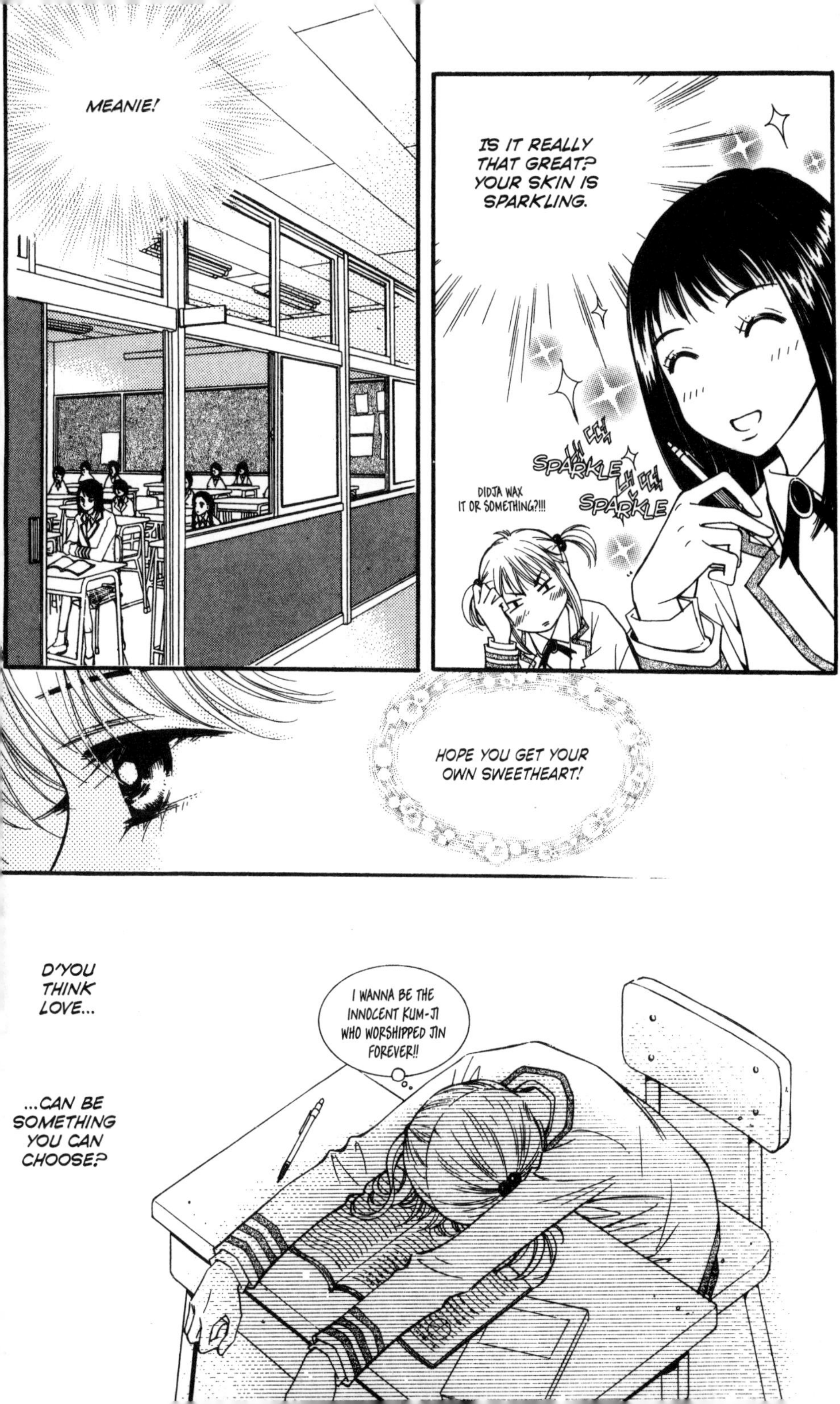
MEANIE!
IS IT REALLY THAT GREAT? YOUR SKIN IS SPARKLING.
DIDJA WAX IT OR SOMETHING?!!!
SPARKLE
SPARKLE
HOPE YOU GET YOUR OWN SWEETHEART!
D'YOU THINK LOVE...
I WANNA BE THE INNOCENT KUM-JI WHO WORSHIPPED JIN FOREVER!!
...CAN BE SOMETHING YOU CAN CHOOSE?

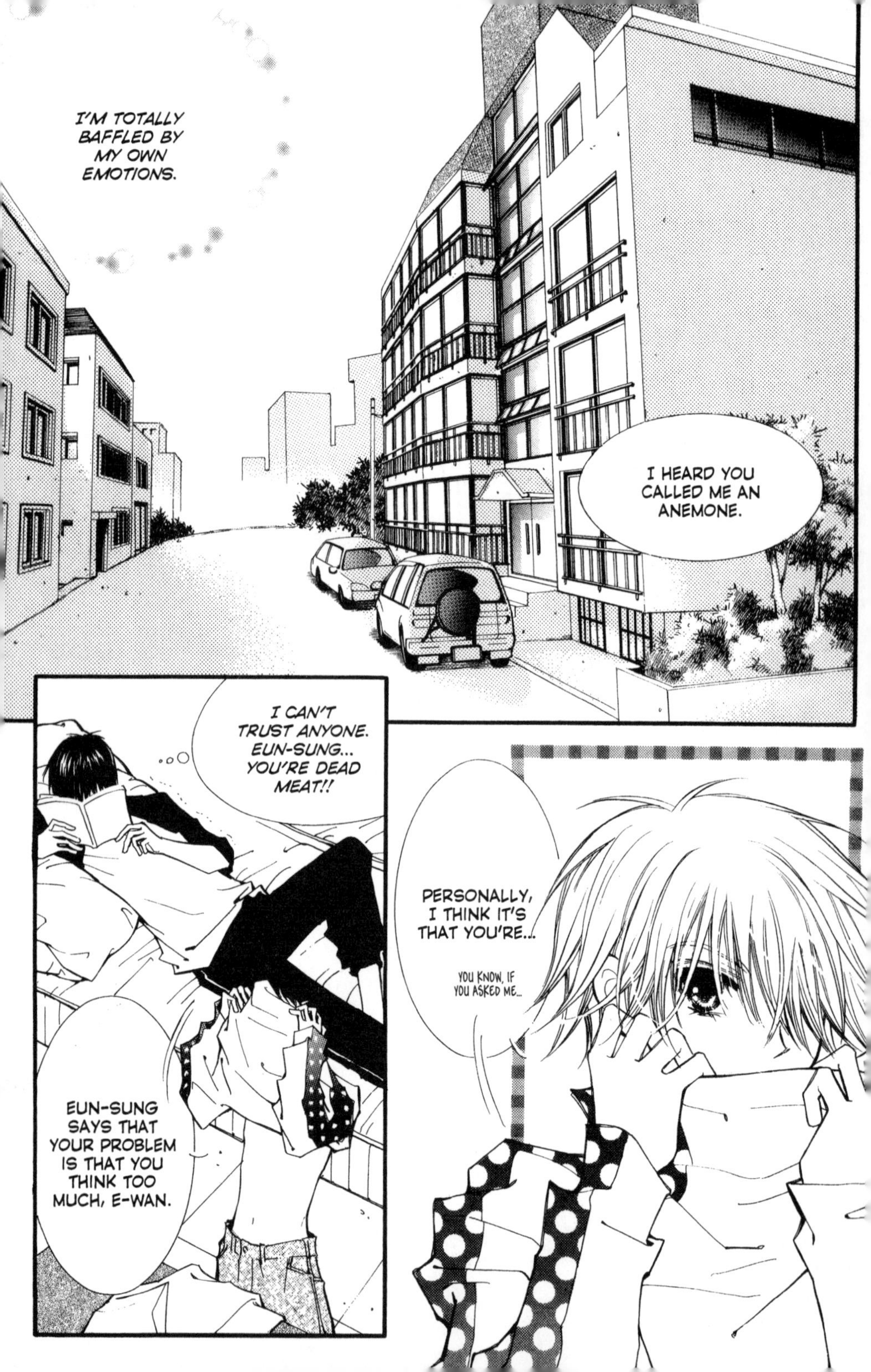
I'M TOTALLY BAFFLED BY MY OWN EMOTIONS.
I HEARD YOU CALLED ME AN ANEMONE.
I CAN'T TRUST ANYONE. EUN-SUNG... YOU'RE DEAD MEAT!!
EUN-SUNG SAYS THAT YOUR PROBLEM IS THAT YOU THINK TOO MUCH, E-WAN.
PERSONALLY, I THINK IT'S THAT YOU'RE...
YOU KNOW, IF YOU ASKED ME...

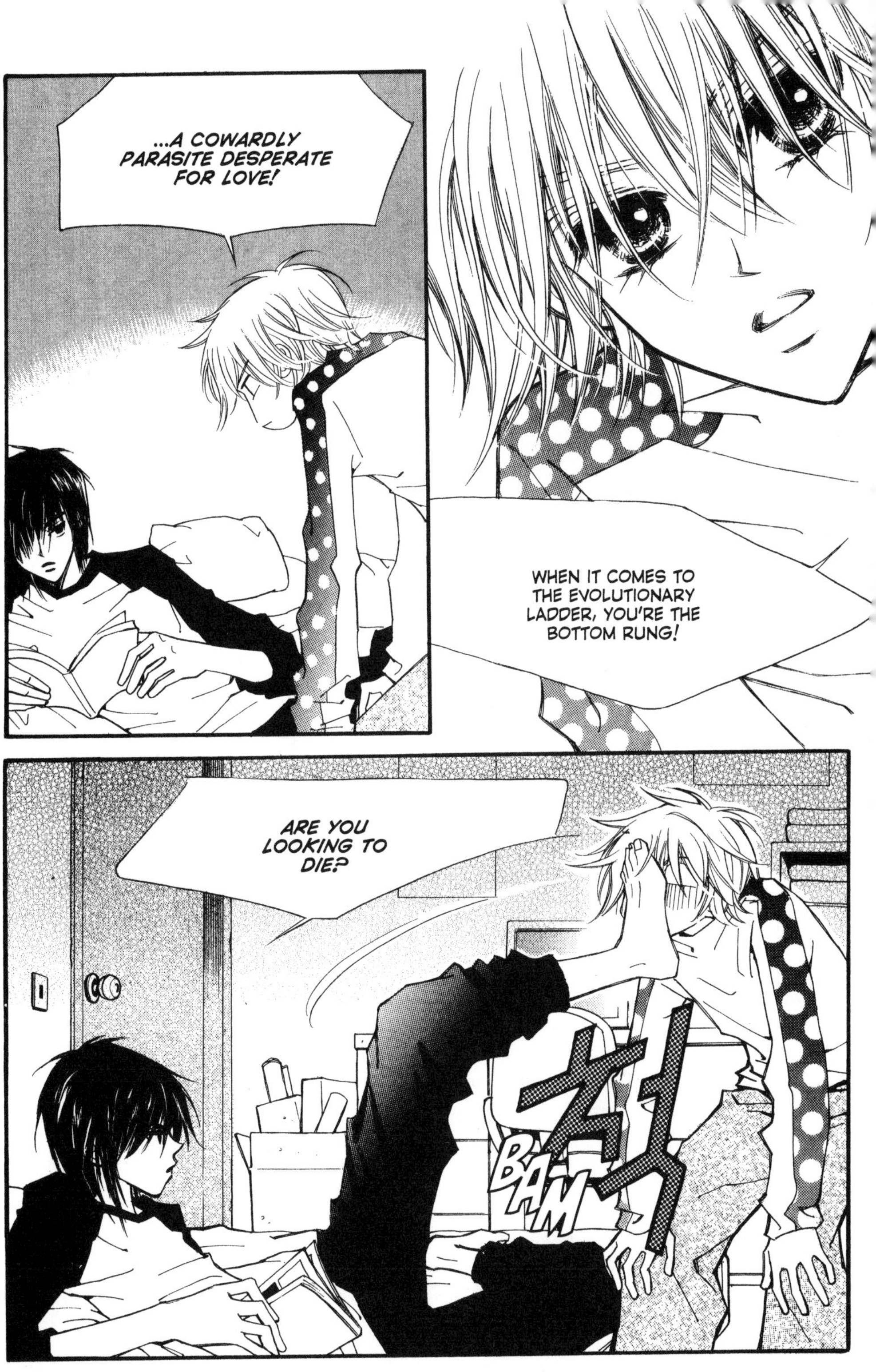
...A COWARDLY PARASITE DESPERATE FOR LOVE!
WHEN IT COMES TO THE EVOLUTIONARY LADDER, YOU'RE THE BOTTOM RUNG!
ARE YOU LOOKING TO DIE?
BAM

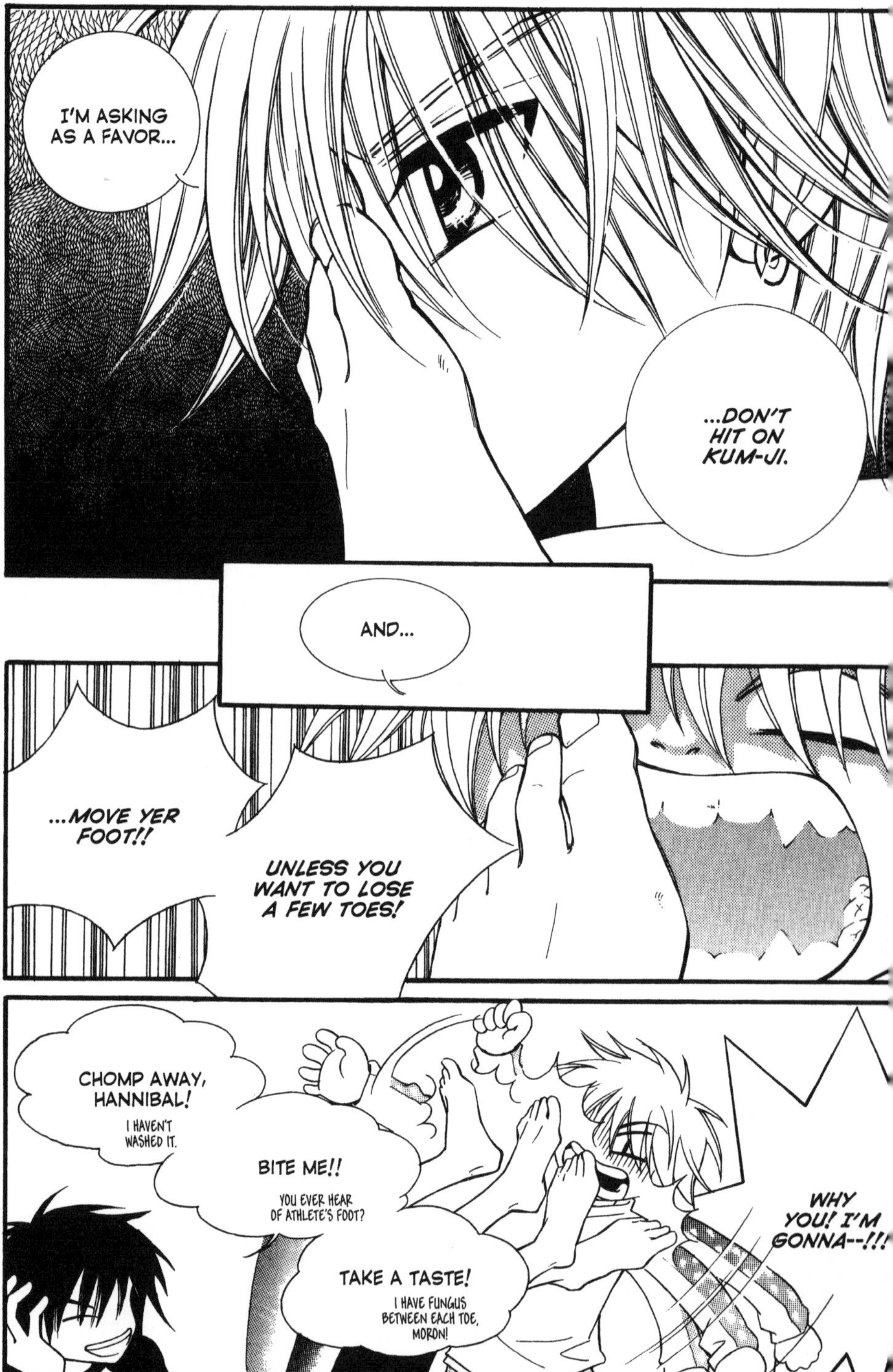
I'M ASKING AS A FAVOR...
...DON'T HIT ON KUM-JI.
AND...
...MOVE YER FOOT!!
UNLESS YOU WANT TO LOSE A FEW TOES!
CHOMP AWAY, HANNIBAL!
I HAVEN'T WASHED IT.
BITE ME!!
YOU EVER HEAR OF ATHLETE'S FOOT?
TAKE A TASTE!
I HAVE FUNGUS BETWEEN EACH TOE, MORON!
WHY YOU! I'M GONNA--!!!

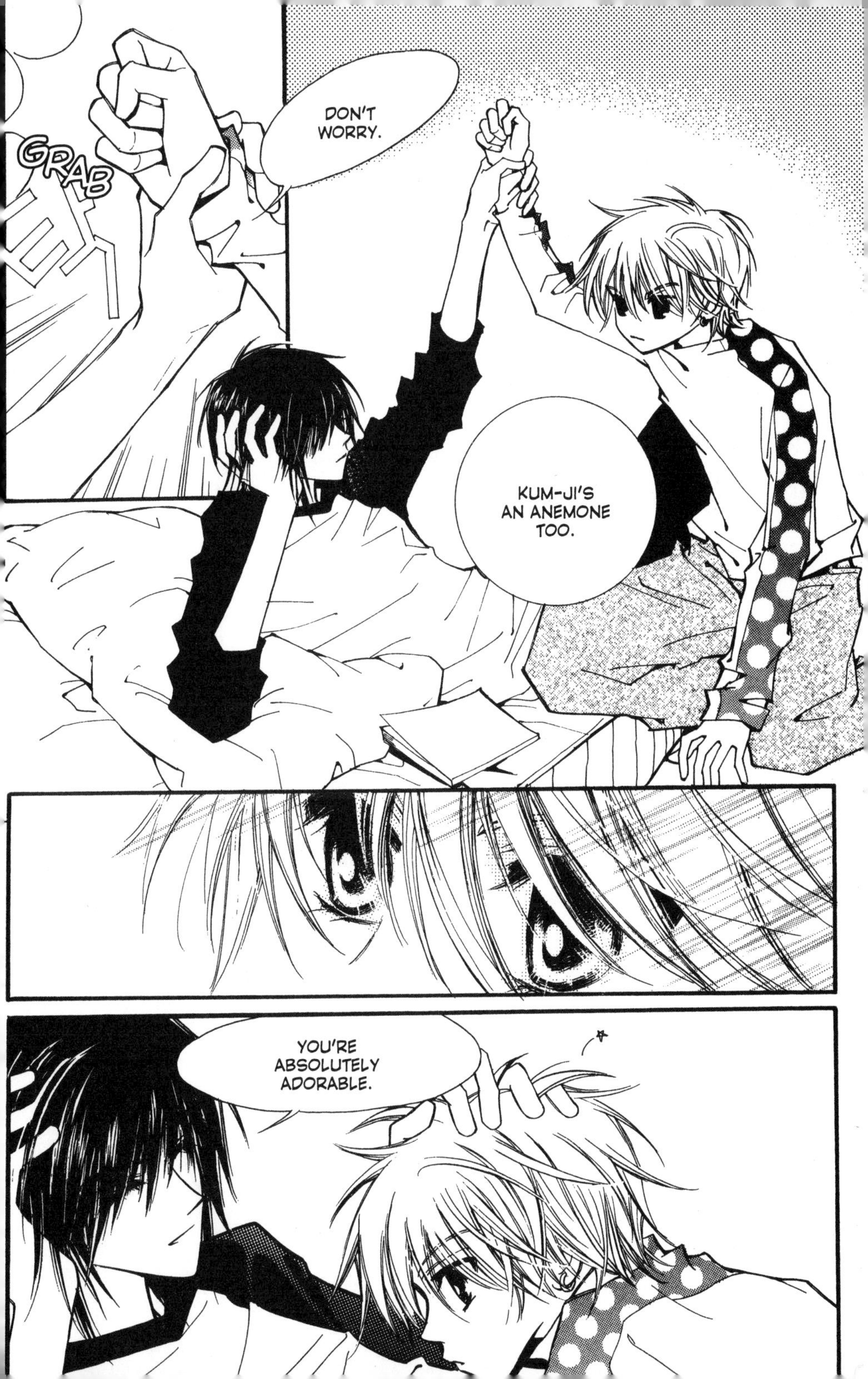
GRAB
DON'T WORRY.
KUM-JI'S AN ANEMONE TOO.
YOU'RE ABSOLUTELY ADORABLE.

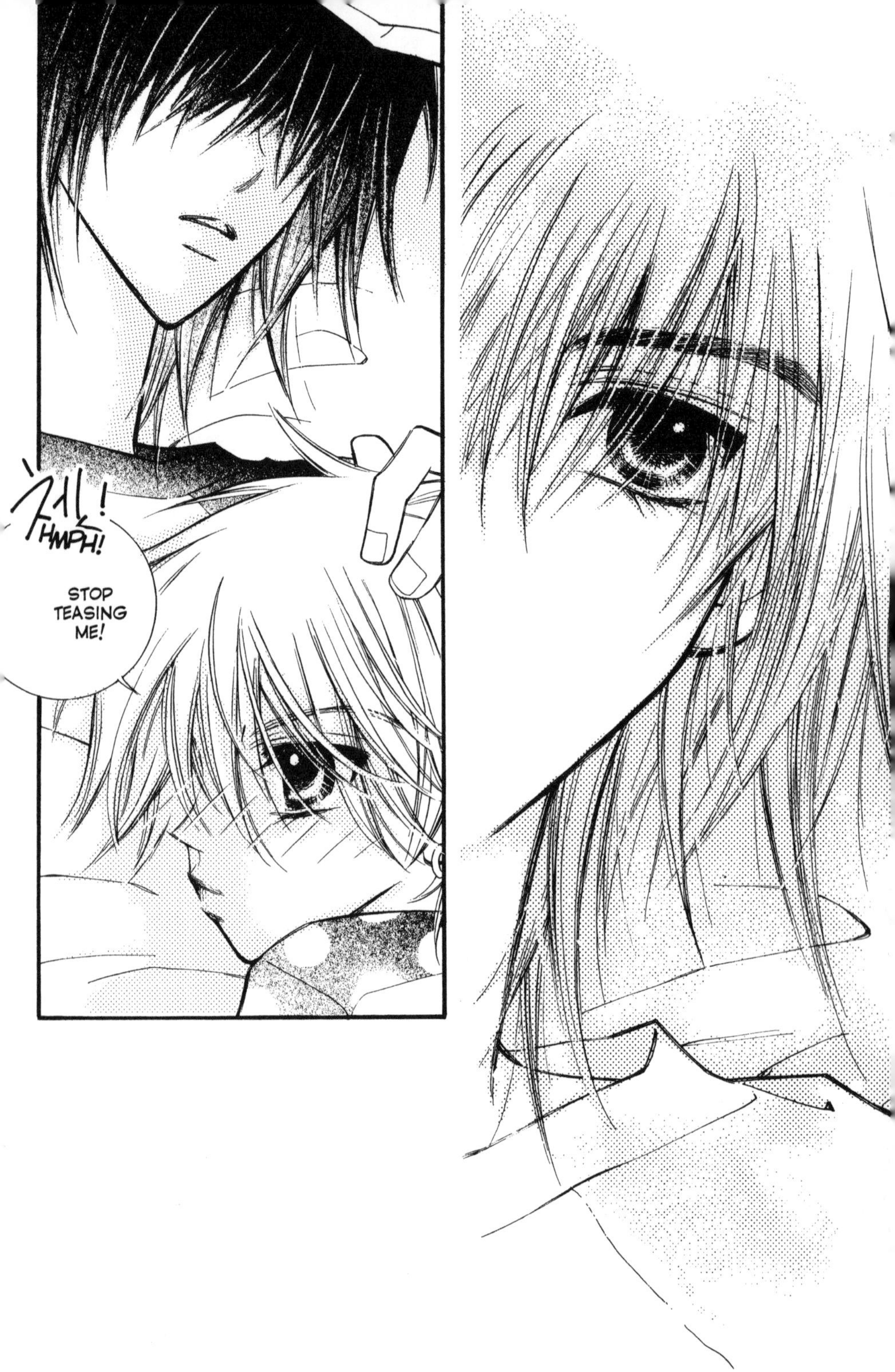
칫!
HMPH!
STOP TEASING ME!

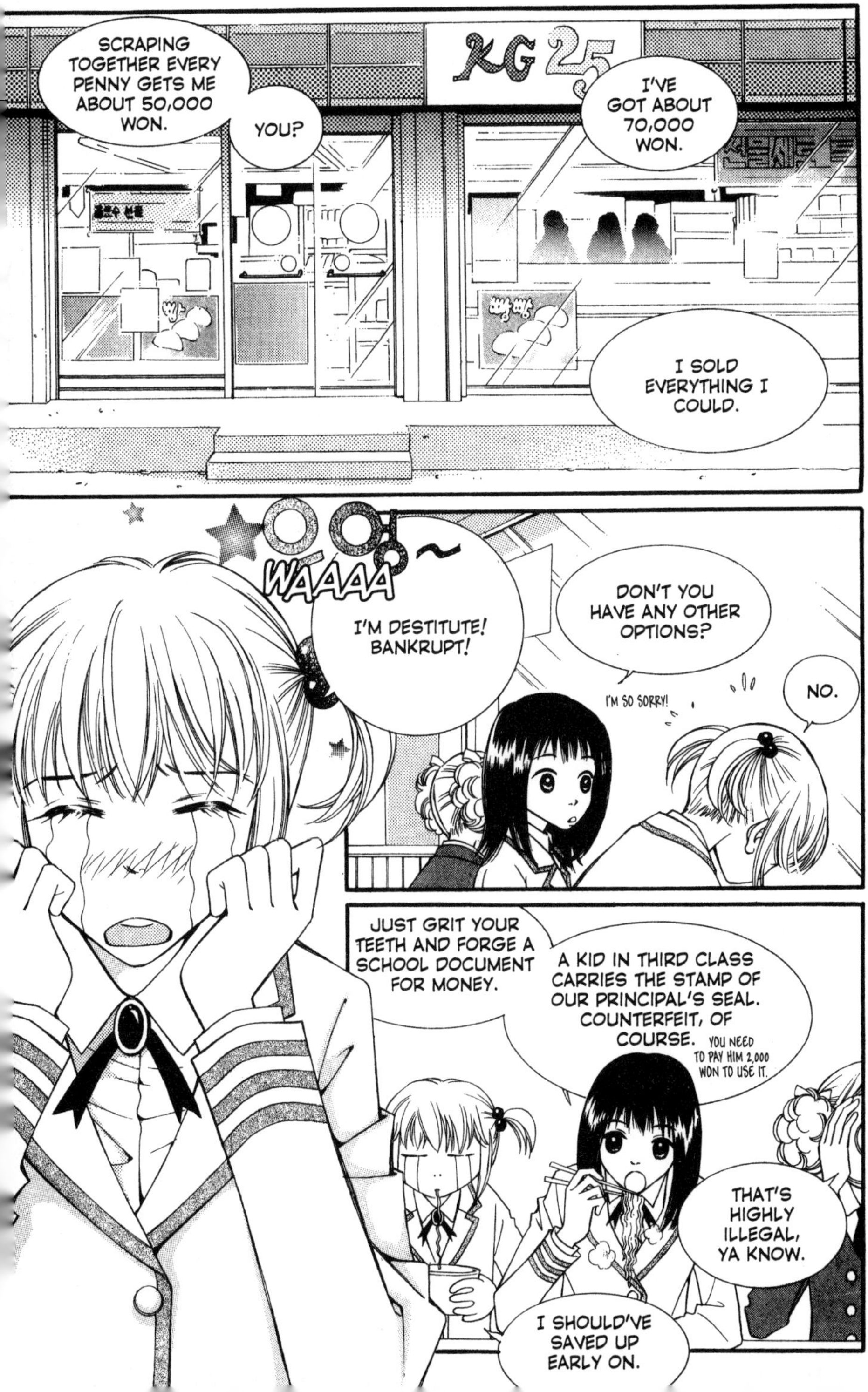
SCRAPING TOGETHER EVERY PENNY GETS ME ABOUT 50,000 WON.
YOU?
KG 25
I'VE GOT ABOUT 70,000 WON.
I SOLD EVERYTHING I COULD.
WAAAA
I'M DESTITUTE! BANKRUPT!
DON'T YOU HAVE ANY OTHER OPTIONS?
I'M SO SORRY!
NO.
JUST GRIT YOUR TEETH AND FORGE A SCHOOL DOCUMENT FOR MONEY.
A KID IN THIRD CLASS CARRIES THE STAMP OF OUR PRINCIPAL'S SEAL. COUNTERFEIT, OF COURSE.
YOU NEED TO PAY HIM 2,000 WON TO USE IT.
THAT'S HIGHLY ILLEGAL, YA KNOW.
I SHOULD'VE SAVED UP EARLY ON.

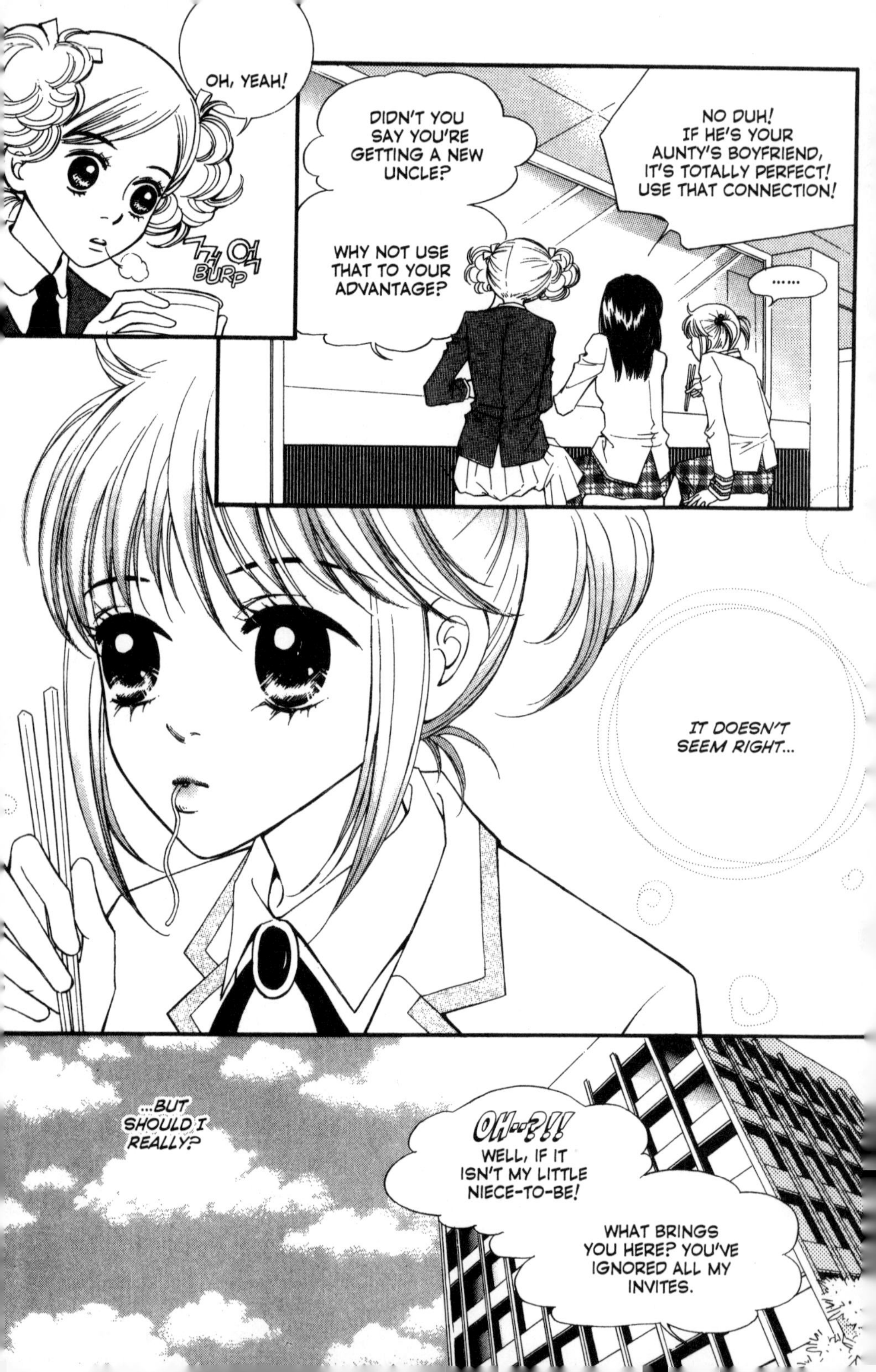
OH, YEAH!
BURP
DIDN'T YOU SAY YOU'RE GETTING A NEW UNCLE?
WHY NOT USE THAT TO YOUR ADVANTAGE?
NO DUH! IF HE'S YOUR AUNTY'S BOYFRIEND, IT'S TOTALLY PERFECT! USE THAT CONNECTION!
......
IT DOESN'T SEEM RIGHT...
...BUT SHOULD I REALLY?
OH--?!!
WELL, IF IT ISN'T MY LITTLE NIECE-TO-BE!
WHAT BRINGS YOU HERE? YOU'VE IGNORED ALL MY INVITES.

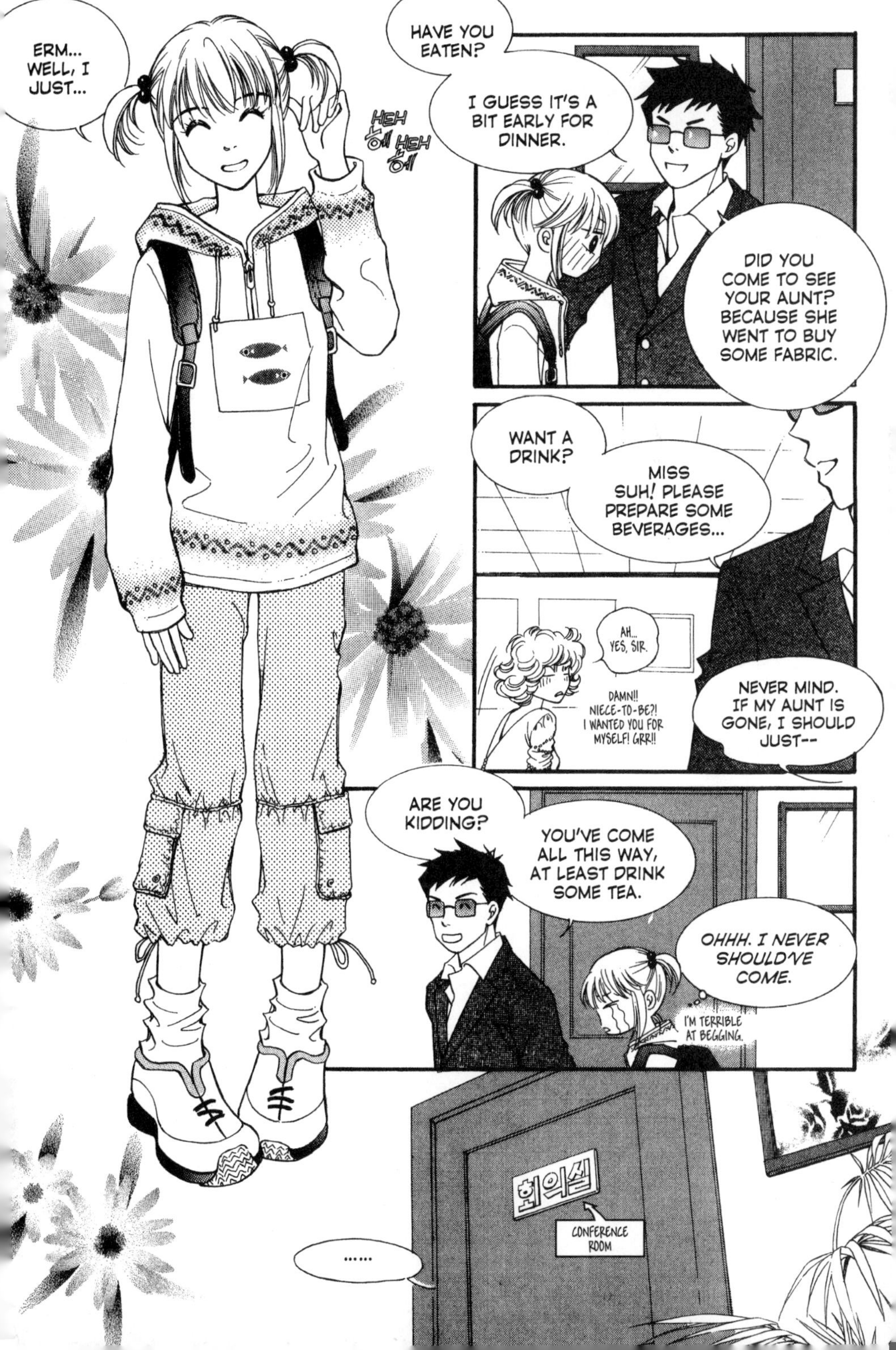
ERM... WELL, I JUST...
HEH HEH
HAVE YOU EATEN?
I GUESS IT'S A BIT EARLY FOR DINNER.
DID YOU COME TO SEE YOUR AUNT? BECAUSE SHE WENT TO BUY SOME FABRIC.
WANT A DRINK?
MISS SUH! PLEASE PREPARE SOME BEVERAGES...
AH... YES, SIR.
DAMN!! NIECE-TO-BE?! I WANTED YOU FOR MYSELF! GRR!!
NEVER MIND. IF MY AUNT IS GONE, I SHOULD JUST--
ARE YOU KIDDING?
YOU'VE COME ALL THIS WAY, AT LEAST DRINK SOME TEA.
OHHH. I NEVER SHOULD'VE COME.
I'M TERRIBLE AT BEGGING.
회의실
CONFERENCE ROOM
......

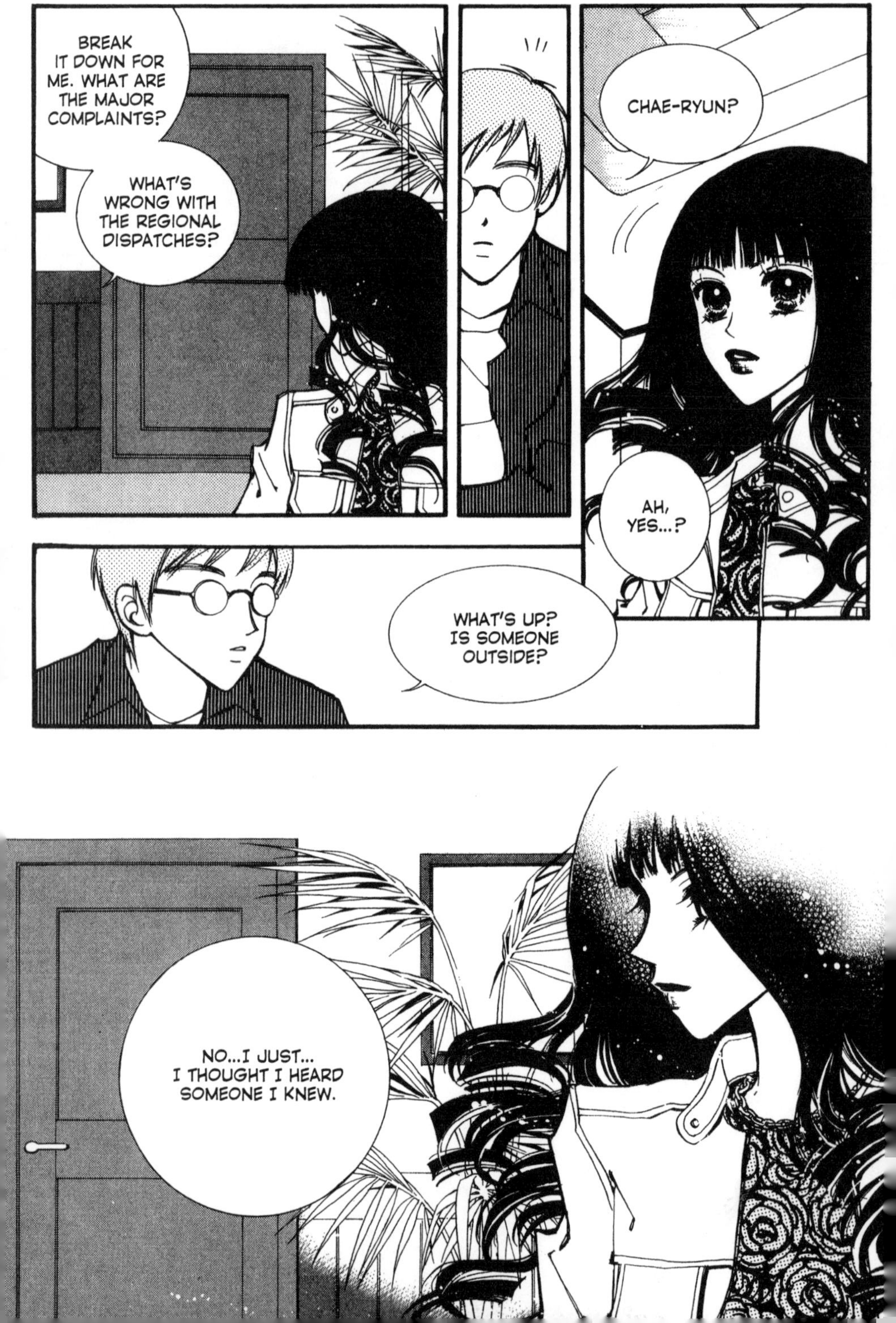
BREAK IT DOWN FOR ME. WHAT ARE THE MAJOR COMPLAINTS?
WHAT'S WRONG WITH THE REGIONAL DISPATCHES?
CHAE-RYUN?
AH, YES...?
WHAT'S UP? IS SOMEONE OUTSIDE?
NO...I JUST... I THOUGHT I HEARD SOMEONE I KNEW.

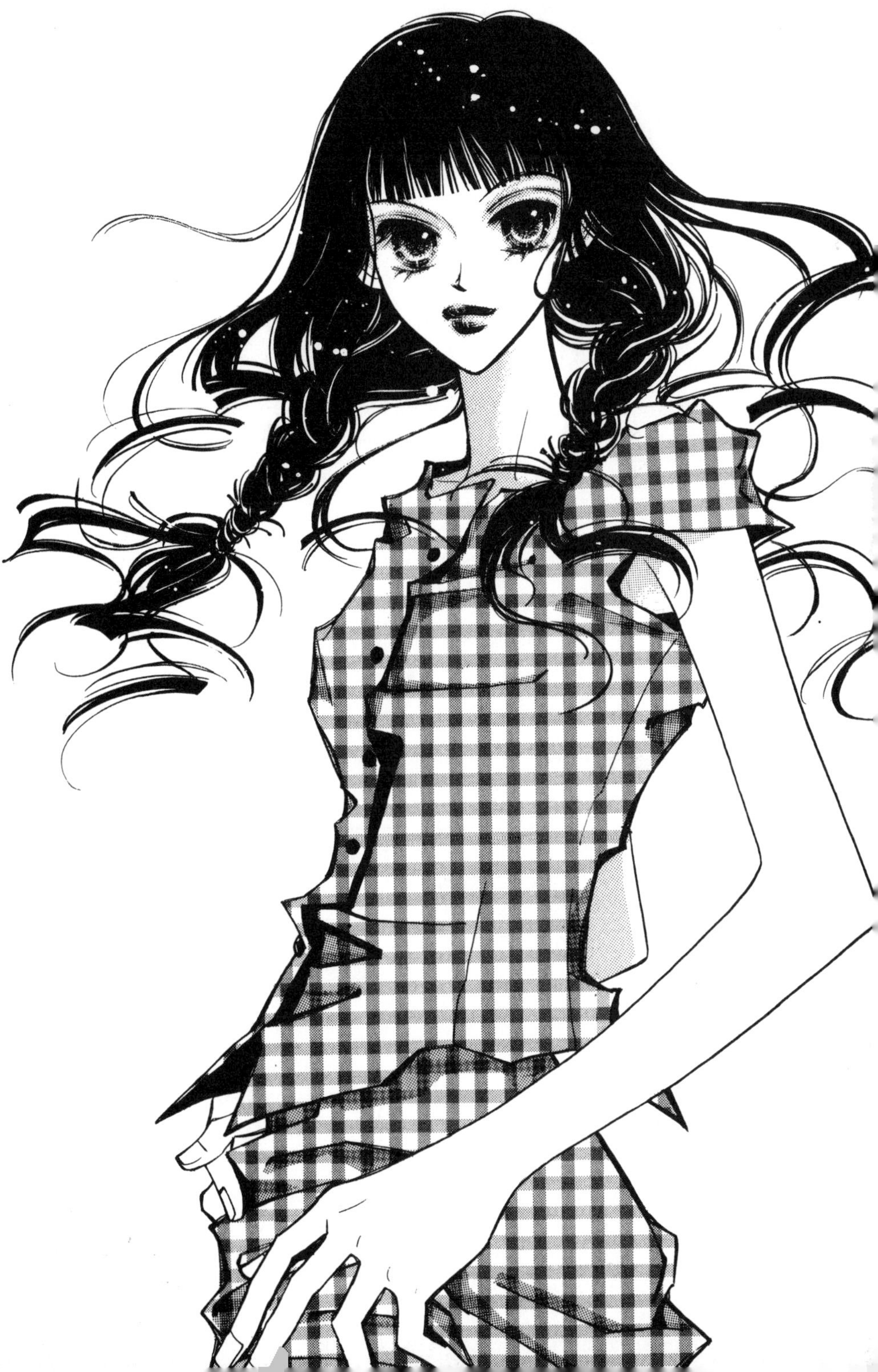

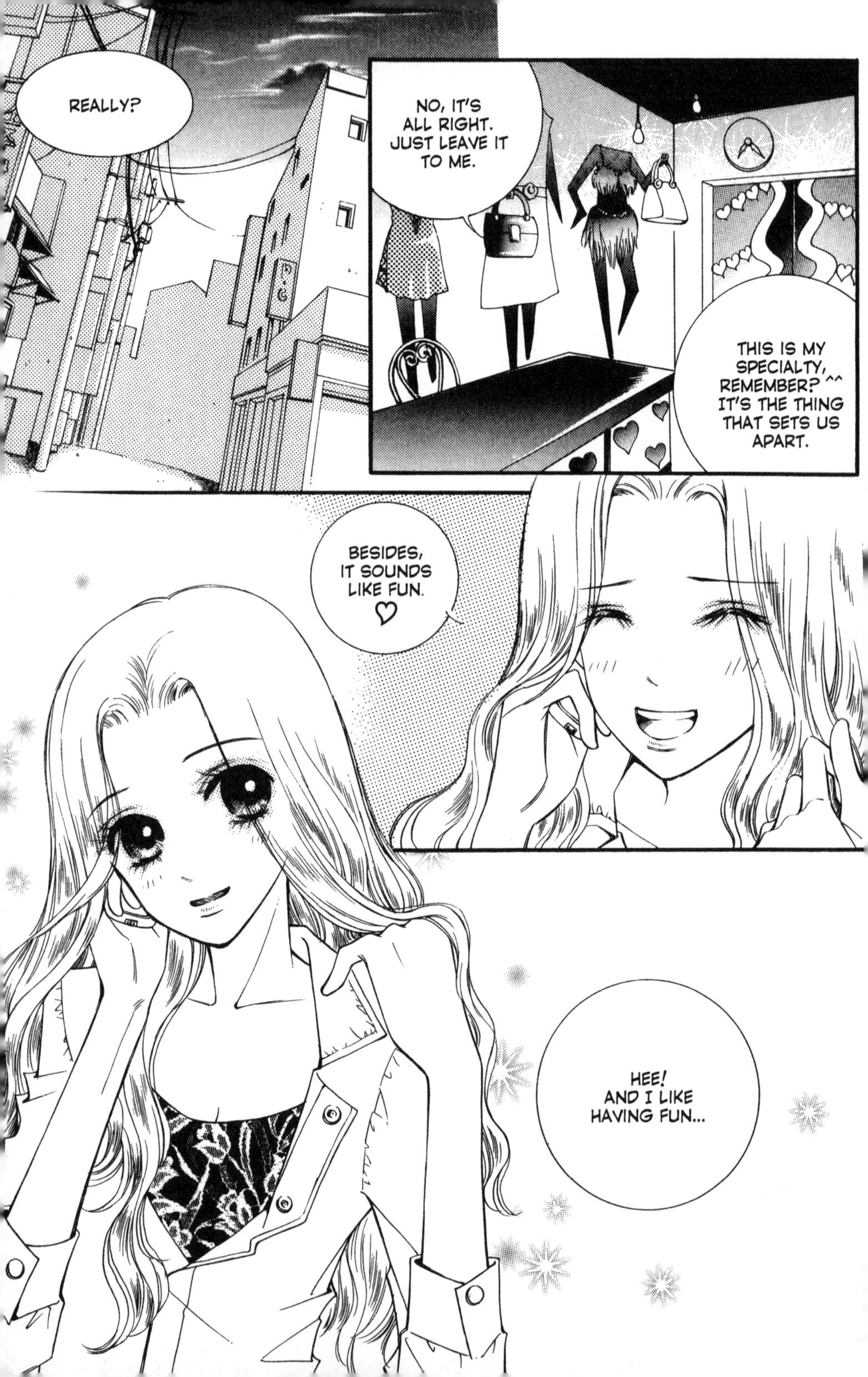
REALLY?
NO, IT'S ALL RIGHT. JUST LEAVE IT TO ME.
THIS IS MY SPECIALTY, REMEMBER? ^^ IT'S THE THING THAT SETS US APART.
BESIDES, IT SOUNDS LIKE FUN. ♡
HEE! AND I LIKE HAVING FUN...

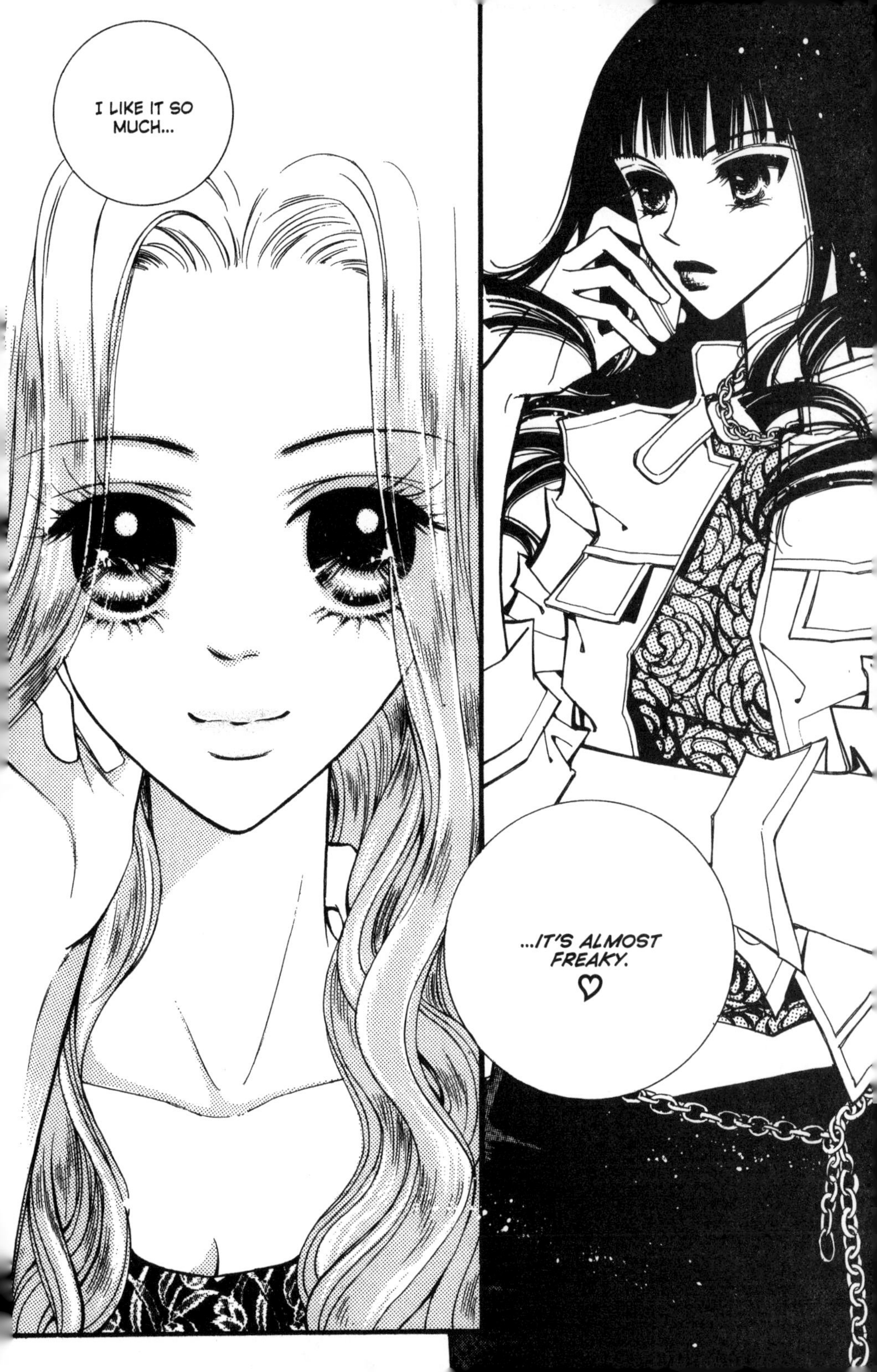
I LIKE IT SO MUCH...
...IT'S ALMOST FREAKY. ♡

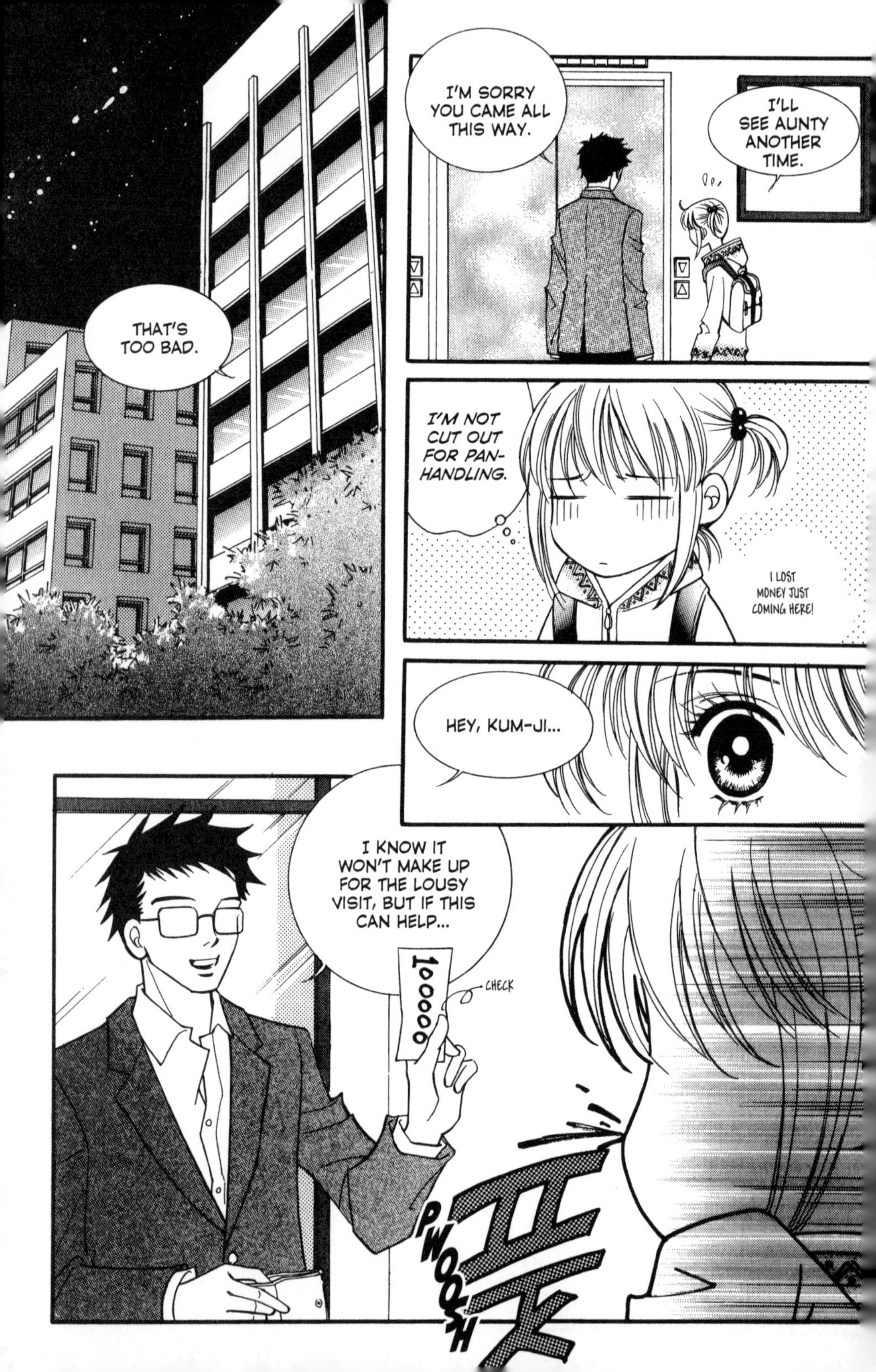
THAT'S TOO BAD.
I'M SORRY YOU CAME ALL THIS WAY.
I'LL SEE AUNTY ANOTHER TIME.
I'M NOT CUT OUT FOR PAN-HANDLING.
I LOST MONEY JUST COMING HERE!
HEY, KUM-JI...
I KNOW IT WON'T MAKE UP FOR THE LOUSY VISIT, BUT IF THIS CAN HELP...
100000
CHECK
PWOOH

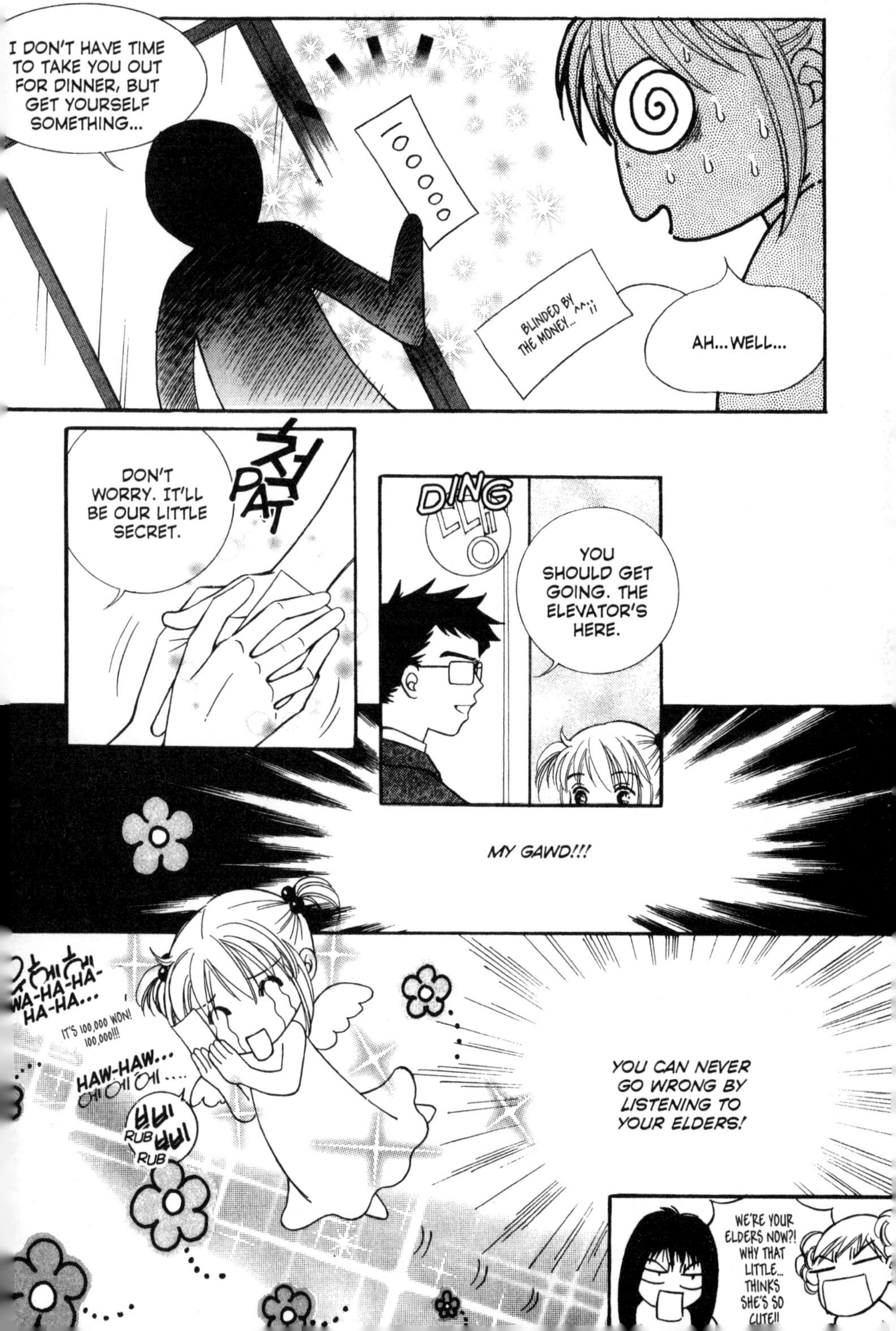

I DON'T HAVE TIME TO TAKE YOU OUT FOR DINNER, BUT GET YOURSELF SOMETHING...
100000
BLINDED BY THE MONEY... ^^;;
AH...WELL...
DON'T WORRY. IT'LL BE OUR LITTLE SECRET.
PAT
DING
YOU SHOULD GET GOING. THE ELEVATOR'S HERE.
MY GAWD!!!
WA-HA-HA-HA-HA-HA...
IT'S 100,000 WON! 100,000!!!
HAW-HAW...
RUB RUB
YOU CAN NEVER GO WRONG BY LISTENING TO YOUR ELDERS!
WE'RE YOUR ELDERS NOW?! WHY THAT LITTLE... THINKS SHE'S SO CUTE!!

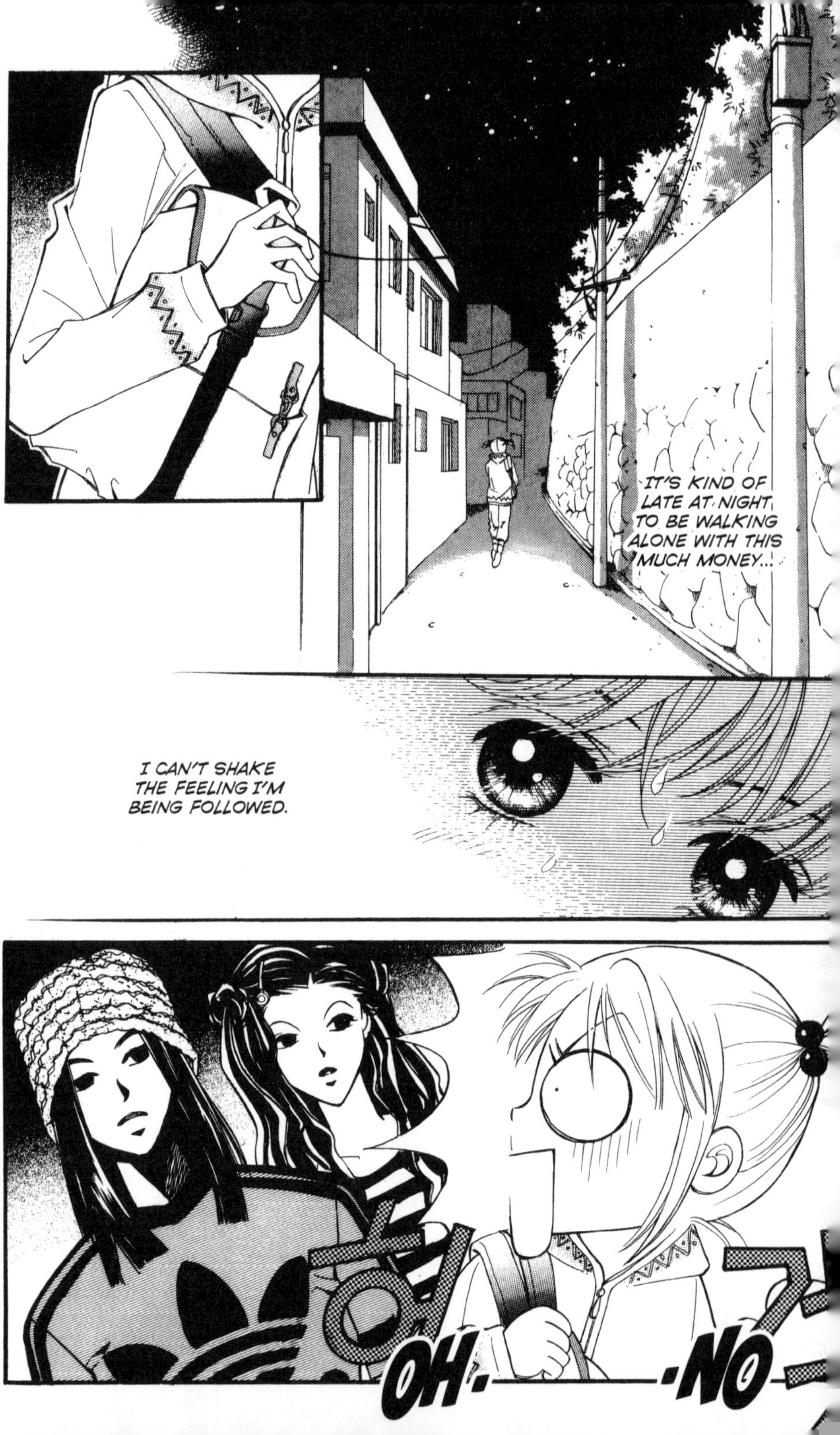
IT'S KIND OF LATE AT NIGHT TO BE WALKING ALONE WITH THIS MUCH MONEY...
I CAN'T SHAKE THE FEELING I'M BEING FOLLOWED.
OH.
.NO--

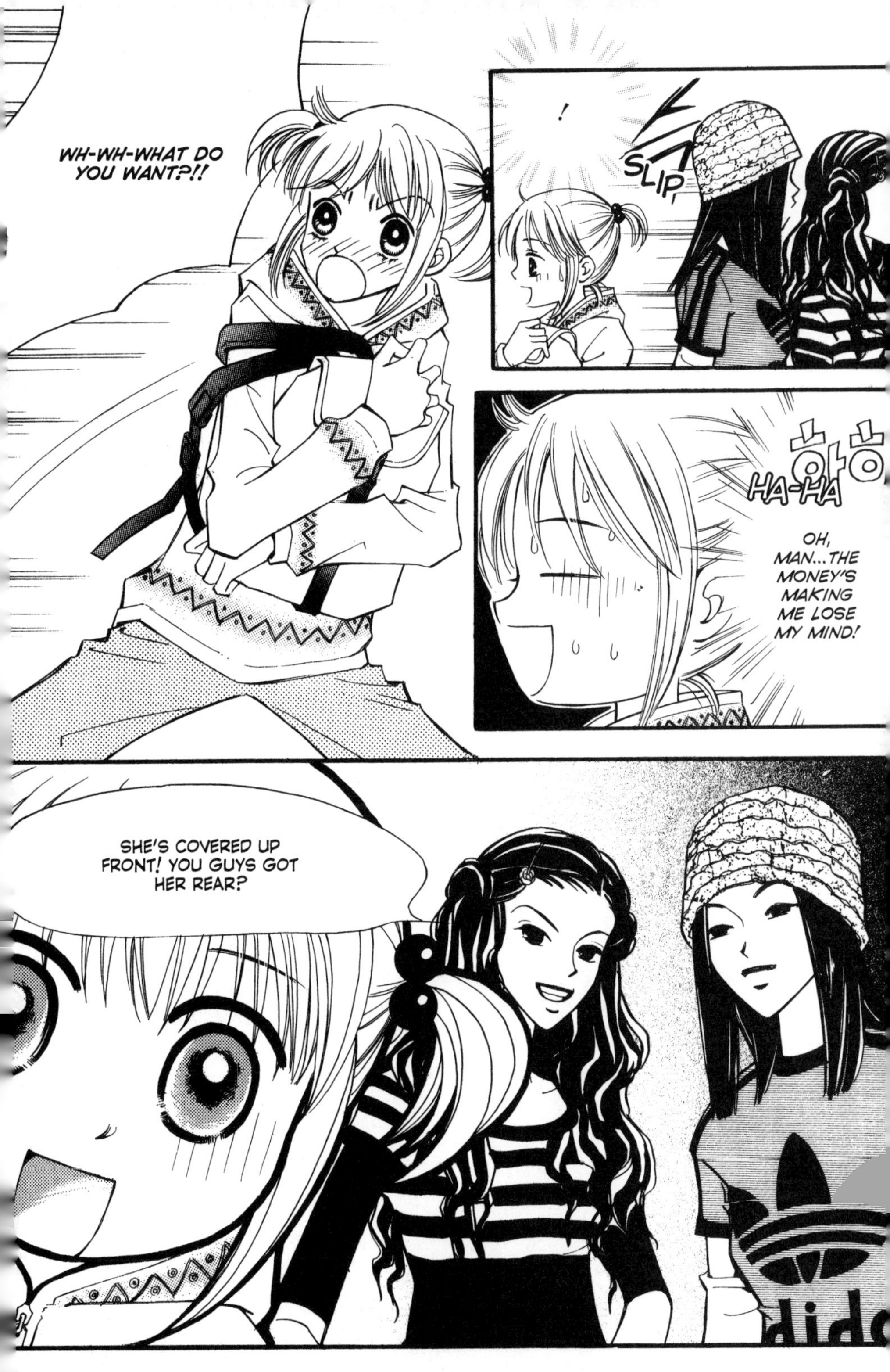
WH-WH-WHAT DO YOU WANT?!!
!
SLIP
HA-HA
OH, MAN...THE MONEY'S MAKING ME LOSE MY MIND!
SHE'S COVERED UP FRONT! YOU GUYS GOT HER REAR?

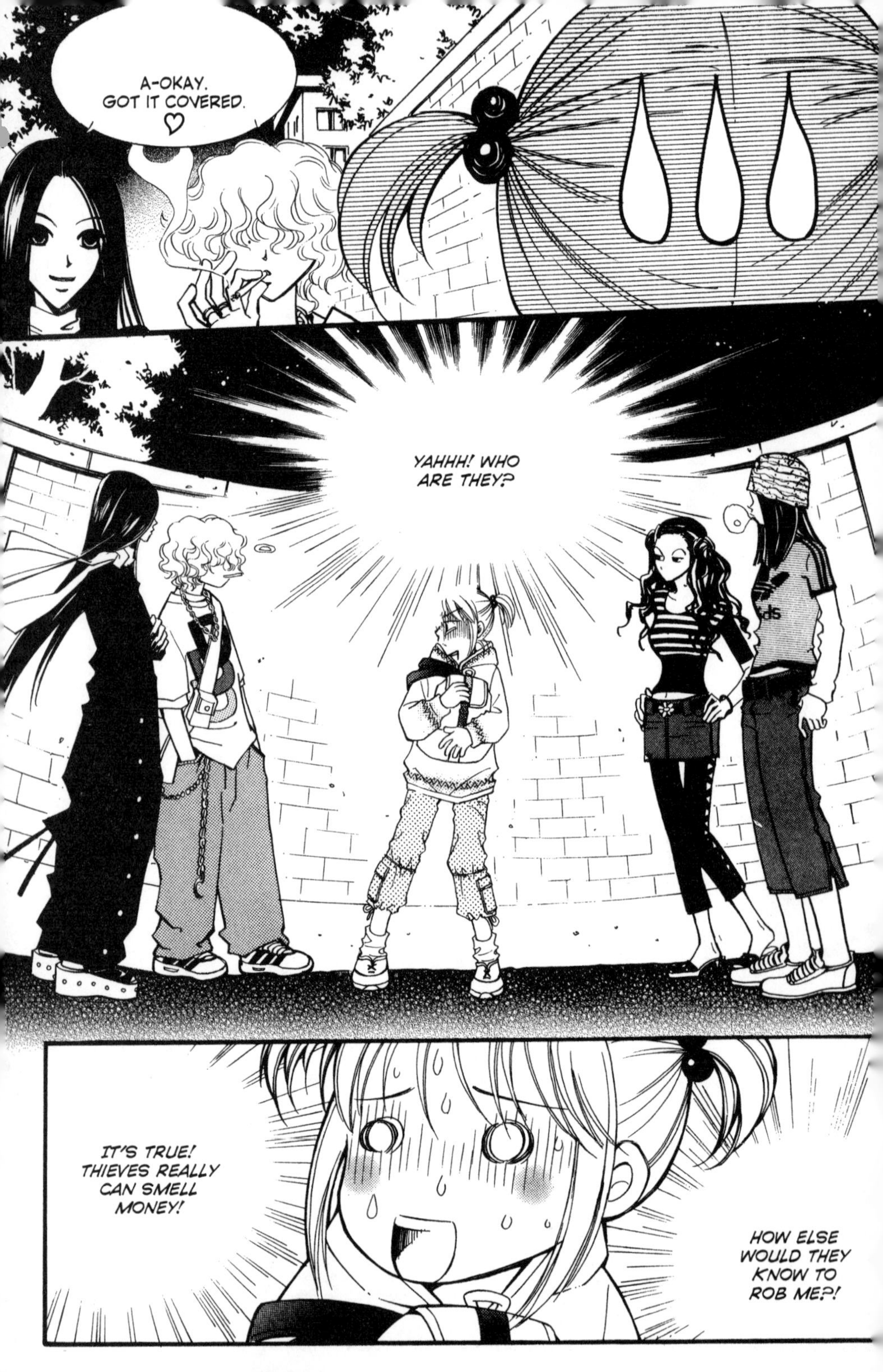
A-OKAY. GOT IT COVERED. ♡
YAHHH! WHO ARE THEY?
IT'S TRUE! THIEVES REALLY CAN SMELL MONEY!
HOW ELSE WOULD THEY KNOW TO ROB ME?!

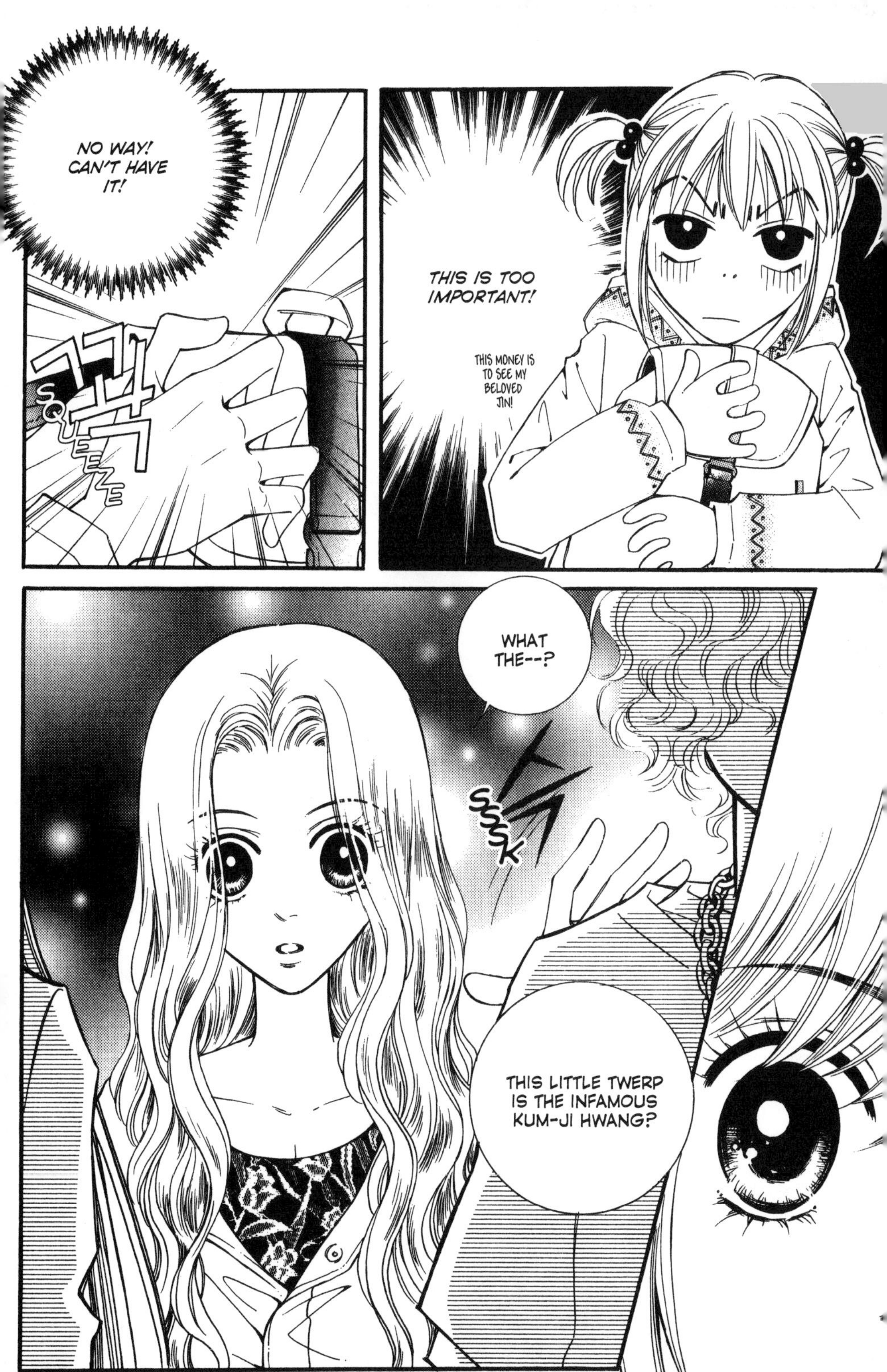NO WAY! CAN'T HAVE IT!
SQUEEZE
THIS IS TOO IMPORTANT!
THIS MONEY IS TO SEE MY BELOVED JIN!
WHAT THE--?
SSSK
THIS LITTLE TWERP IS THE INFAMOUS KUM-JI HWANG?

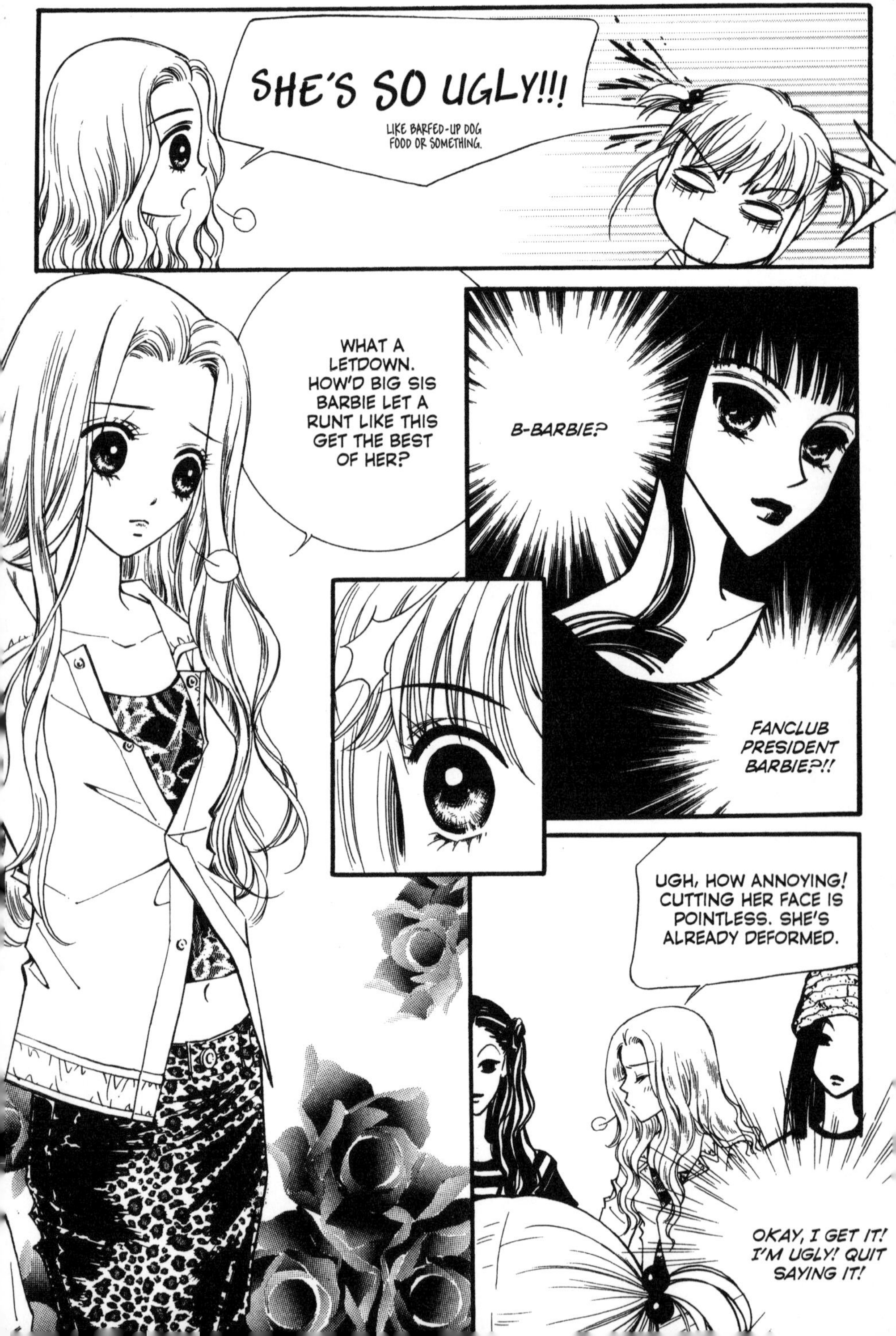
SHE'S SO UGLY!!!
LIKE BARFED-UP DOG FOOD OR SOMETHING.
WHAT A LETDOWN. HOW'D BIG SIS BARBIE LET A RUNT LIKE THIS GET THE BEST OF HER?
B-BARBIE?
FANCLUB PRESIDENT BARBIE?!!
UGH, HOW ANNOYING! CUTTING HER FACE IS POINTLESS. SHE'S ALREADY DEFORMED.
OKAY, I GET IT! I'M UGLY! QUIT SAYING IT!

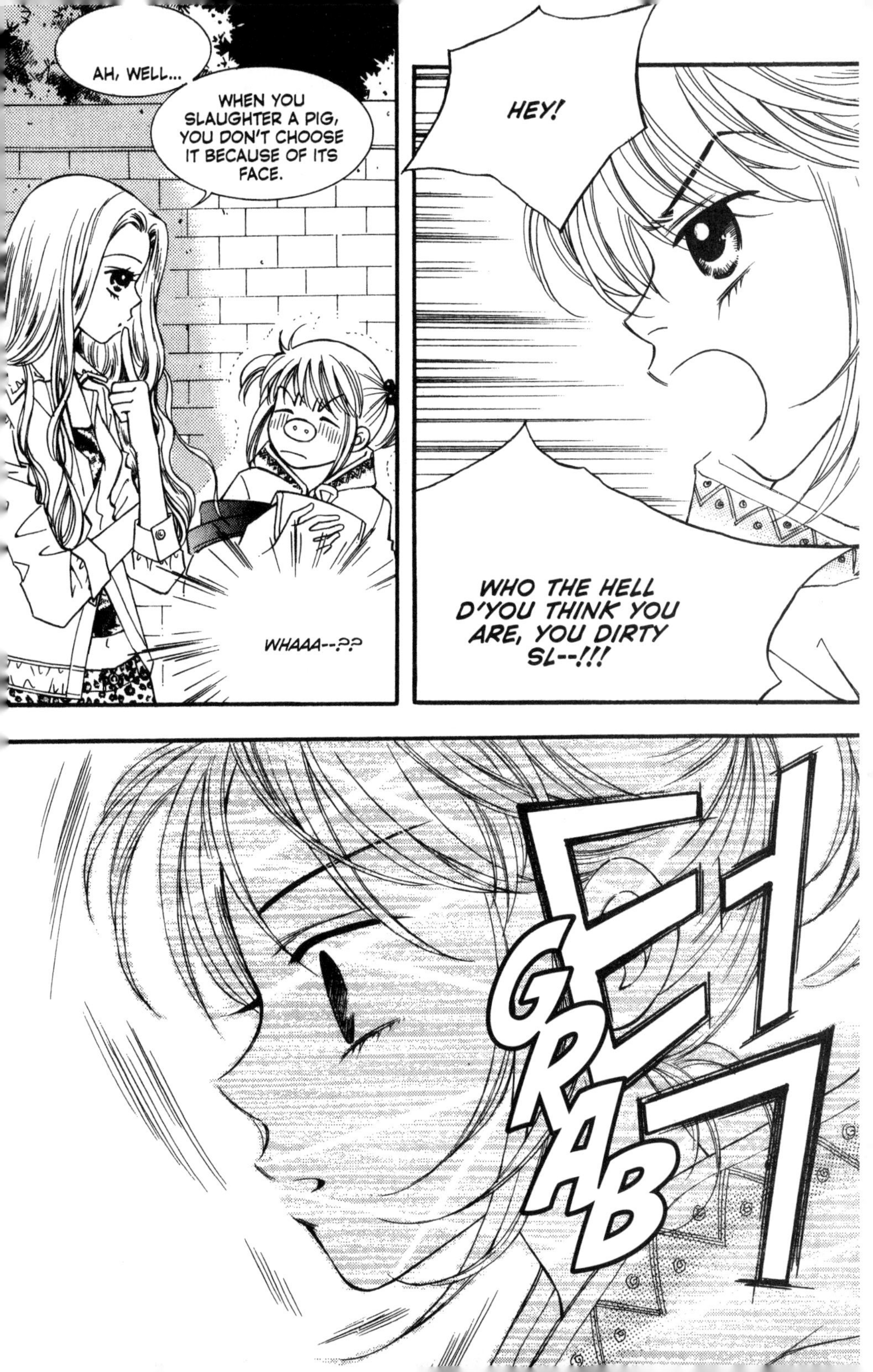
AH, WELL...
WHEN YOU SLAUGHTER A PIG, YOU DON'T CHOOSE IT BECAUSE OF ITS FACE.
WHAAA--?!?
HEY!
WHO THE HELL D'YOU THINK YOU ARE, YOU DIRTY SL--!!!
GRAB

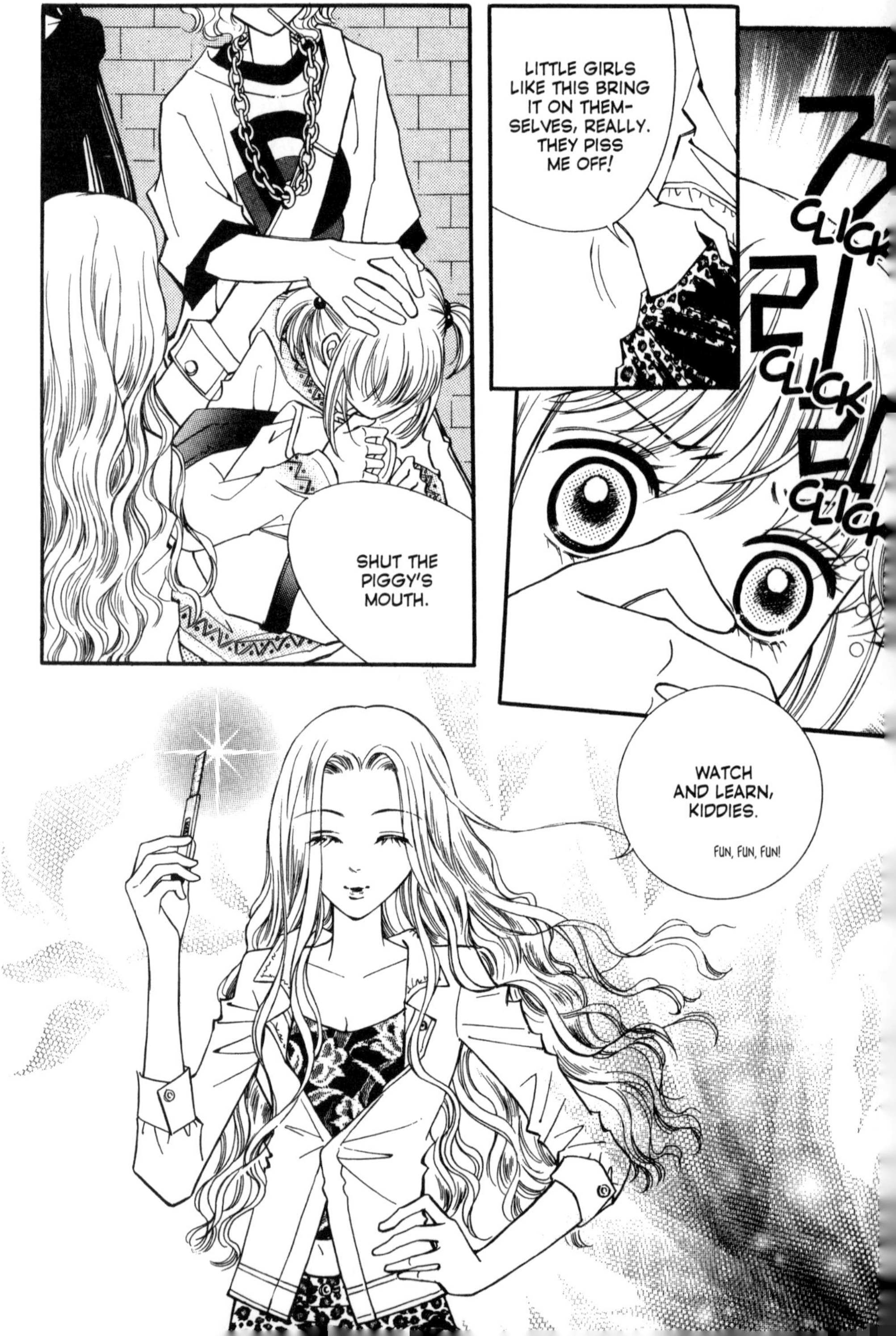
SHUT THE PIGGY'S MOUTH.
LITTLE GIRLS LIKE THIS BRING IT ON THEMSELVES, REALLY. THEY PISS ME OFF!
CLICK
CLICK
CLICK
WATCH AND LEARN, KIDDIES.
FUN, FUN, FUN!

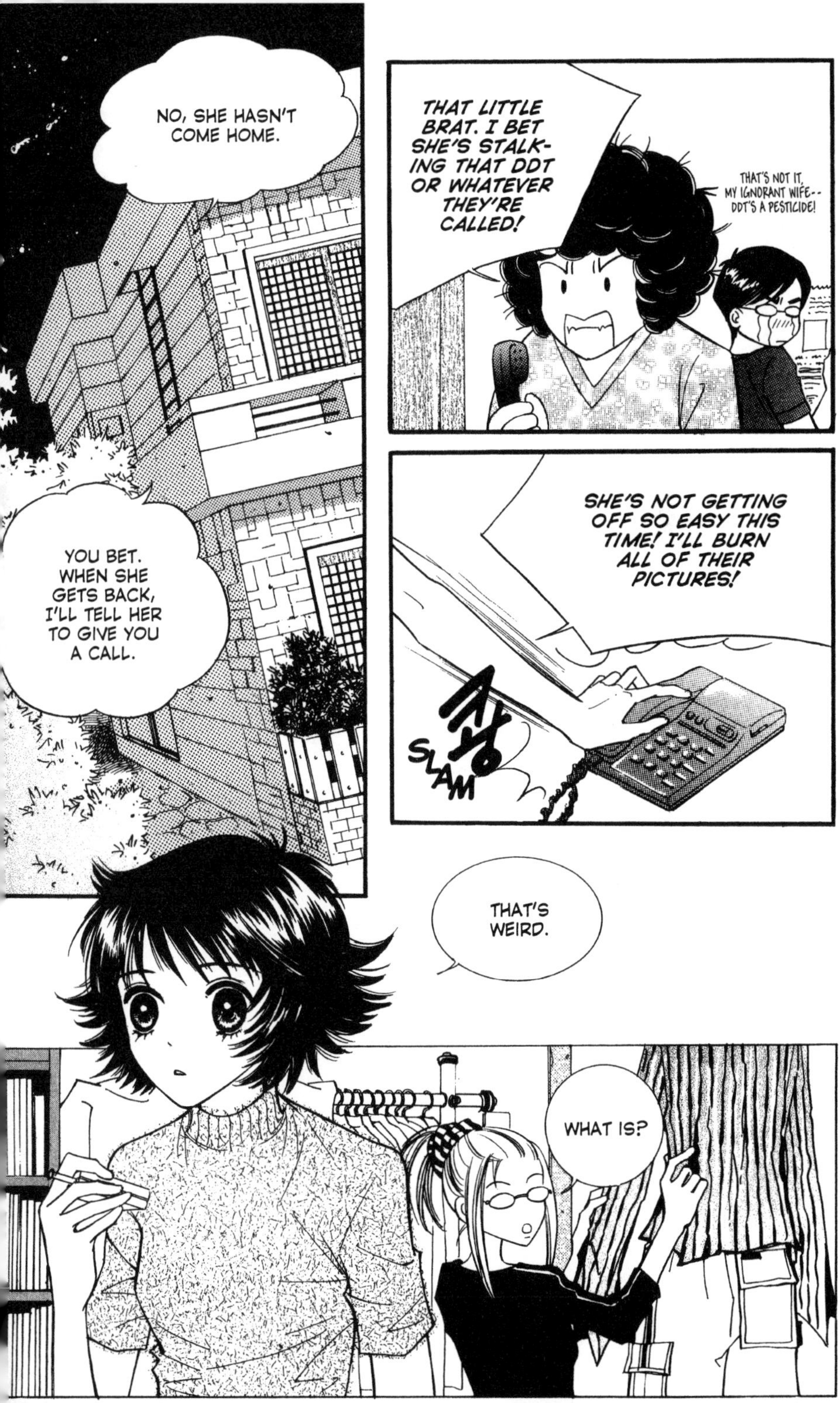
NO, SHE HASN'T COME HOME.
YOU BET. WHEN SHE GETS BACK, I'LL TELL HER TO GIVE YOU A CALL.
THAT LITTLE BRAT. I BET SHE'S STALKING THAT DDT OR WHATEVER THEY'RE CALLED!
THAT'S NOT IT, MY IGNORANT WIFE--DDT'S A PESTICIDE!
SHE'S NOT GETTING OFF SO EASY THIS TIME! I'LL BURN ALL OF THEIR PICTURES!
SLAM
THAT'S WEIRD.
WHAT IS?

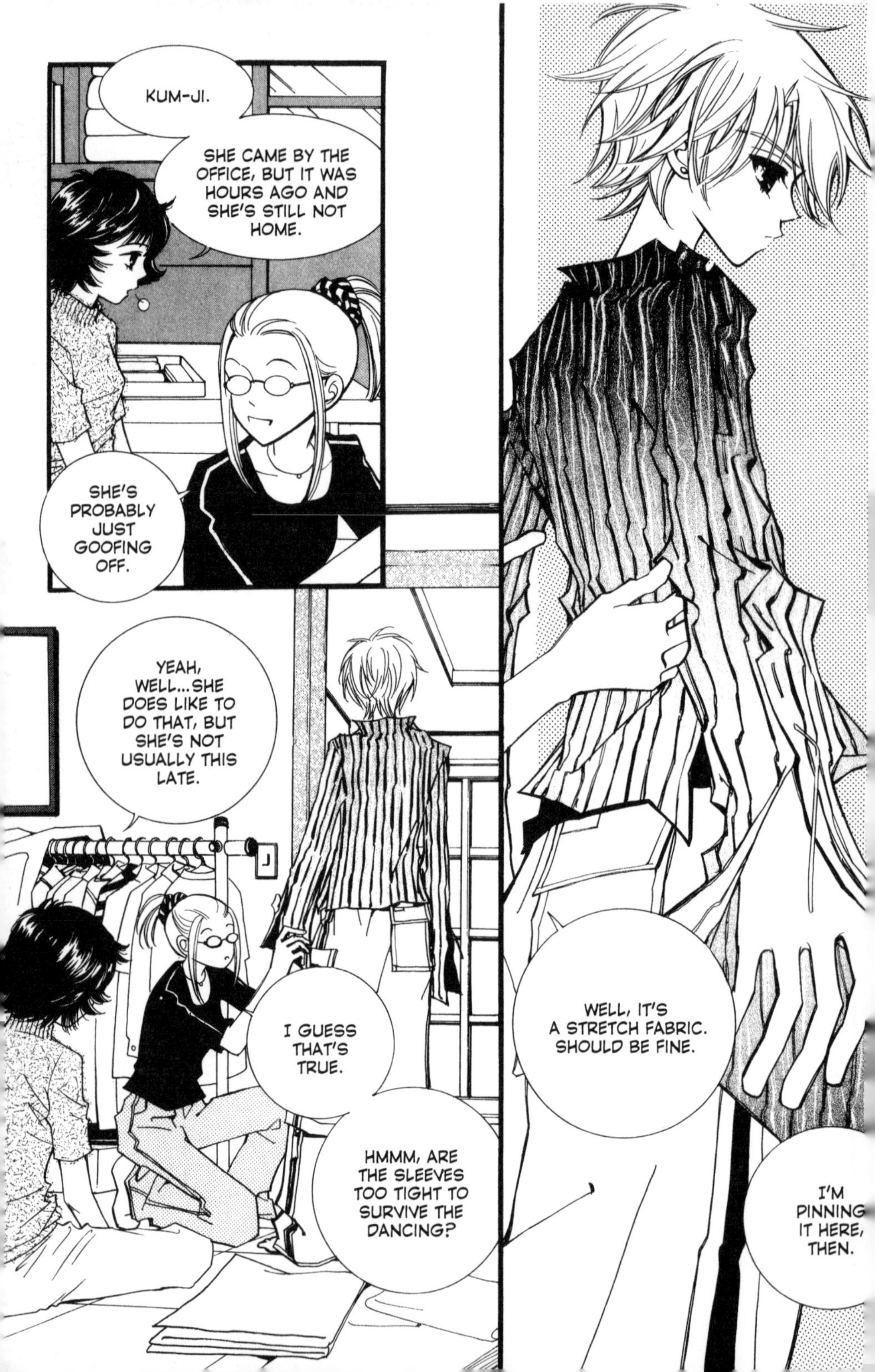
KUM-JI.
SHE CAME BY THE OFFICE, BUT IT WAS HOURS AGO AND SHE'S STILL NOT HOME.
SHE'S PROBABLY JUST GOOFING OFF.
YEAH, WELL...SHE DOES LIKE TO DO THAT, BUT SHE'S NOT USUALLY THIS LATE.
I GUESS THAT'S TRUE.
HMMM, ARE THE SLEEVES TOO TIGHT TO SURVIVE THE DANCING?
WELL, IT'S A STRETCH FABRIC. SHOULD BE FINE.
I'M PINNING IT HERE, THEN.

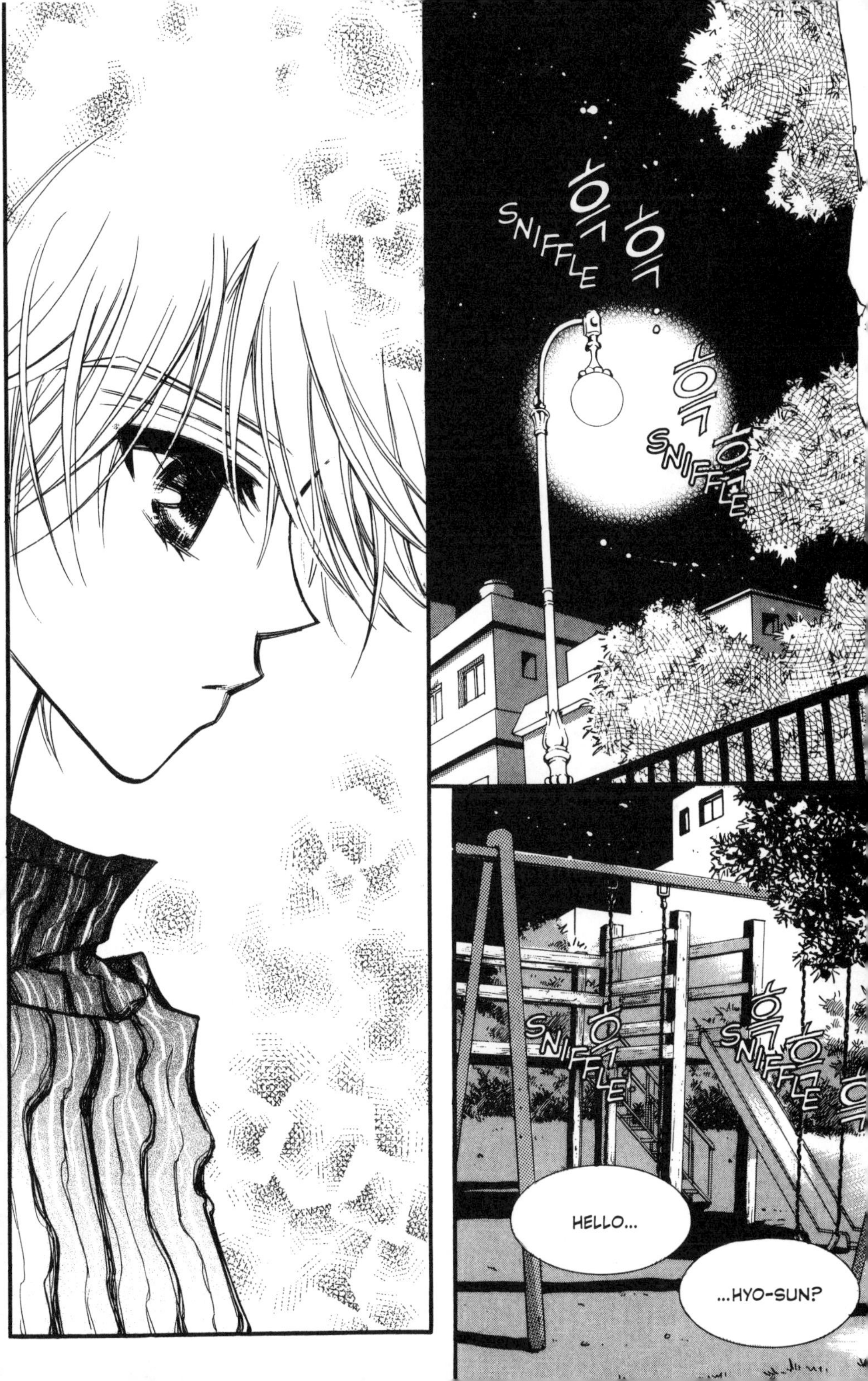
SNIFFLE
SNIFFLE
SNIFFLE
SNIFFLE
HELLO...
...HYO-SUN?

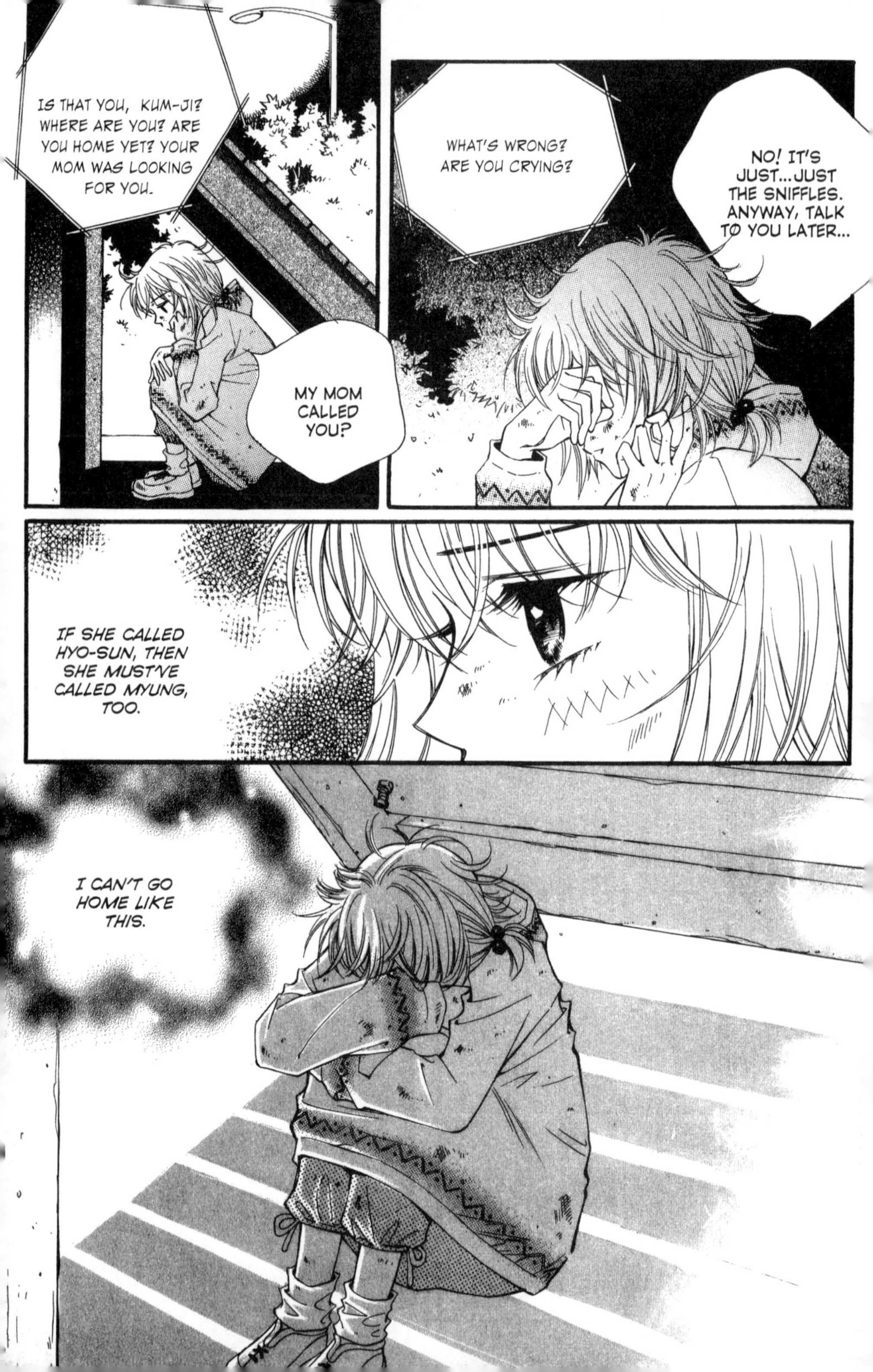
IS THAT YOU, KUM-JI? WHERE ARE YOU? ARE YOU HOME YET? YOUR MOM WAS LOOKING FOR YOU.
MY MOM CALLED YOU?
WHAT'S WRONG? ARE YOU CRYING?
NO! IT'S JUST...JUST THE SNIFFLES. ANYWAY, TALK TO YOU LATER...
IF SHE CALLED HYO-SUN, THEN SHE MUST'VE CALLED MYUNG, TOO.
I CAN'T GO HOME LIKE THIS.

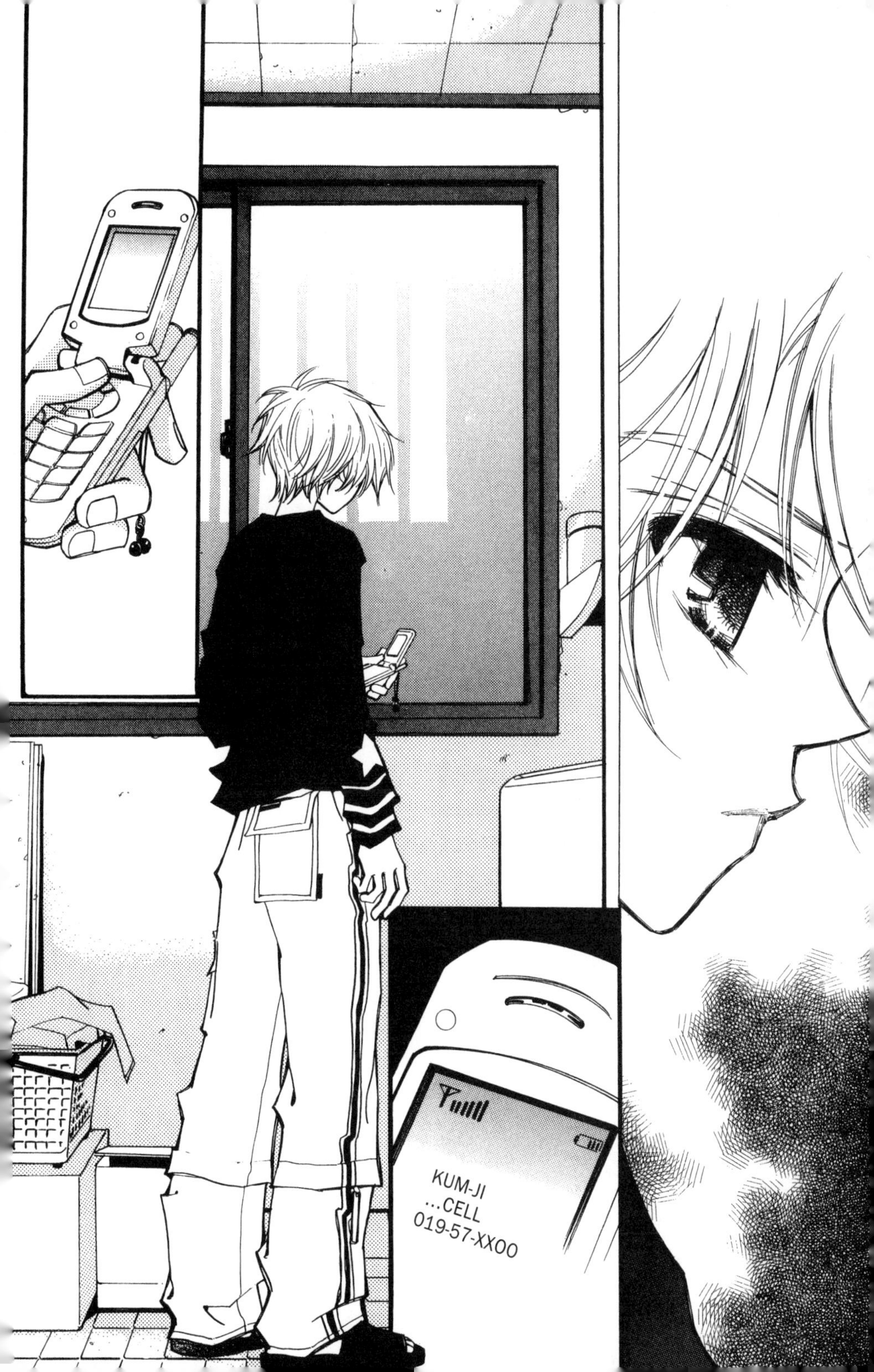
KUM-JI
...CELL
019-57-XX00

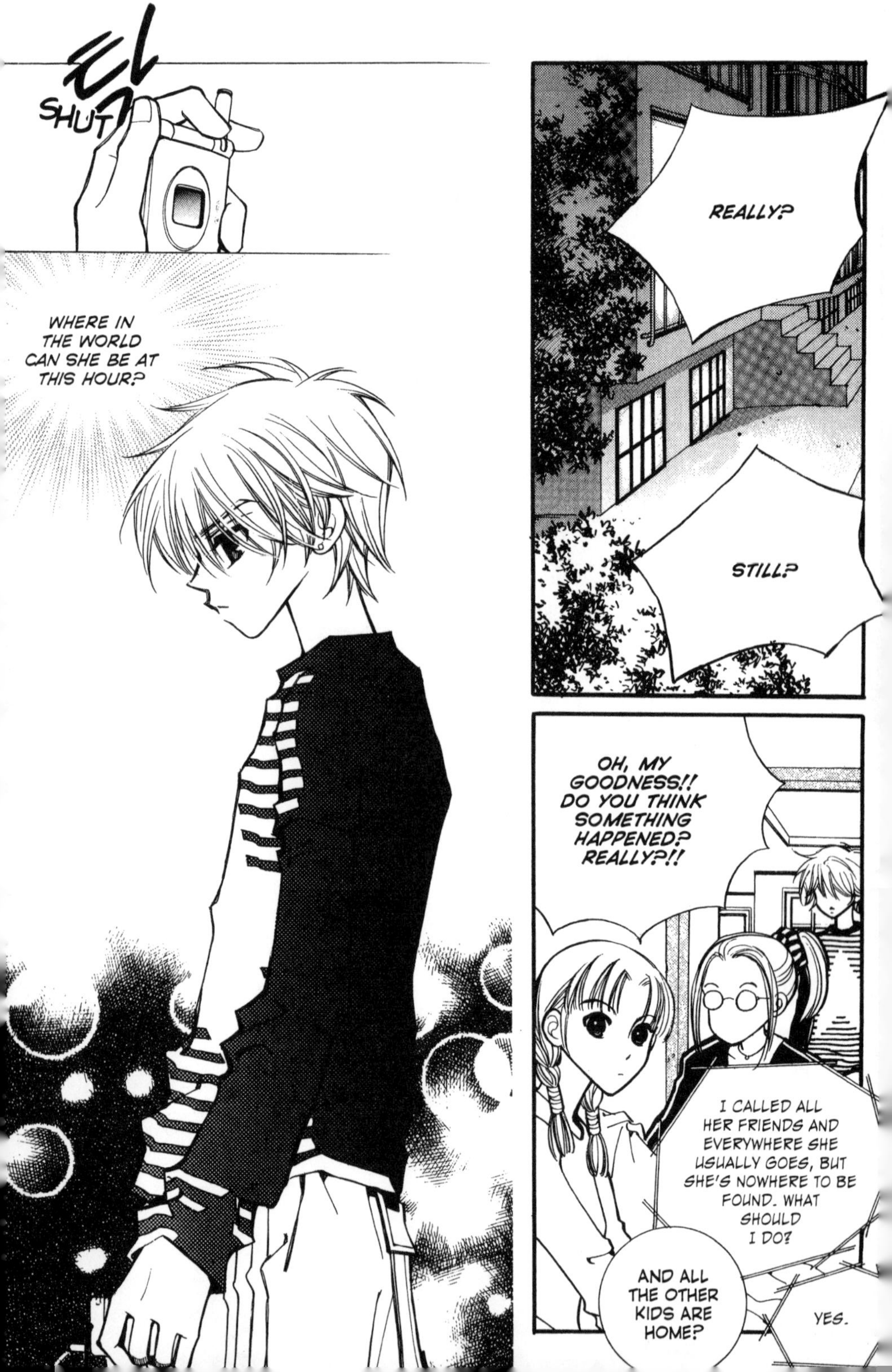
SHUT
WHERE IN THE WORLD CAN SHE BE AT THIS HOUR?
REALLY?
STILL?
OH, MY GOODNESS!! DO YOU THINK SOMETHING HAPPENED? REALLY?!!
I CALLED ALL HER FRIENDS AND EVERYWHERE SHE USUALLY GOES, BUT SHE'S NOWHERE TO BE FOUND. WHAT SHOULD I DO?
AND ALL THE OTHER KIDS ARE HOME?
YES.

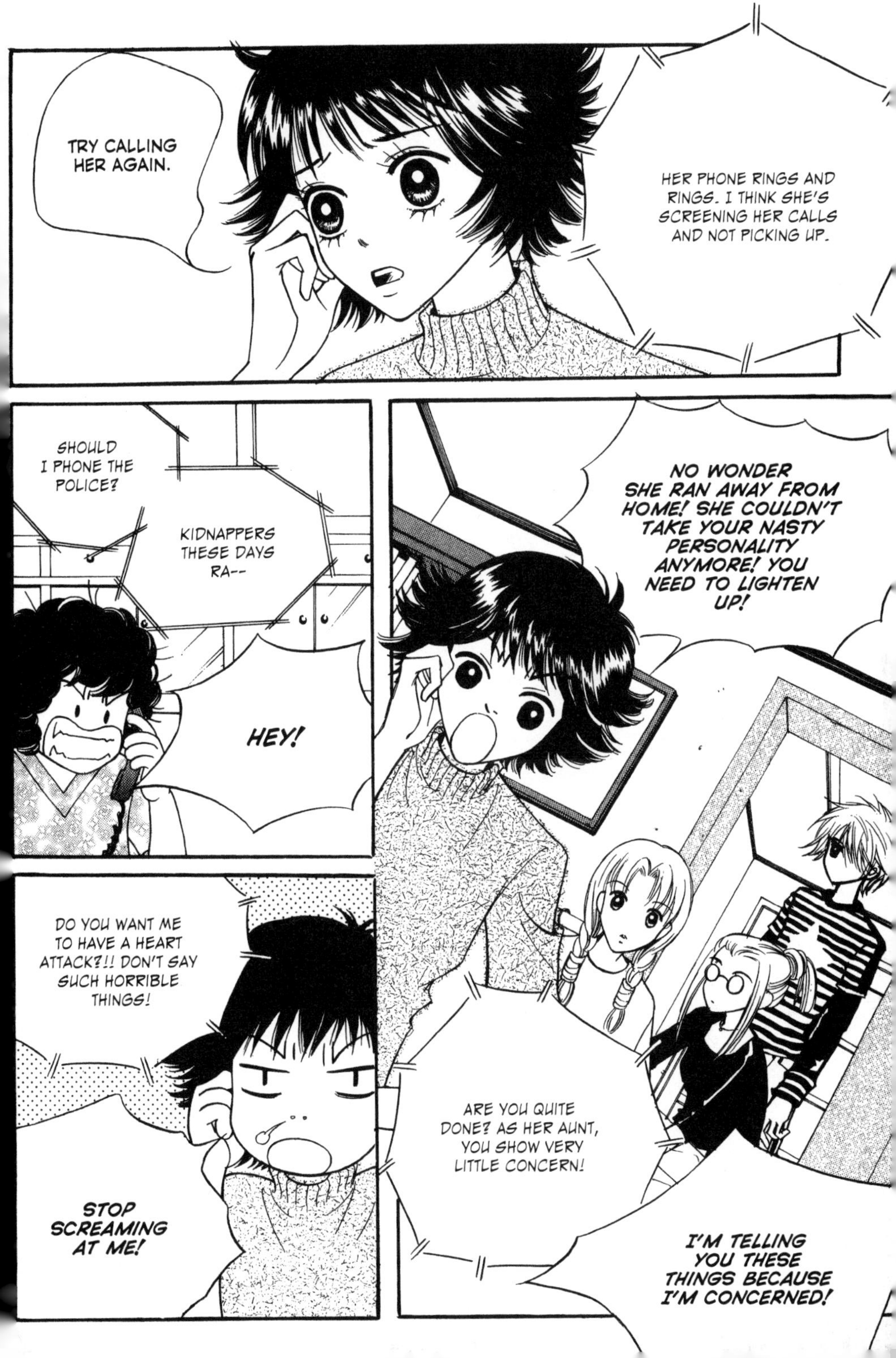
TRY CALLING HER AGAIN.
HER PHONE RINGS AND RINGS. I THINK SHE'S SCREENING HER CALLS AND NOT PICKING UP.
SHOULD I PHONE THE POLICE?
KIDNAPPERS THESE DAYS RA--
HEY!
DO YOU WANT ME TO HAVE A HEART ATTACK?!! DON'T SAY SUCH HORRIBLE THINGS!
STOP SCREAMING AT ME!
NO WONDER SHE RAN AWAY FROM HOME! SHE COULDN'T TAKE YOUR NASTY PERSONALITY ANYMORE! YOU NEED TO LIGHTEN UP!
ARE YOU QUITE DONE? AS HER AUNT, YOU SHOW VERY LITTLE CONCERN!
I'M TELLING YOU THESE THINGS BECAUSE I'M CONCERNED!

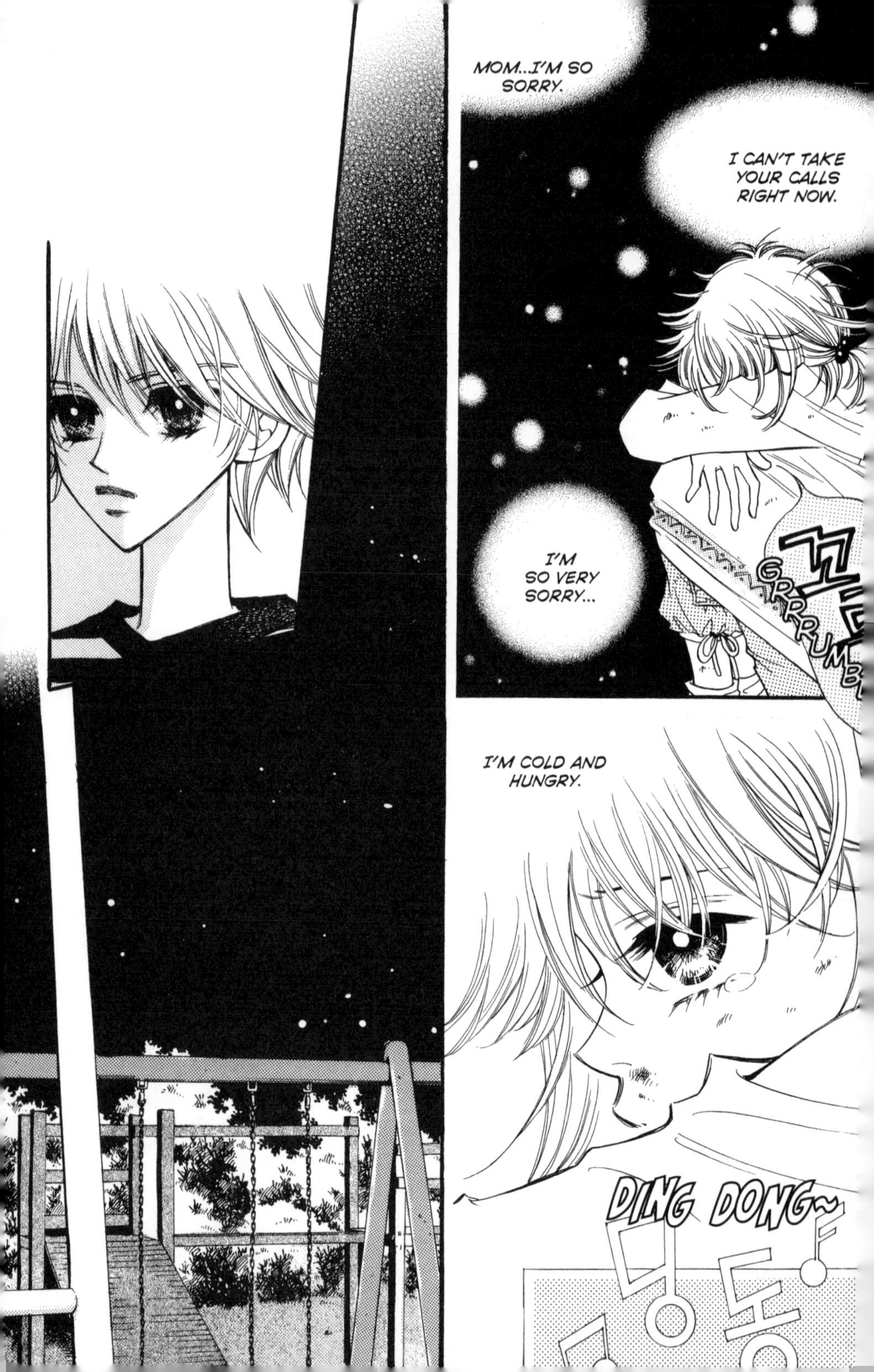
MOM...I'M SO SORRY.
I CAN'T TAKE YOUR CALLS RIGHT NOW.
I'M SO VERY SORRY...
GRRRUMB
I'M COLD AND HUNGRY.
DING DONG~

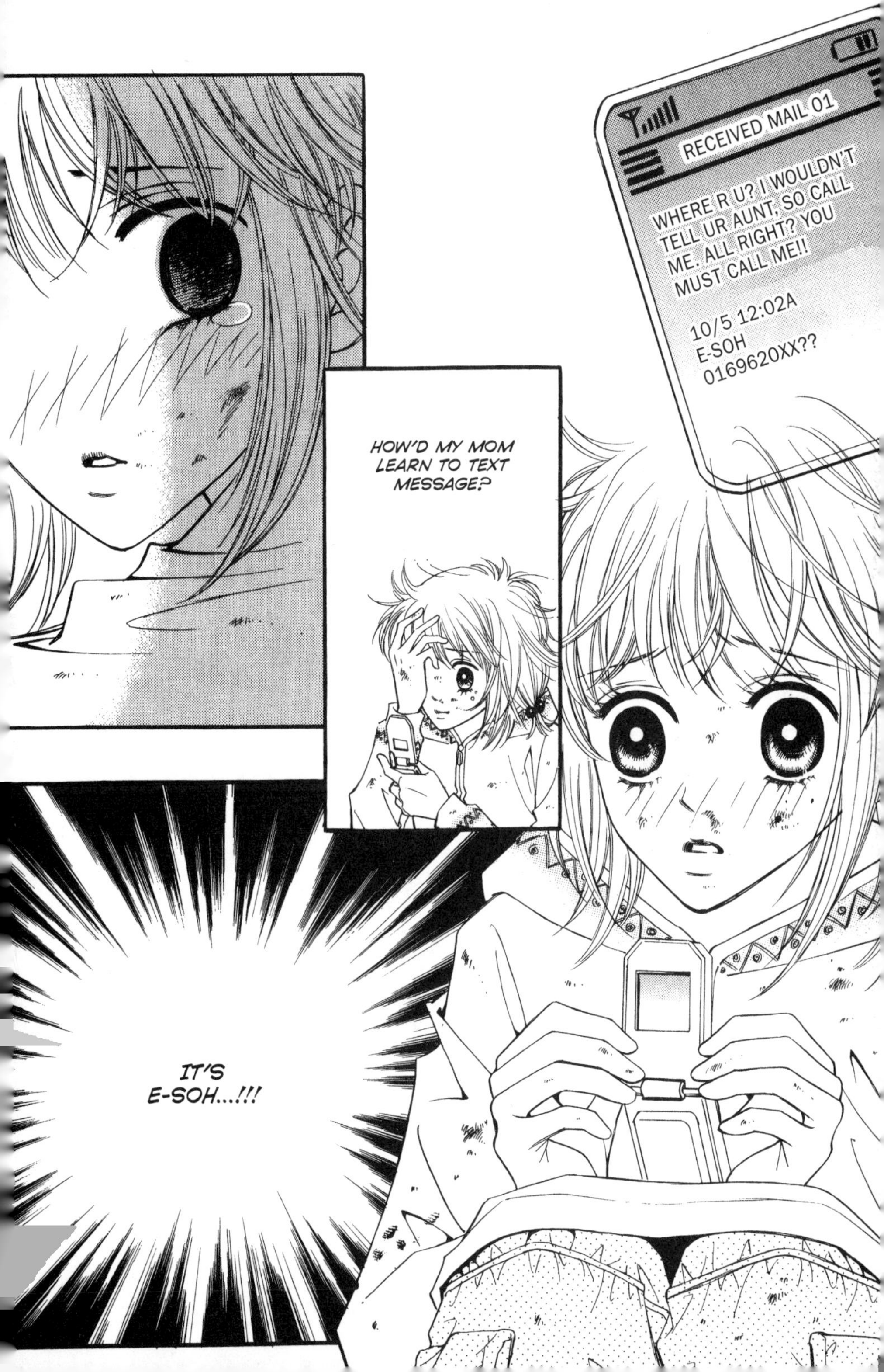
HOW'D MY MOM LEARN TO TEXT MESSAGE?
RECEIVED MAIL 01
WHERE R U? I WOULDN'T TELL UR AUNT, SO CALL ME. ALL RIGHT? YOU MUST CALL ME!!
10/5 12:02A
E-SOH
0169620XX??
IT'S E-SOH...!!!

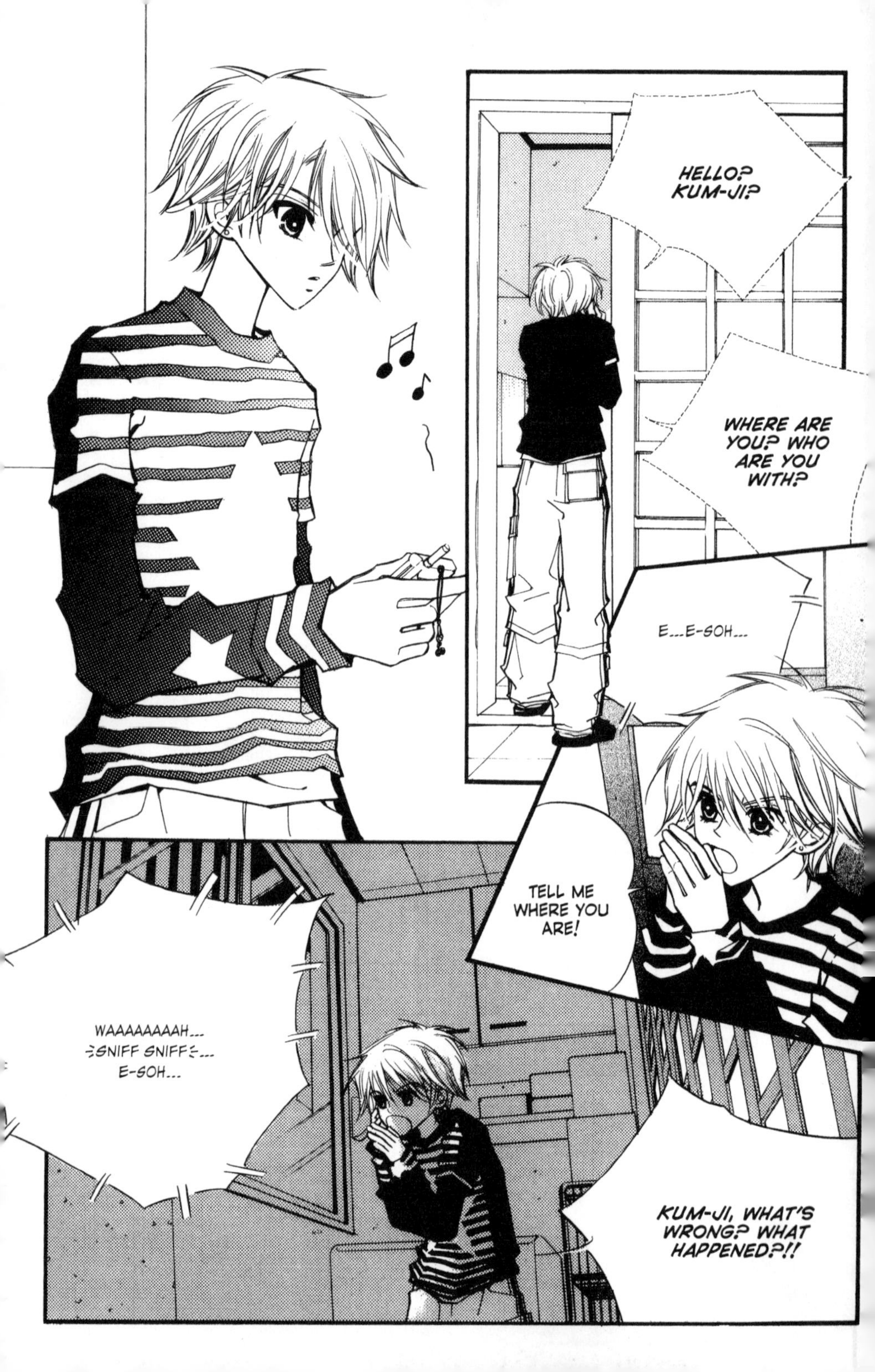
HELLO? KUM-JI?
WHERE ARE YOU? WHO ARE YOU WITH?
E...E-SOH...
TELL ME WHERE YOU ARE!
WAAAAAAAAH... ≡SNIFF SNIFF≡... E-SOH...
KUM-JI, WHAT'S WRONG? WHAT HAPPENED?!!

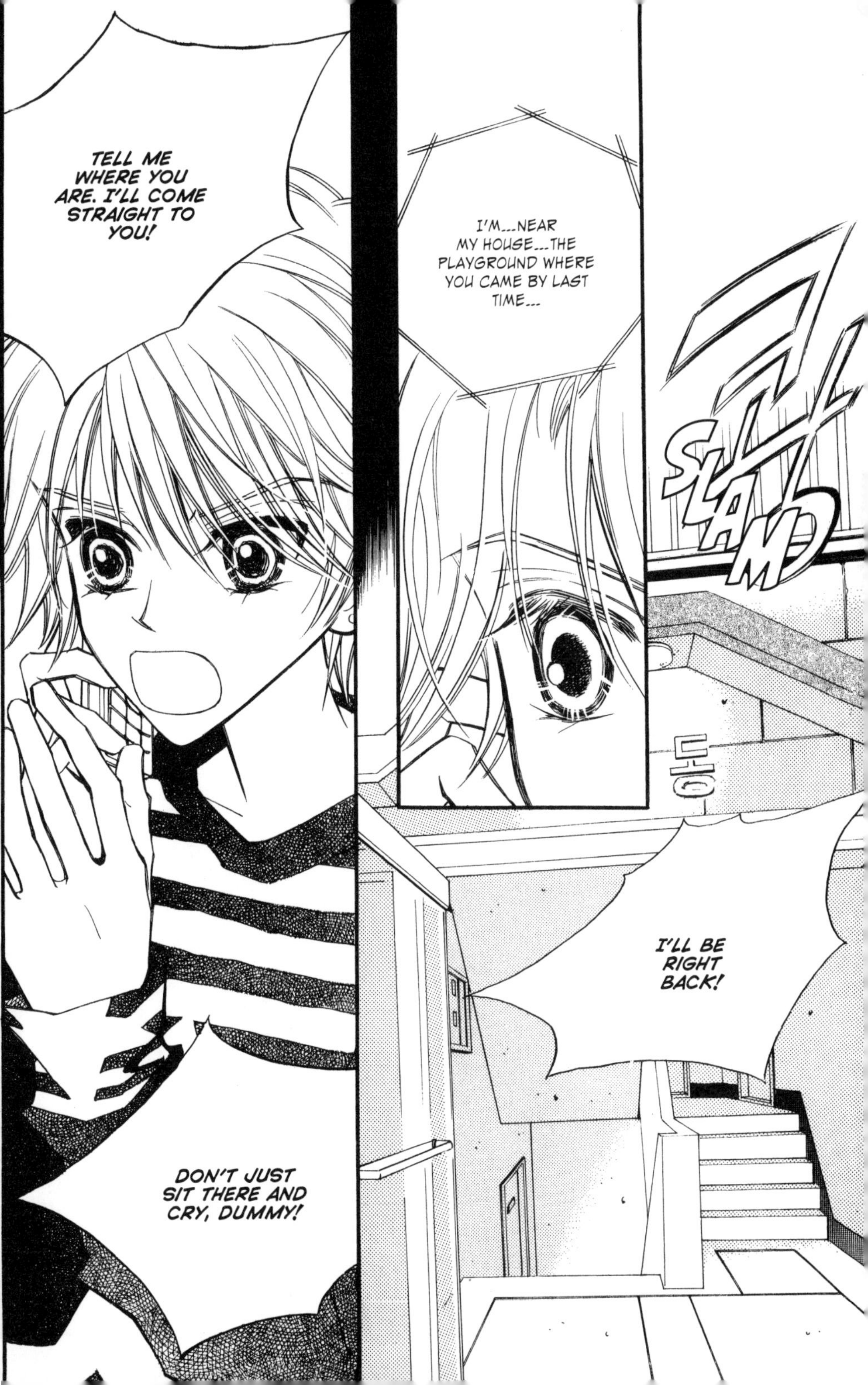
I'M...NEAR MY HOUSE...THE PLAYGROUND WHERE YOU CAME BY LAST TIME...
TELL ME WHERE YOU ARE. I'LL COME STRAIGHT TO YOU!
DON'T JUST SIT THERE AND CRY, DUMMY!
SLAM
I'LL BE RIGHT BACK!

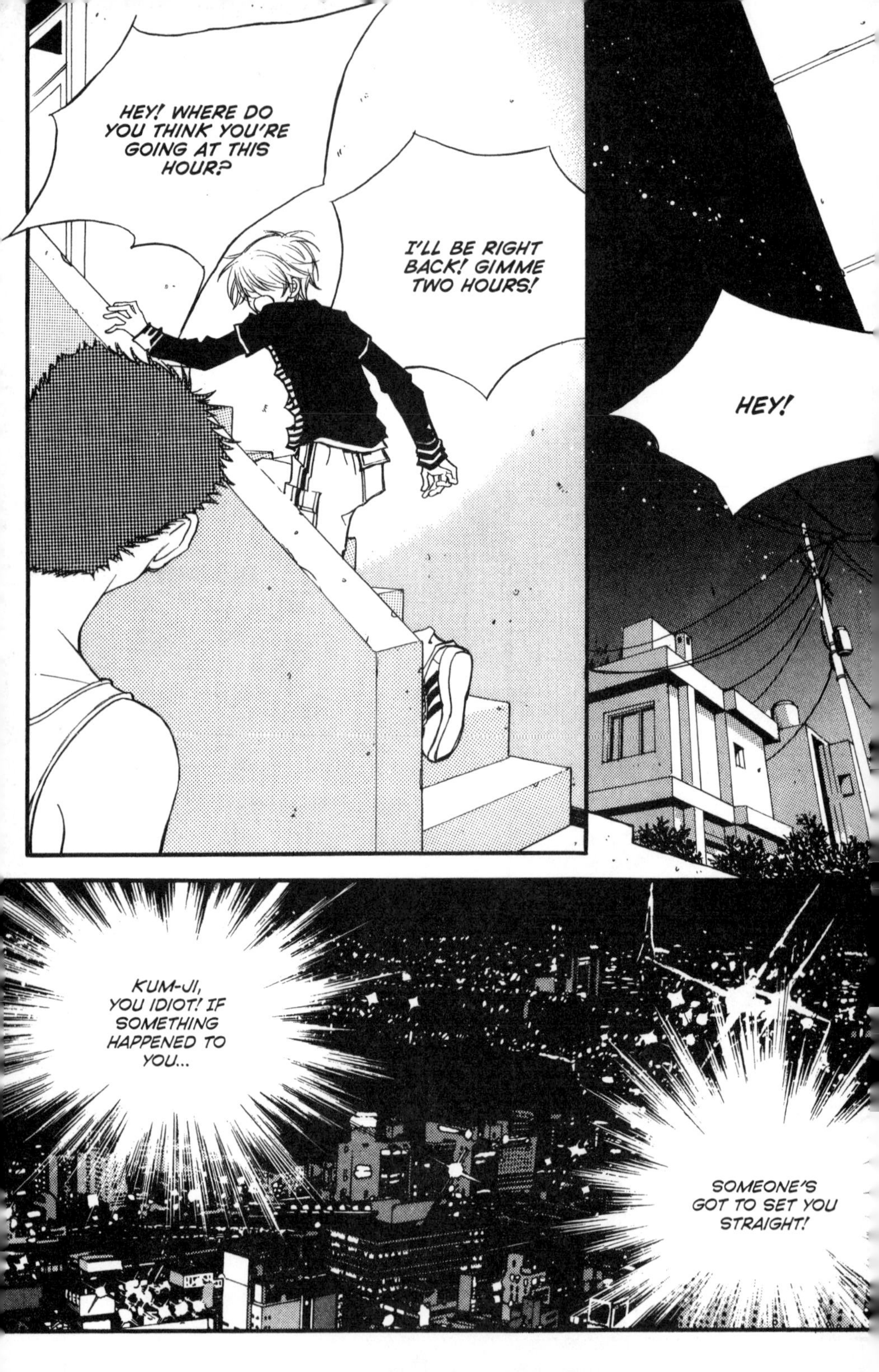
HEY! WHERE DO YOU THINK YOU'RE GOING AT THIS HOUR?
I'LL BE RIGHT BACK! GIMME TWO HOURS!
HEY!
KUM-JI, YOU IDIOT! IF SOMETHING HAPPENED TO YOU...
SOMEONE'S GOT TO SET YOU STRAIGHT!

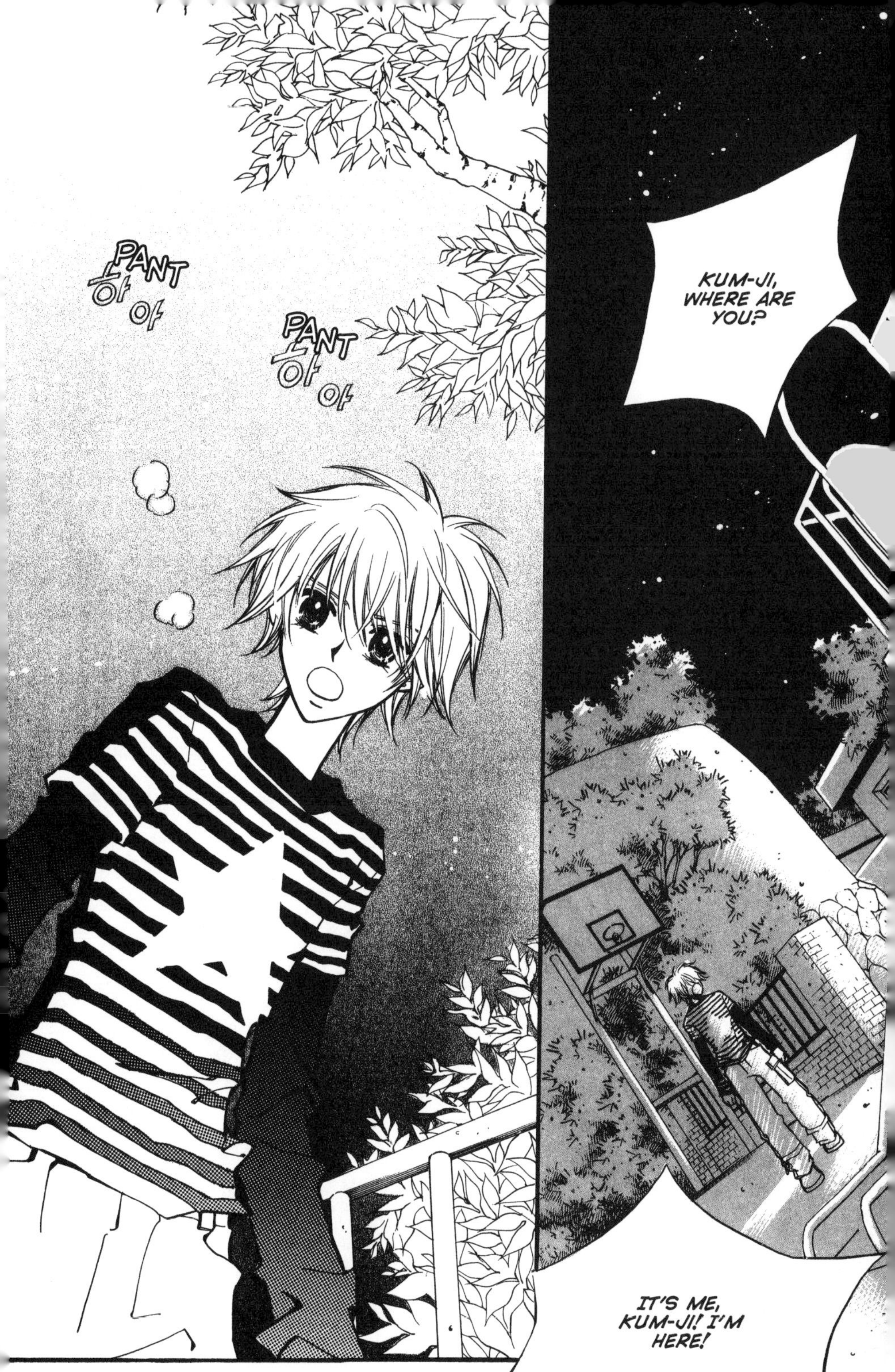
PANT
PANT
KUM-JI, WHERE ARE YOU?
IT'S ME, KUM-JI! I'M HERE!

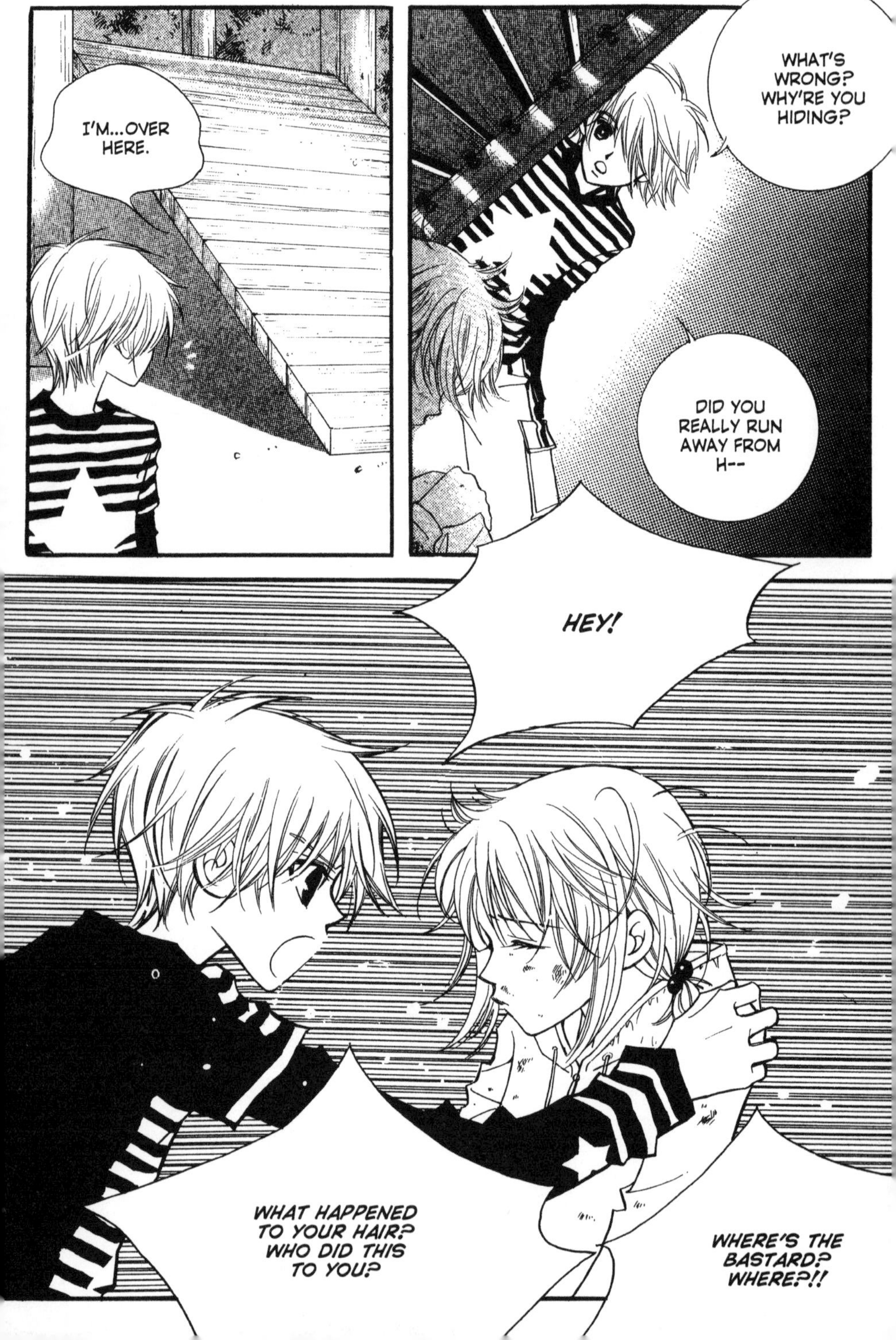
I'M...OVER HERE.
WHAT'S WRONG? WHY'RE YOU HIDING?
DID YOU REALLY RUN AWAY FROM H--
HEY!
WHAT HAPPENED TO YOUR HAIR? WHO DID THIS TO YOU?
WHERE'S THE BASTARD? WHERE?!!

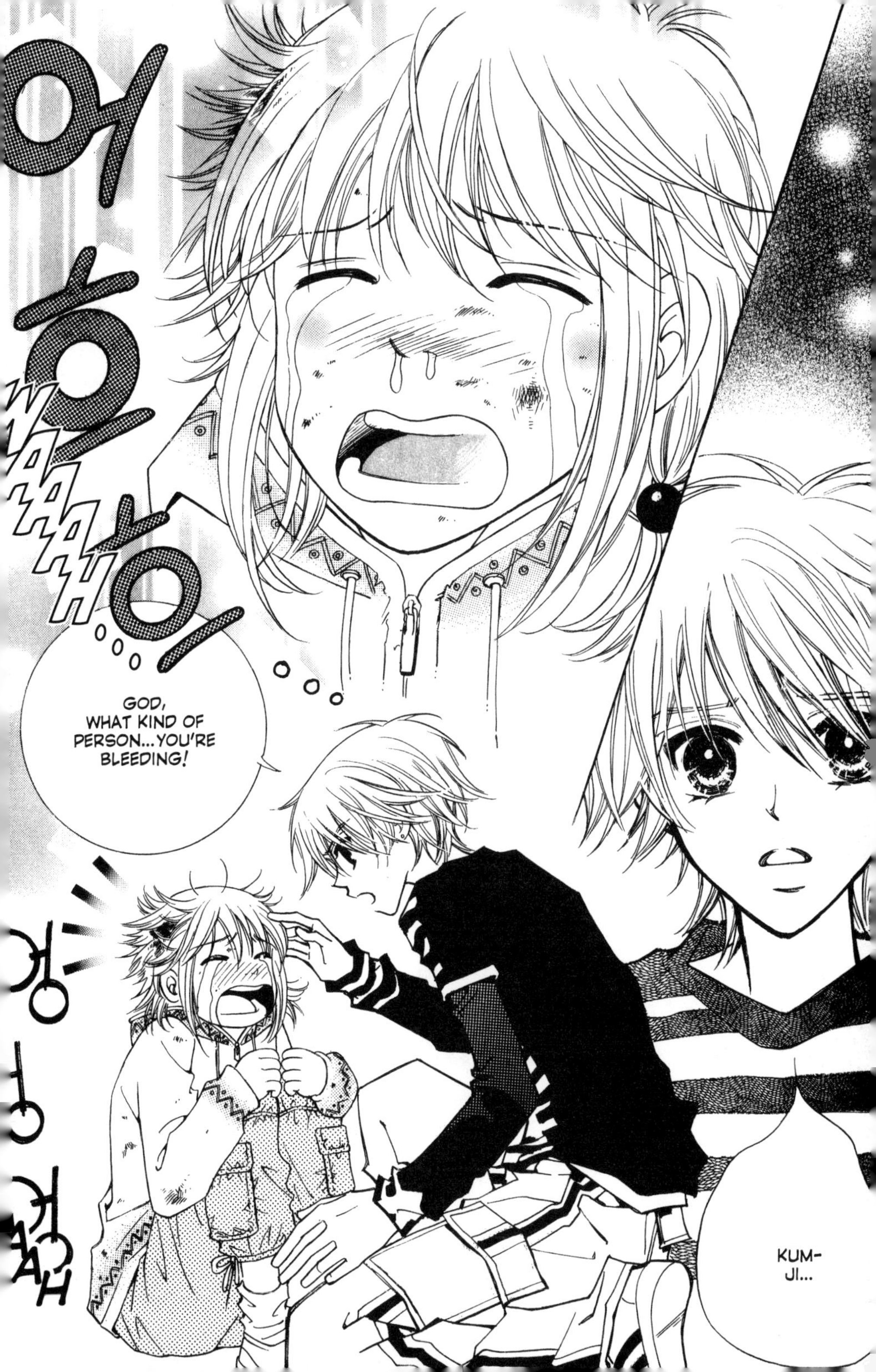
WAAAH
GOD, WHAT KIND OF PERSON...YOU'RE BLEEDING!
KUM-JI...

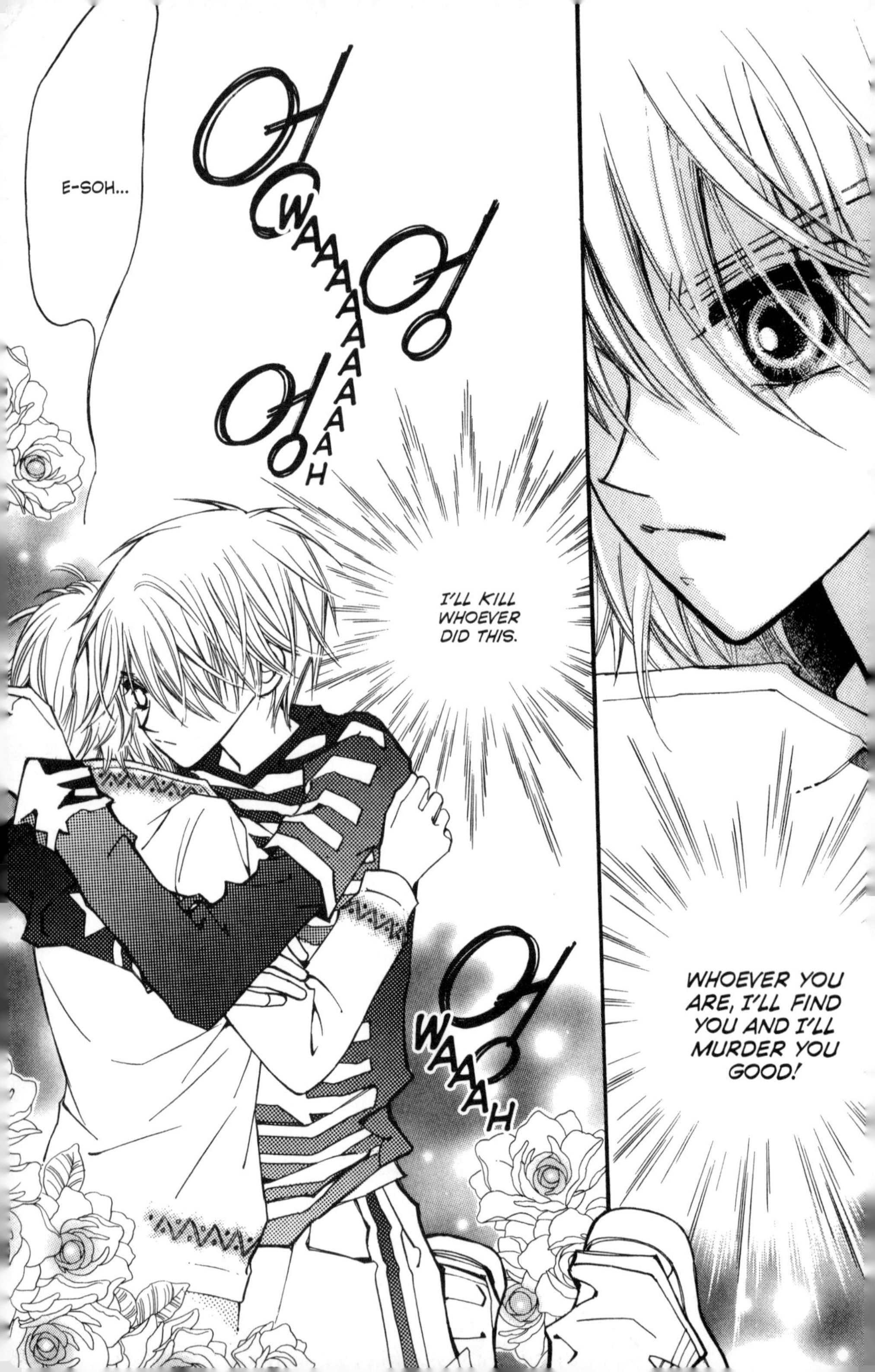
E-SOH...
WAAAAAAAAAAAAH
I'LL KILL WHOEVER DID THIS.
WAAAH
WHOEVER YOU ARE, I'LL FIND YOU AND I'LL MURDER YOU GOOD!

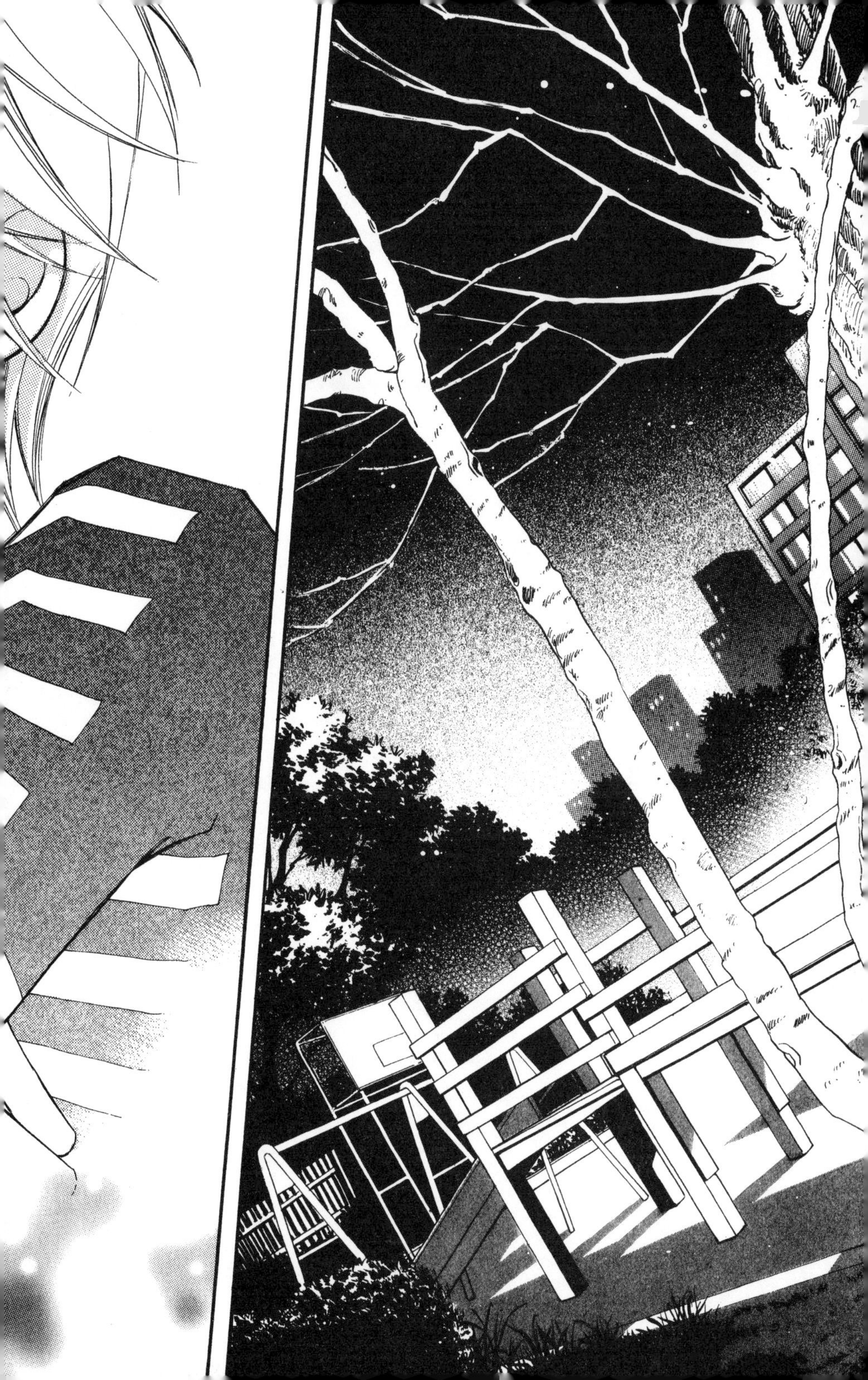

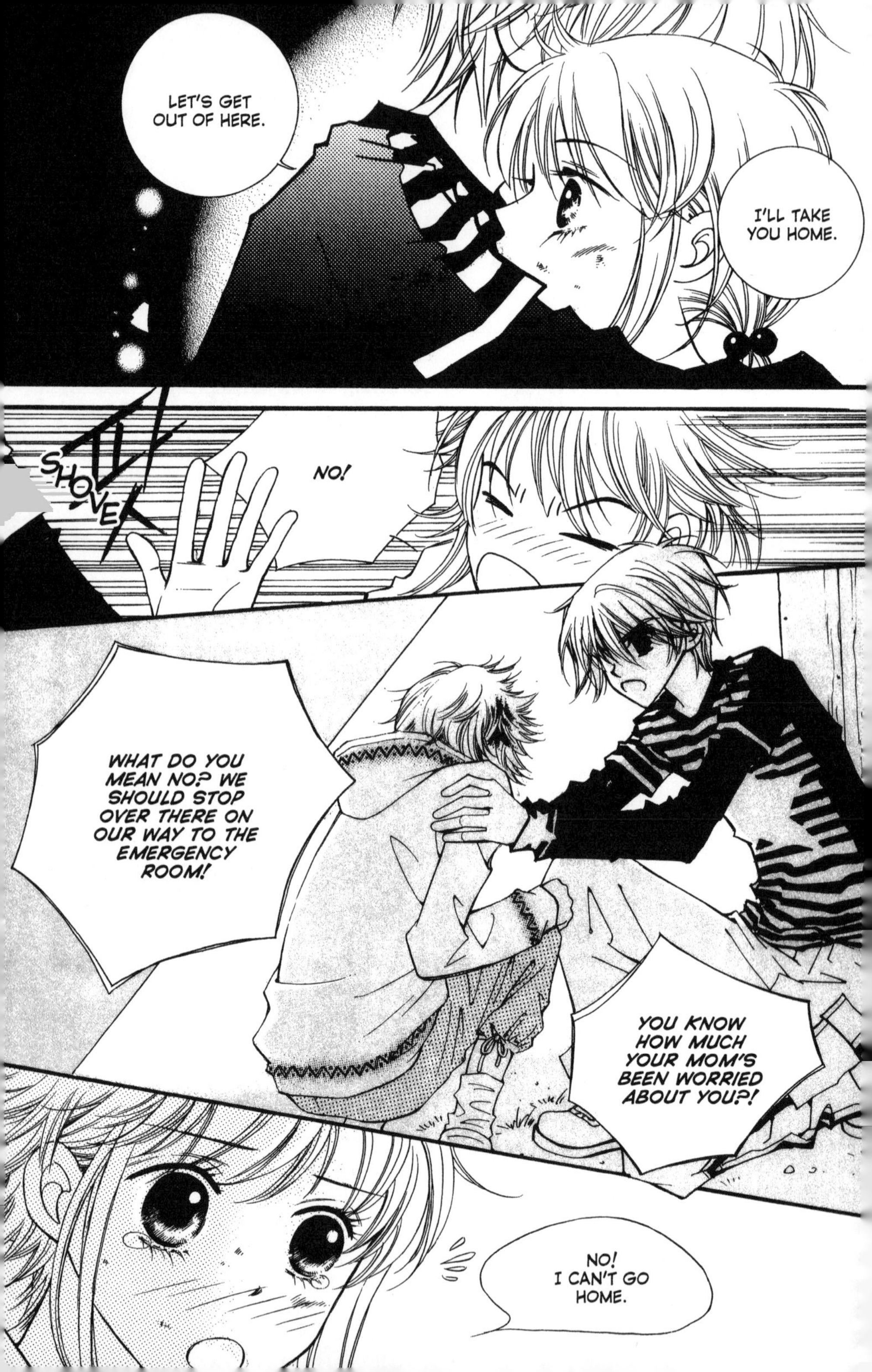
LET'S GET OUT OF HERE.
I'LL TAKE YOU HOME.
SHOVE
NO!
WHAT DO YOU MEAN NO? WE SHOULD STOP OVER THERE ON OUR WAY TO THE EMERGENCY ROOM!
YOU KNOW HOW MUCH YOUR MOM'S BEEN WORRIED ABOUT YOU?!
NO! I CAN'T GO HOME.

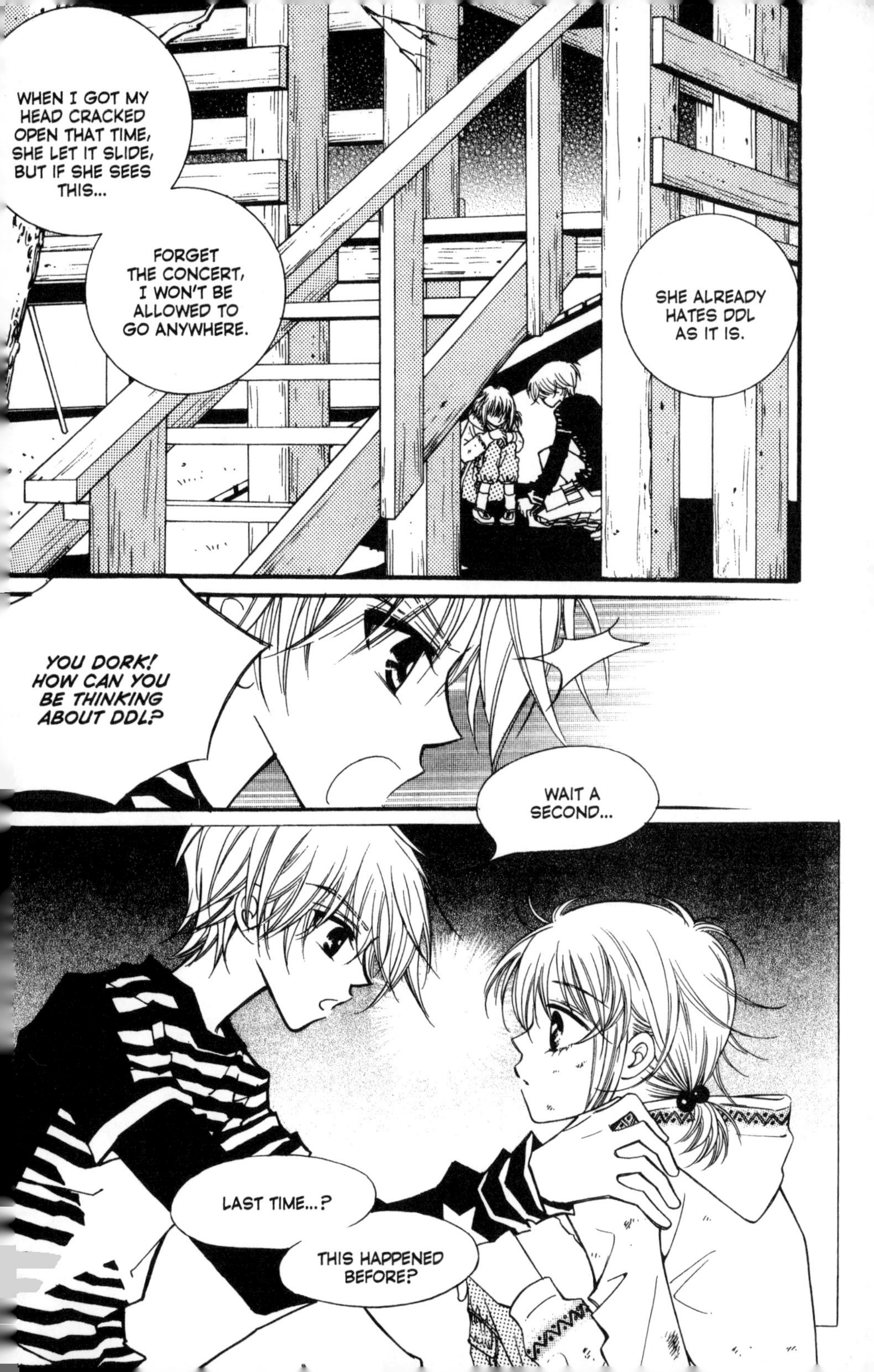
WHEN I GOT MY HEAD CRACKED OPEN THAT TIME, SHE LET IT SLIDE, BUT IF SHE SEES THIS...
FORGET THE CONCERT, I WON'T BE ALLOWED TO GO ANYWHERE.
SHE ALREADY HATES DDL AS IT IS.
YOU DORK! HOW CAN YOU BE THINKING ABOUT DDL?
WAIT A SECOND...
LAST TIME...?
THIS HAPPENED BEFORE?

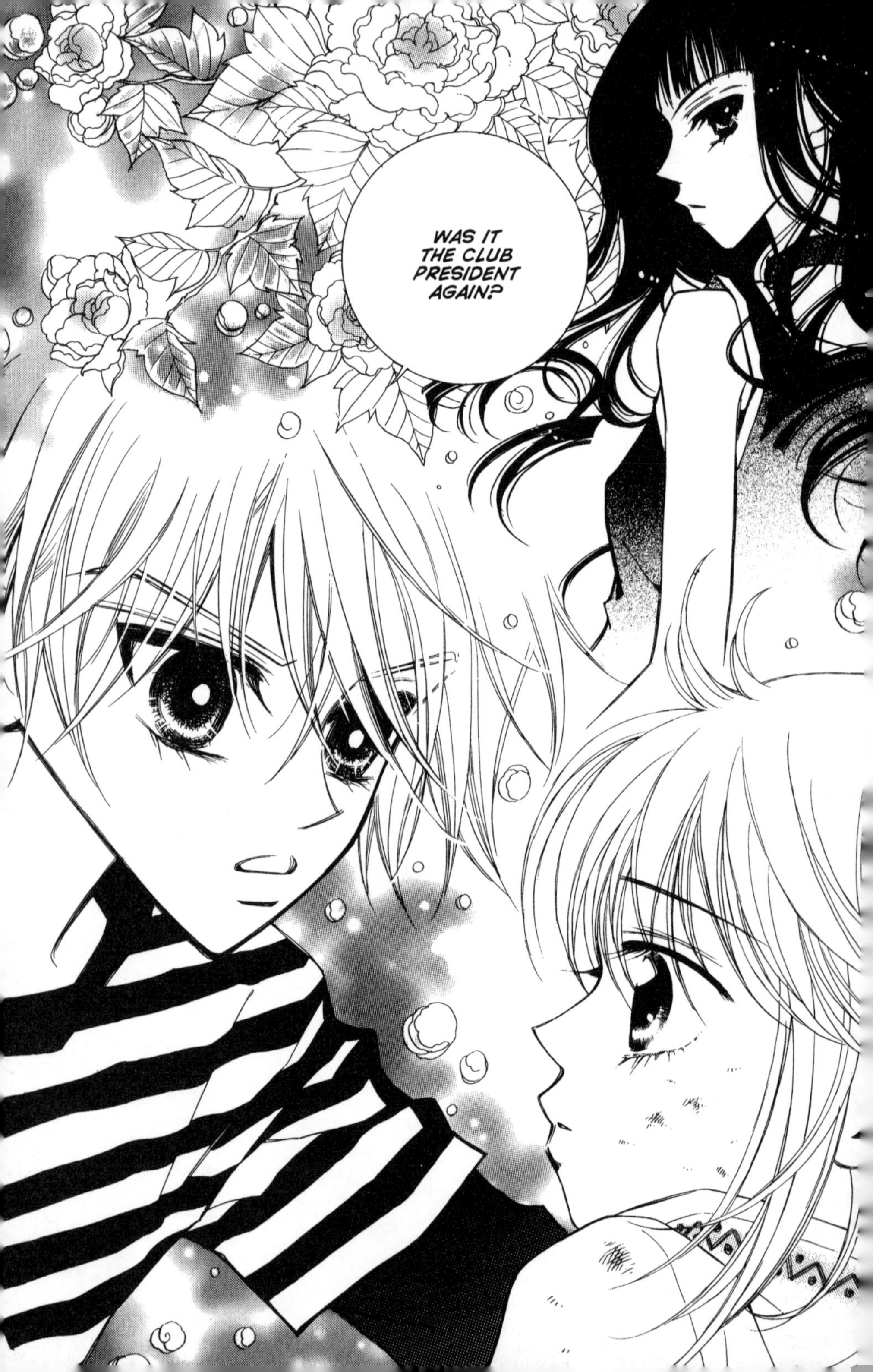
WAS IT THE CLUB PRESIDENT AGAIN?

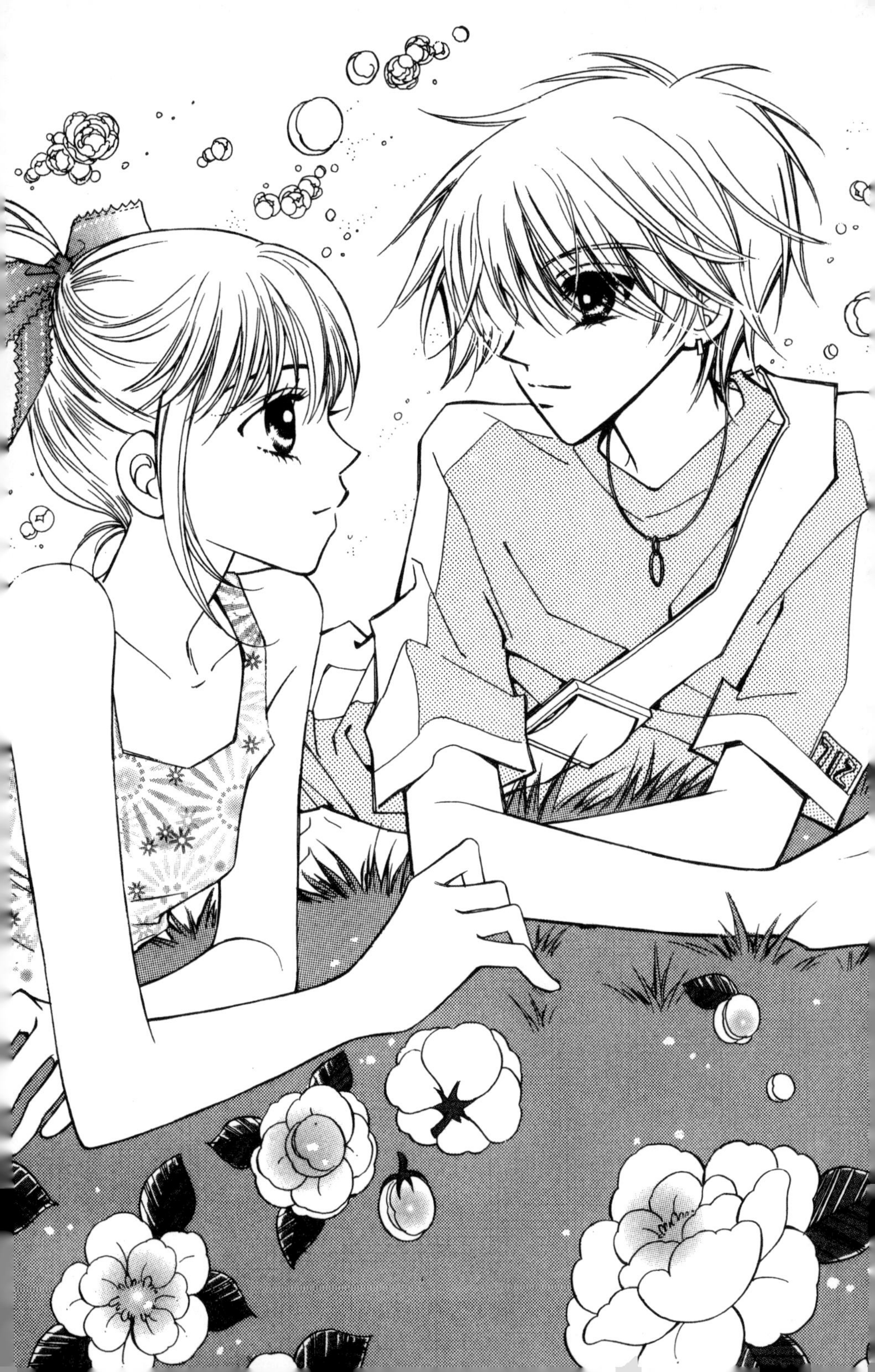

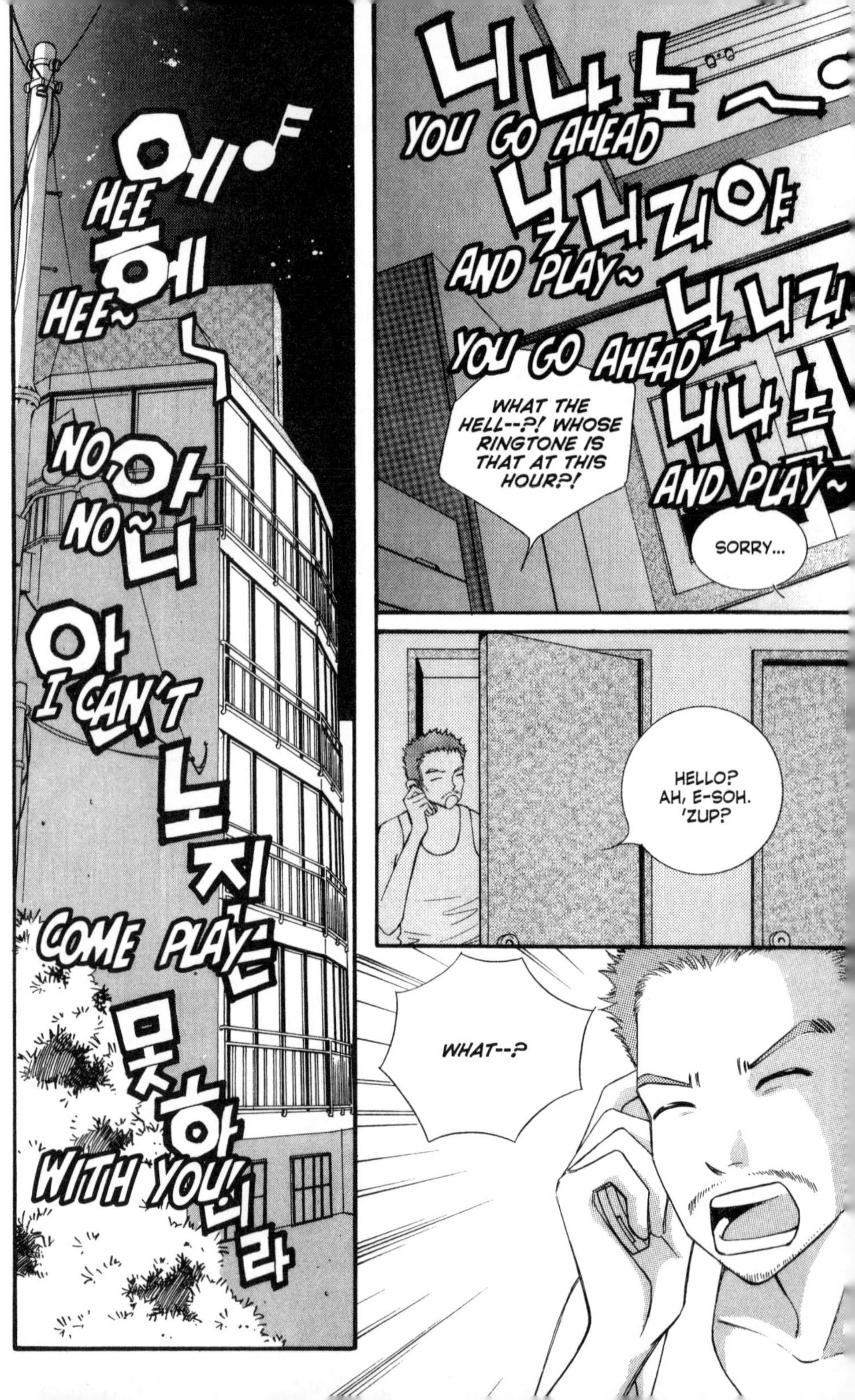
HEE
HEE~
NO, NO~
I CAN'T
COME PLAY
WITH YOU!
니나노~
YOU GO AHEAD
닐니리야
AND PLAY~
YOU GO AHEAD
닐니리
니나노
AND PLAY~
WHAT THE HELL--?! WHOSE RINGTONE IS THAT AT THIS HOUR?!
SORRY...
HELLO? AH, E-SOH. 'ZUP?
WHAT--?

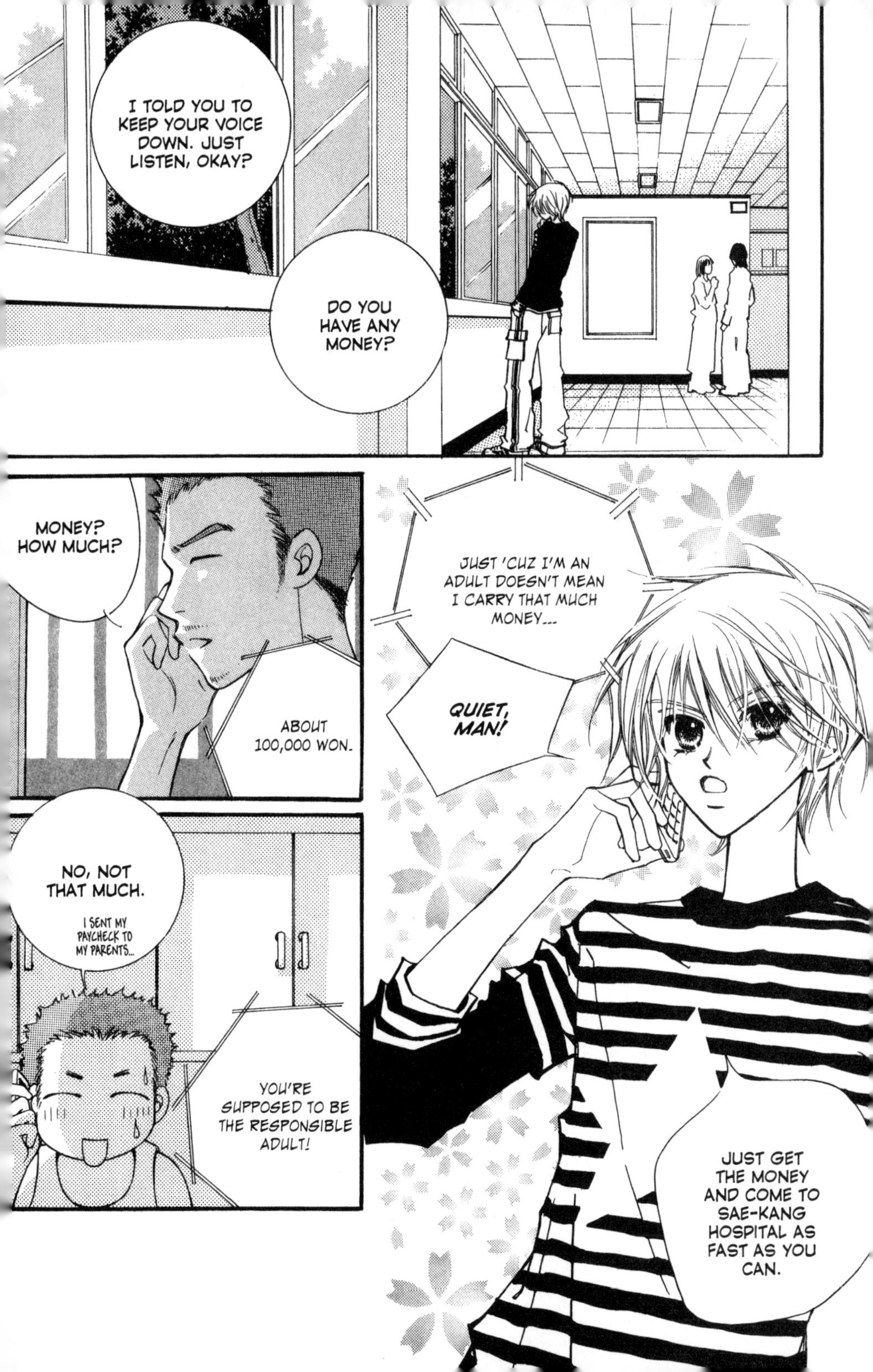
I TOLD YOU TO KEEP YOUR VOICE DOWN. JUST LISTEN, OKAY?
DO YOU HAVE ANY MONEY?
MONEY? HOW MUCH?
ABOUT 100,000 WON.
NO, NOT THAT MUCH.
I SENT MY PAYCHECK TO MY PARENTS...
YOU'RE SUPPOSED TO BE THE RESPONSIBLE ADULT!
JUST 'CUZ I'M AN ADULT DOESN'T MEAN I CARRY THAT MUCH MONEY...
QUIET, MAN!
JUST GET THE MONEY AND COME TO SAE-KANG HOSPITAL AS FAST AS YOU CAN.

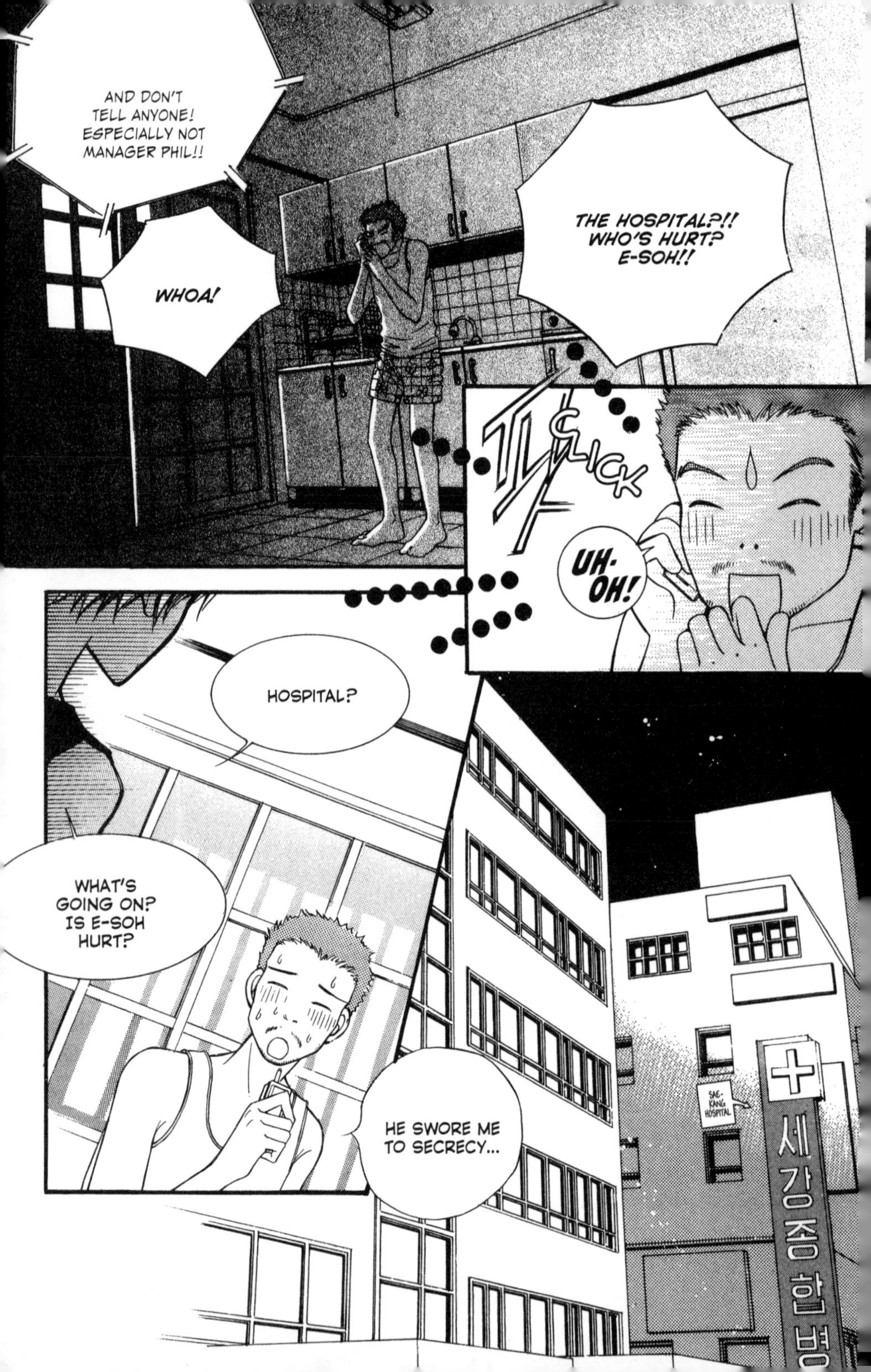
AND DON'T TELL ANYONE! ESPECIALLY NOT MANAGER PHIL!!
WHOA!
THE HOSPITAL?!! WHO'S HURT? E-SOH!!
CLICK
UH-OH!
HOSPITAL?
WHAT'S GOING ON? IS E-SOH HURT?
HE SWORE ME TO SECRECY...
SAE-KANG HOSPITAL
세강종합병

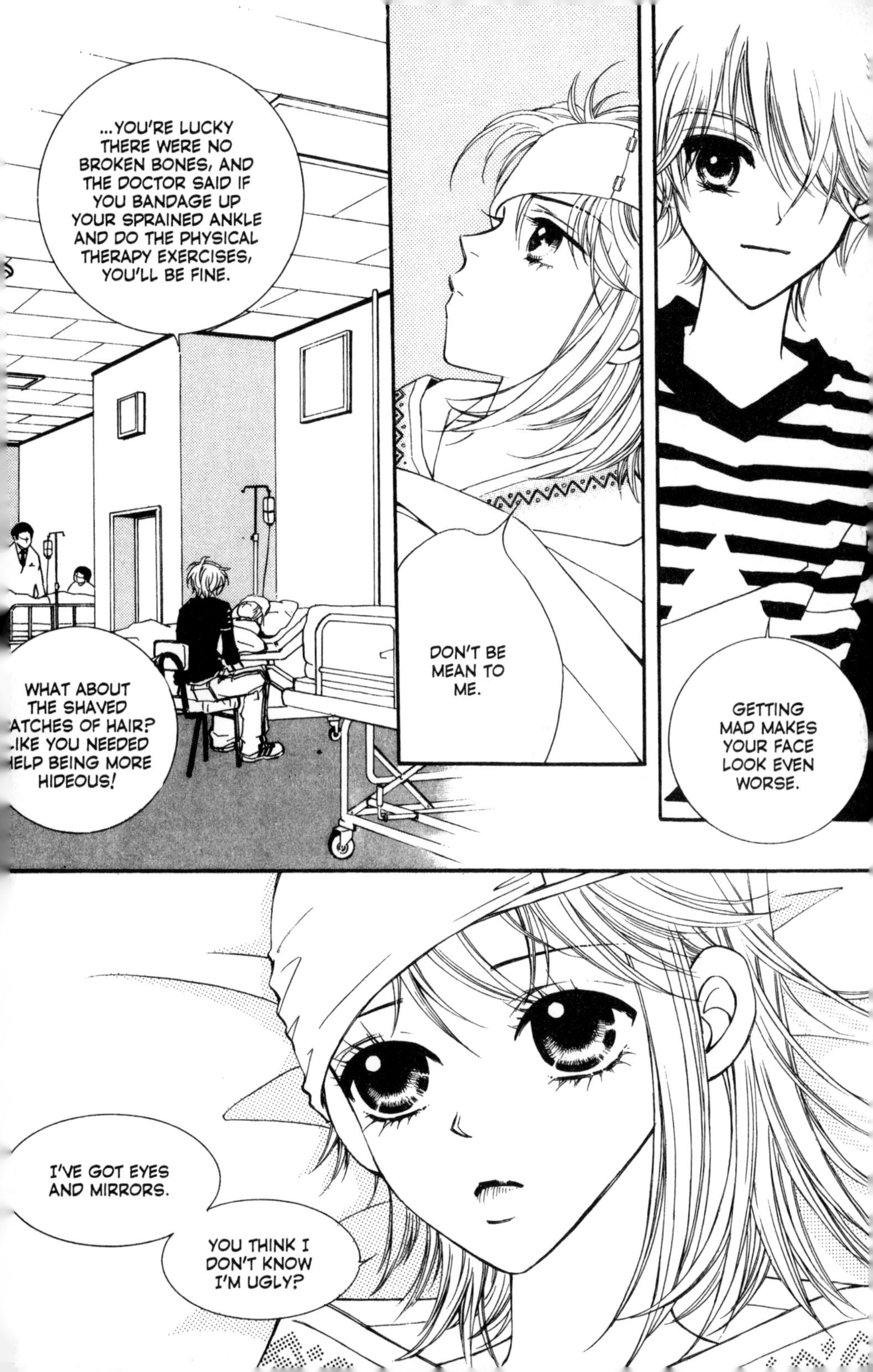
...YOU'RE LUCKY THERE WERE NO BROKEN BONES, AND THE DOCTOR SAID IF YOU BANDAGE UP YOUR SPRAINED ANKLE AND DO THE PHYSICAL THERAPY EXERCISES, YOU'LL BE FINE.
WHAT ABOUT THE SHAVED ATCHES OF HAIR? IKE YOU NEEDED ELP BEING MORE HIDEOUS!
DON'T BE MEAN TO ME.
GETTING MAD MAKES YOUR FACE LOOK EVEN WORSE.
I'VE GOT EYES AND MIRRORS.
YOU THINK I DON'T KNOW I'M UGLY?

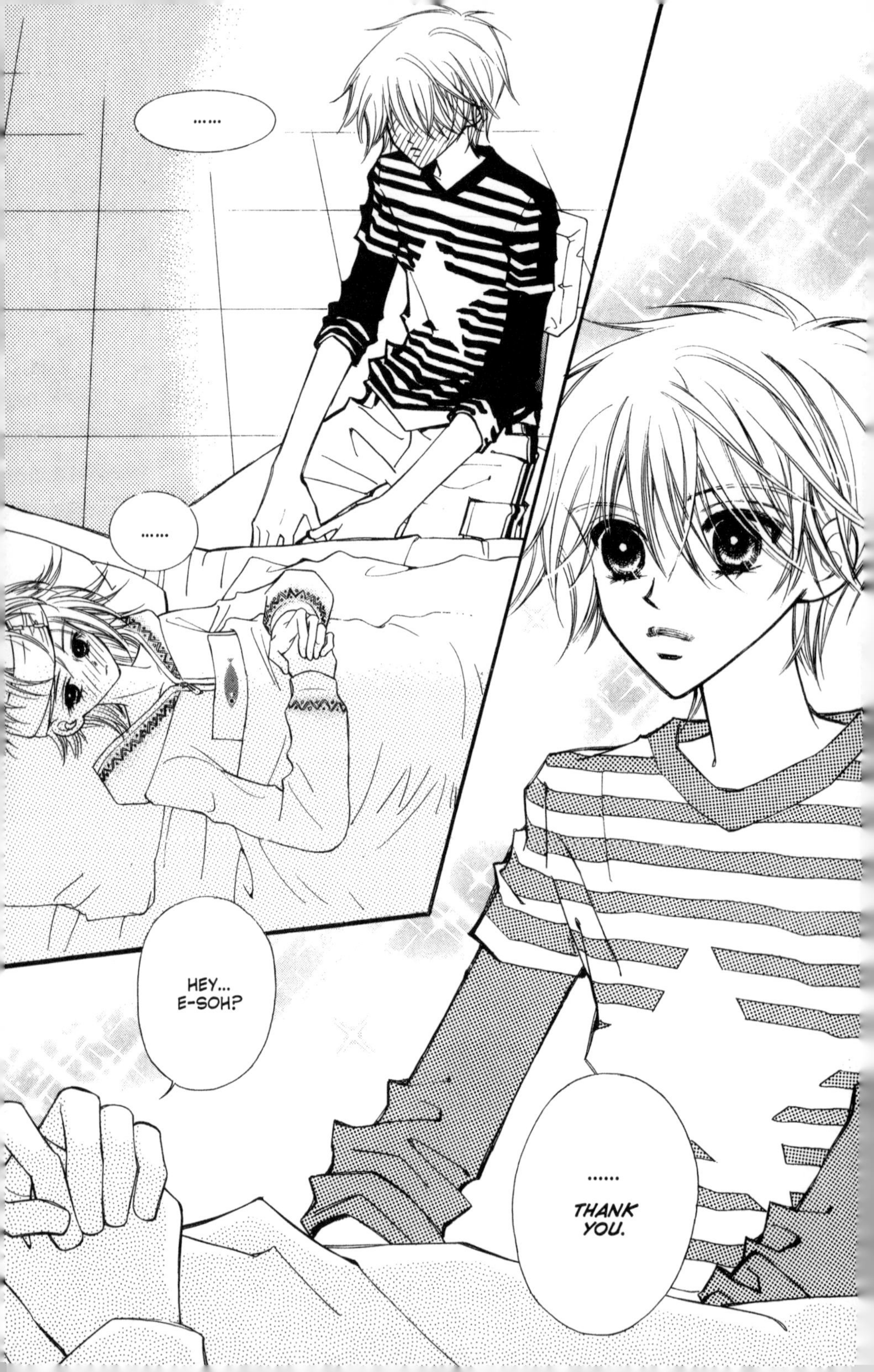
......
......
HEY... E-SOH?
...... THANK YOU.

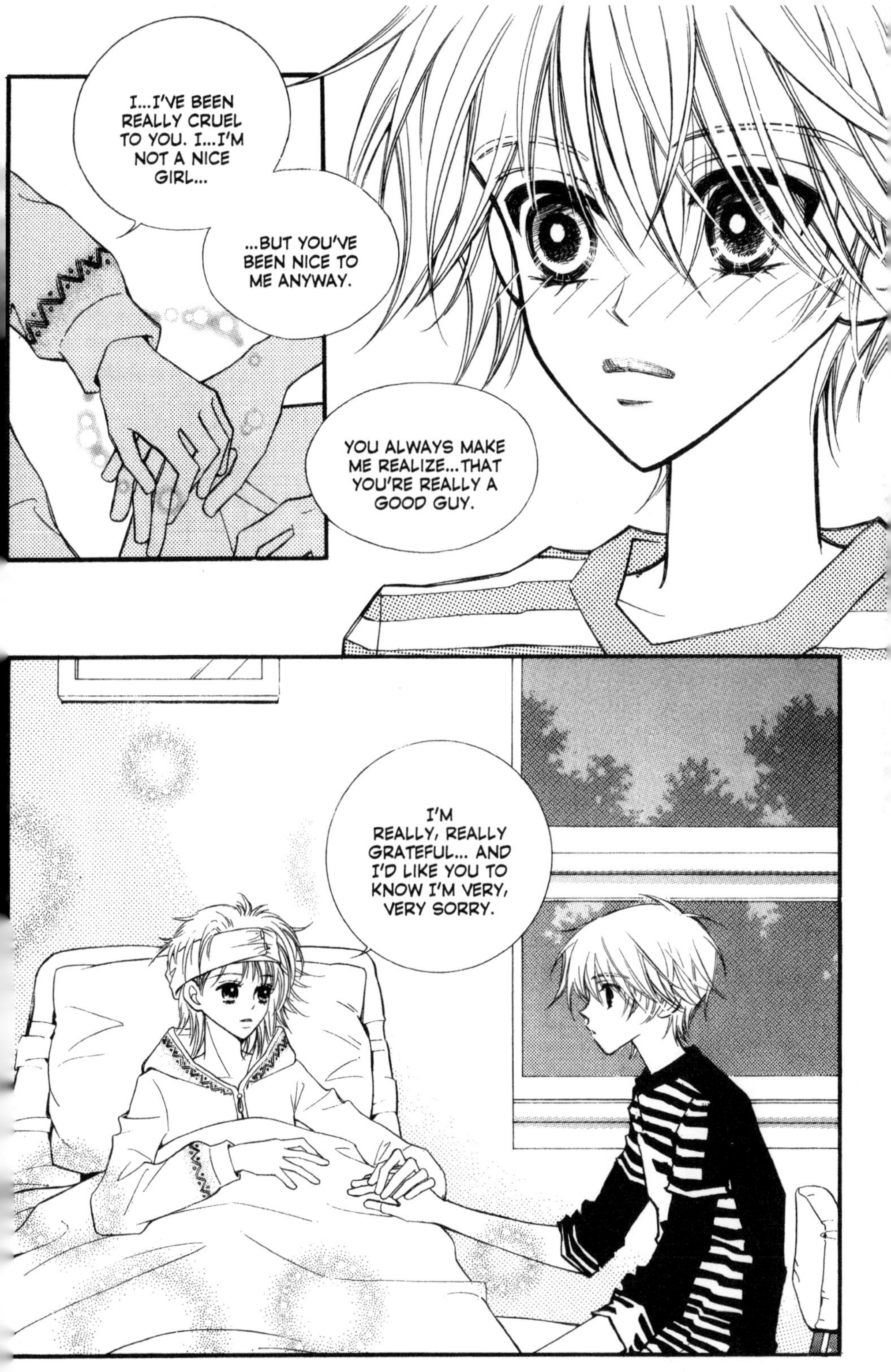
I...I'VE BEEN REALLY CRUEL TO YOU. I...I'M NOT A NICE GIRL...
...BUT YOU'VE BEEN NICE TO ME ANYWAY.
YOU ALWAYS MAKE ME REALIZE...THAT YOU'RE REALLY A GOOD GUY.
I'M REALLY, REALLY GRATEFUL... AND I'D LIKE YOU TO KNOW I'M VERY, VERY SORRY.

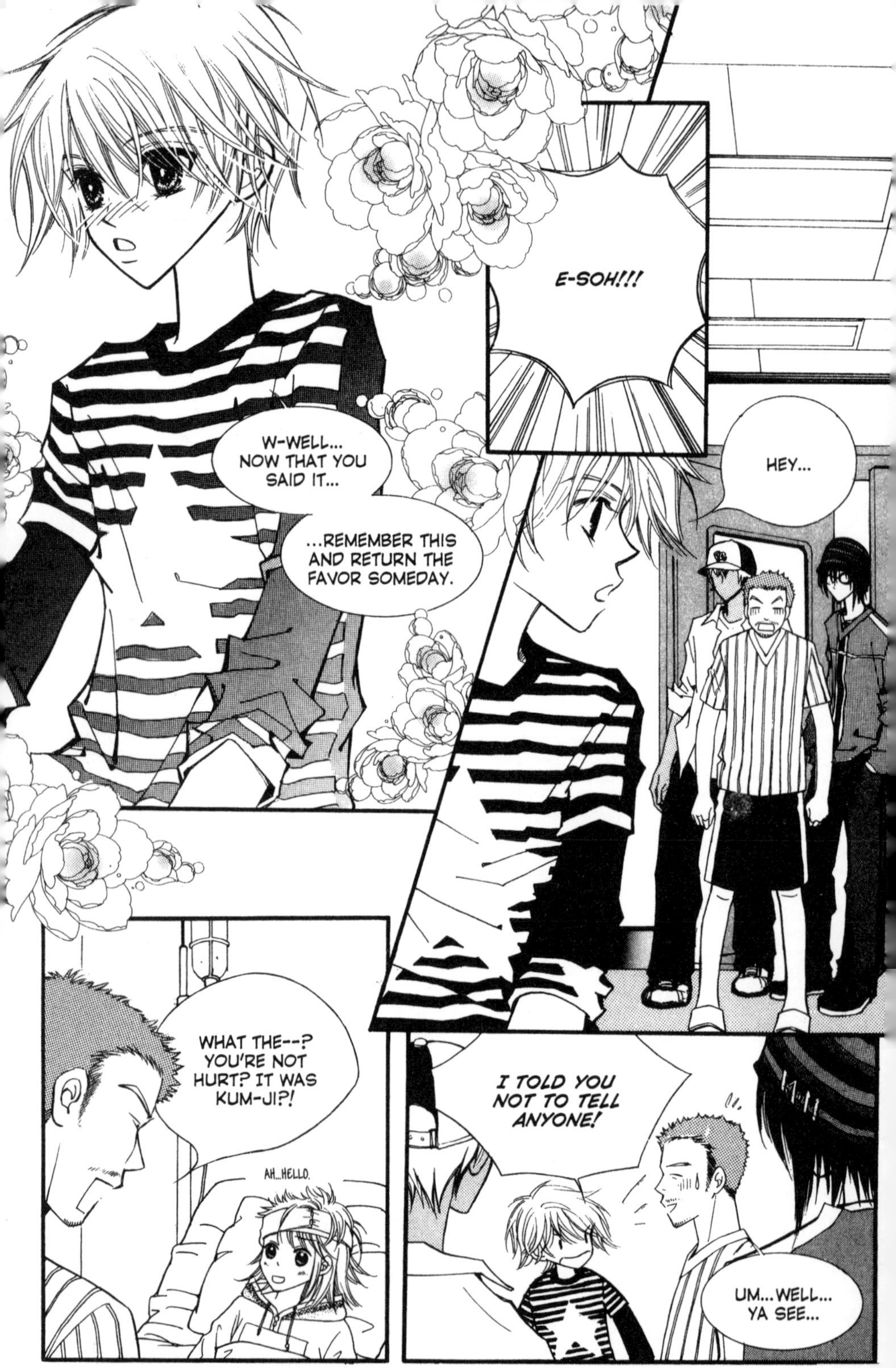
W-WELL... NOW THAT YOU SAID IT...
...REMEMBER THIS AND RETURN THE FAVOR SOMEDAY.
E-SOH!!!
HEY...
WHAT THE--? YOU'RE NOT HURT? IT WAS KUM-JI?!
AH...HELLO.
I TOLD YOU NOT TO TELL ANYONE!
UM...WELL... YA SEE...

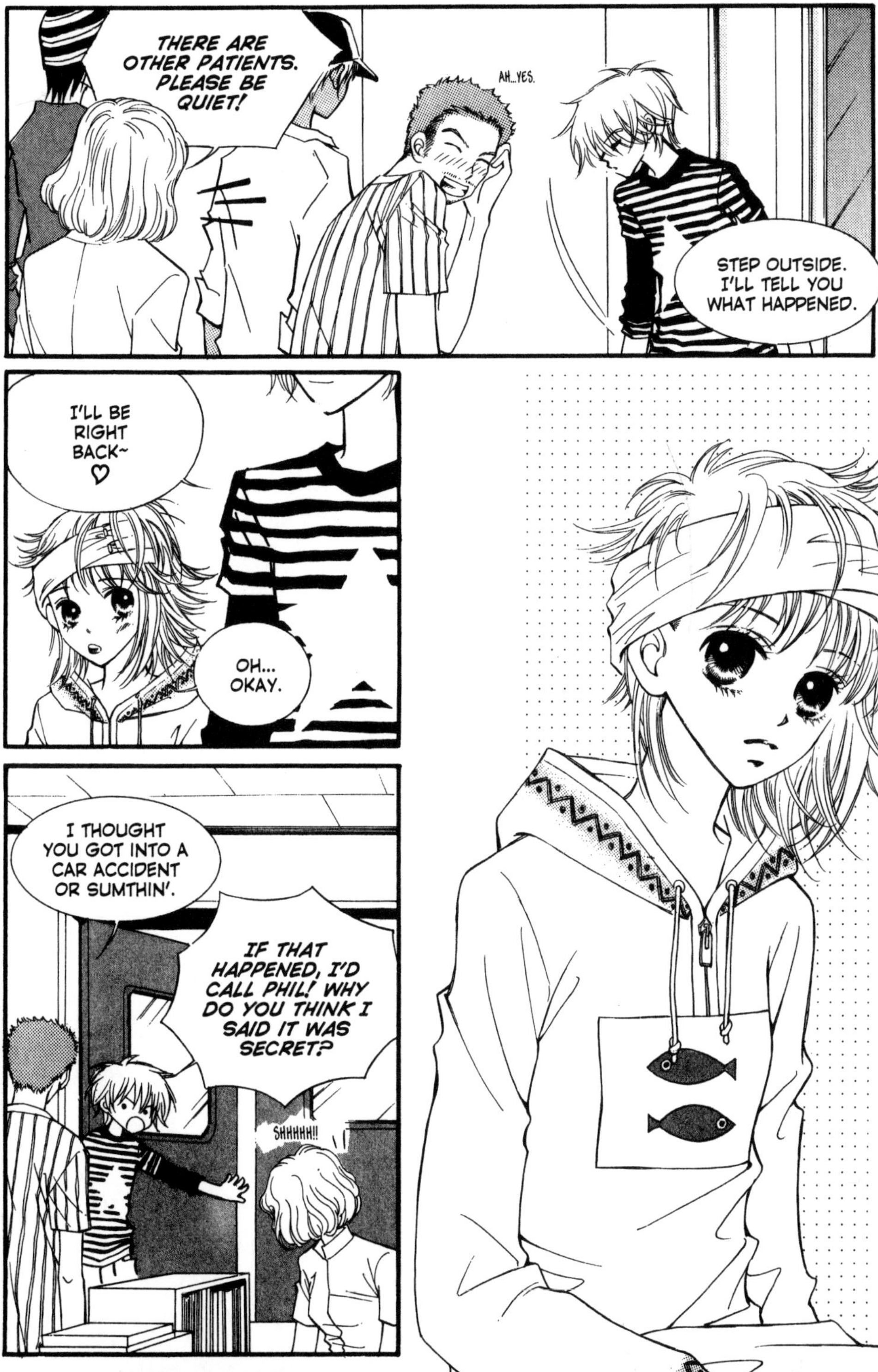
THERE ARE OTHER PATIENTS. PLEASE BE QUIET!
AH...YES.
STEP OUTSIDE. I'LL TELL YOU WHAT HAPPENED.
I'LL BE RIGHT BACK~ ♡
OH... OKAY.
I THOUGHT YOU GOT INTO A CAR ACCIDENT OR SUMTHIN'.
IF THAT HAPPENED, I'D CALL PHIL! WHY DO YOU THINK I SAID IT WAS SECRET?
SHHHHH!!

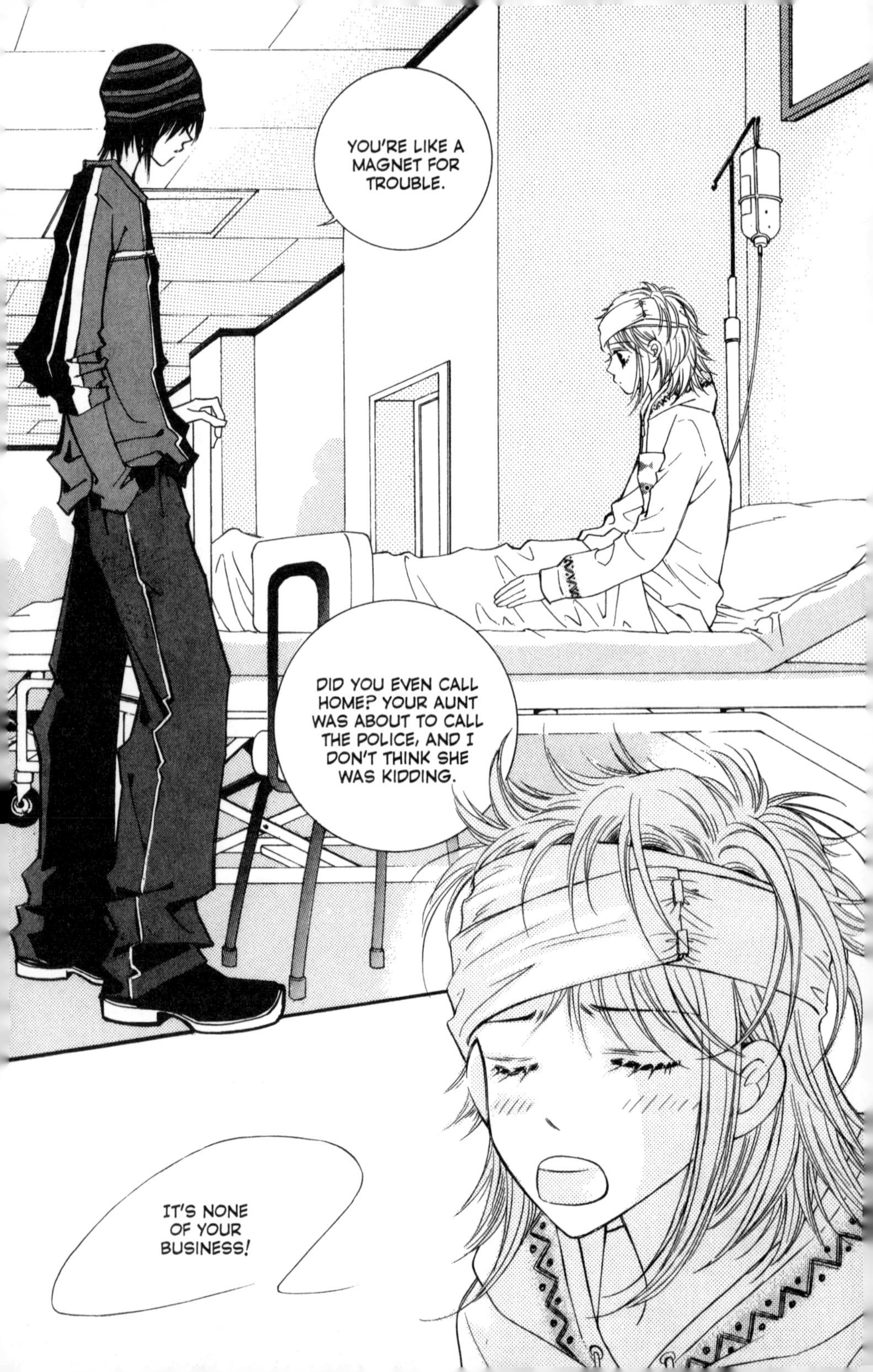
YOU'RE LIKE A MAGNET FOR TROUBLE.
DID YOU EVEN CALL HOME? YOUR AUNT WAS ABOUT TO CALL THE POLICE, AND I DON'T THINK SHE WAS KIDDING.
IT'S NONE OF YOUR BUSINESS!

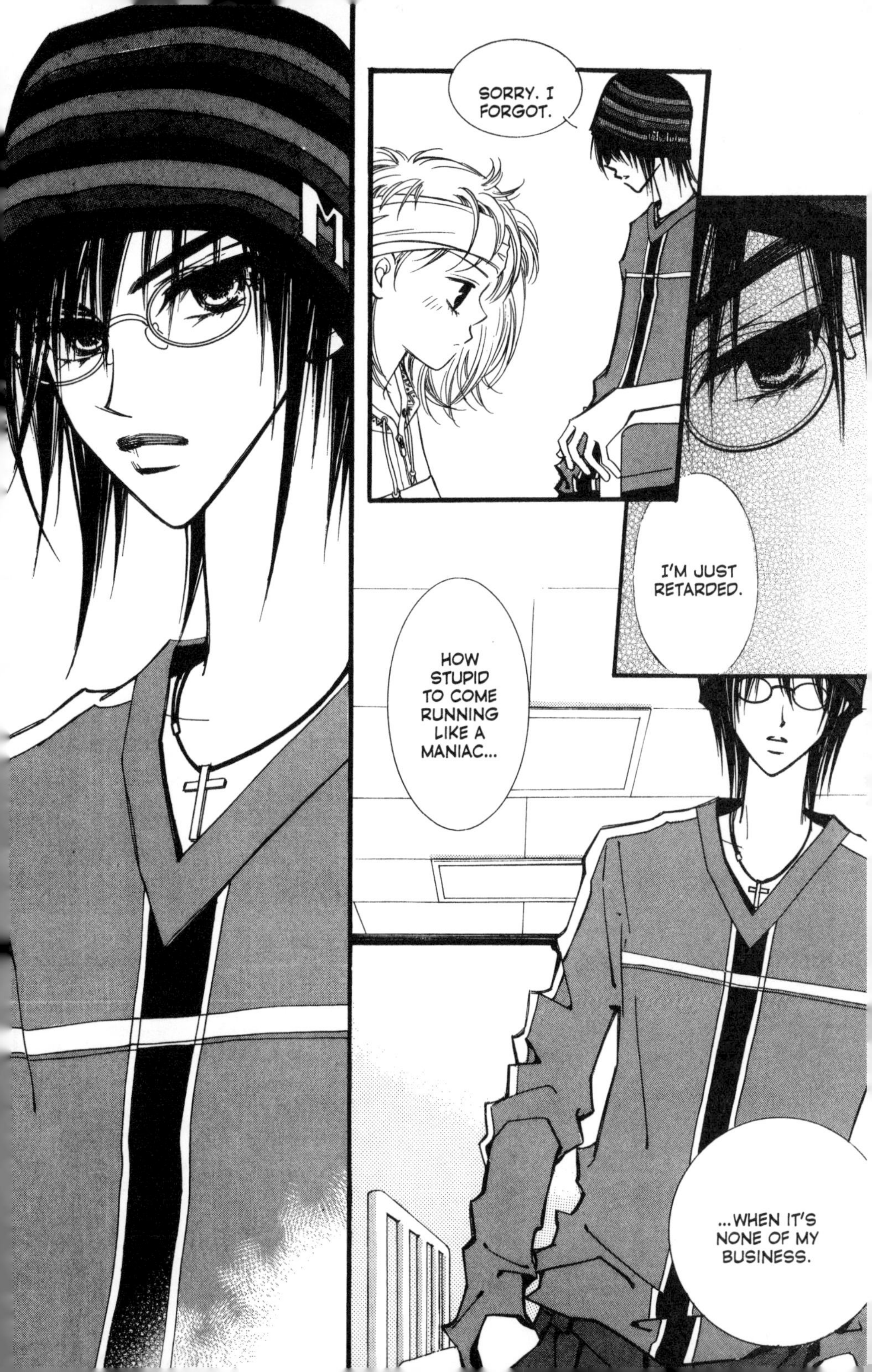
SORRY. I FORGOT.
I'M JUST RETARDED.
HOW STUPID TO COME RUNNING LIKE A MANIAC...
...WHEN IT'S NONE OF MY BUSINESS.

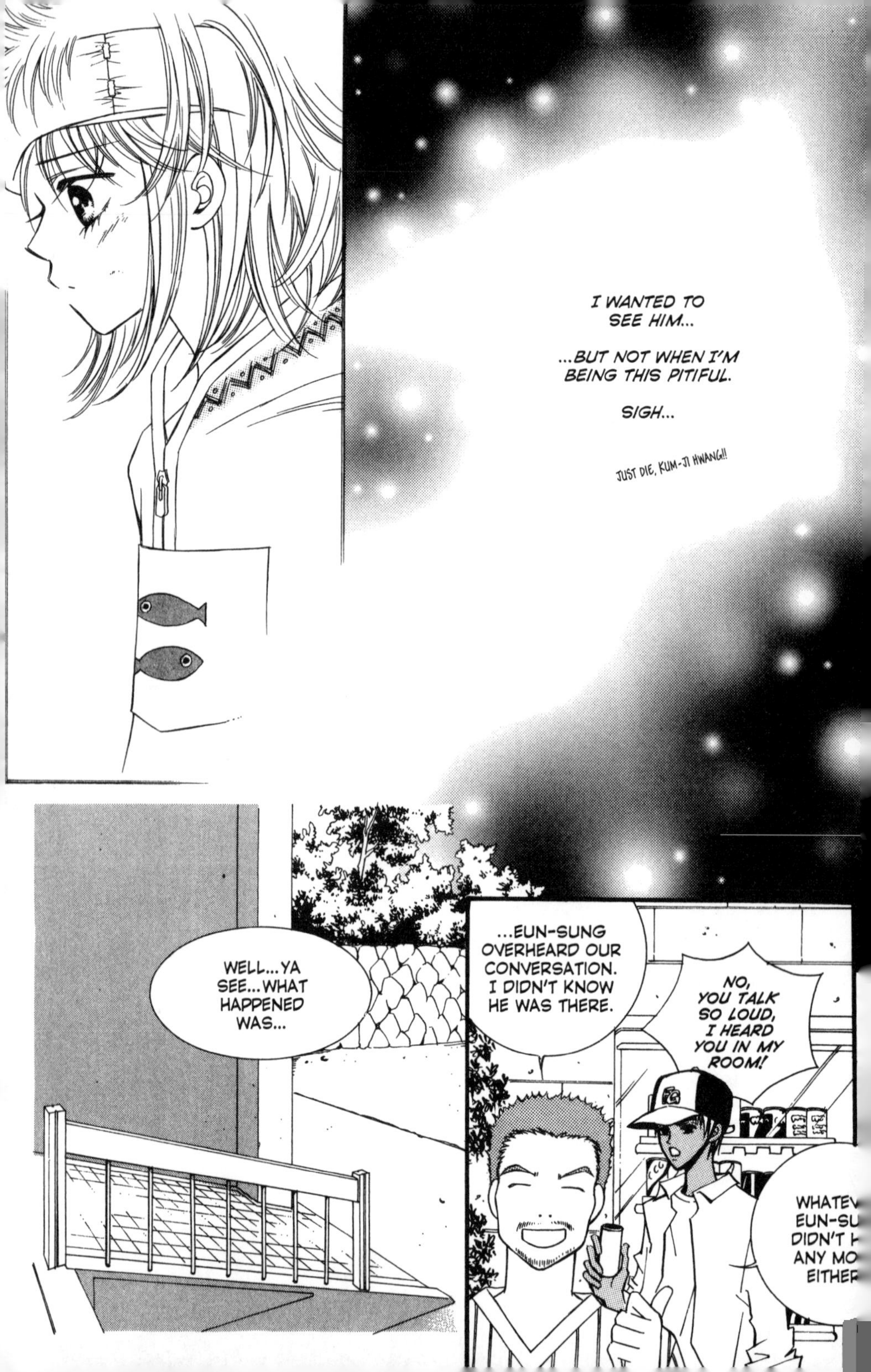
I WANTED TO SEE HIM...
...BUT NOT WHEN I'M BEING THIS PITIFUL.
SIGH...
JUST DIE, KUM-JI HWANG!!
WELL...YA SEE...WHAT HAPPENED WAS...
...EUN-SUNG OVERHEARD OUR CONVERSATION. I DIDN'T KNOW HE WAS THERE.
NO, YOU TALK SO LOUD, I HEARD YOU IN MY ROOM!
WHATEV EUN-SU DIDN'T ANY MO EITHER

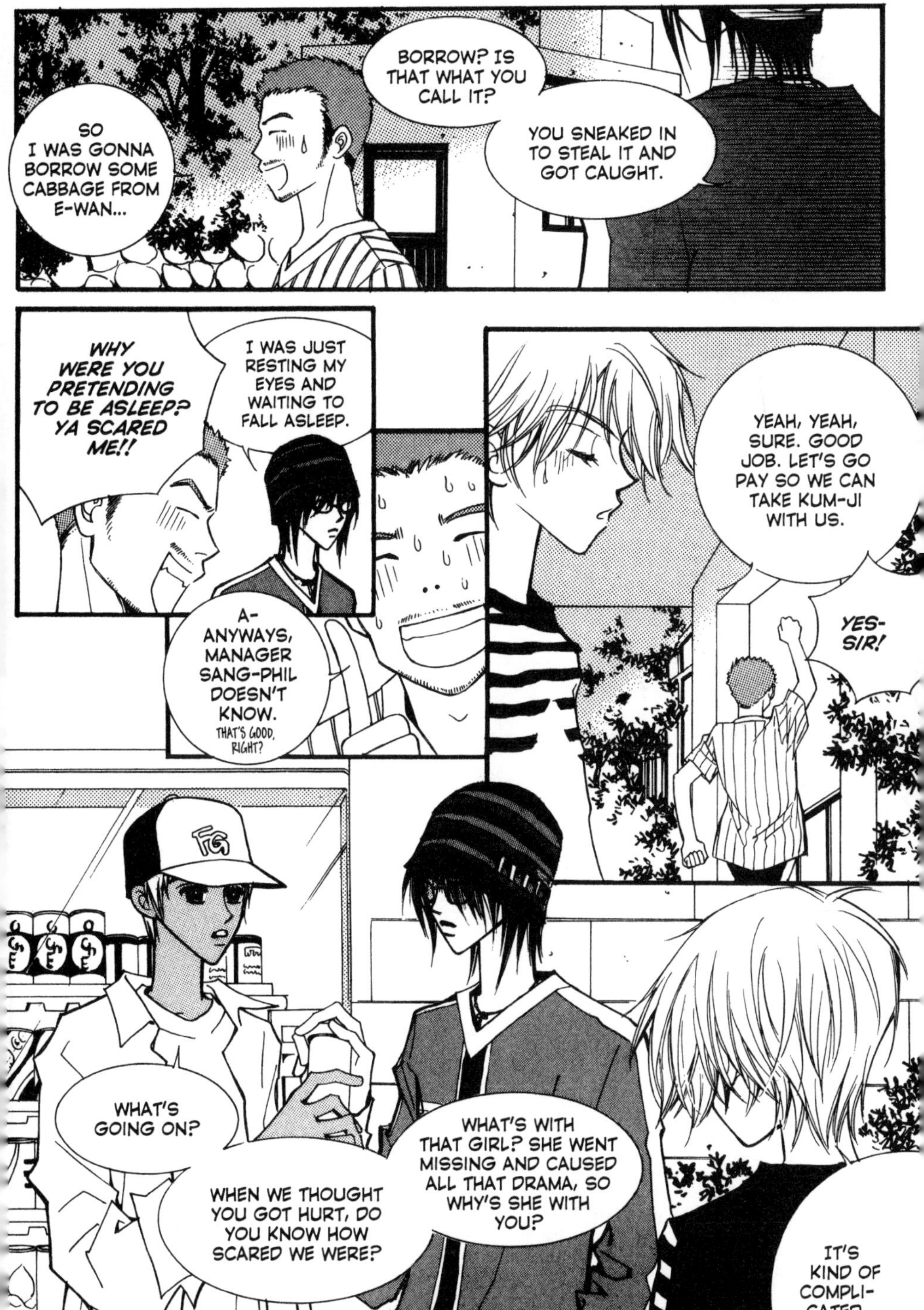
SO I WAS GONNA BORROW SOME CABBAGE FROM E-WAN...
BORROW? IS THAT WHAT YOU CALL IT?
YOU SNEAKED IN TO STEAL IT AND GOT CAUGHT.
WHY WERE YOU PRETENDING TO BE ASLEEP? YA SCARED ME!!
I WAS JUST RESTING MY EYES AND WAITING TO FALL ASLEEP.
A- ANYWAYS, MANAGER SANG-PHIL DOESN'T KNOW.
THAT'S GOOD, RIGHT?
YEAH, YEAH, SURE. GOOD JOB. LET'S GO PAY SO WE CAN TAKE KUM-JI WITH US.
YES-SIR!
WHAT'S GOING ON?
WHEN WE THOUGHT YOU GOT HURT, DO YOU KNOW HOW SCARED WE WERE?
WHAT'S WITH THAT GIRL? SHE WENT MISSING AND CAUSED ALL THAT DRAMA, SO WHY'S SHE WITH YOU?
IT'S KIND OF COMPLI-CATED...

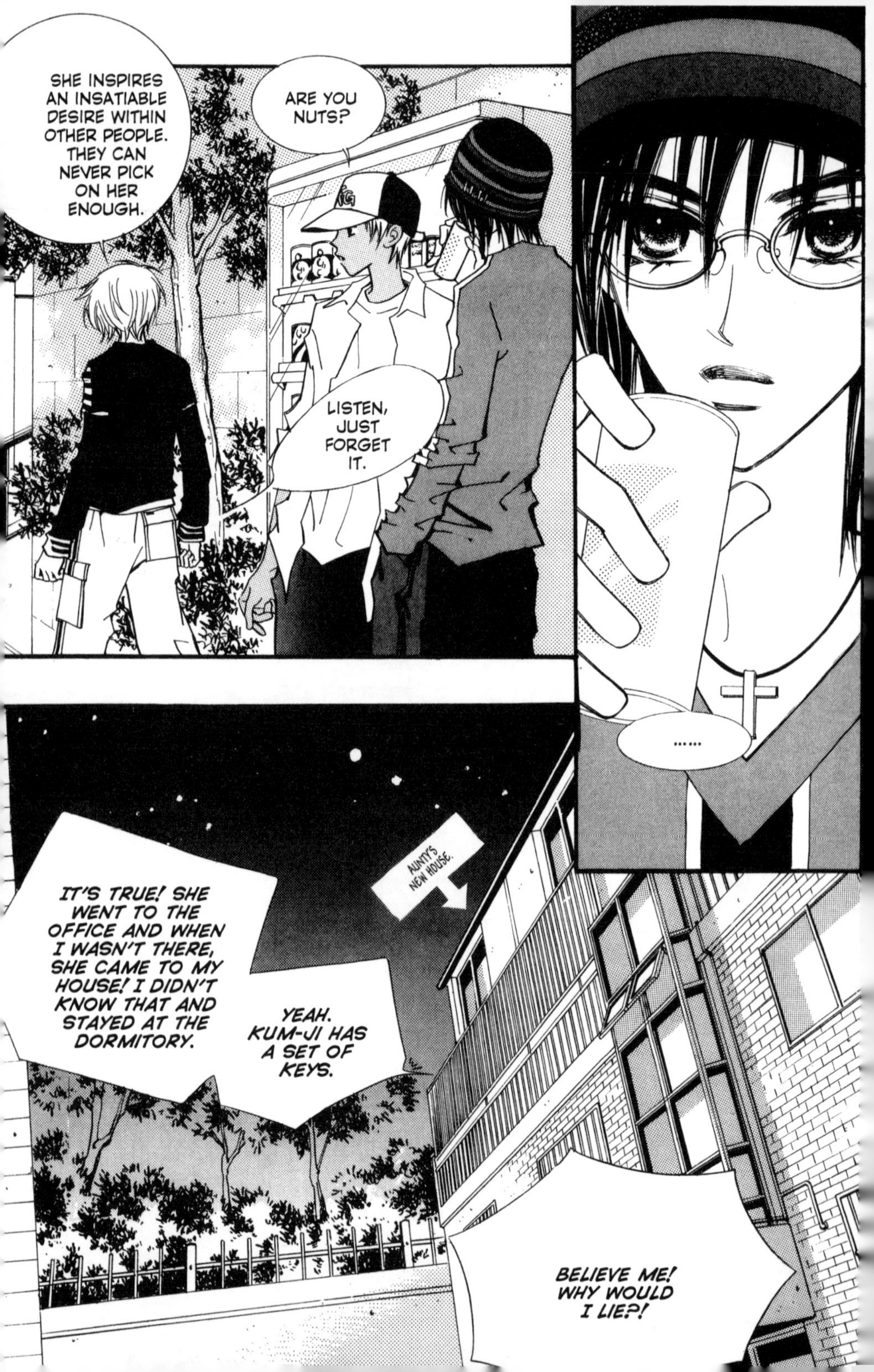
SHE INSPIRES AN INSATIABLE DESIRE WITHIN OTHER PEOPLE. THEY CAN NEVER PICK ON HER ENOUGH.
ARE YOU NUTS?
LISTEN, JUST FORGET IT.
......
IT'S TRUE! SHE WENT TO THE OFFICE AND WHEN I WASN'T THERE, SHE CAME TO MY HOUSE! I DIDN'T KNOW THAT AND STAYED AT THE DORMITORY.
AUNTY'S NEW HOUSE.
YEAH. KUM-JI HAS A SET OF KEYS.
BELIEVE ME! WHY WOULD I LIE?!

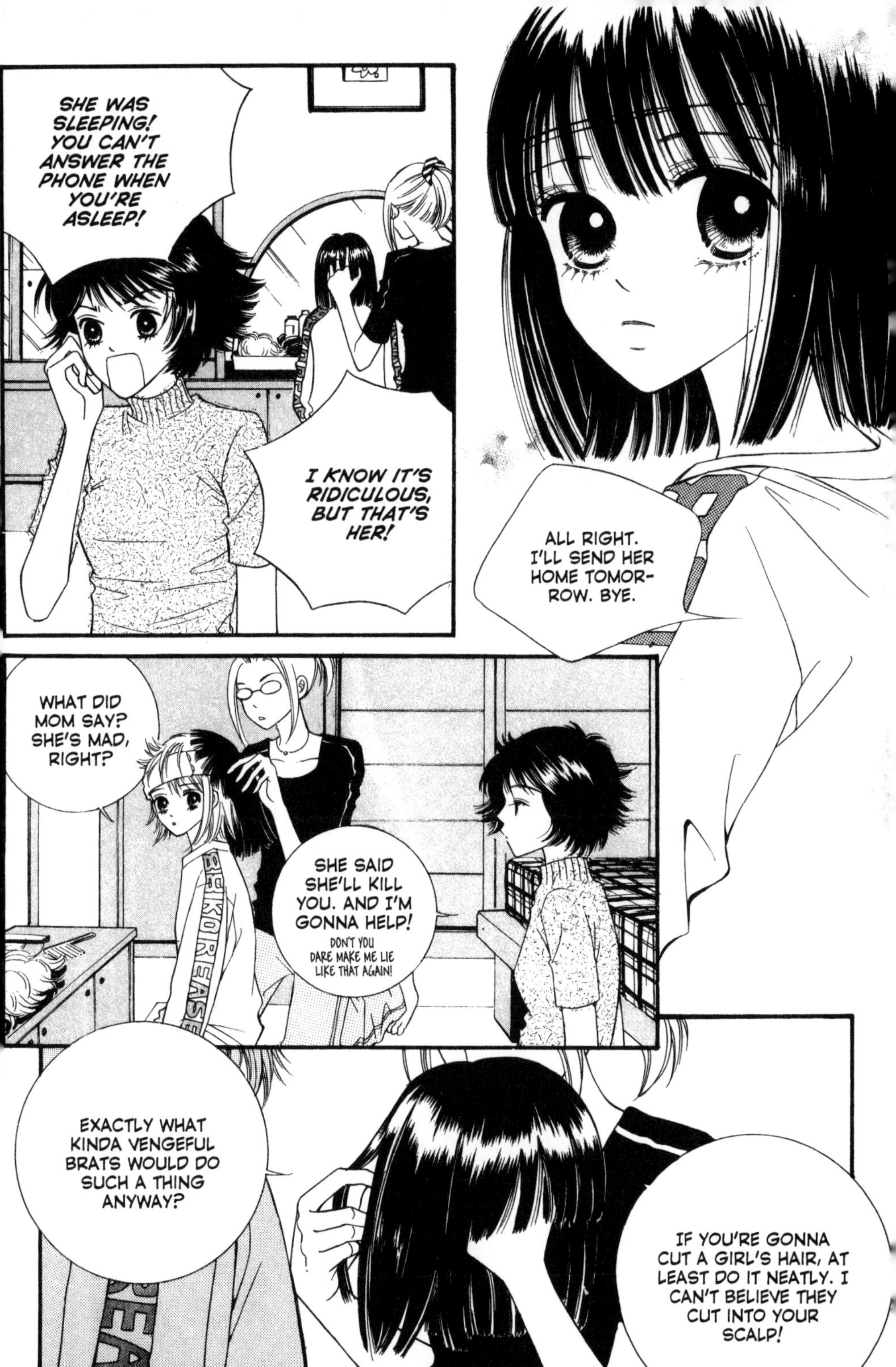
SHE WAS SLEEPING! YOU CAN'T ANSWER THE PHONE WHEN YOU'RE ASLEEP!
I KNOW IT'S RIDICULOUS, BUT THAT'S HER!
ALL RIGHT. I'LL SEND HER HOME TOMORROW. BYE.
WHAT DID MOM SAY? SHE'S MAD, RIGHT?
SHE SAID SHE'LL KILL YOU. AND I'M GONNA HELP!
DON'T YOU DARE MAKE ME LIE LIKE THAT AGAIN!
EXACTLY WHAT KINDA VENGEFUL BRATS WOULD DO SUCH A THING ANYWAY?
IF YOU'RE GONNA CUT A GIRL'S HAIR, AT LEAST DO IT NEATLY. I CAN'T BELIEVE THEY CUT INTO YOUR SCALP!

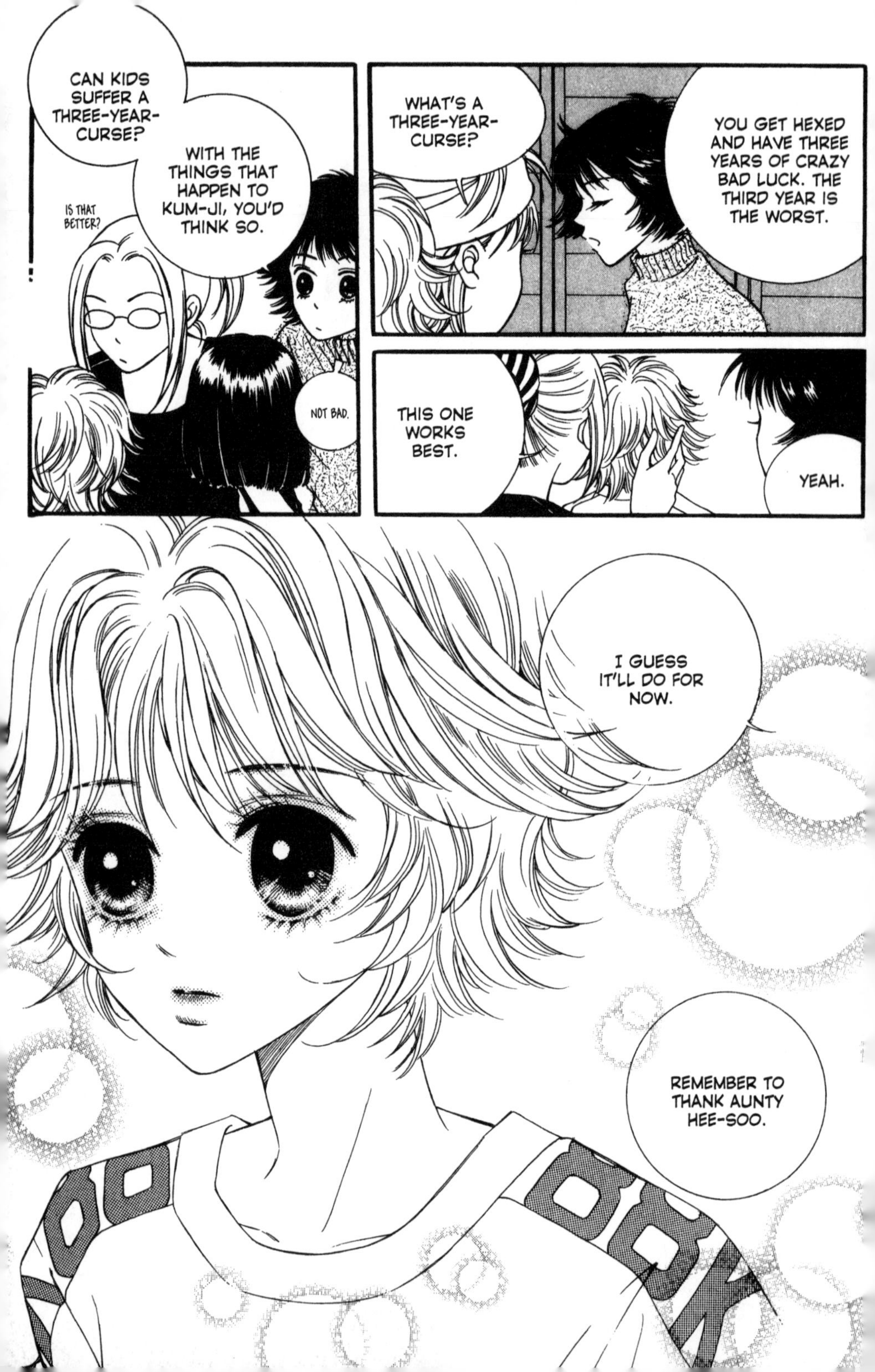
CAN KIDS SUFFER A THREE-YEAR-CURSE?
WITH THE THINGS THAT HAPPEN TO KUM-JI, YOU'D THINK SO.
IS THAT BETTER?
NOT BAD.
WHAT'S A THREE-YEAR-CURSE?
YOU GET HEXED AND HAVE THREE YEARS OF CRAZY BAD LUCK. THE THIRD YEAR IS THE WORST.
THIS ONE WORKS BEST.
YEAH.
I GUESS IT'LL DO FOR NOW.
REMEMBER TO THANK AUNTY HEE-SOO.

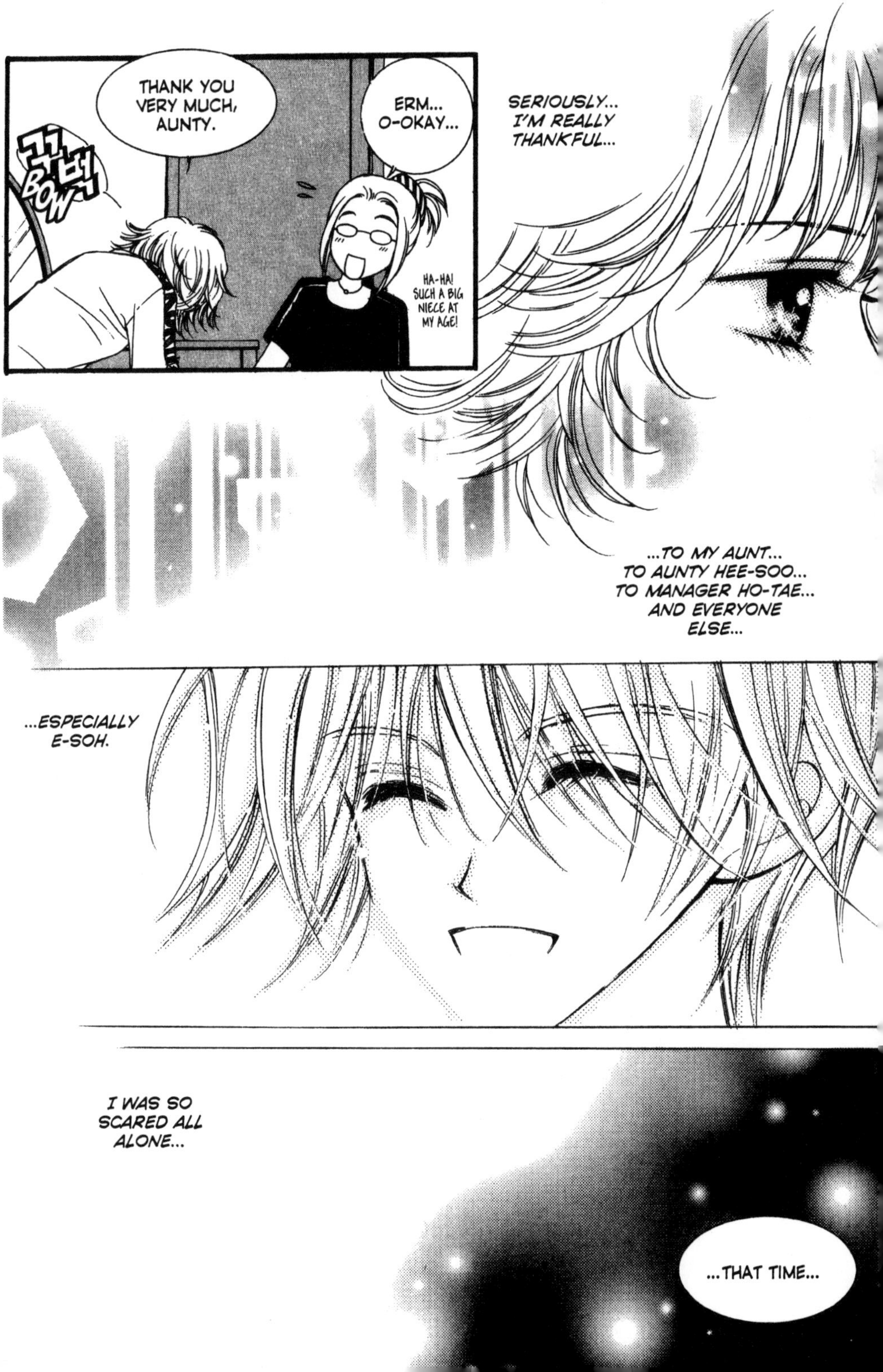
THANK YOU VERY MUCH, AUNTY.
BOW
ERM... O-OKAY...
HA-HA! SUCH A BIG NIECE AT MY AGE!
SERIOUSLY... I'M REALLY THANKFUL...
...TO MY AUNT... TO AUNTY HEE-SOO... TO MANAGER HO-TAE... AND EVERYONE ELSE...
...ESPECIALLY E-SOH.
I WAS SO SCARED ALL ALONE...
...THAT TIME...

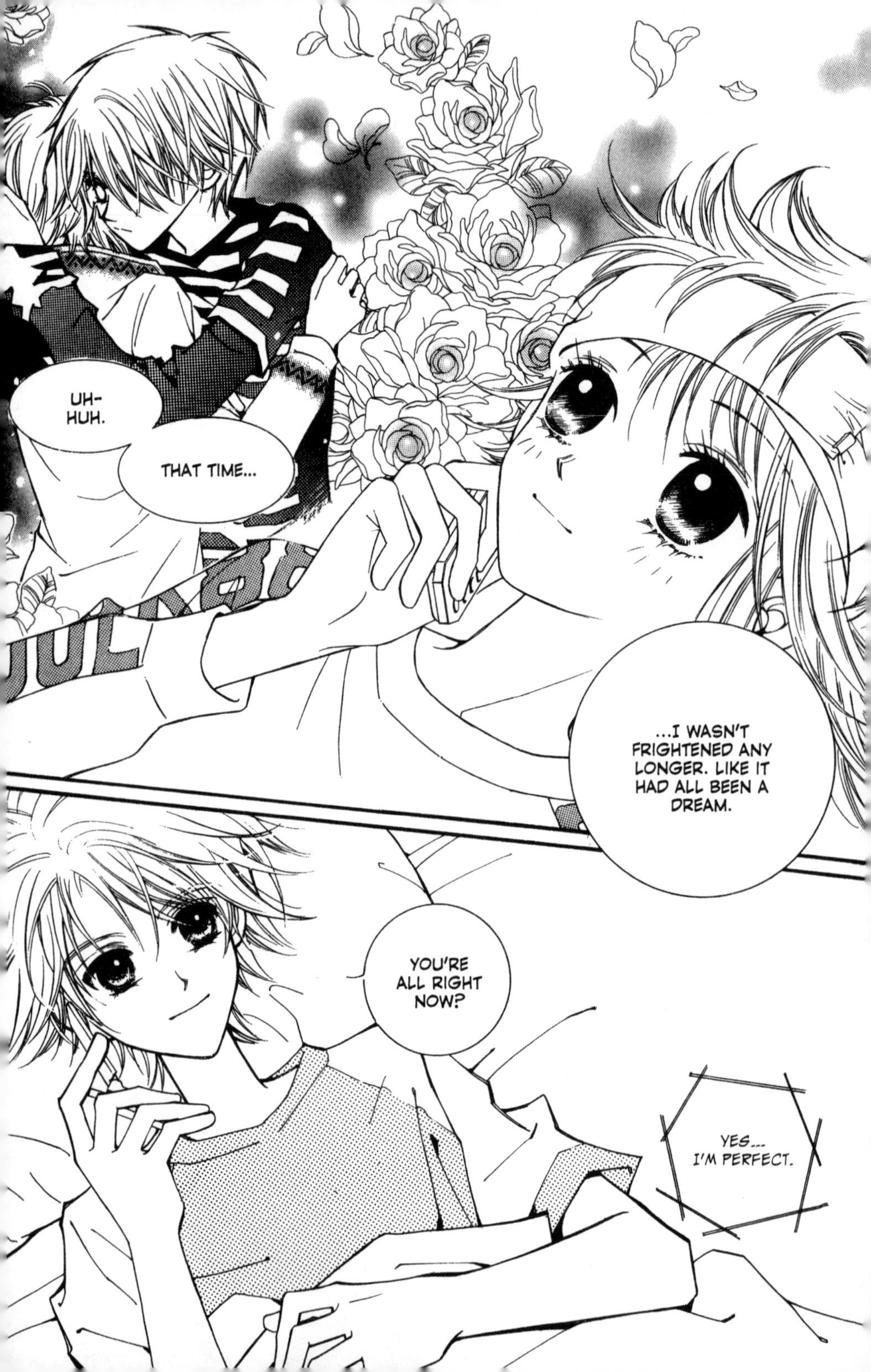
UH-HUH.
THAT TIME...
...I WASN'T FRIGHTENED ANY LONGER. LIKE IT HAD ALL BEEN A DREAM.
YOU'RE ALL RIGHT NOW?
YES... I'M PERFECT.

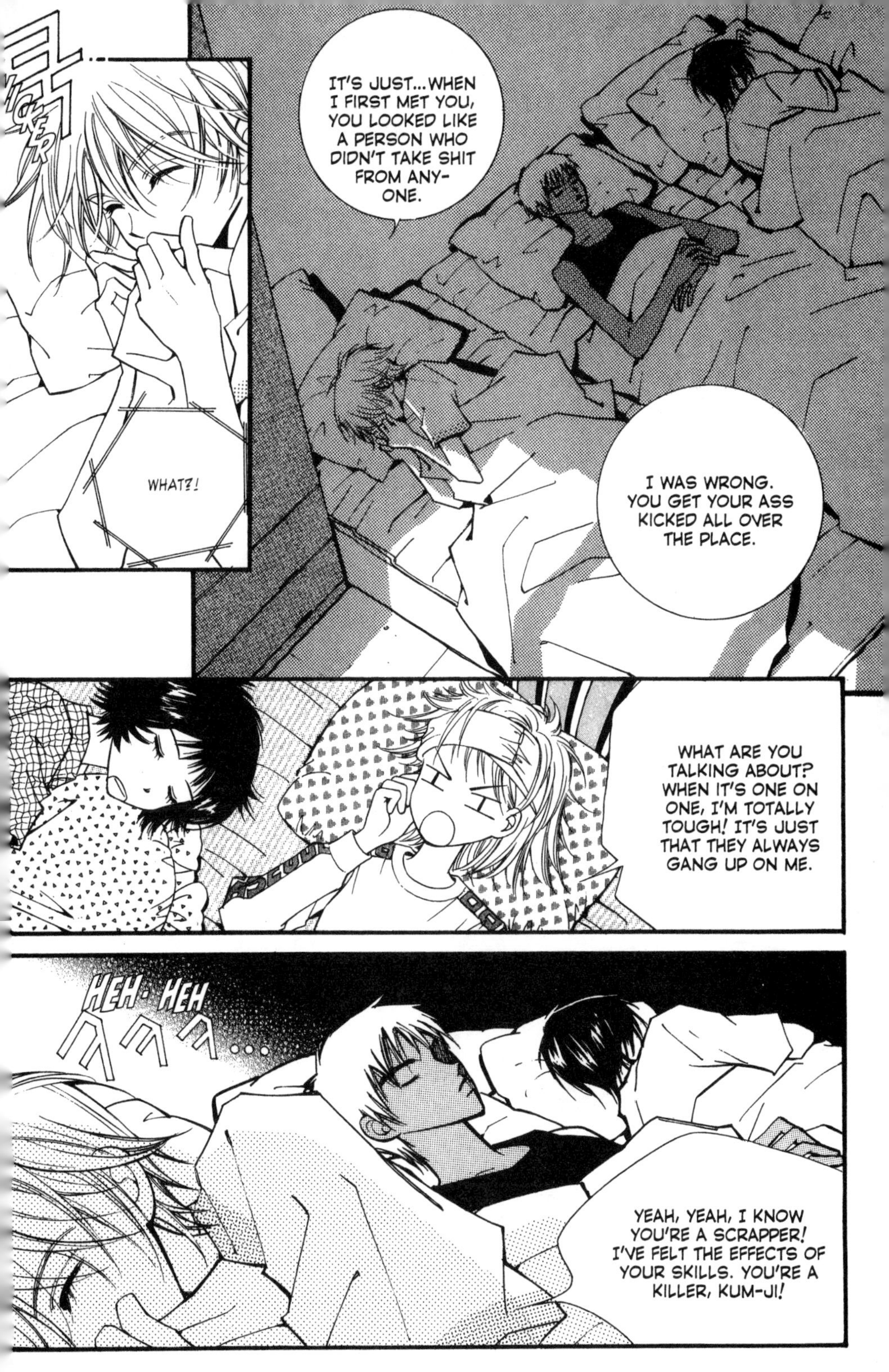
FLICKER
WHAT?!
IT'S JUST...WHEN I FIRST MET YOU, YOU LOOKED LIKE A PERSON WHO DIDN'T TAKE SHIT FROM ANY-ONE.
I WAS WRONG. YOU GET YOUR ASS KICKED ALL OVER THE PLACE.
WHAT ARE YOU TALKING ABOUT? WHEN IT'S ONE ON ONE, I'M TOTALLY TOUGH! IT'S JUST THAT THEY ALWAYS GANG UP ON ME.
HEH · HEH
YEAH, YEAH, I KNOW YOU'RE A SCRAPPER! I'VE FELT THE EFFECTS OF YOUR SKILLS. YOU'RE A KILLER, KUM-JI!

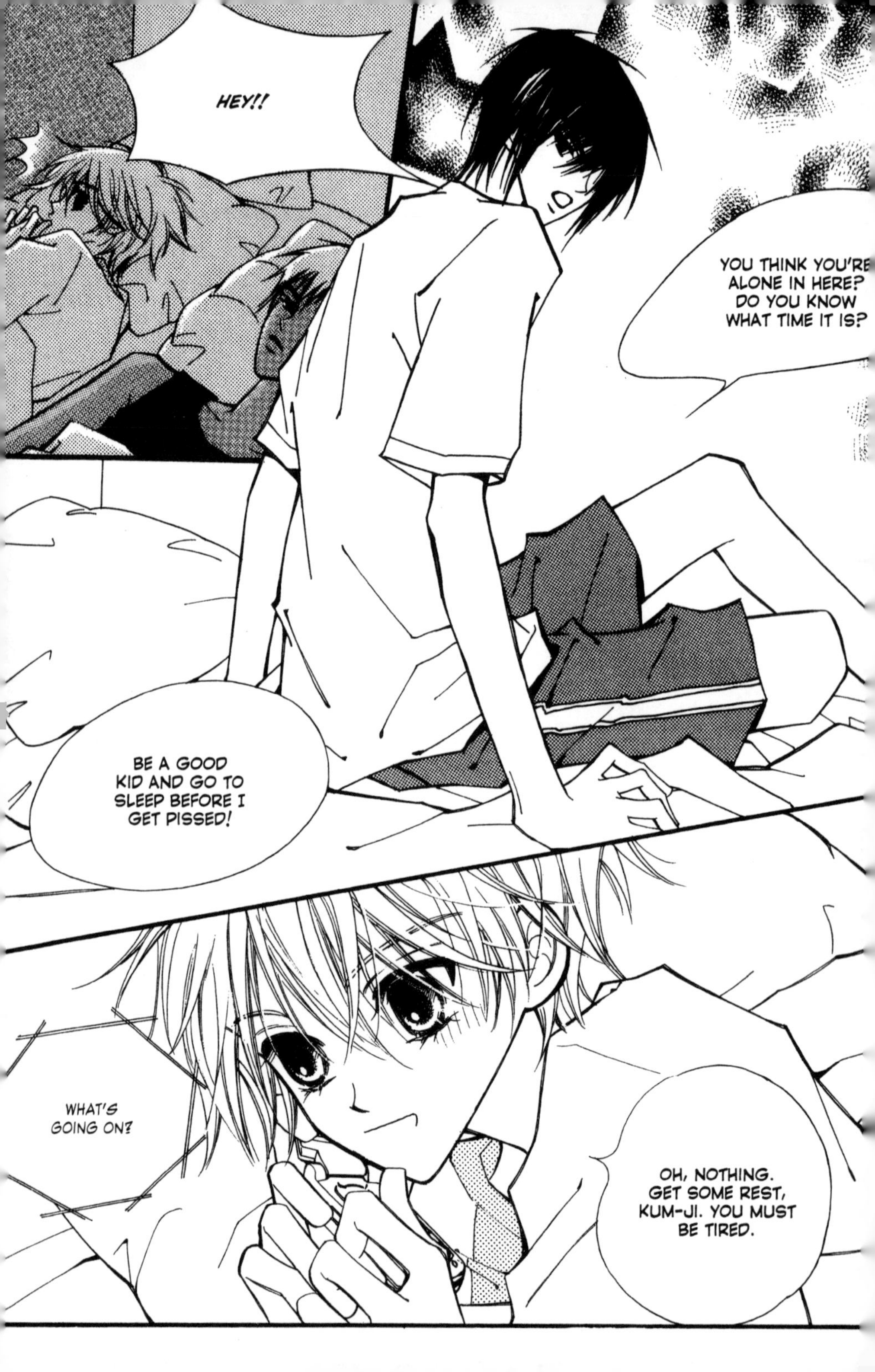
HEY!!
YOU THINK YOU'RE ALONE IN HERE? DO YOU KNOW WHAT TIME IT IS?
BE A GOOD KID AND GO TO SLEEP BEFORE I GET PISSED!
WHAT'S GOING ON?
OH, NOTHING. GET SOME REST, KUM-JI. YOU MUST BE TIRED.

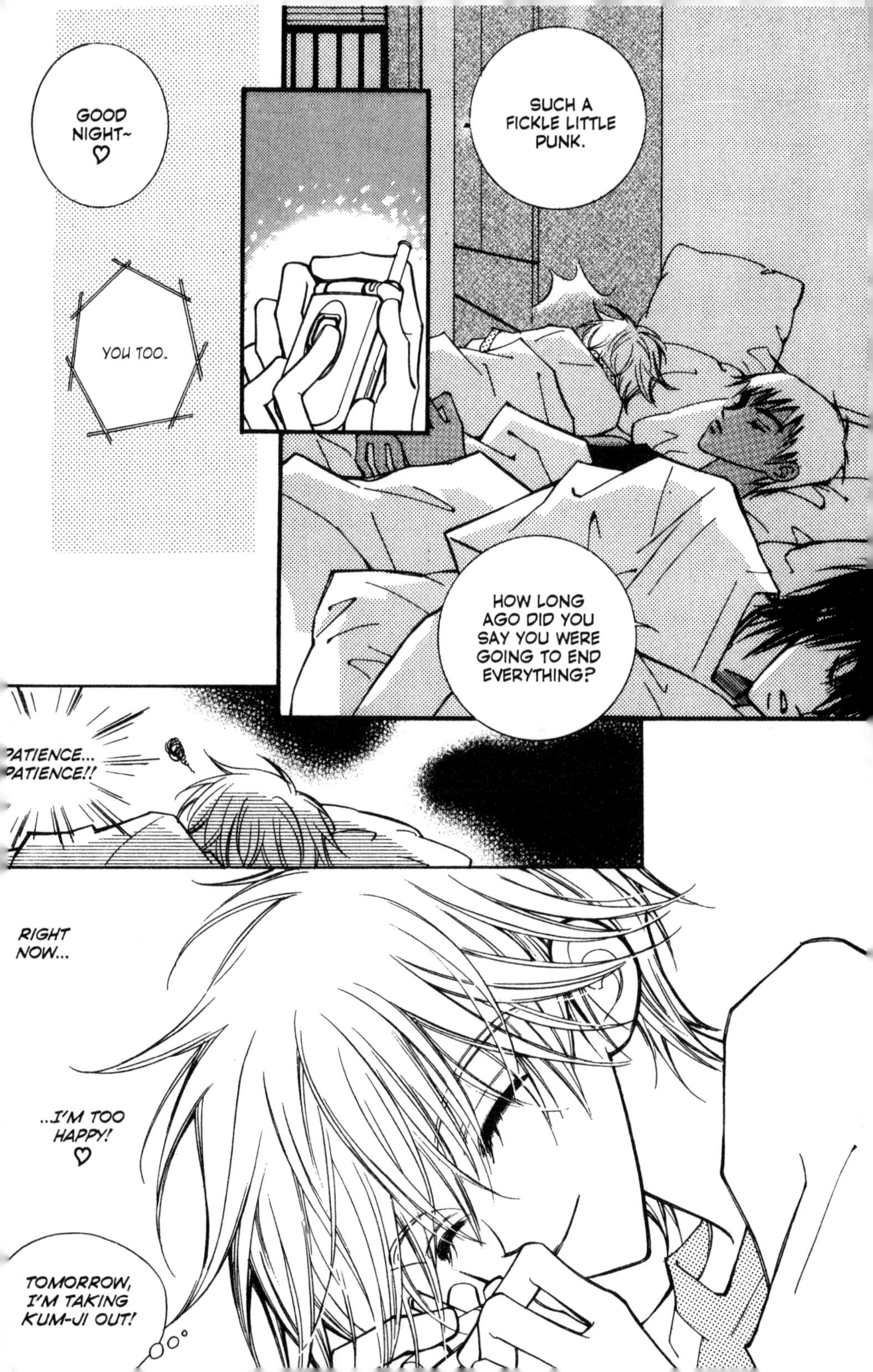
GOOD NIGHT~ ♡
YOU TOO.
SUCH A FICKLE LITTLE PUNK.
HOW LONG AGO DID YOU SAY YOU WERE GOING TO END EVERYTHING?
PATIENCE... PATIENCE!!
RIGHT NOW...
...I'M TOO HAPPY! ♡
TOMORROW, I'M TAKING KUM-JI OUT!

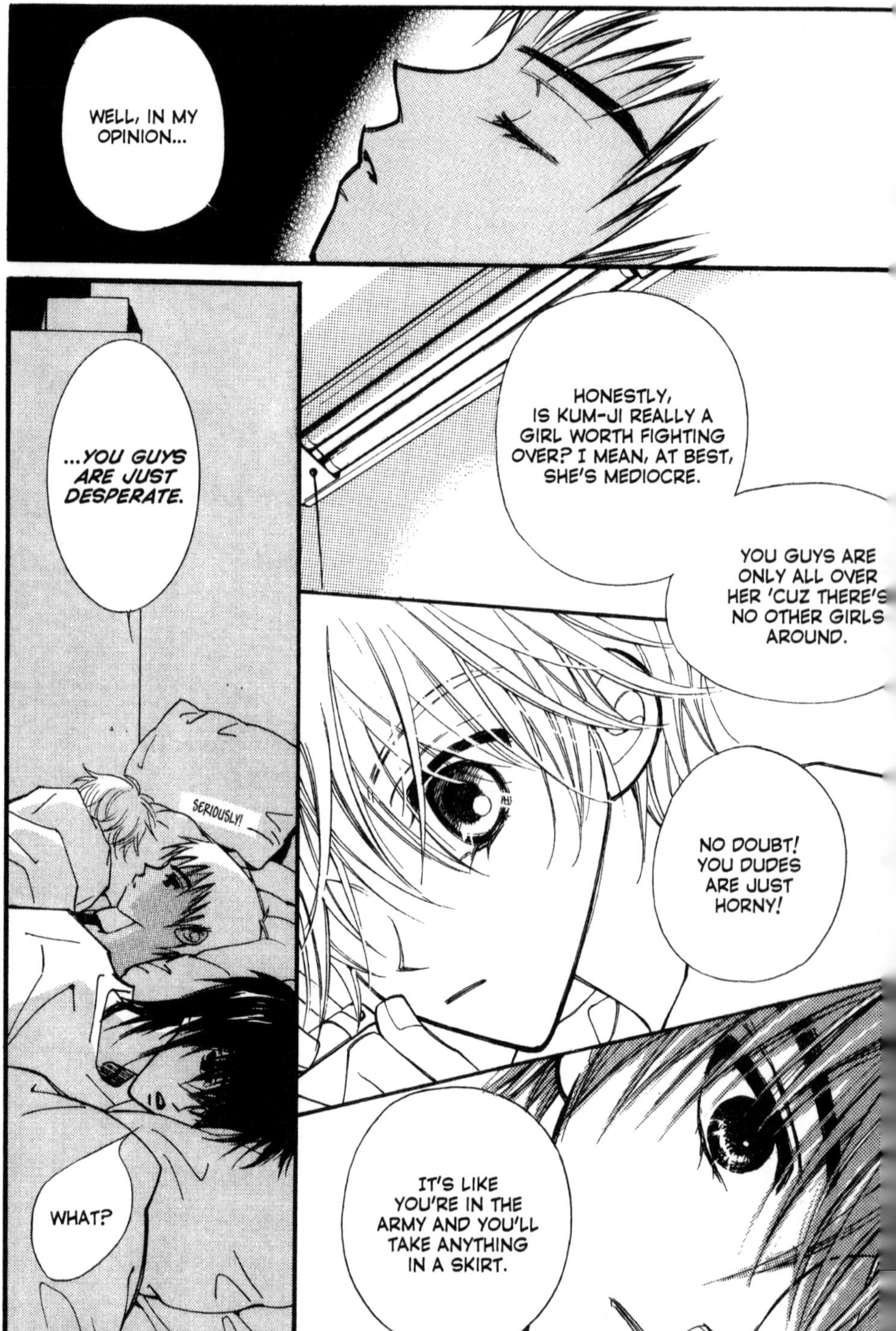
WELL, IN MY OPINION...
...YOU GUYS ARE JUST DESPERATE.
SERIOUSLY!
WHAT?
HONESTLY, IS KUM-JI REALLY A GIRL WORTH FIGHTING OVER? I MEAN, AT BEST, SHE'S MEDIOCRE.
YOU GUYS ARE ONLY ALL OVER HER 'CUZ THERE'S NO OTHER GIRLS AROUND.
NO DOUBT! YOU DUDES ARE JUST HORNY!
IT'S LIKE YOU'RE IN THE ARMY AND YOU'LL TAKE ANYTHING IN A SKIRT.

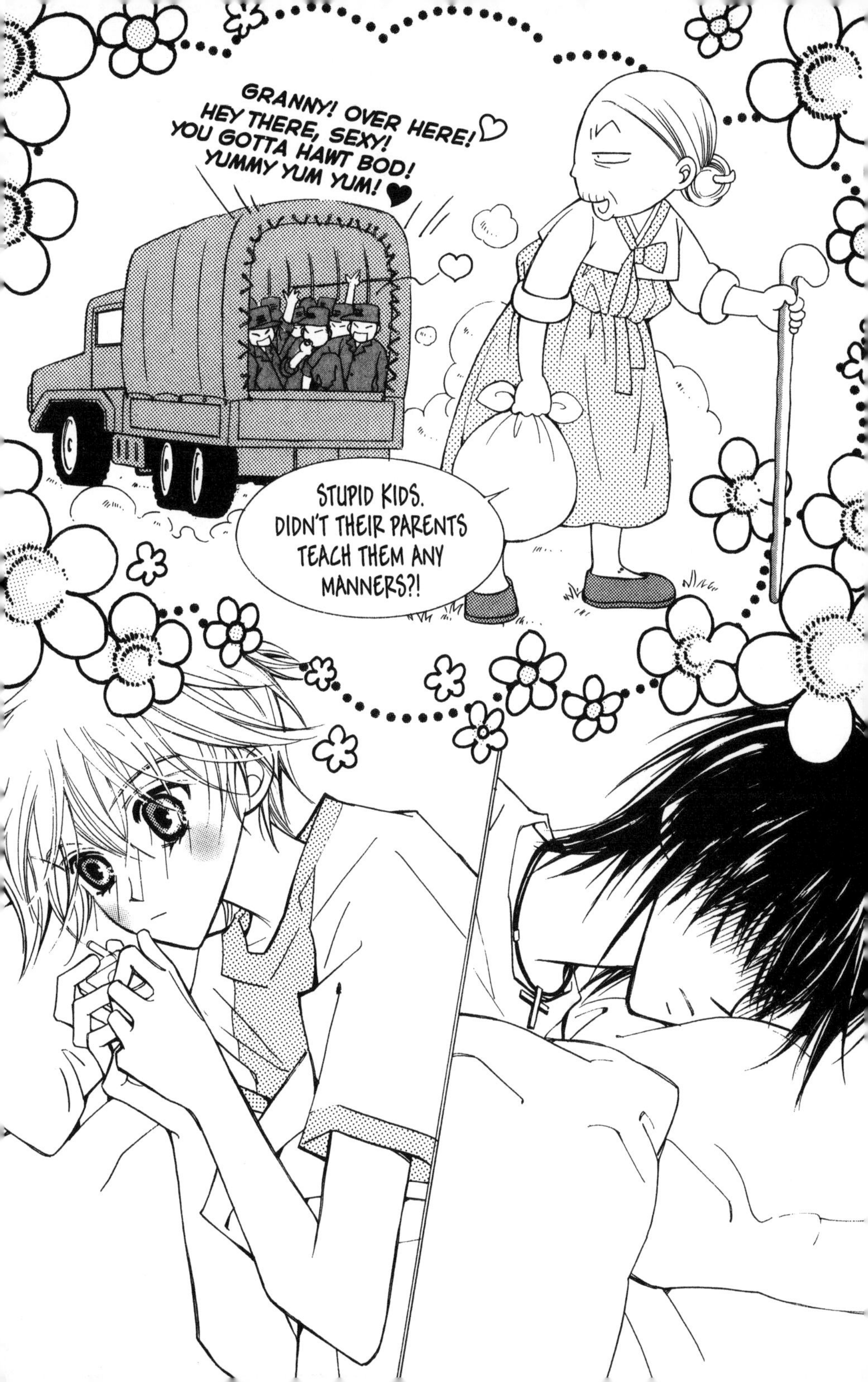
GRANNY! OVER HERE! HEY THERE, SEXY! YOU GOTTA HAWT BOD! YUMMY YUM YUM!
STUPID KIDS. DIDN'T THEIR PARENTS TEACH THEM ANY MANNERS?!

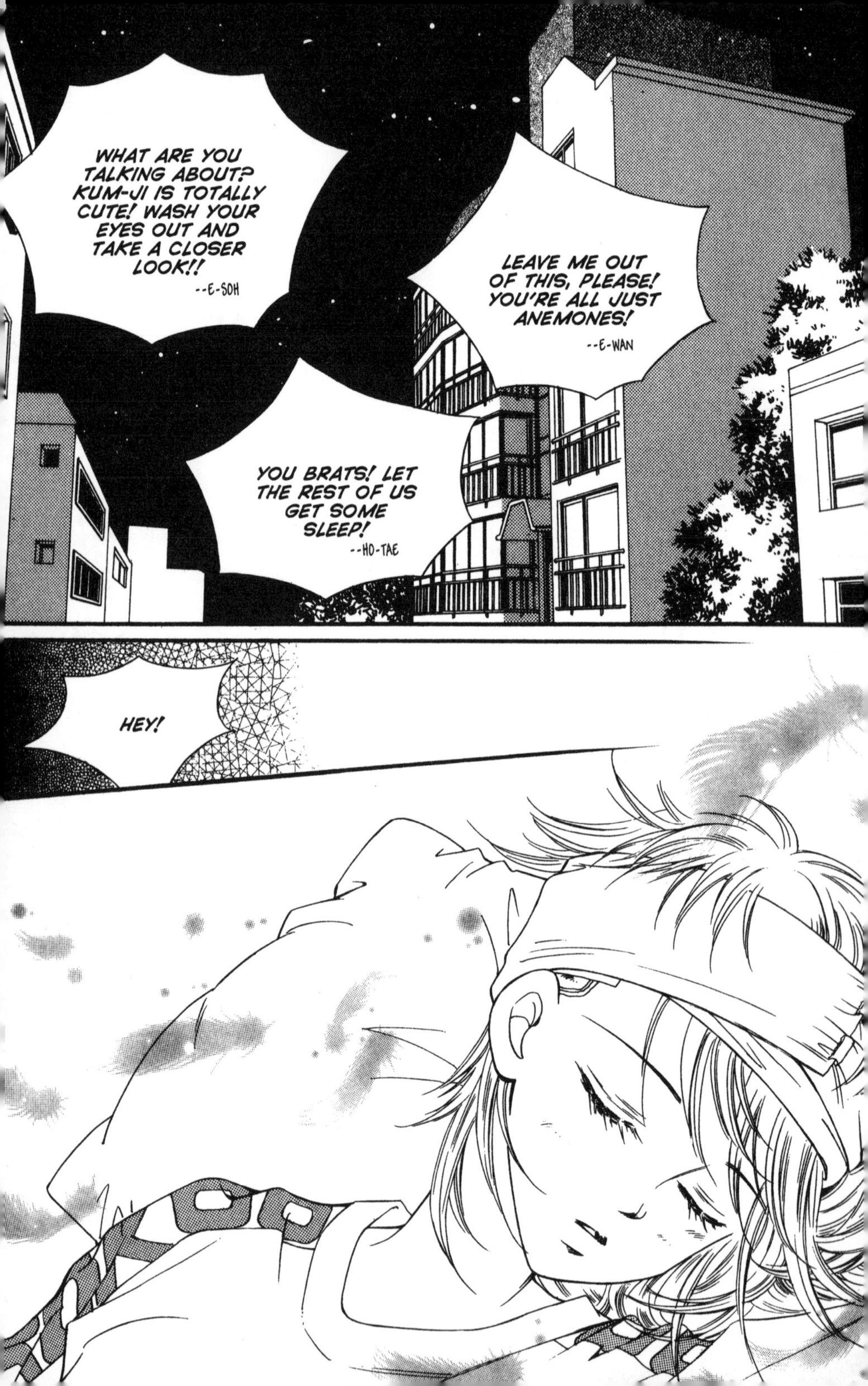
WHAT ARE YOU TALKING ABOUT? KUM-JI IS TOTALLY CUTE! WASH YOUR EYES OUT AND TAKE A CLOSER LOOK!!
--E-SOH
LEAVE ME OUT OF THIS, PLEASE! YOU'RE ALL JUST ANEMONES!
--E-WAN
YOU BRATS! LET THE REST OF US GET SOME SLEEP!
--HO-TAE
HEY!

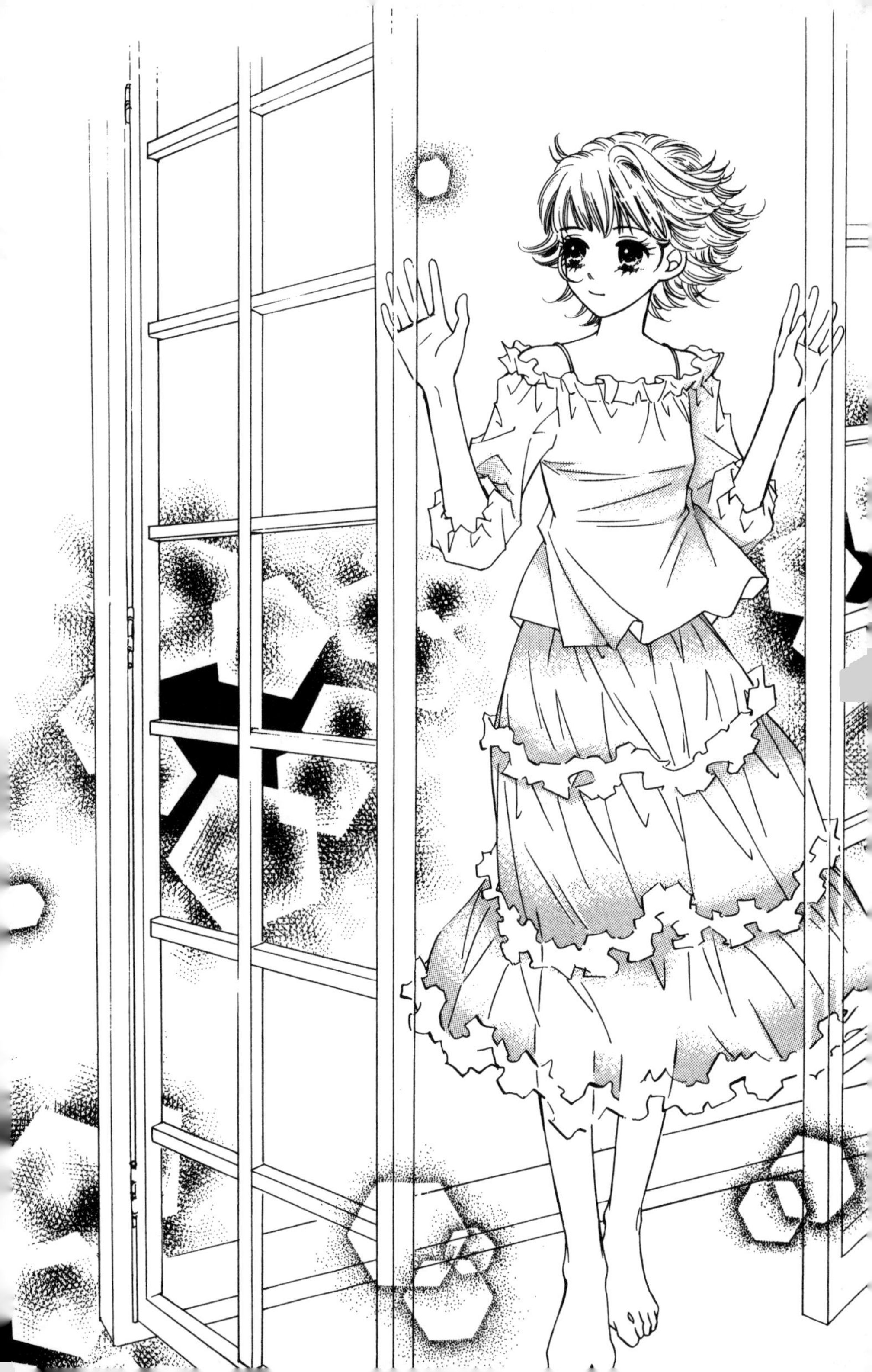

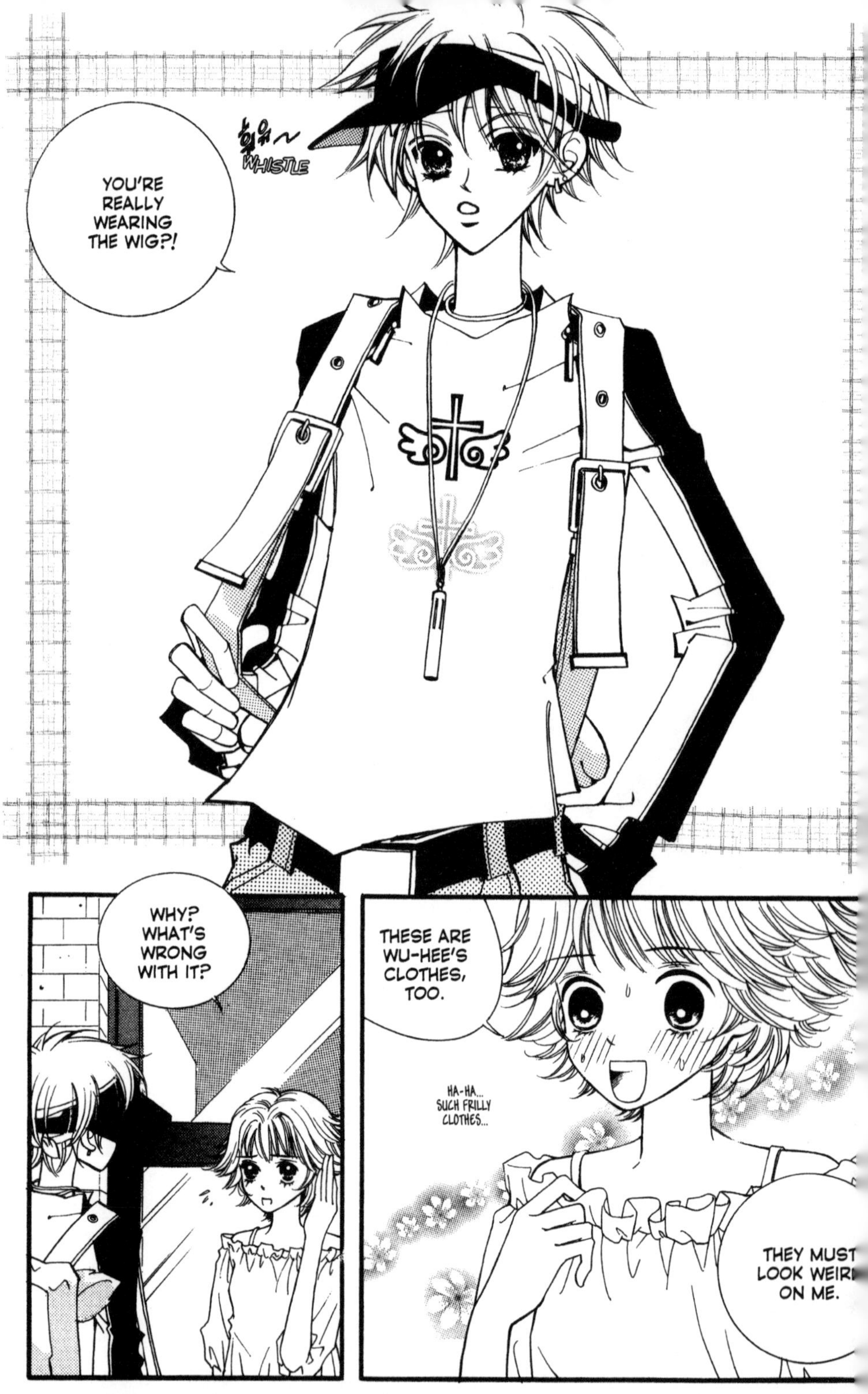

YOU'RE REALLY WEARING THE WIG?!
휘유~
WHISTLE
WHY? WHAT'S WRONG WITH IT?
THESE ARE WU-HEE'S CLOTHES, TOO.
HA-HA... SUCH FRILLY CLOTHES...
THEY MUST LOOK WEIRD ON ME.

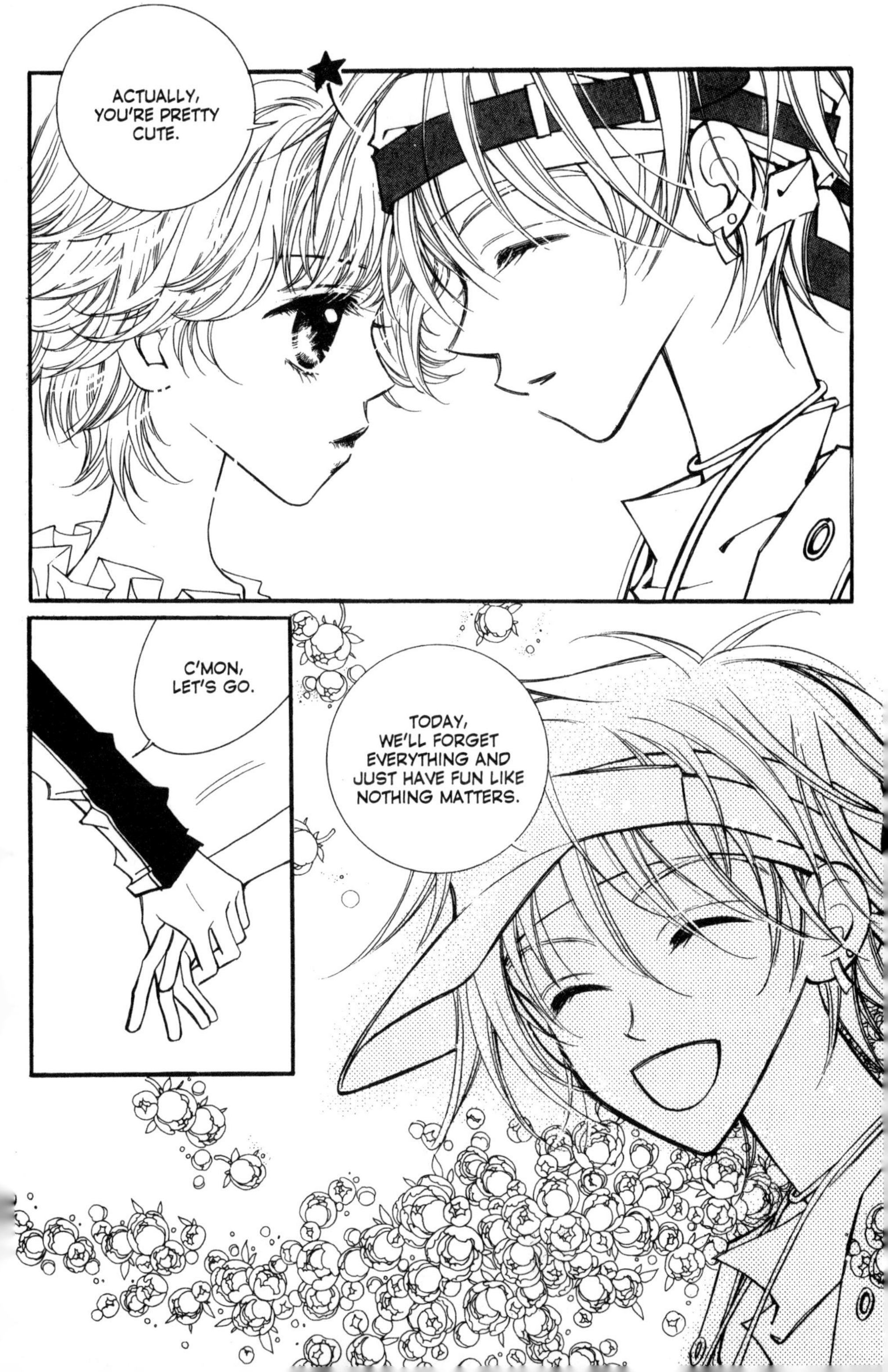
ACTUALLY, YOU'RE PRETTY CUTE.
C'MON, LET'S GO.
TODAY, WE'LL FORGET EVERYTHING AND JUST HAVE FUN LIKE NOTHING MATTERS.

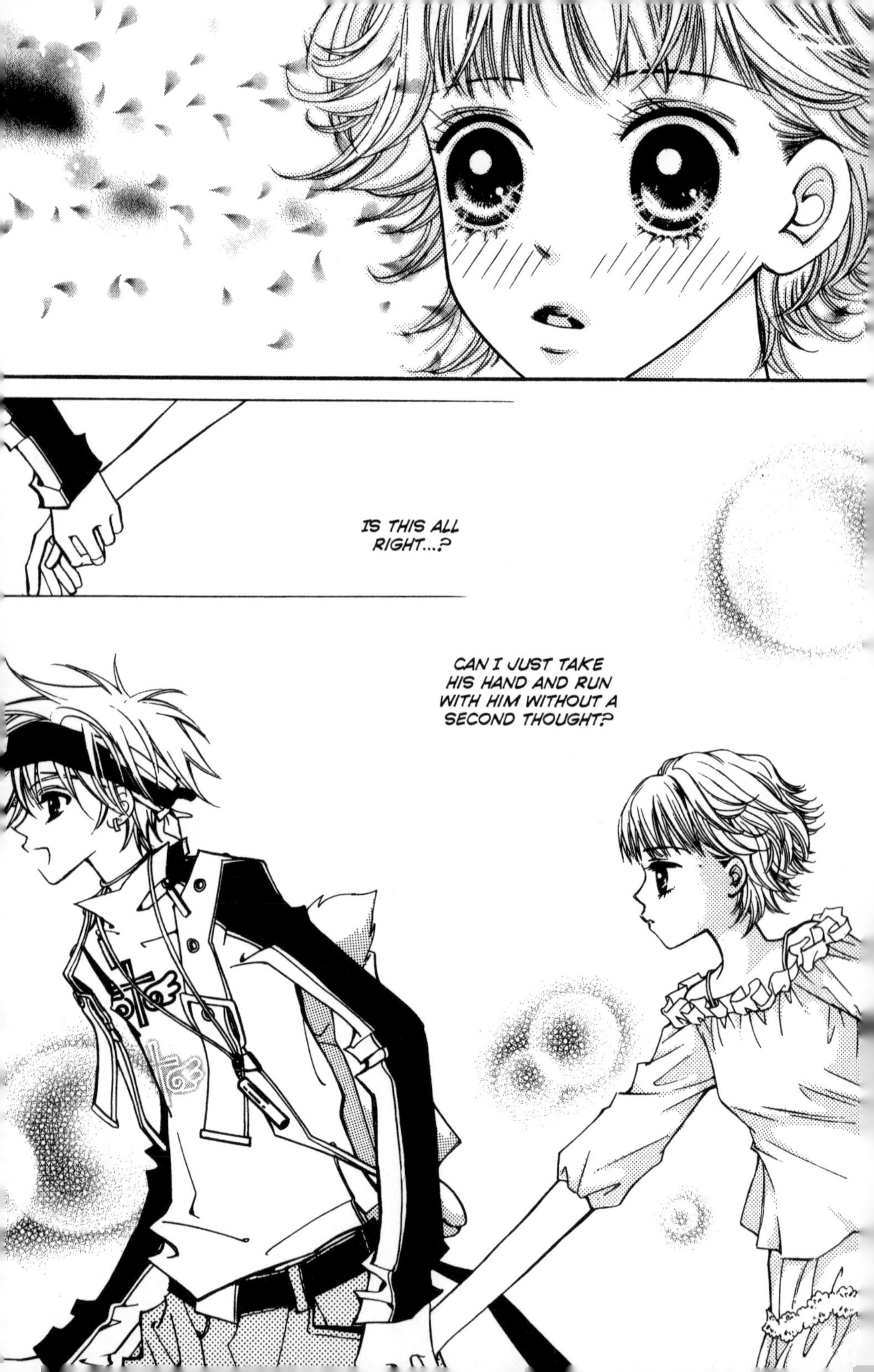
IS THIS ALL RIGHT...?
CAN I JUST TAKE HIS HAND AND RUN WITH HIM WITHOUT A SECOND THOUGHT?

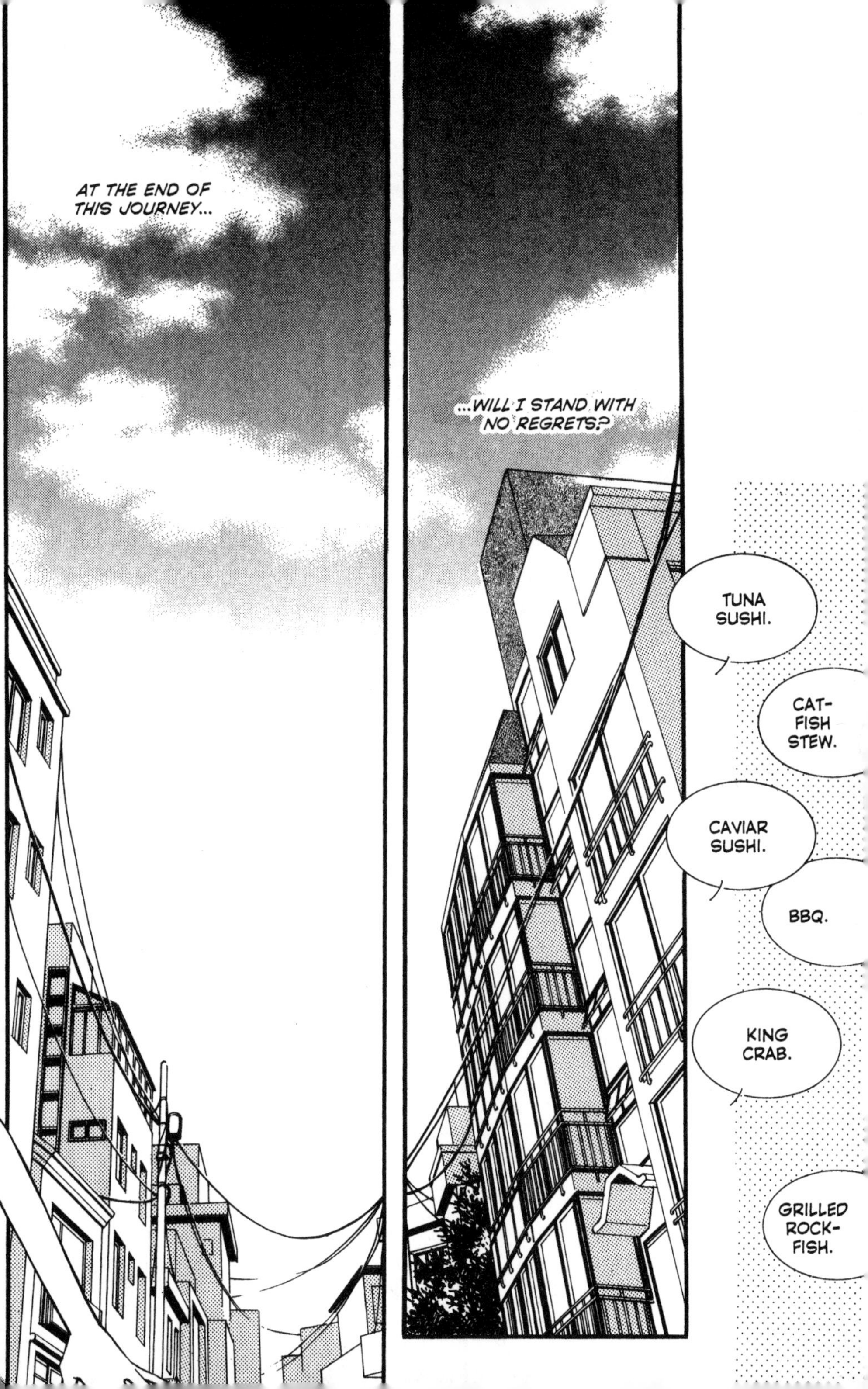
AT THE END OF THIS JOURNEY...
...WILL I STAND WITH NO REGRETS?
TUNA SUSHI.
CAT-FISH STEW.
CAVIAR SUSHI.
BBQ.
KING CRAB.
GRILLED ROCK-FISH.

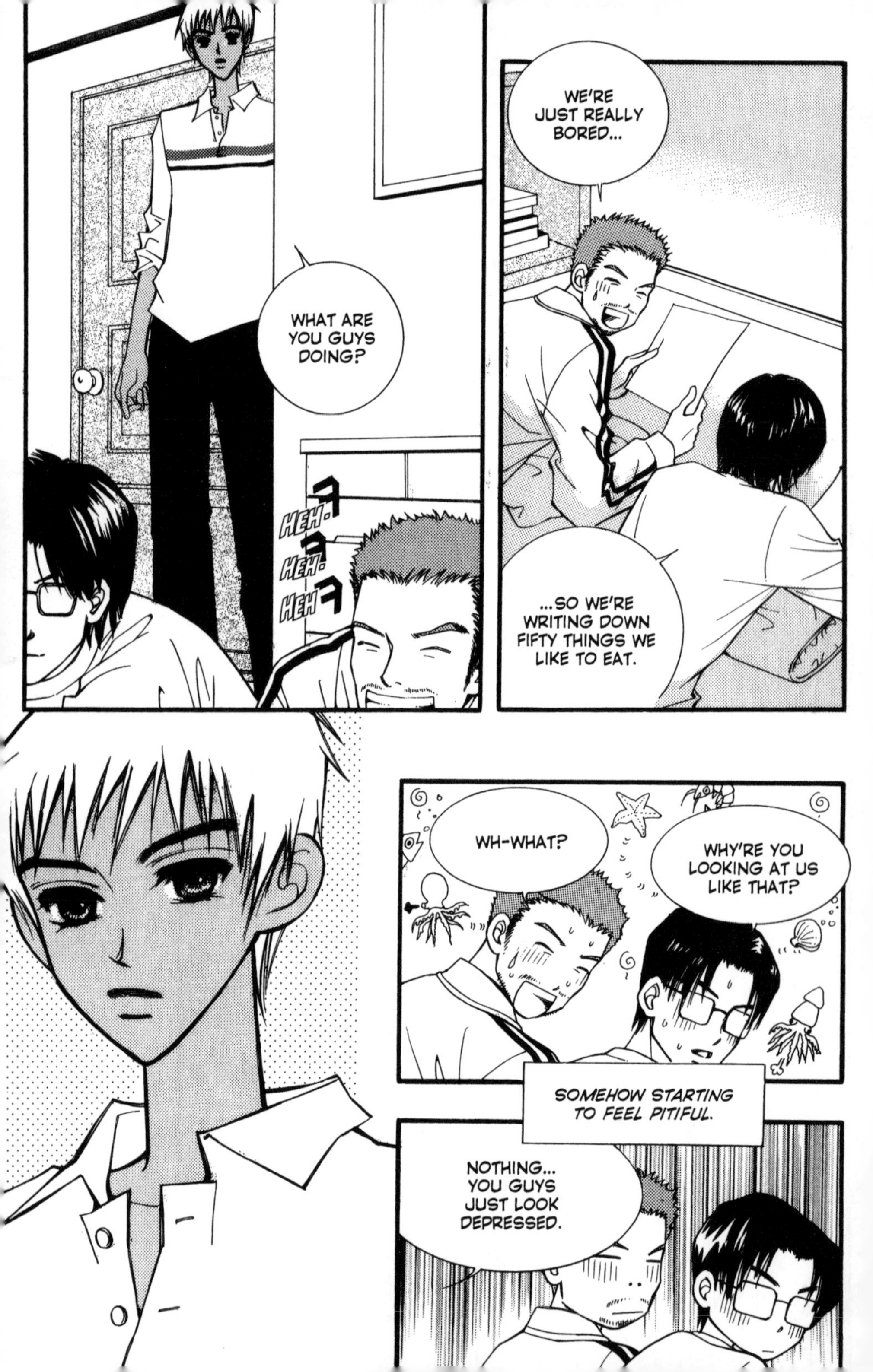
WHAT ARE YOU GUYS DOING?
HEH. HEH. HEH
WE'RE JUST REALLY BORED...
...SO WE'RE WRITING DOWN FIFTY THINGS WE LIKE TO EAT.
WH-WHAT?
WHY'RE YOU LOOKING AT US LIKE THAT?
SOMEHOW STARTING TO FEEL PITIFUL.
NOTHING... YOU GUYS JUST LOOK DEPRESSED.

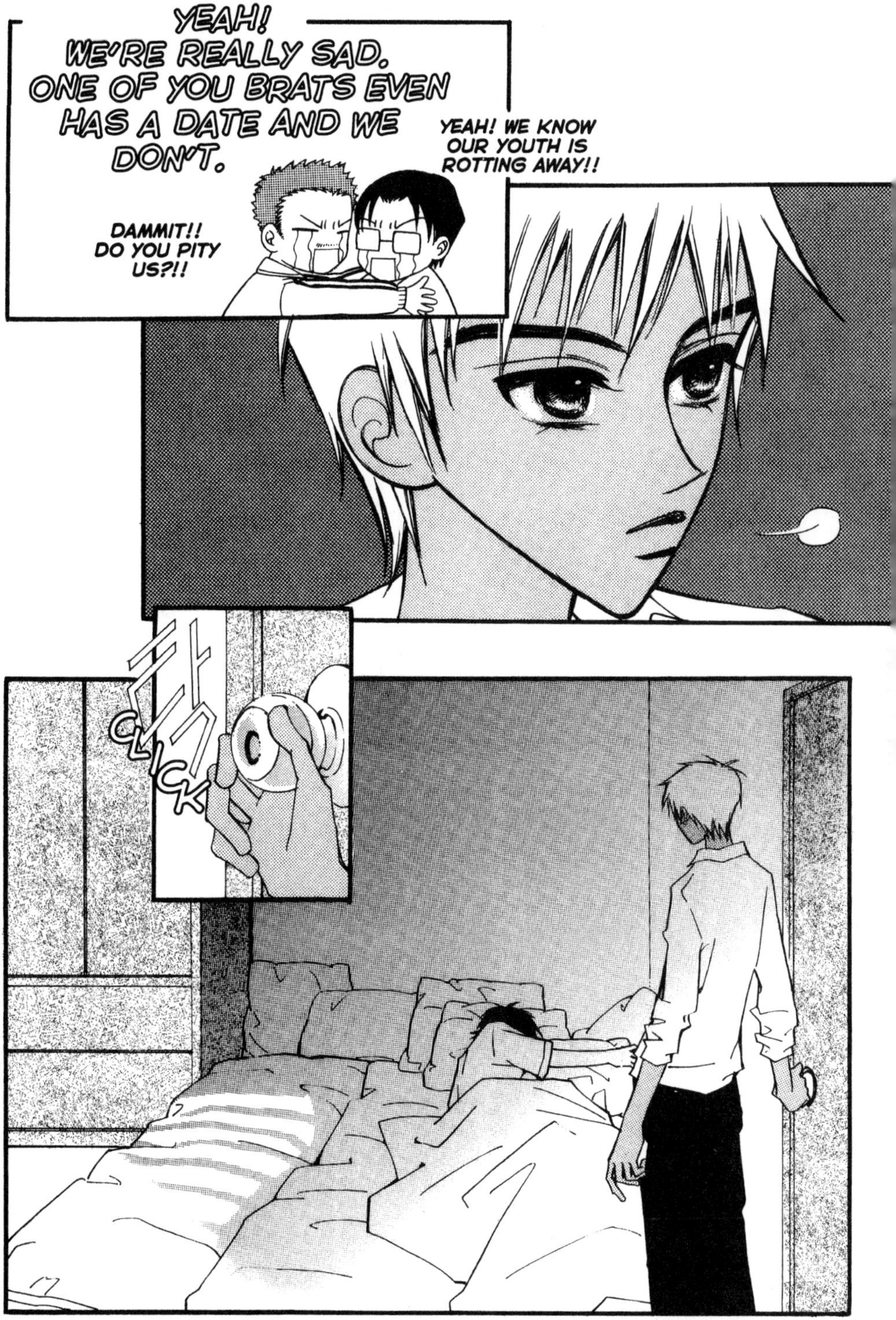
YEAH! WE'RE REALLY SAD. ONE OF YOU BRATS EVEN HAS A DATE AND WE DON'T.
YEAH! WE KNOW OUR YOUTH IS ROTTING AWAY!!
DAMMIT!! DO YOU PITY US?!!
CLICK

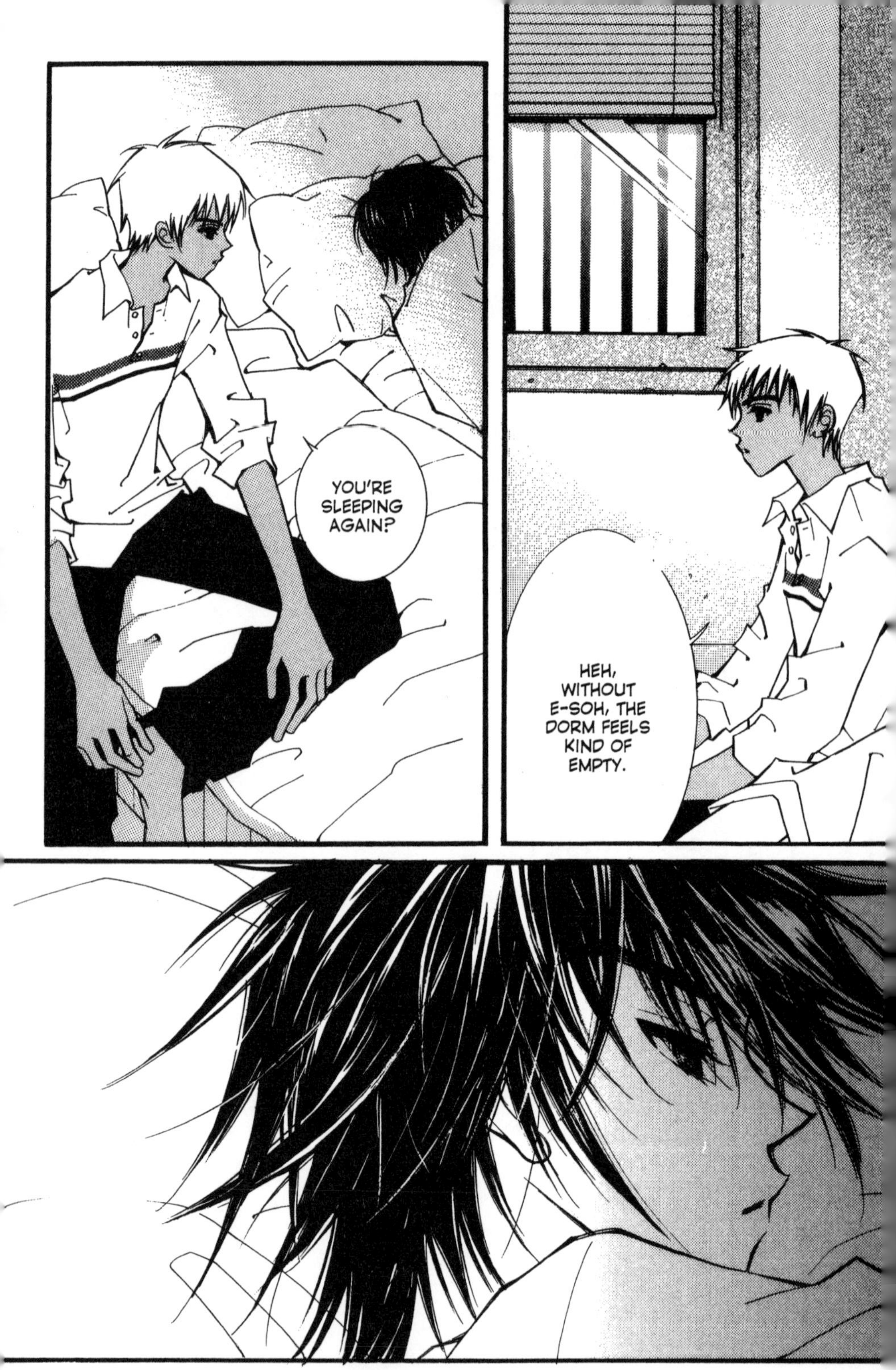
YOU'RE SLEEPING AGAIN?
HEH, WITHOUT E-SOH, THE DORM FEELS KIND OF EMPTY.

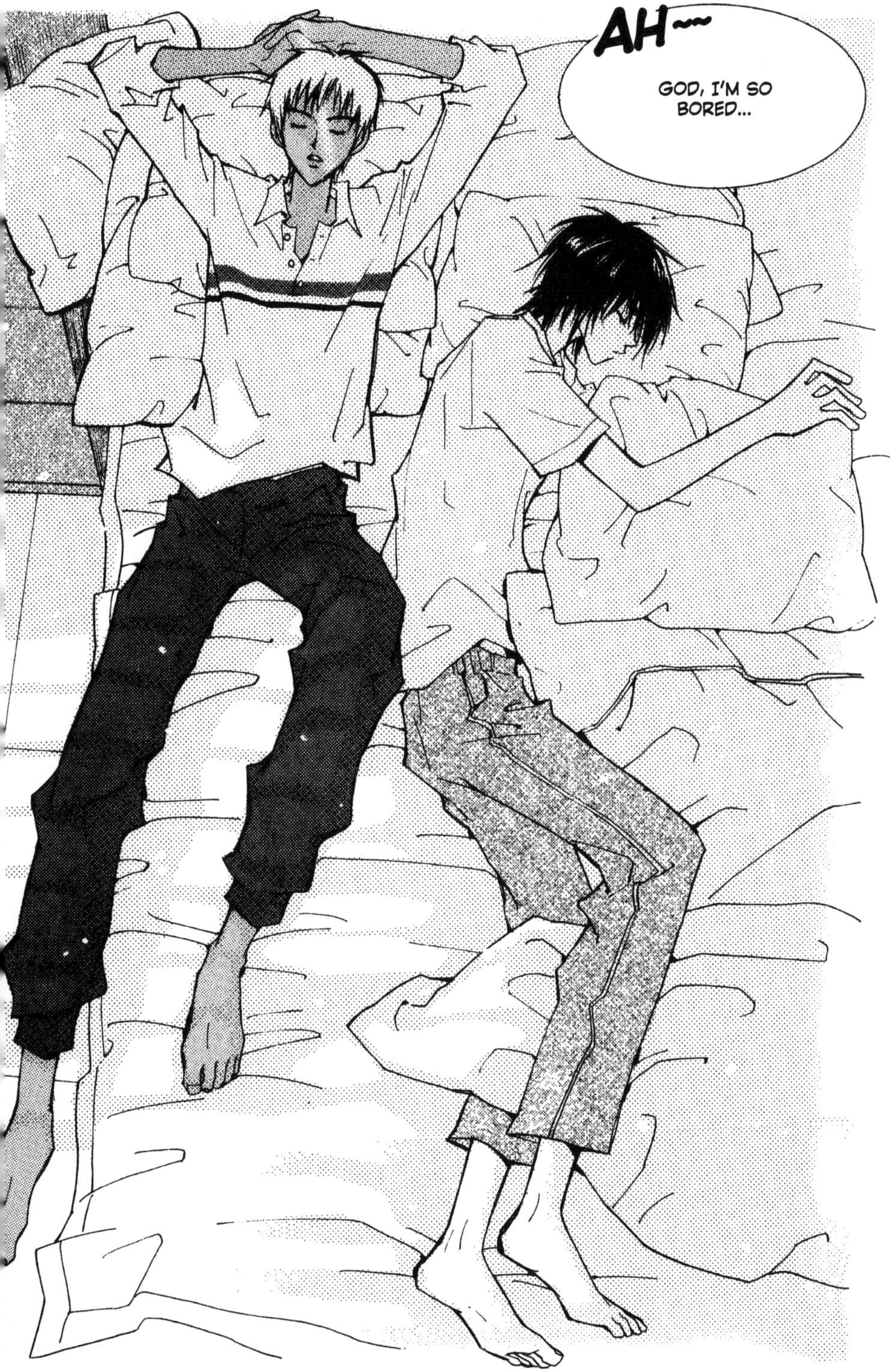
AH~~
GOD, I'M SO BORED...

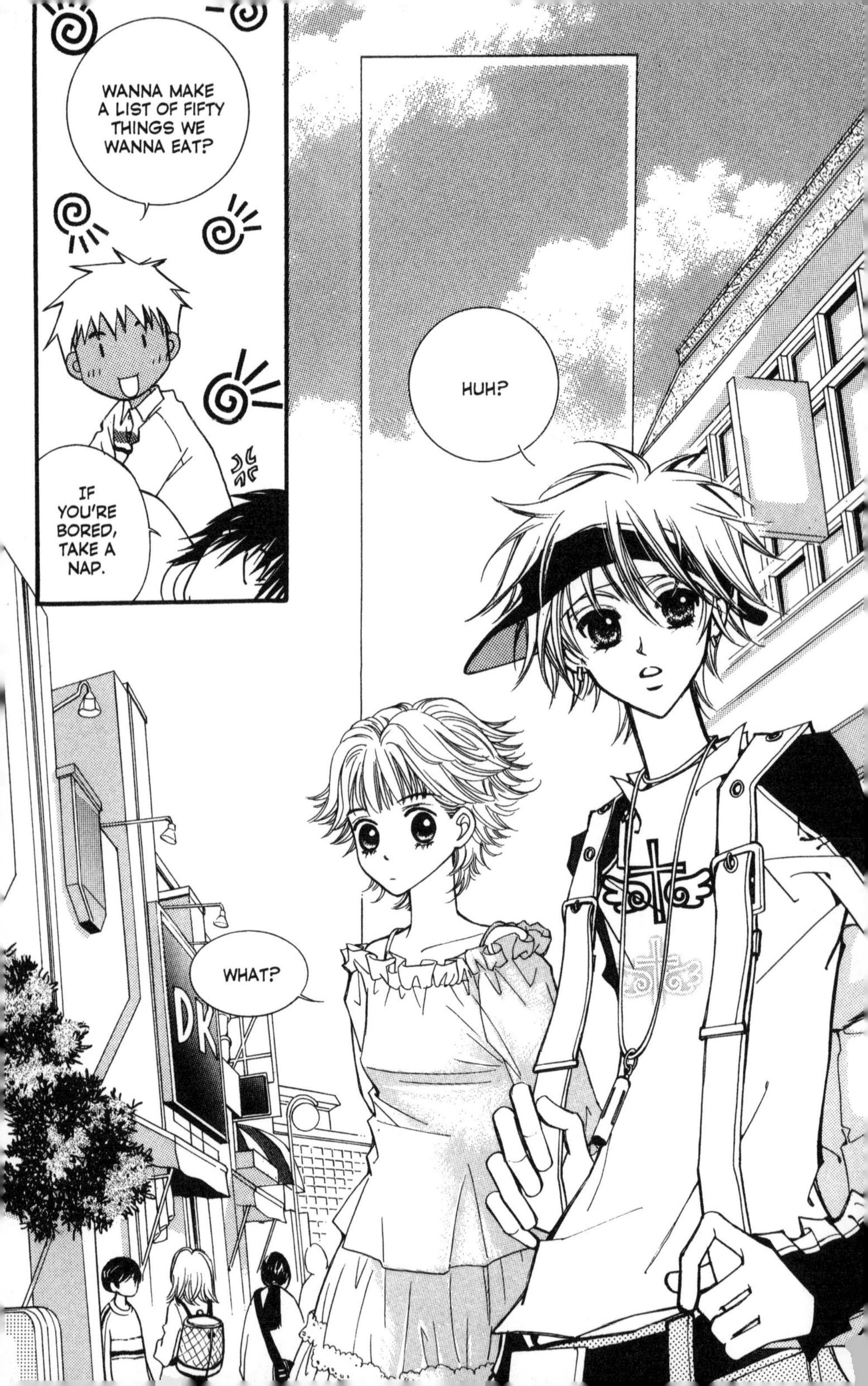
WANNA MAKE A LIST OF FIFTY THINGS WE WANNA EAT?
IF YOU'RE BORED, TAKE A NAP.
HUH?
WHAT?

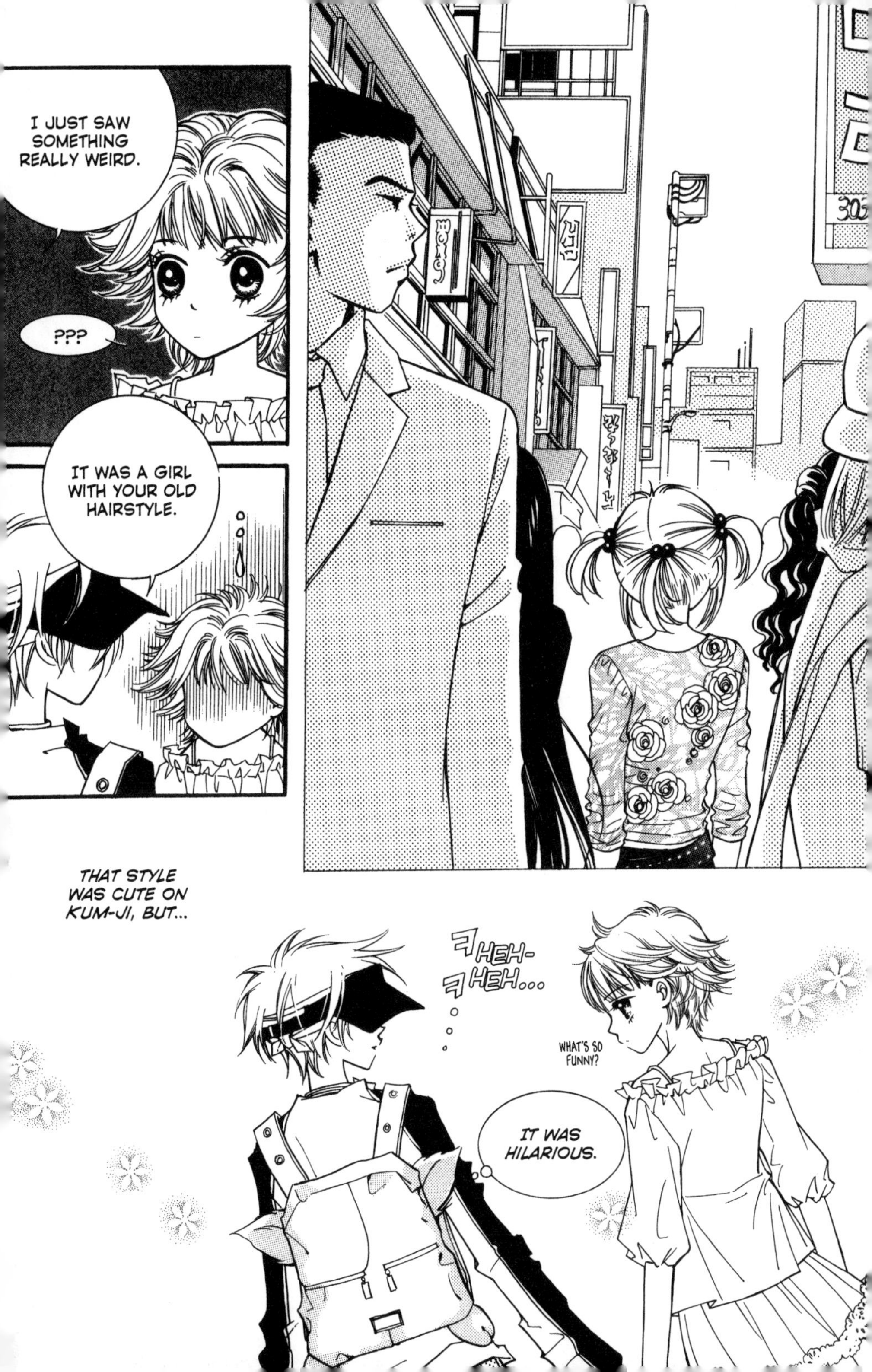
I JUST SAW SOMETHING REALLY WEIRD.
???
IT WAS A GIRL WITH YOUR OLD HAIRSTYLE.
THAT STYLE WAS CUTE ON KUM-JI, BUT...
ㅋHEH-ㅋHEH...
WHAT'S SO FUNNY?
IT WAS HILARIOUS.

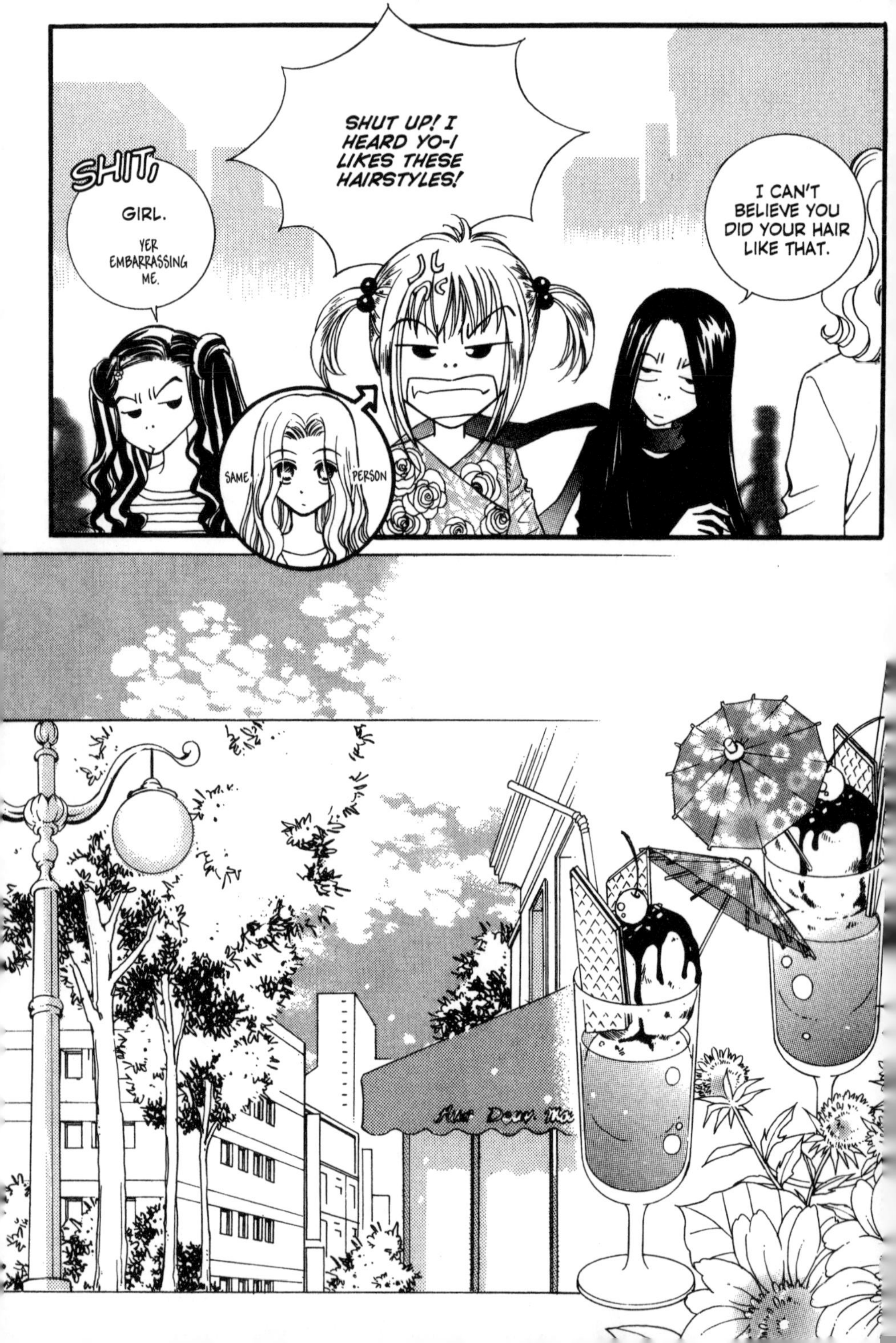
SHIT,
GIRL.
YER EMBARRASSING ME.
SHUT UP! I HEARD YO-I LIKES THESE HAIRSTYLES!
SAME
PERSON
I CAN'T BELIEVE YOU DID YOUR HAIR LIKE THAT.

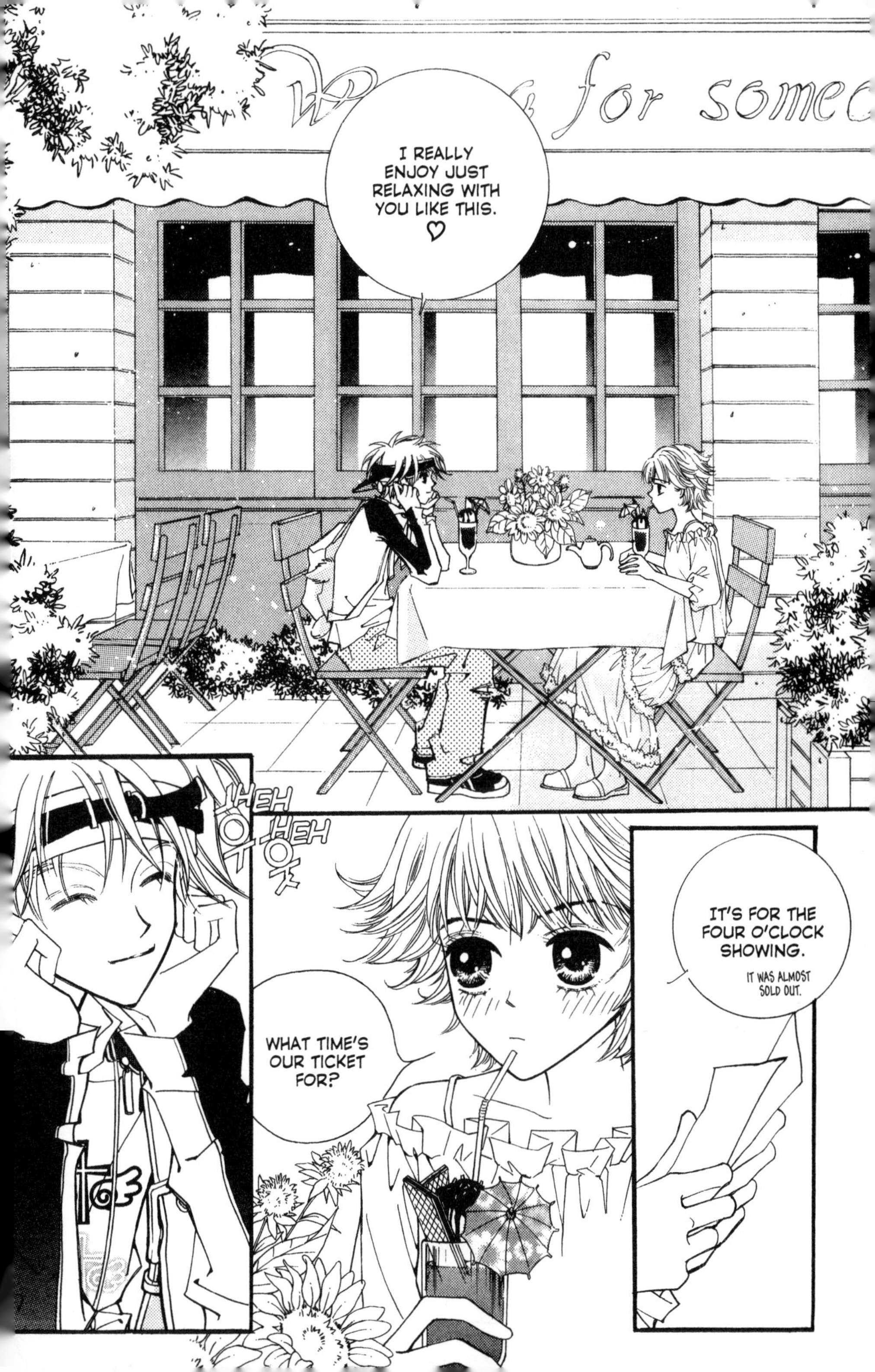

I REALLY ENJOY JUST RELAXING WITH YOU LIKE THIS. ♡
HEH HEH
WHAT TIME'S OUR TICKET FOR?
IT'S FOR THE FOUR O'CLOCK SHOWING.
IT WAS ALMOST SOLD OUT.

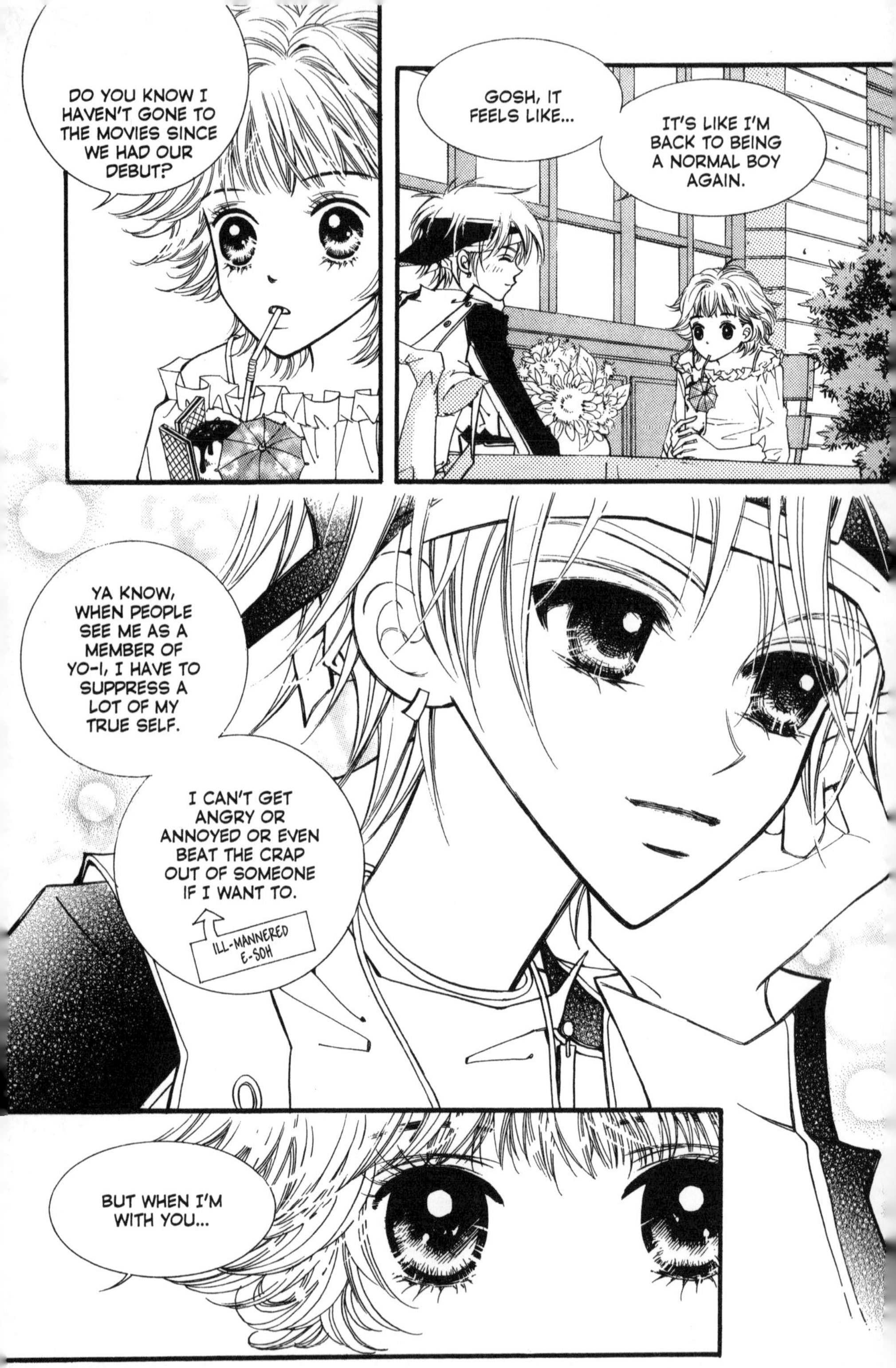

DO YOU KNOW I HAVEN'T GONE TO THE MOVIES SINCE WE HAD OUR DEBUT?
GOSH, IT FEELS LIKE...
IT'S LIKE I'M BACK TO BEING A NORMAL BOY AGAIN.
YA KNOW, WHEN PEOPLE SEE ME AS A MEMBER OF YO-I, I HAVE TO SUPPRESS A LOT OF MY TRUE SELF.
I CAN'T GET ANGRY OR ANNOYED OR EVEN BEAT THE CRAP OUT OF SOMEONE IF I WANT TO.
ILL-MANNERED E-SOH
BUT WHEN I'M WITH YOU...

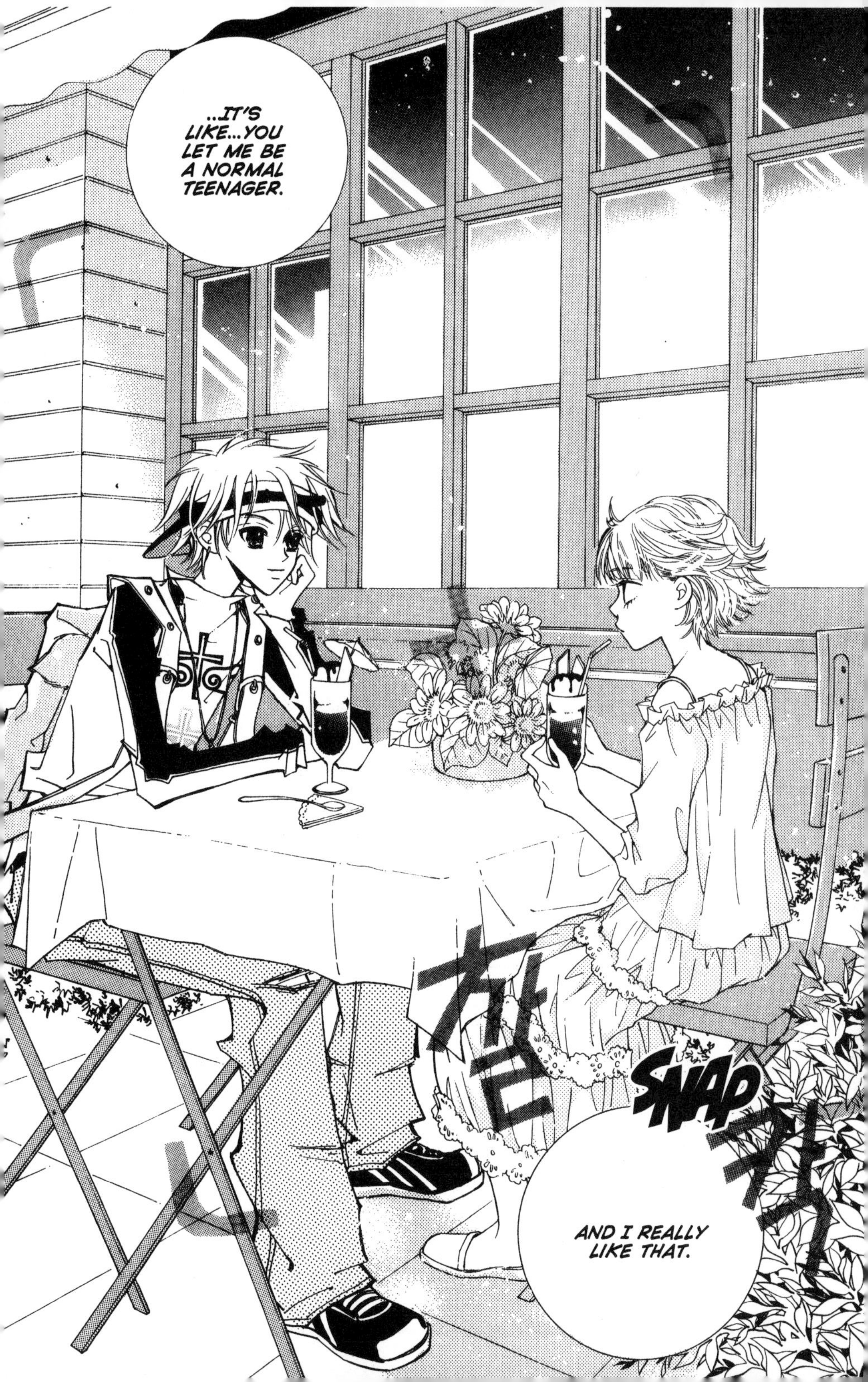
..IT'S LIKE...YOU LET ME BE A NORMAL TEENAGER.
SNAP
AND I REALLY LIKE THAT.

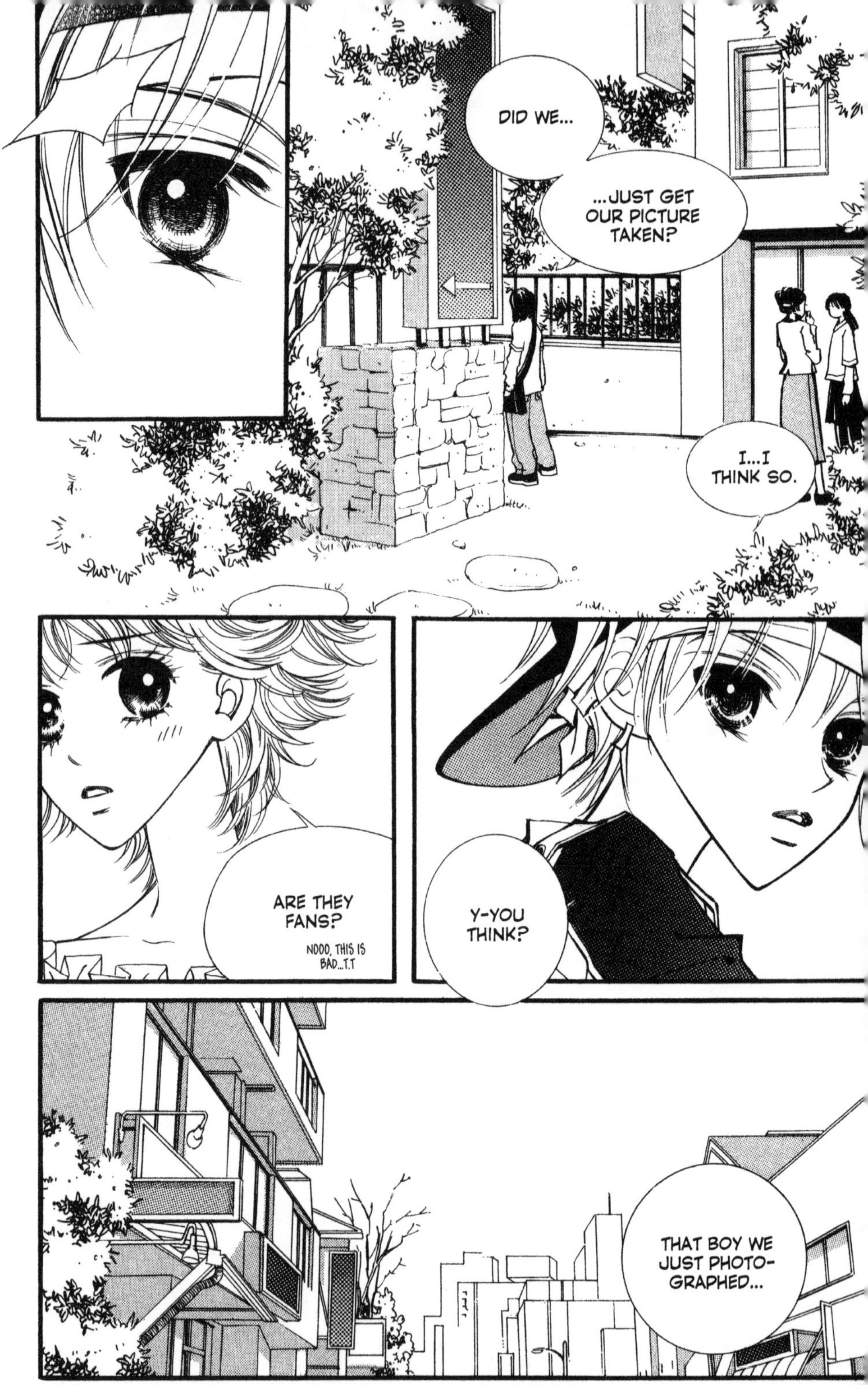
DID WE...
...JUST GET OUR PICTURE TAKEN?
I...I THINK SO.
ARE THEY FANS?
NOOO, THIS IS BAD...T.T
Y-YOU THINK?
THAT BOY WE JUST PHOTO-GRAPHED...

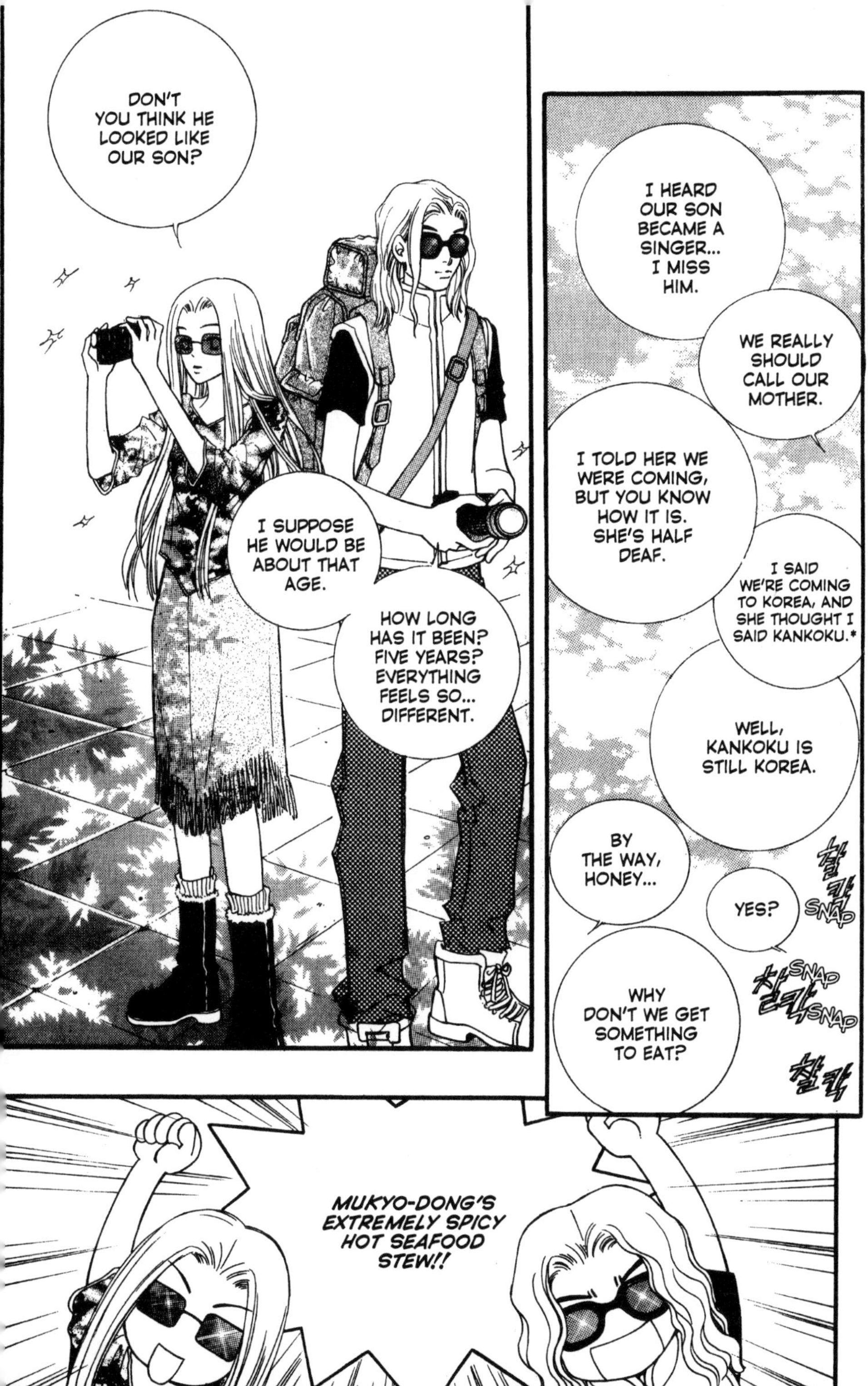
DON'T YOU THINK HE LOOKED LIKE OUR SON?
I SUPPOSE HE WOULD BE ABOUT THAT AGE.
HOW LONG HAS IT BEEN? FIVE YEARS? EVERYTHING FEELS SO... DIFFERENT.
I HEARD OUR SON BECAME A SINGER... I MISS HIM.
WE REALLY SHOULD CALL OUR MOTHER.
I TOLD HER WE WERE COMING, BUT YOU KNOW HOW IT IS. SHE'S HALF DEAF.
I SAID WE'RE COMING TO KOREA, AND SHE THOUGHT I SAID KANKOKU.*
WELL, KANKOKU IS STILL KOREA.
BY THE WAY, HONEY...
YES?
찰칵
SNAP
WHY DON'T WE GET SOMETHING TO EAT?
찰칵
SNAP
찰칵
SNAP
찰칵
MUKYO-DONG'S EXTREMELY SPICY HOT SEAFOOD STEW!!

EDITOR'S NOTE: "KANKOKU" IS THE JAPANESE WORD FOR KOREA. AROUND THE TIME OF WORLD WAR II, JAPAN TOOK OVER KOREA FOR EVERAL DECADES AND FORCED KOREANS TO SPEAK ONLY JAPANESE. AS A RESULT, MANY GRANDPARENTS IN KOREA SWITCH ETWEEN SPEAKING IN KOREAN AND JAPANESE REGULARLY.

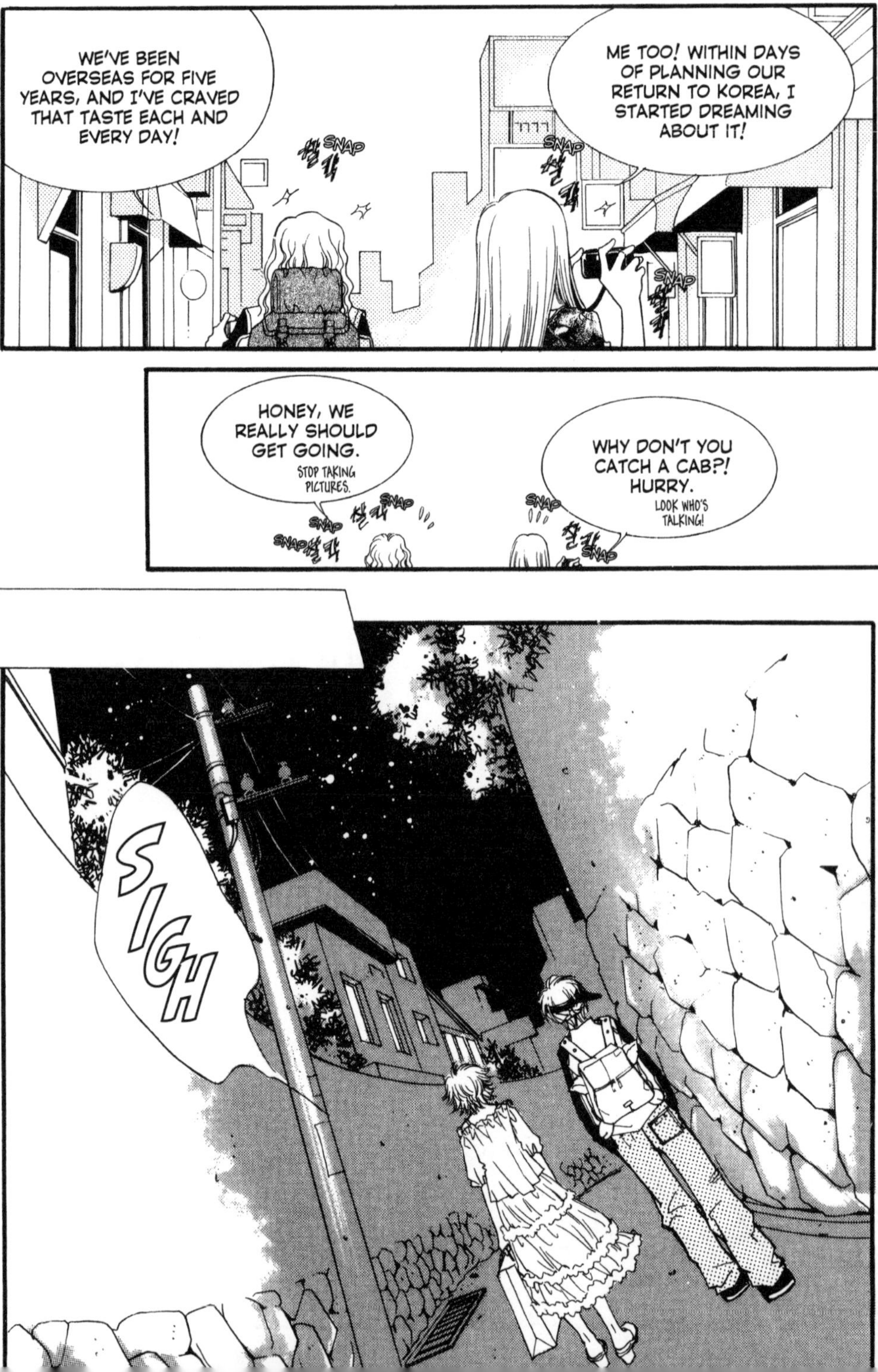
WE'VE BEEN OVERSEAS FOR FIVE YEARS, AND I'VE CRAVED THAT TASTE EACH AND EVERY DAY!
SNAP
ME TOO! WITHIN DAYS OF PLANNING OUR RETURN TO KOREA, I STARTED DREAMING ABOUT IT!
SNAP
SNAP
HONEY, WE REALLY SHOULD GET GOING.
STOP TAKING PICTURES.
SNAP
SNAP
SNAP
WHY DON'T YOU CATCH A CAB?! HURRY.
LOOK WHO'S TALKING!
SNAP
SNAP
SIGH

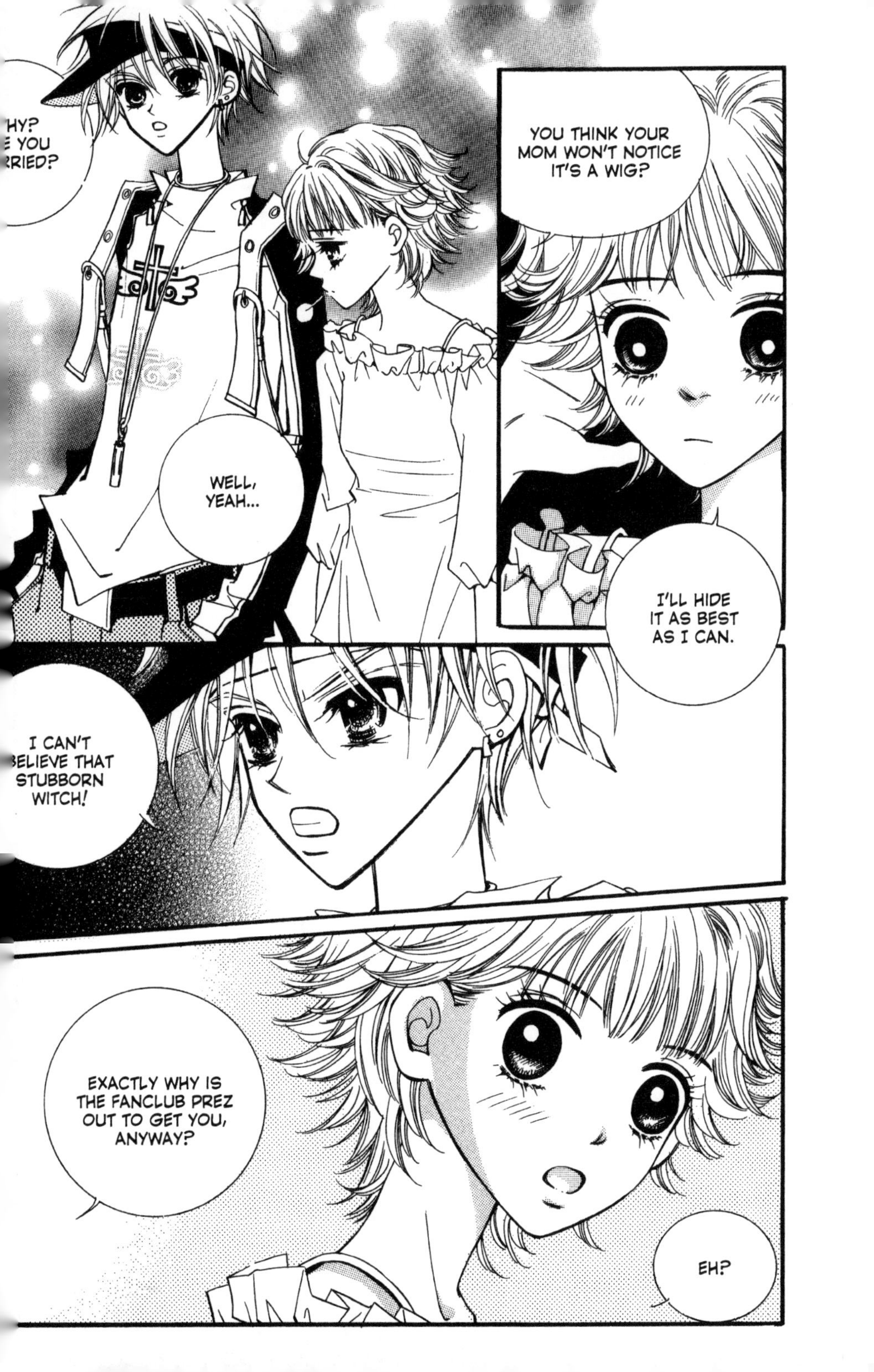
HY? E YOU RRIED?
WELL, YEAH...
YOU THINK YOUR MOM WON'T NOTICE IT'S A WIG?
I'LL HIDE IT AS BEST AS I CAN.
I CAN'T ELIEVE THAT STUBBORN WITCH!
EXACTLY WHY IS THE FANCLUB PREZ OUT TO GET YOU, ANYWAY?
EH?

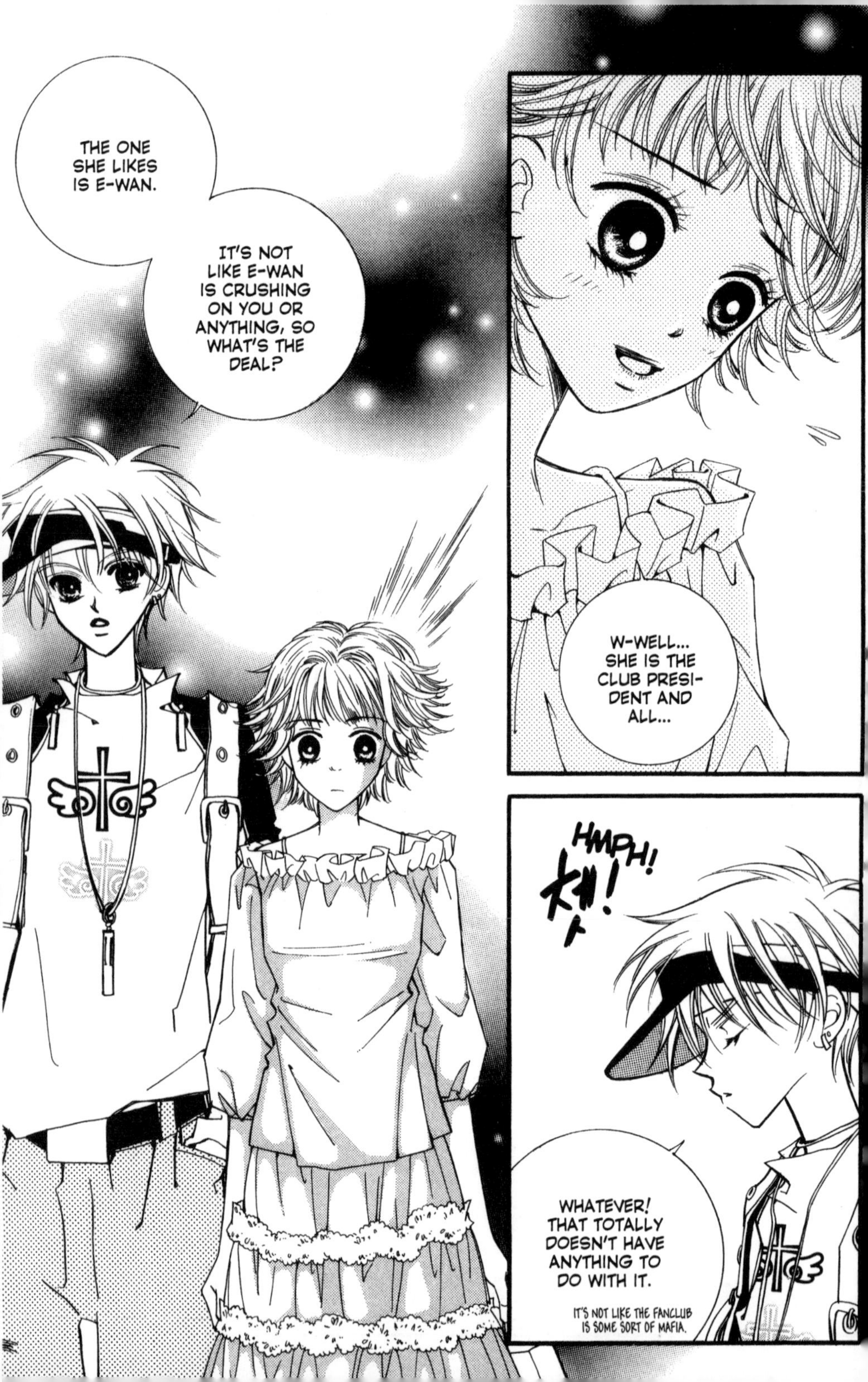
THE ONE SHE LIKES IS E-WAN.
IT'S NOT LIKE E-WAN IS CRUSHING ON YOU OR ANYTHING, SO WHAT'S THE DEAL?
W-WELL... SHE IS THE CLUB PRESI-DENT AND ALL...
HMPH!
칫!
WHATEVER! THAT TOTALLY DOESN'T HAVE ANYTHING TO DO WITH IT.
IT'S NOT LIKE THE FANCLUB IS SOME SORT OF MAFIA.

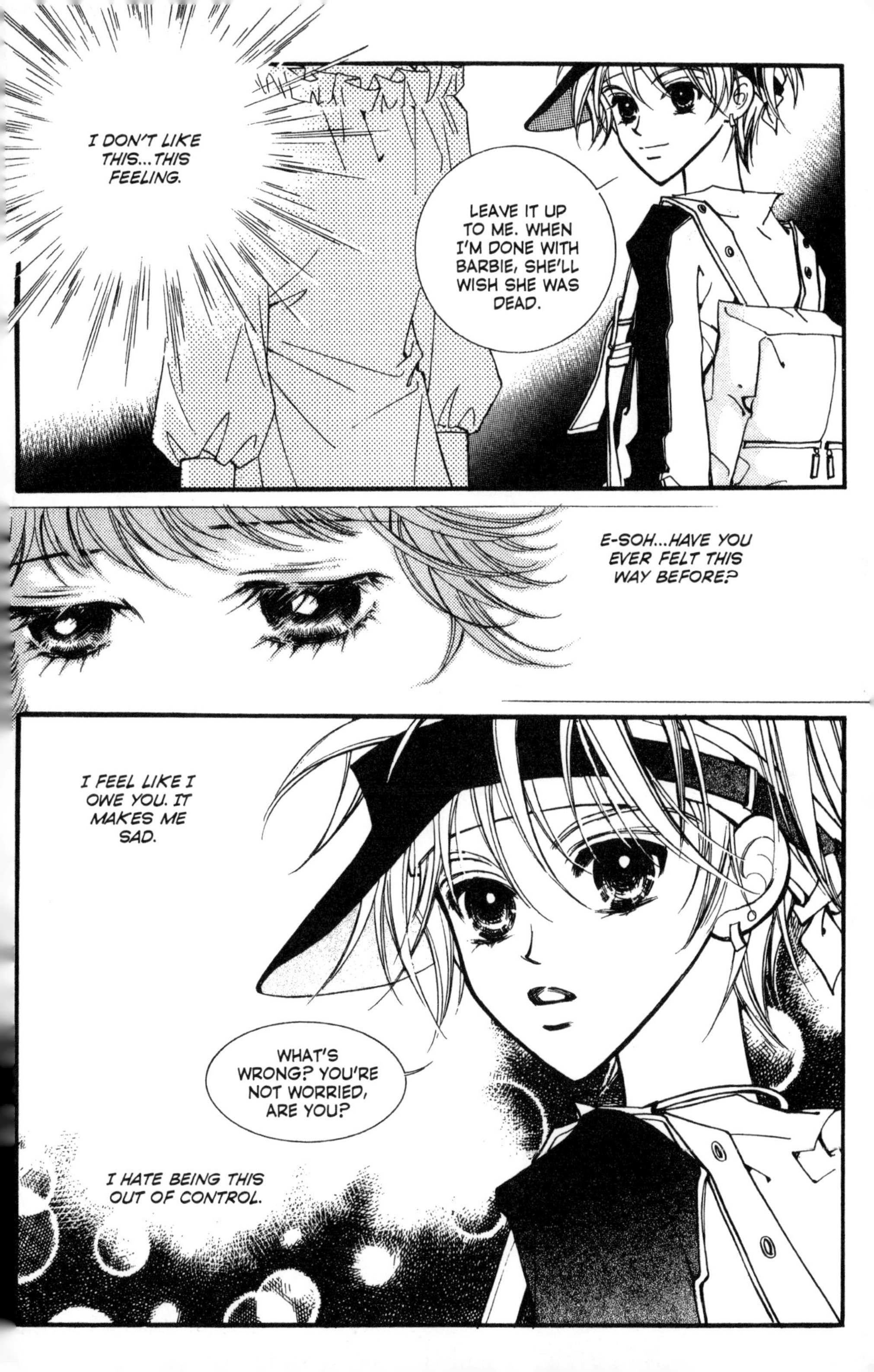
I DON'T LIKE THIS...THIS FEELING.
LEAVE IT UP TO ME. WHEN I'M DONE WITH BARBIE, SHE'LL WISH SHE WAS DEAD.
E-SOH...HAVE YOU EVER FELT THIS WAY BEFORE?
I FEEL LIKE I OWE YOU. IT MAKES ME SAD.
WHAT'S WRONG? YOU'RE NOT WORRIED, ARE YOU?
I HATE BEING THIS OUT OF CONTROL.

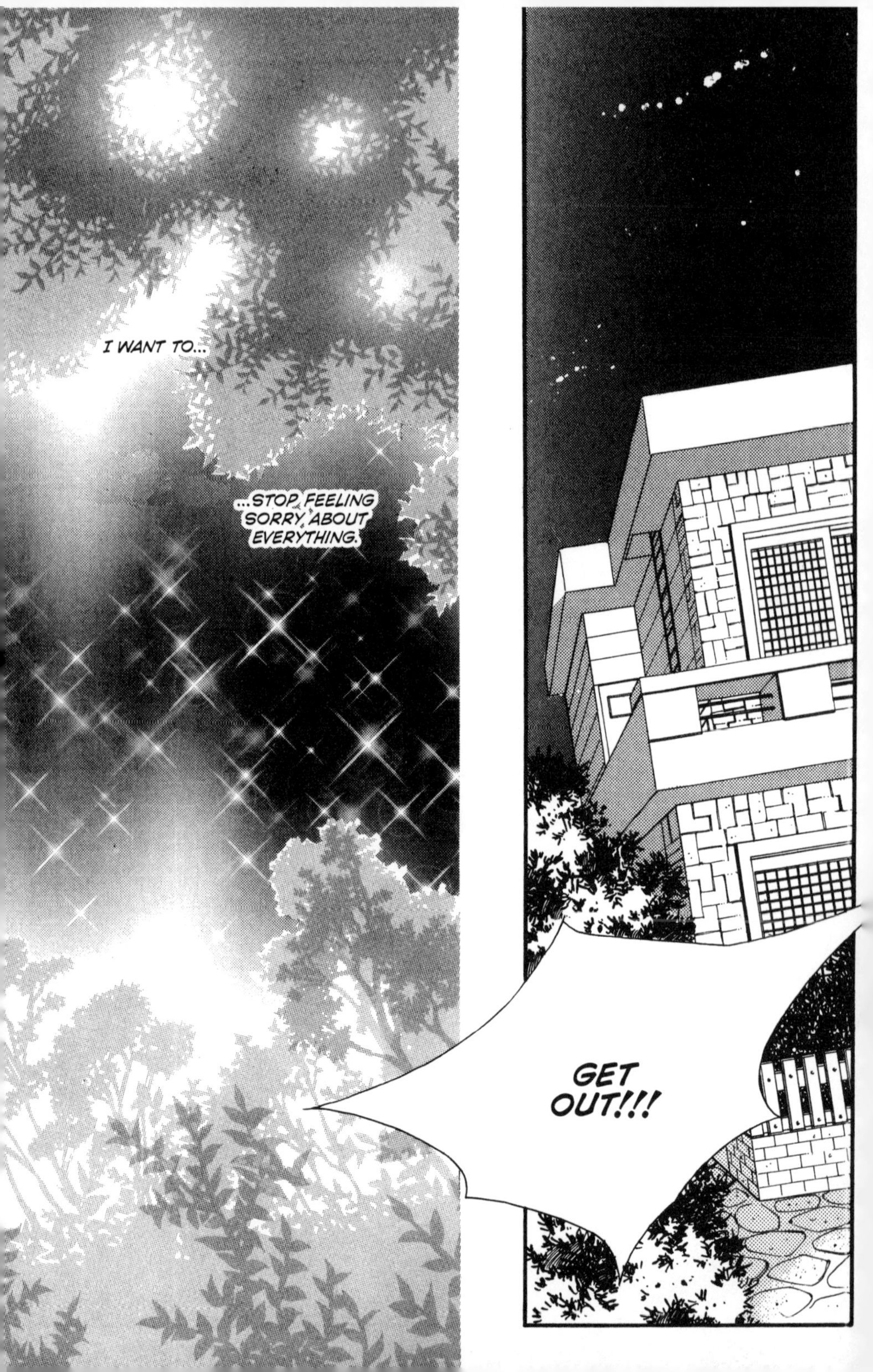
I WANT TO...
...STOP FEELING SORRY ABOUT EVERYTHING.
GET OUT!!!

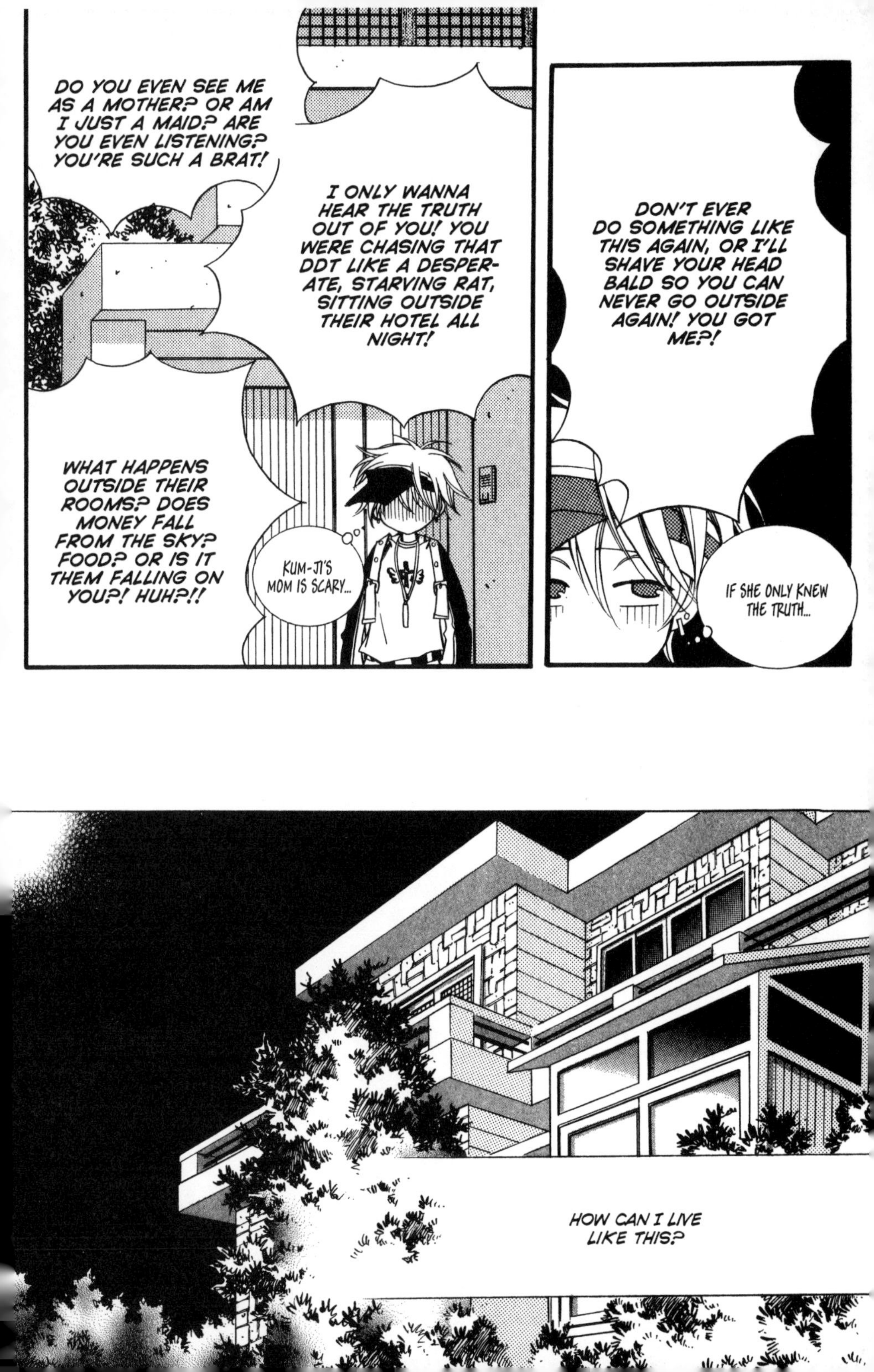
DO YOU EVEN SEE ME AS A MOTHER? OR AM I JUST A MAID? ARE YOU EVEN LISTENING? YOU'RE SUCH A BRAT!
I ONLY WANNA HEAR THE TRUTH OUT OF YOU! YOU WERE CHASING THAT DDT LIKE A DESPER-ATE, STARVING RAT, SITTING OUTSIDE THEIR HOTEL ALL NIGHT!
WHAT HAPPENS OUTSIDE THEIR ROOMS? DOES MONEY FALL FROM THE SKY? FOOD? OR IS IT THEM FALLING ON YOU?! HUH?!!
KUM-JI'S MOM IS SCARY...
DON'T EVER DO SOMETHING LIKE THIS AGAIN, OR I'LL SHAVE YOUR HEAD BALD SO YOU CAN NEVER GO OUTSIDE AGAIN! YOU GOT ME?!
IF SHE ONLY KNEW THE TRUTH...
HOW CAN I LIVE LIKE THIS?

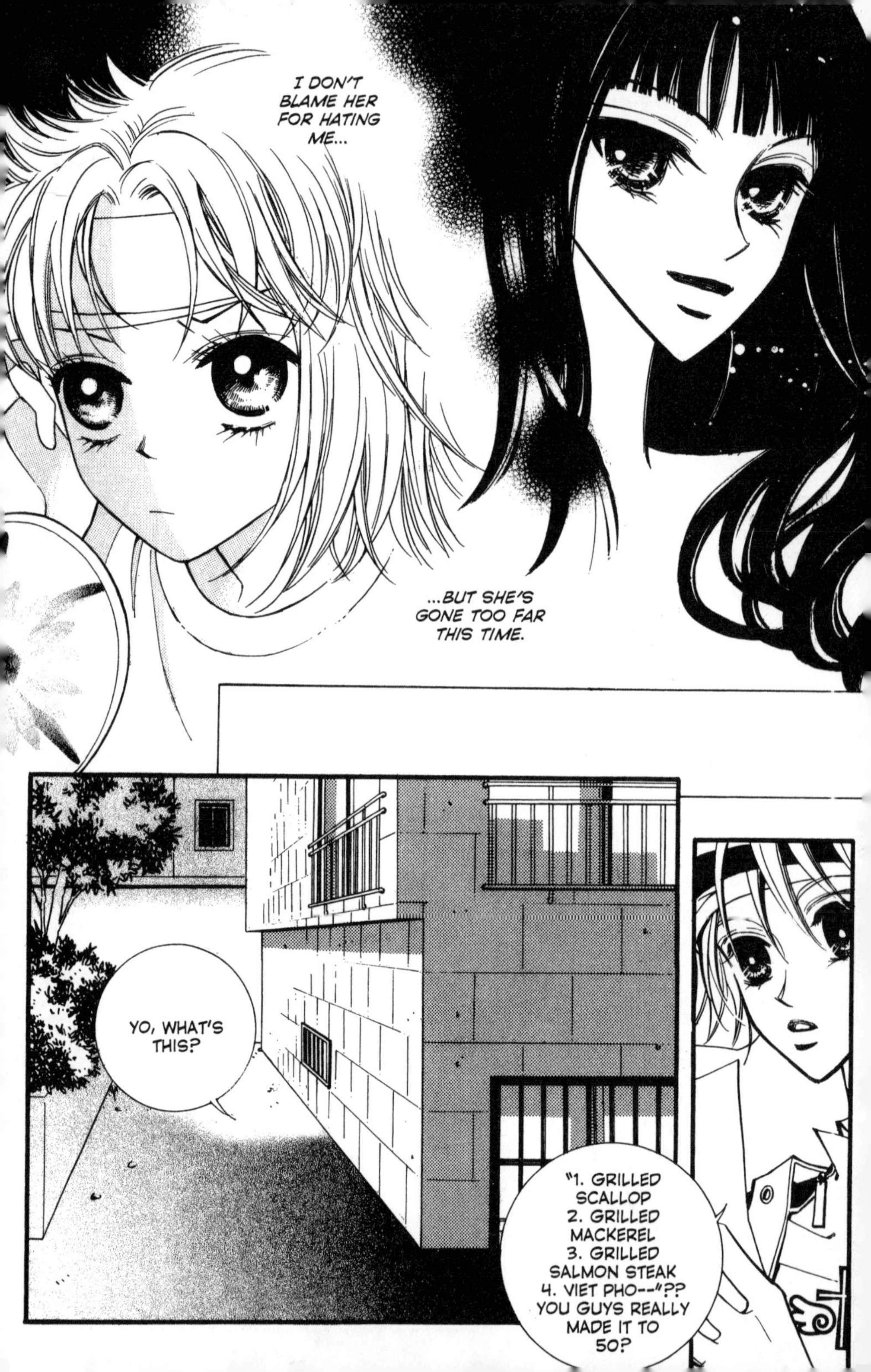
I DON'T BLAME HER FOR HATING ME...
...BUT SHE'S GONE TOO FAR THIS TIME.
YO, WHAT'S THIS?
"1. GRILLED SCALLOP 2. GRILLED MACKEREL 3. GRILLED SALMON STEAK 4. VIET PHO--"?? YOU GUYS REALLY MADE IT TO 50?

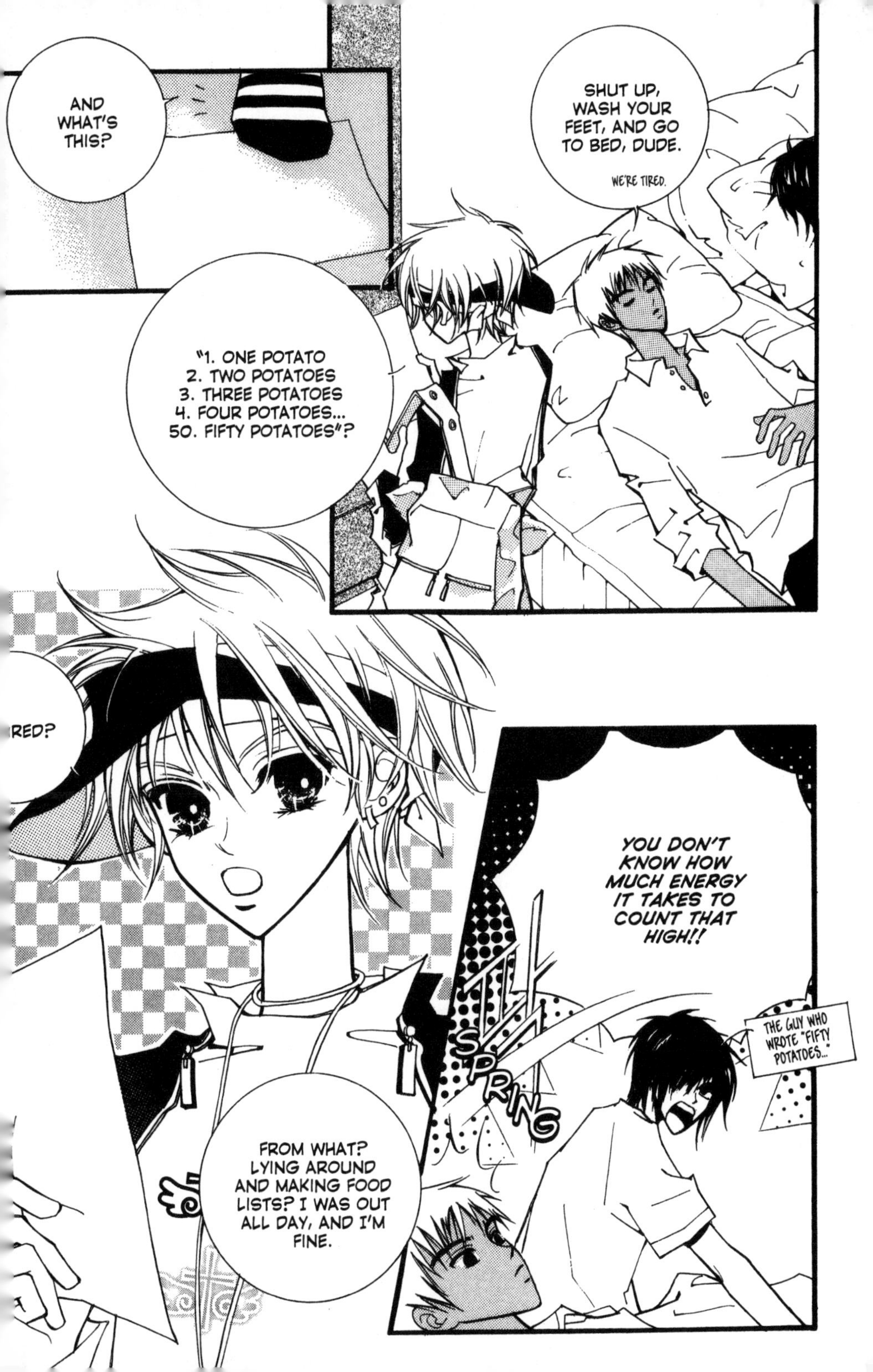
AND WHAT'S THIS?
"1. ONE POTATO
2. TWO POTATOES
3. THREE POTATOES
4. FOUR POTATOES...
50. FIFTY POTATOES"?
SHUT UP, WASH YOUR FEET, AND GO TO BED, DUDE.
WE'RE TIRED.
RED?
FROM WHAT? LYING AROUND AND MAKING FOOD LISTS? I WAS OUT ALL DAY, AND I'M FINE.
YOU DON'T KNOW HOW MUCH ENERGY IT TAKES TO COUNT THAT HIGH!!
SPRING
THE GUY WHO WROTE "FIFTY POTATOES..."

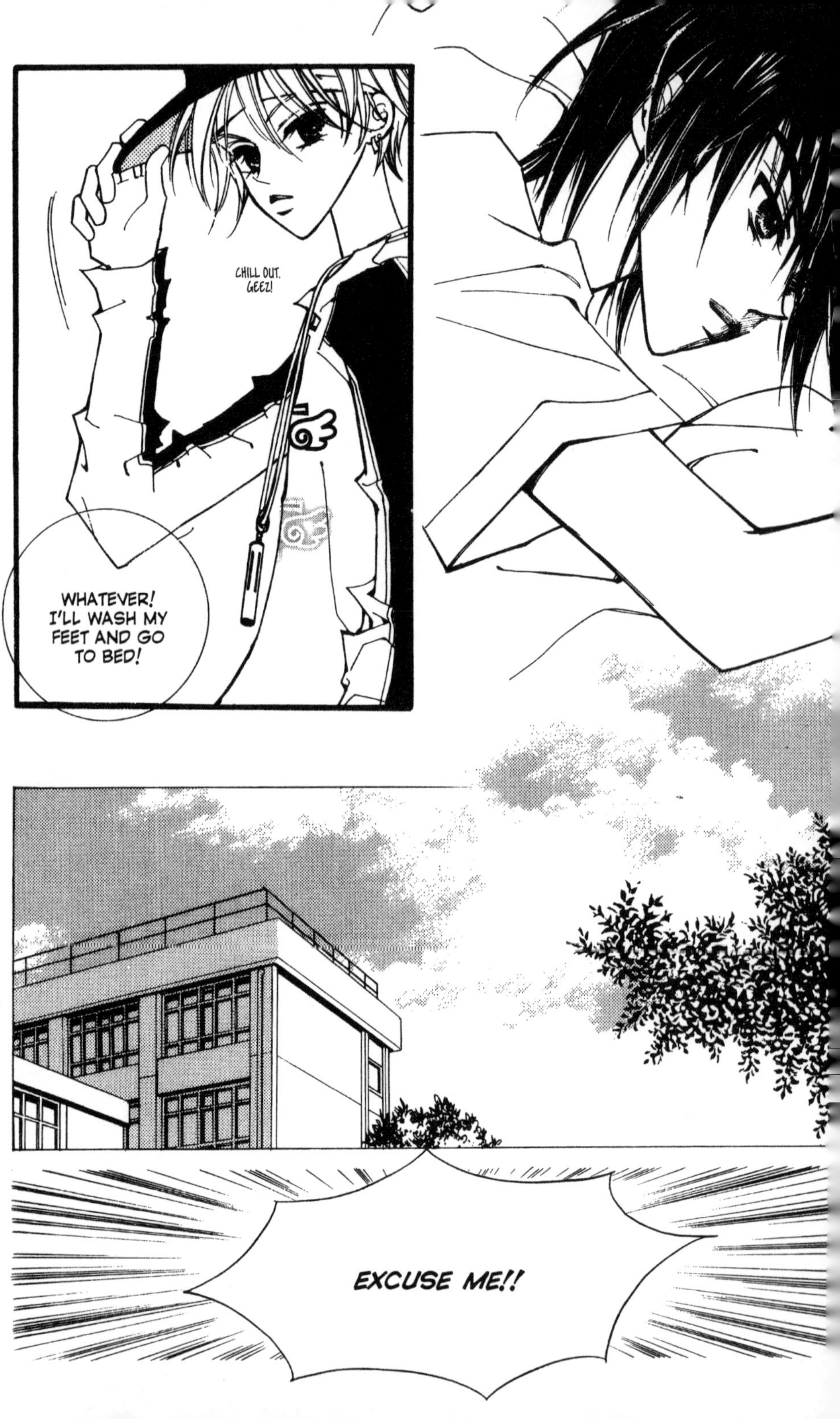
CHILL OUT. GEEZ!
WHATEVER! I'LL WASH MY FEET AND GO TO BED!
EXCUSE ME!!

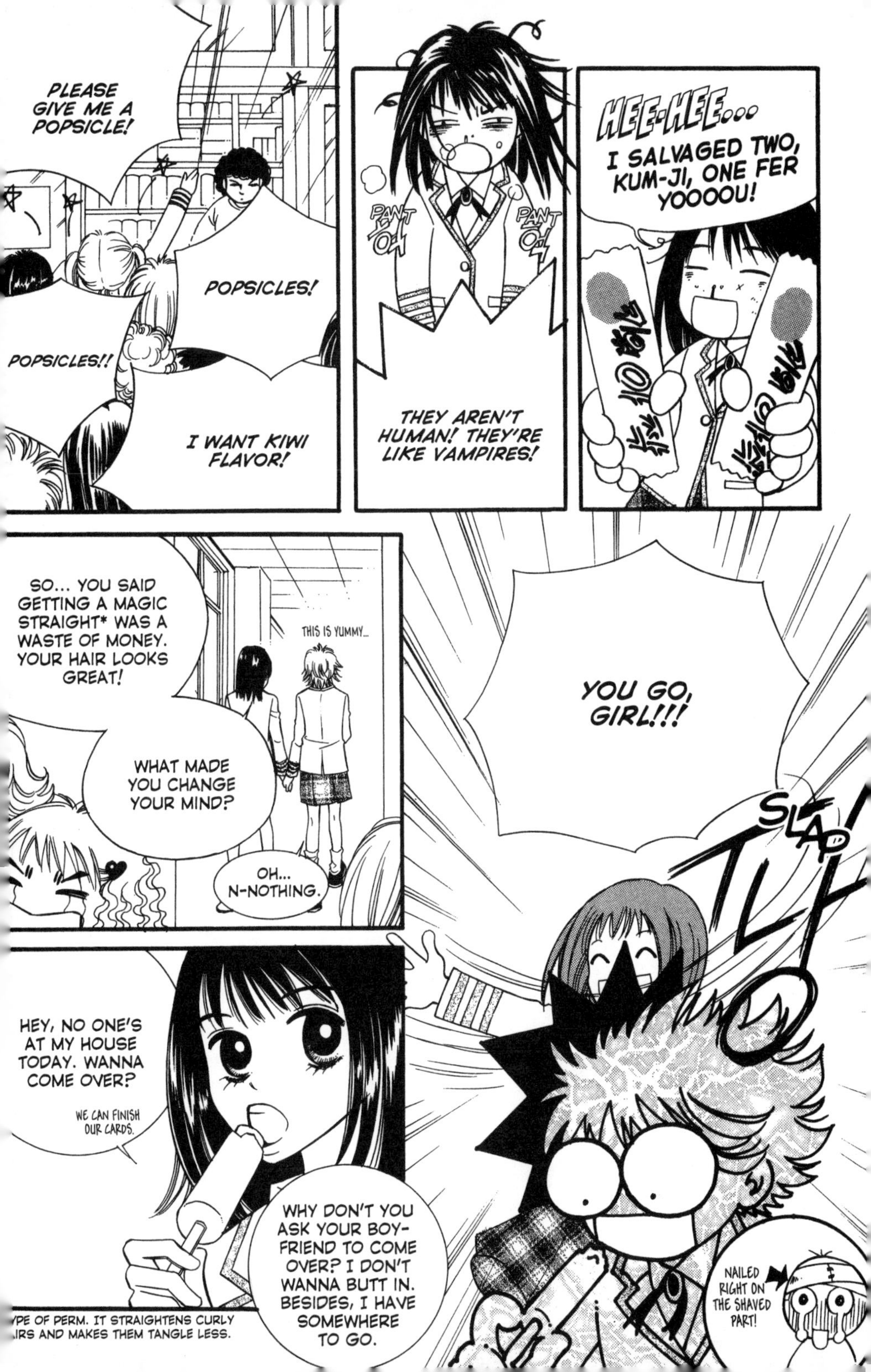
PLEASE GIVE ME A POPSICLE!
POPSICLES!
POPSICLES!!
I WANT KIWI FLAVOR!
PANT
PANT
THEY AREN'T HUMAN! THEY'RE LIKE VAMPIRES!
HEE-HEE...
I SALVAGED TWO, KUM-JI, ONE FER YOOOOU!
SO... YOU SAID GETTING A MAGIC STRAIGHT* WAS A WASTE OF MONEY. YOUR HAIR LOOKS GREAT!
THIS IS YUMMY...
WHAT MADE YOU CHANGE YOUR MIND?
OH... N-NOTHING.
HEY, NO ONE'S AT MY HOUSE TODAY. WANNA COME OVER?
WE CAN FINISH OUR CARDS.
WHY DON'T YOU ASK YOUR BOY-FRIEND TO COME OVER? I DON'T WANNA BUTT IN. BESIDES, I HAVE SOMEWHERE TO GO.
YPE OF PERM. IT STRAIGHTENS CURLY
AIRS AND MAKES THEM TANGLE LESS.
YOU GO, GIRL!!!
SLAP
NAILED RIGHT ON THE SHAVED PART!

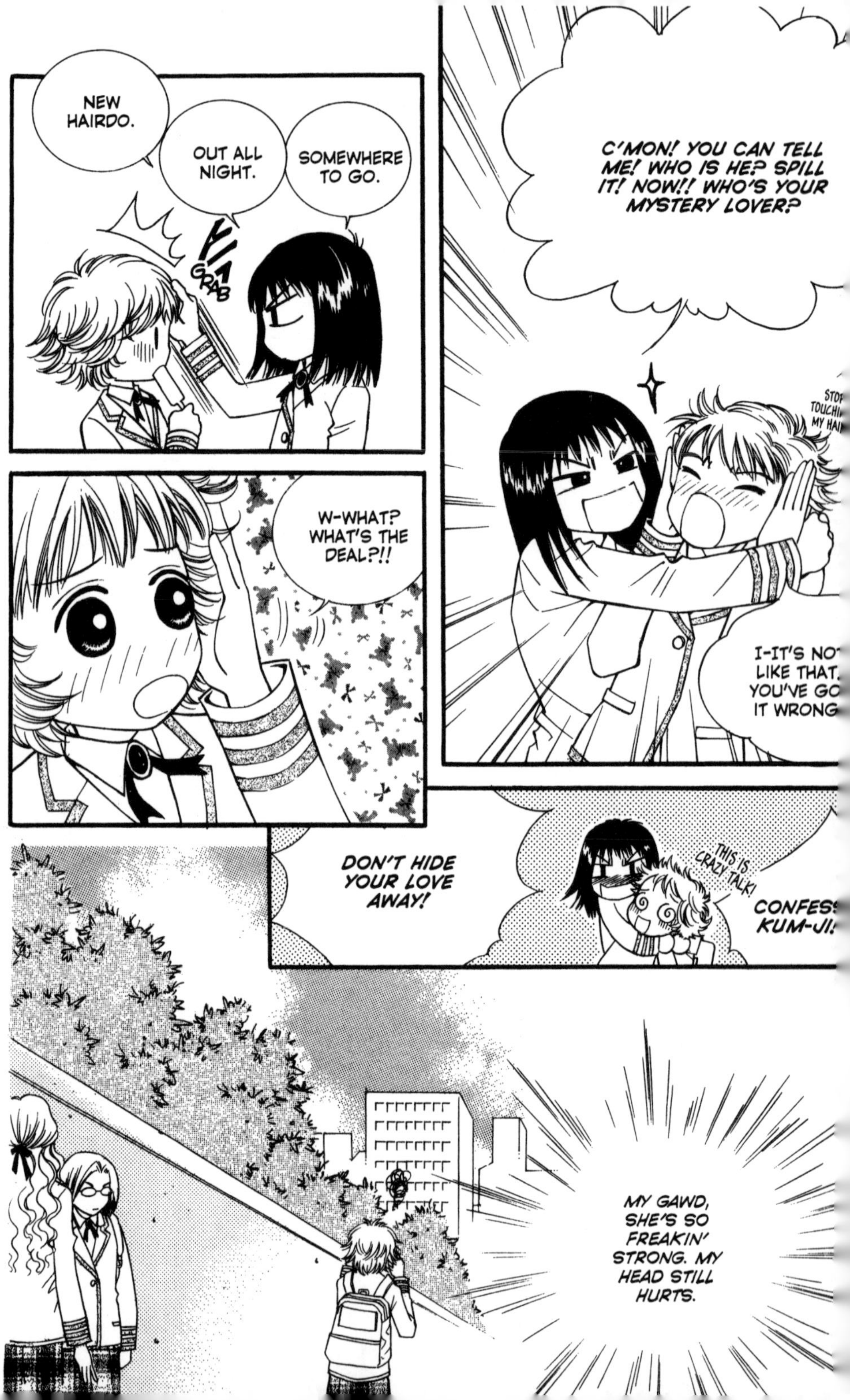
NEW HAIRDO.
OUT ALL NIGHT.
SOMEWHERE TO GO.
GRAB
W-WHAT? WHAT'S THE DEAL?!!
C'MON! YOU CAN TELL ME! WHO IS HE? SPILL IT! NOW!! WHO'S YOUR MYSTERY LOVER?
STOP TOUCHI MY HAI
I-IT'S NOT LIKE THAT. YOU'VE GO IT WRONG
DON'T HIDE YOUR LOVE AWAY!
THIS IS CRAZY TALK!
CONFESS KUM-JI!
MY GAWD, SHE'S SO FREAKIN' STRONG. MY HEAD STILL HURTS.

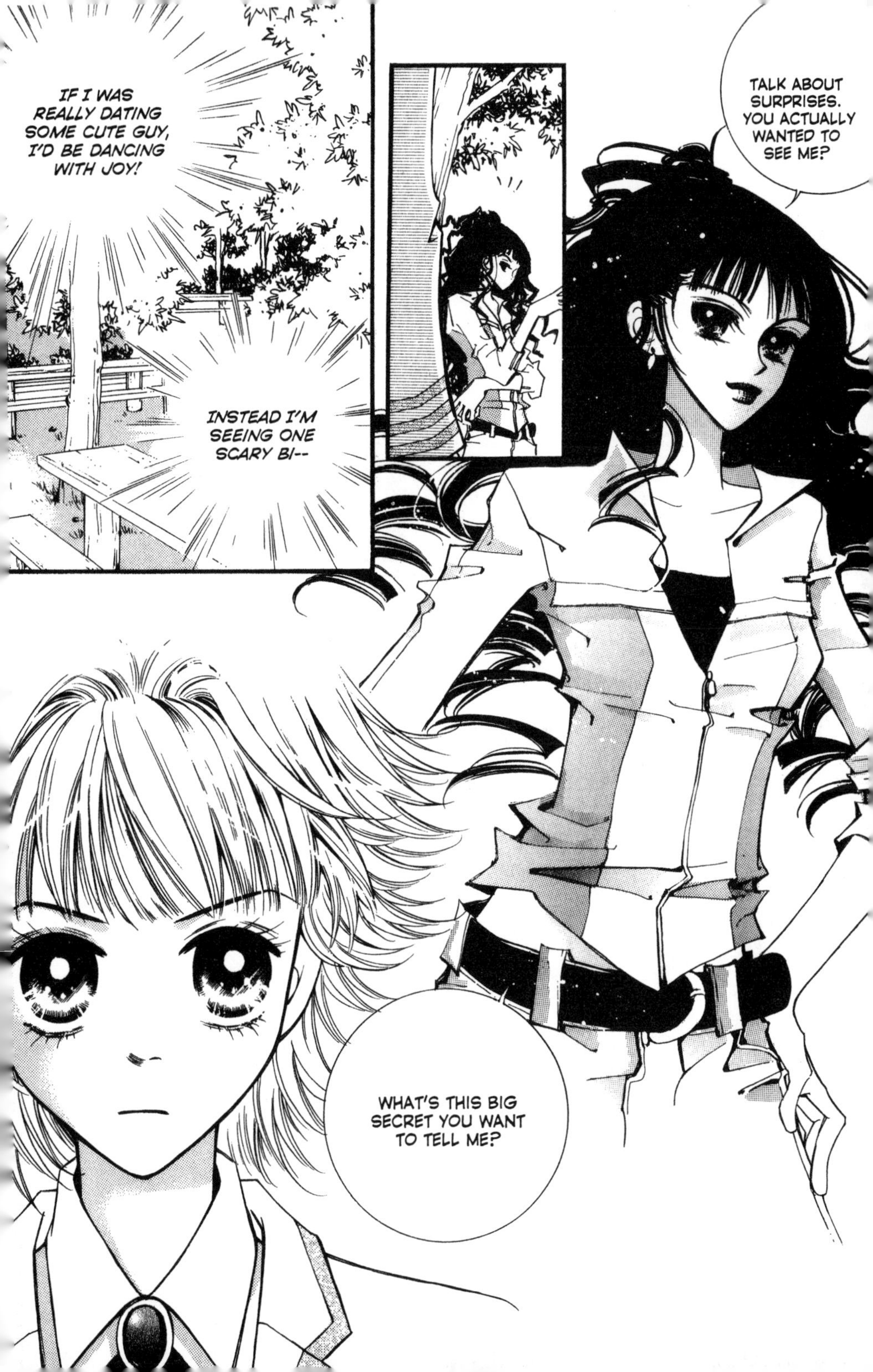
IF I WAS REALLY DATING SOME CUTE GUY, I'D BE DANCING WITH JOY!
INSTEAD I'M SEEING ONE SCARY BI--
TALK ABOUT SURPRISES. YOU ACTUALLY WANTED TO SEE ME?
WHAT'S THIS BIG SECRET YOU WANT TO TELL ME?

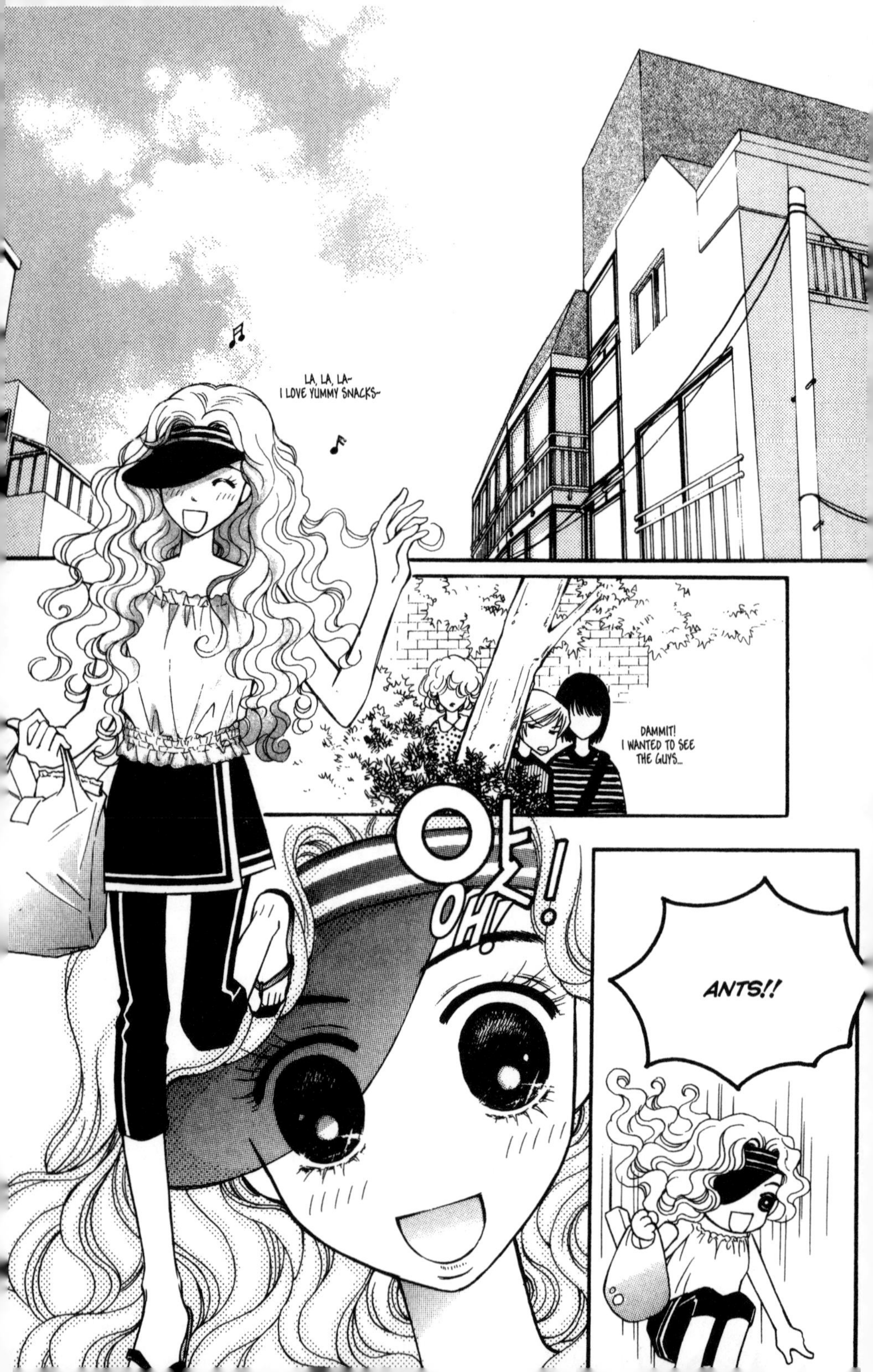
LA, LA, LA~ I LOVE YUMMY SNACKS~
DAMMIT! I WANTED TO SEE THE GUYS...
ANTS!!

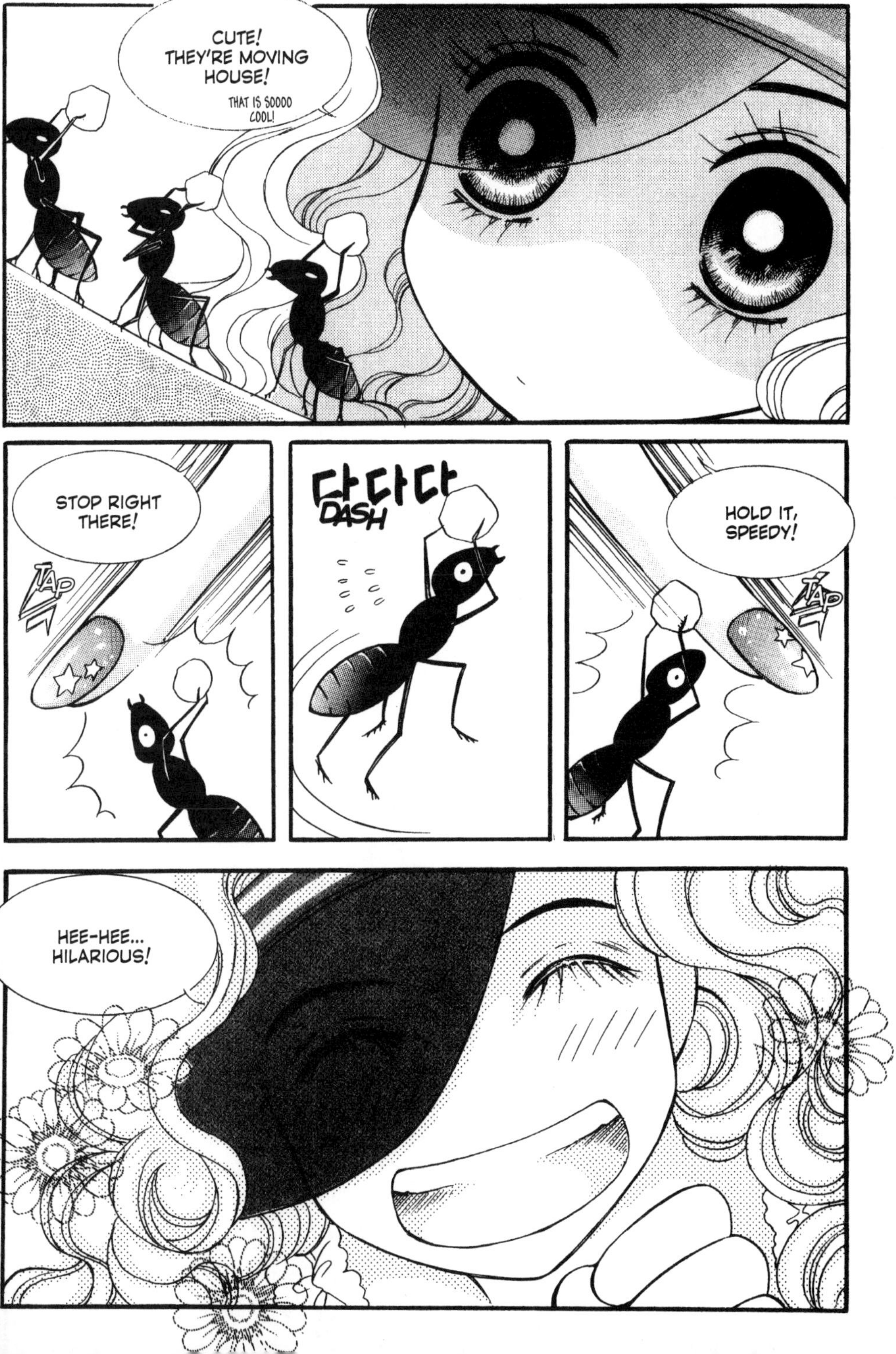
CUTE! THEY'RE MOVING HOUSE!
THAT IS SOOOO COOL!
STOP RIGHT THERE!
TAP
다다다
DASH
HOLD IT, SPEEDY!
TAP
HEE-HEE... HILARIOUS!

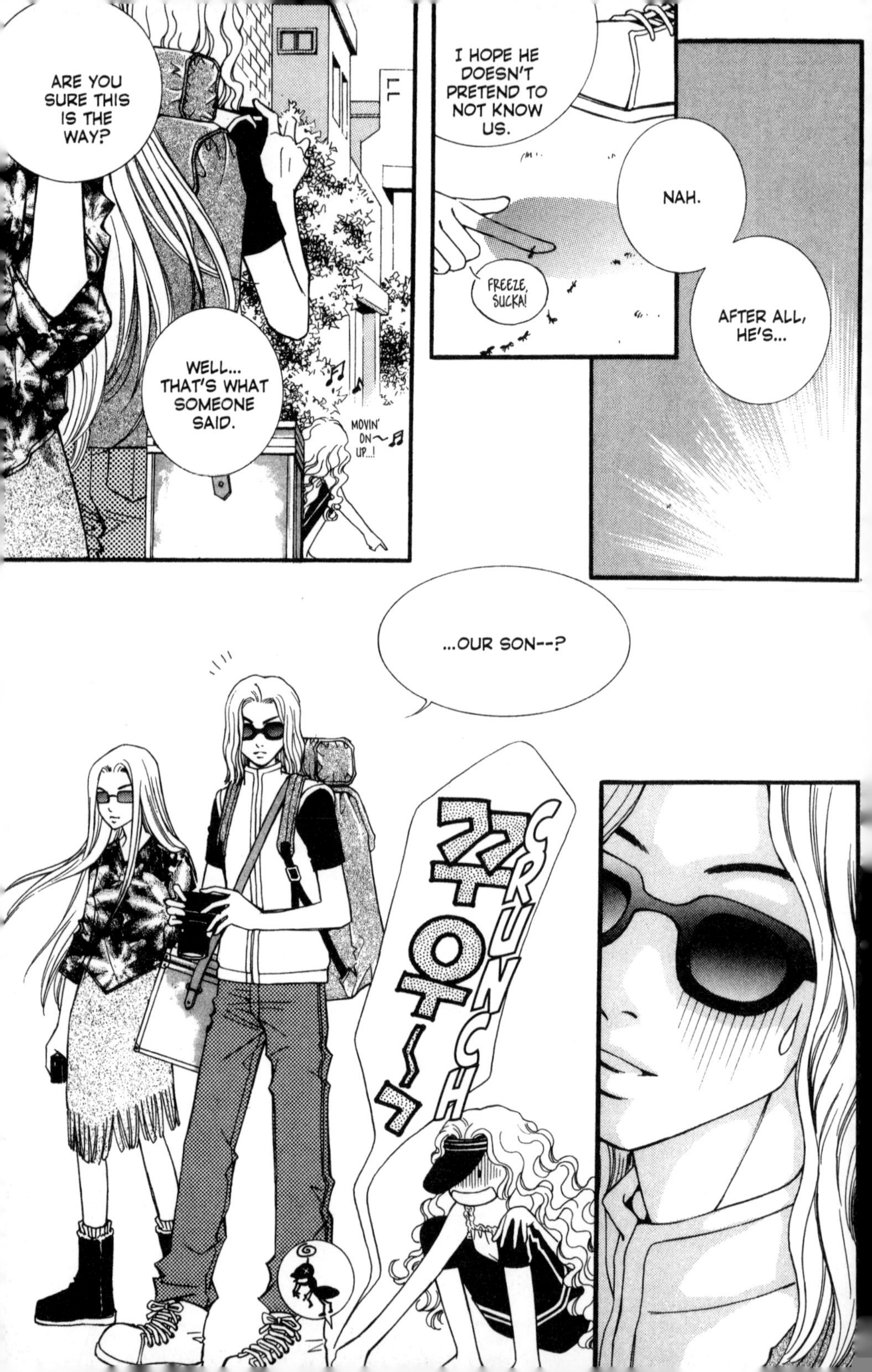
ARE YOU SURE THIS IS THE WAY?
WELL... THAT'S WHAT SOMEONE SAID.
MOVIN' ON~ UP...!
I HOPE HE DOESN'T PRETEND TO NOT KNOW US.
FREEZE, SUCKA!
NAH.
AFTER ALL, HE'S...
...OUR SON--?
CRUNCH

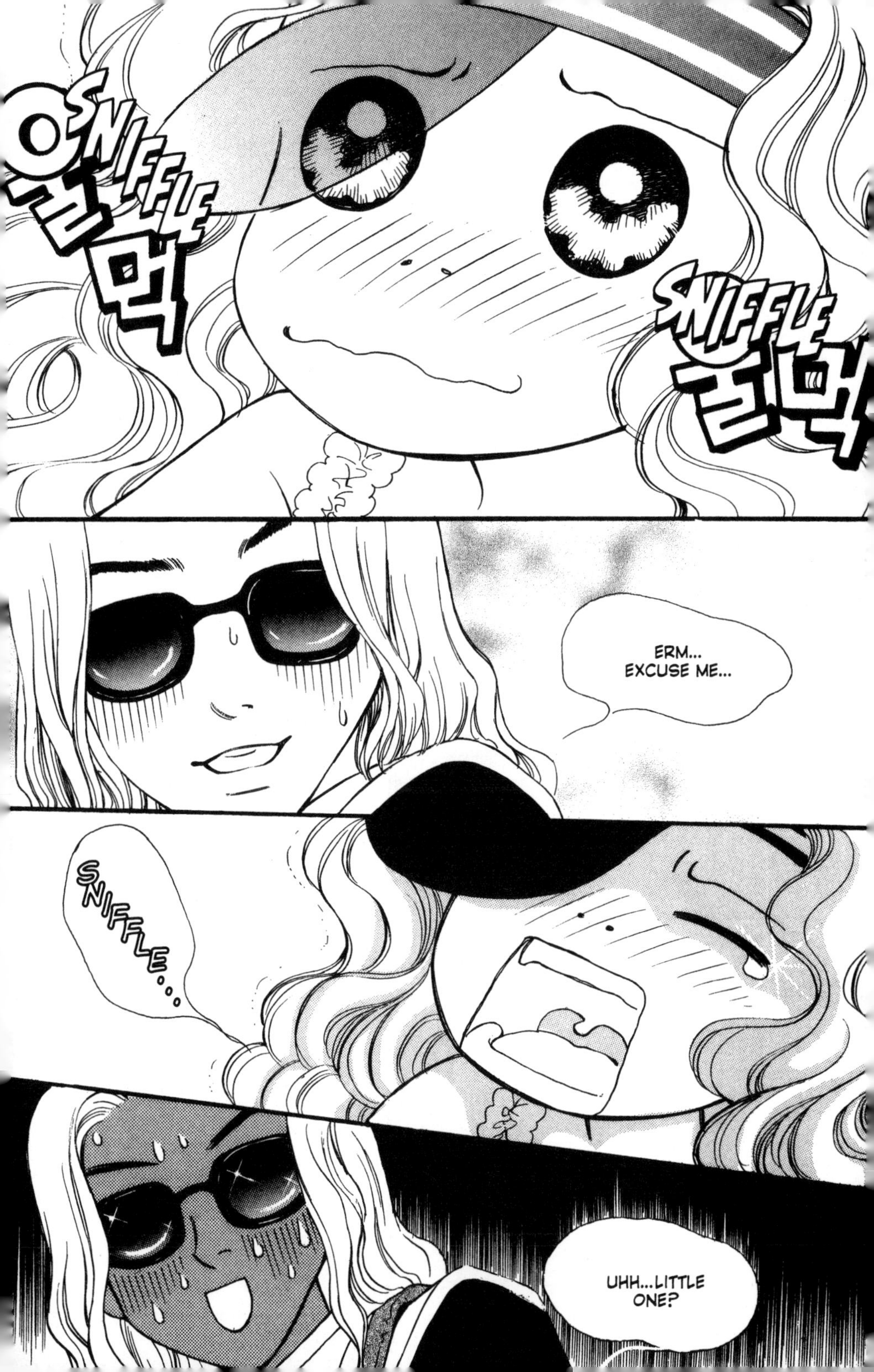
SNIFFLE
SNIFFLE
ERM... EXCUSE ME...
SNIFFLE...
UHH...LITTLE ONE?

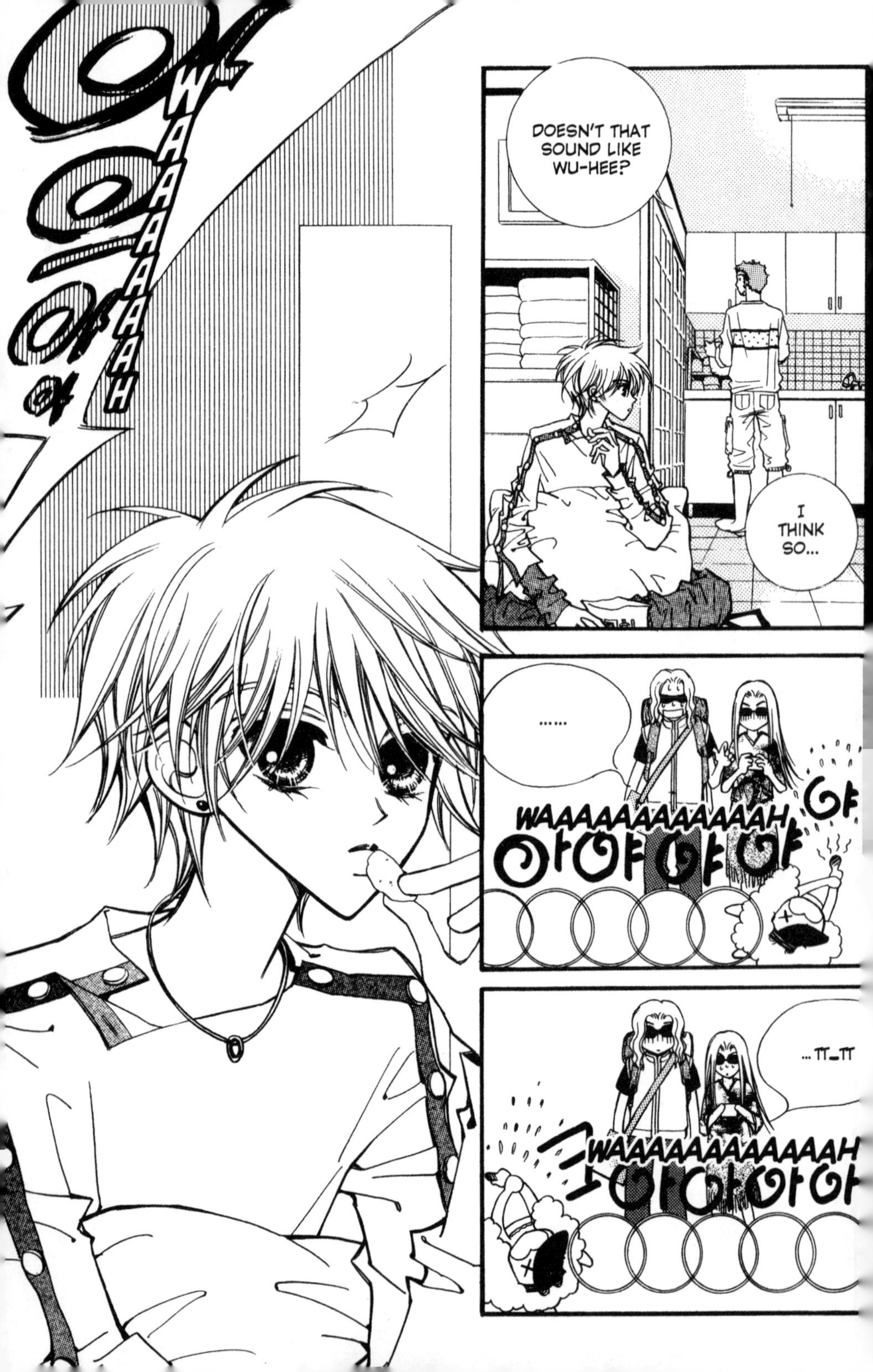
WAAAAAAAAAAAH
DOESN'T THAT SOUND LIKE WU-HEE?
I THINK SO...
......
WAAAAAAAAAAAAH
...ㅠ_ㅠ
WAAAAAAAAAAAAH

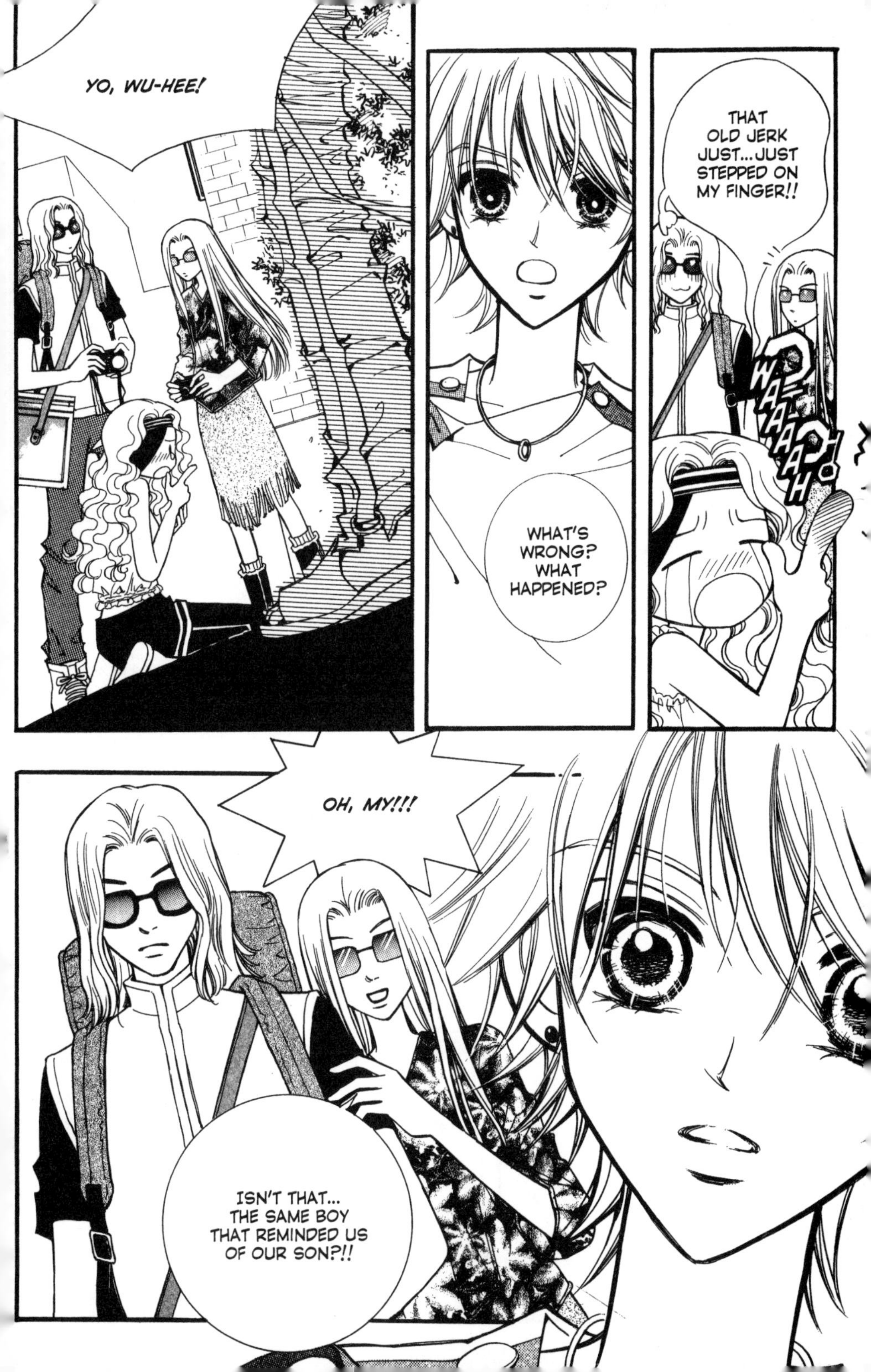
YO, WU-HEE!
WHAT'S WRONG? WHAT HAPPENED?
THAT OLD JERK JUST...JUST STEPPED ON MY FINGER!!
WAAAAAH!
OH, MY!!!
ISN'T THAT... THE SAME BOY THAT REMINDED US OF OUR SON?!!

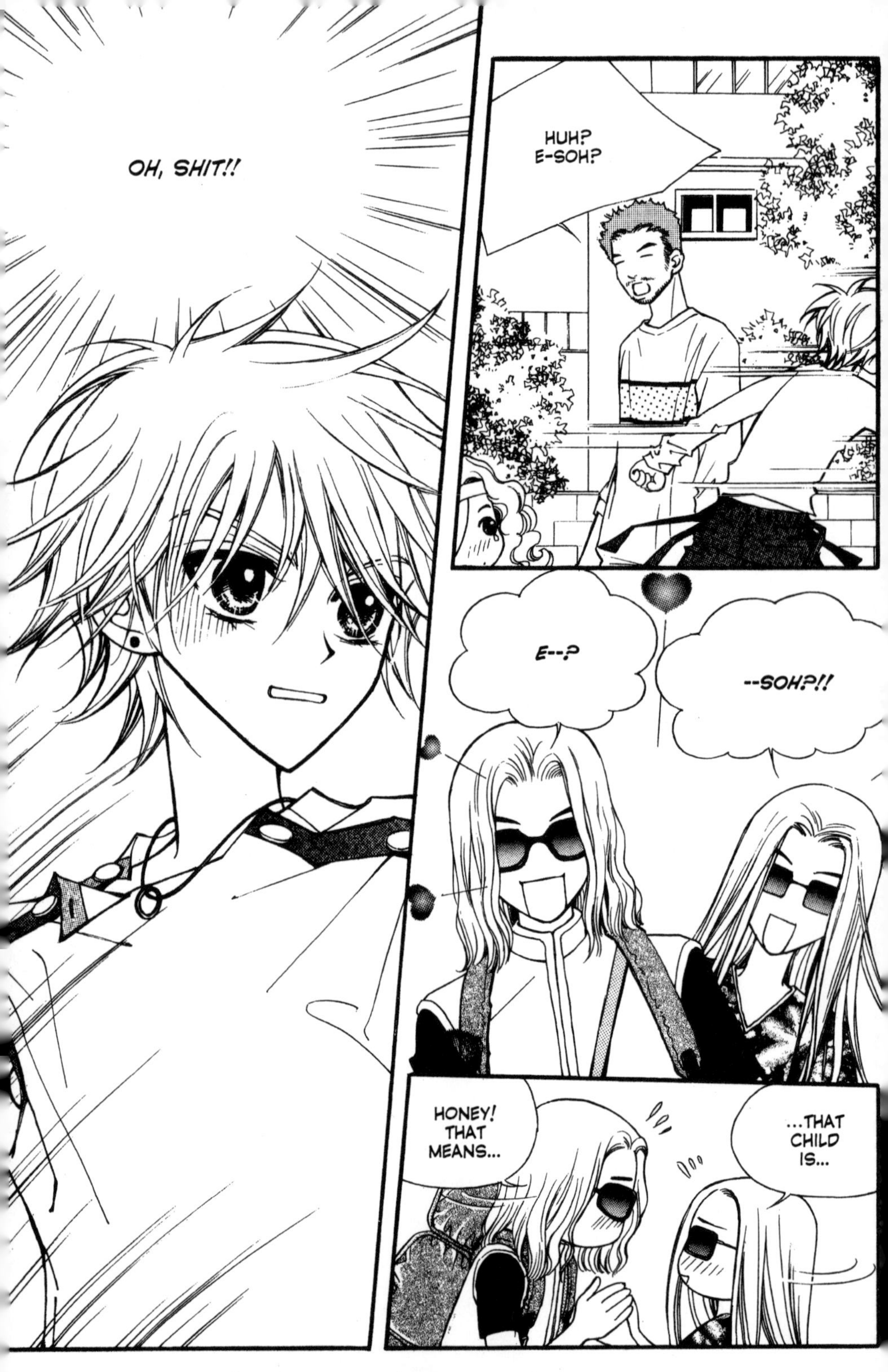
OH, SHIT!!
HUH? E-SOH?
E--?
--SOH?!!
HONEY! THAT MEANS...
...THAT CHILD IS...

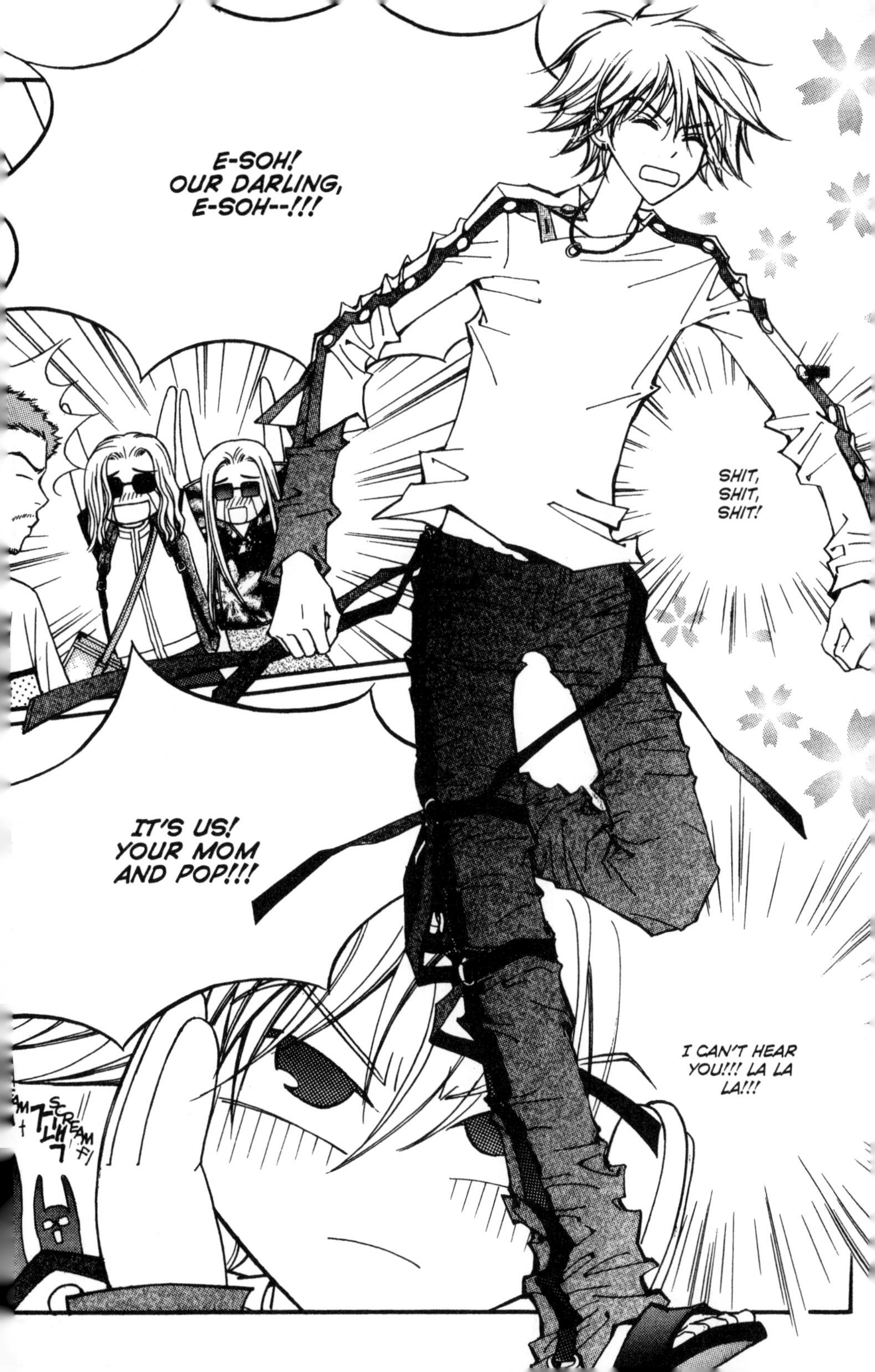
E-SOH! OUR DARLING, E-SOH--!!!
SHIT, SHIT, SHIT!
IT'S US! YOUR MOM AND POP!!!
SCREAM
I CAN'T HEAR YOU!!! LA LA LA!!!

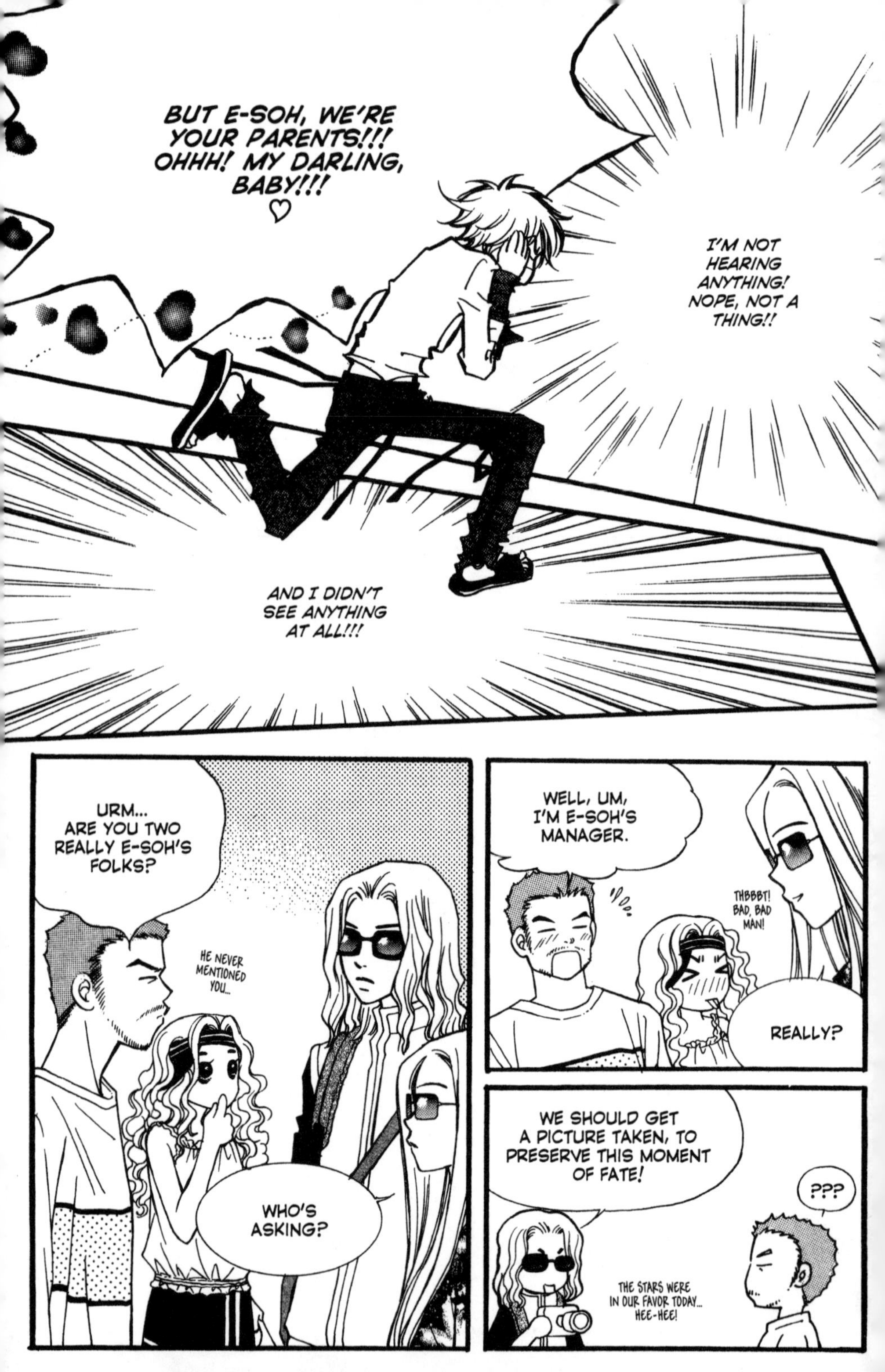
BUT E-SOH, WE'RE YOUR PARENTS!!! OHHH! MY DARLING, BABY!!! ♡
I'M NOT HEARING ANYTHING! NOPE, NOT A THING!!
AND I DIDN'T SEE ANYTHING AT ALL!!!
URM... ARE YOU TWO REALLY E-SOH'S FOLKS?
HE NEVER MENTIONED YOU...
WHO'S ASKING?
WELL, UM, I'M E-SOH'S MANAGER.
THBBBT! BAD, BAD MAN!
REALLY?
WE SHOULD GET A PICTURE TAKEN, TO PRESERVE THIS MOMENT OF FATE!
???
THE STARS WERE IN OUR FAVOR TODAY... HEE-HEE!

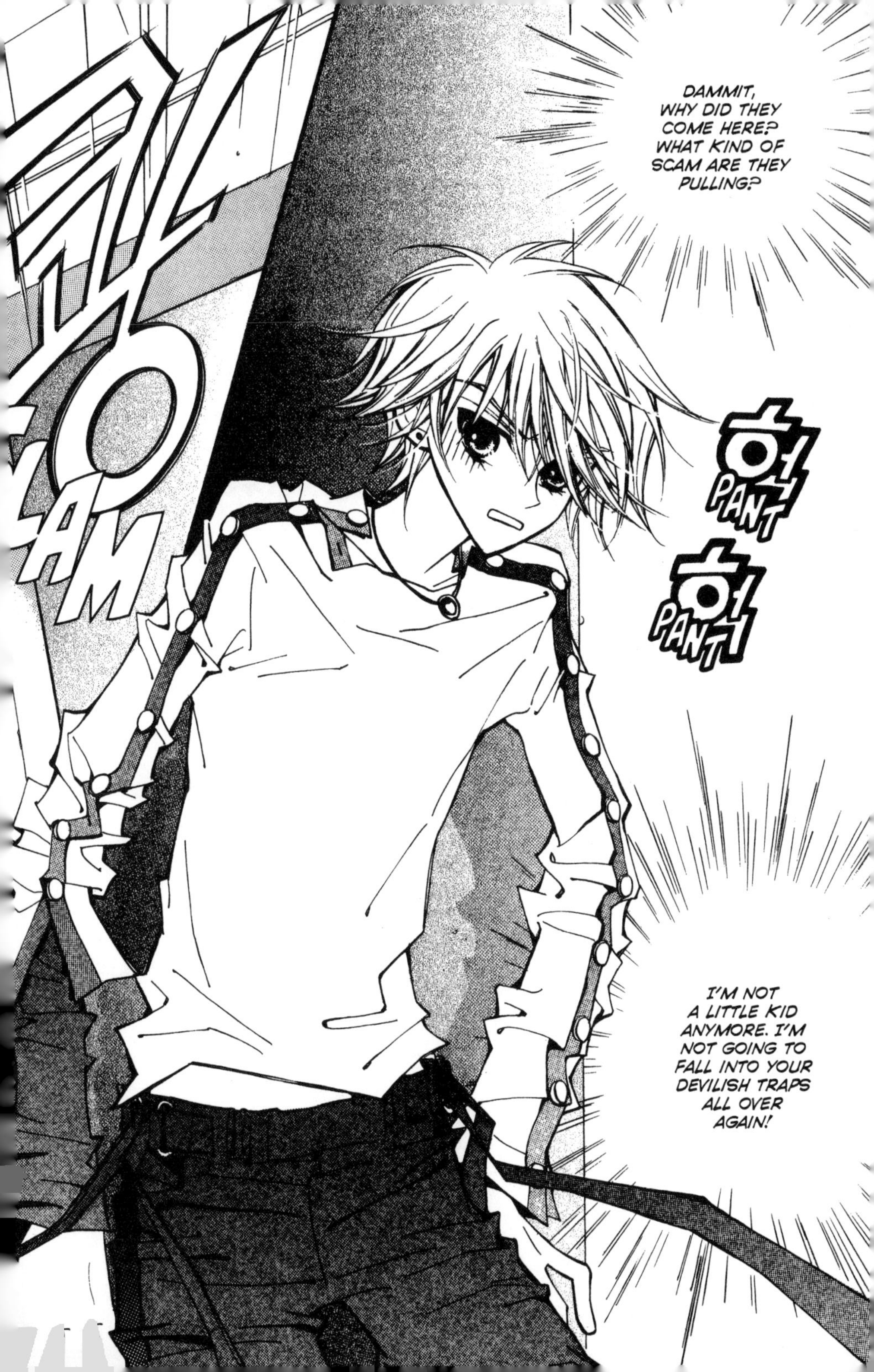
SLAM
DAMMIT, WHY DID THEY COME HERE? WHAT KIND OF SCAM ARE THEY PULLING?
헉 PANT
헉 PANT
I'M NOT A LITTLE KID ANYMORE. I'M NOT GOING TO FALL INTO YOUR DEVILISH TRAPS ALL OVER AGAIN!

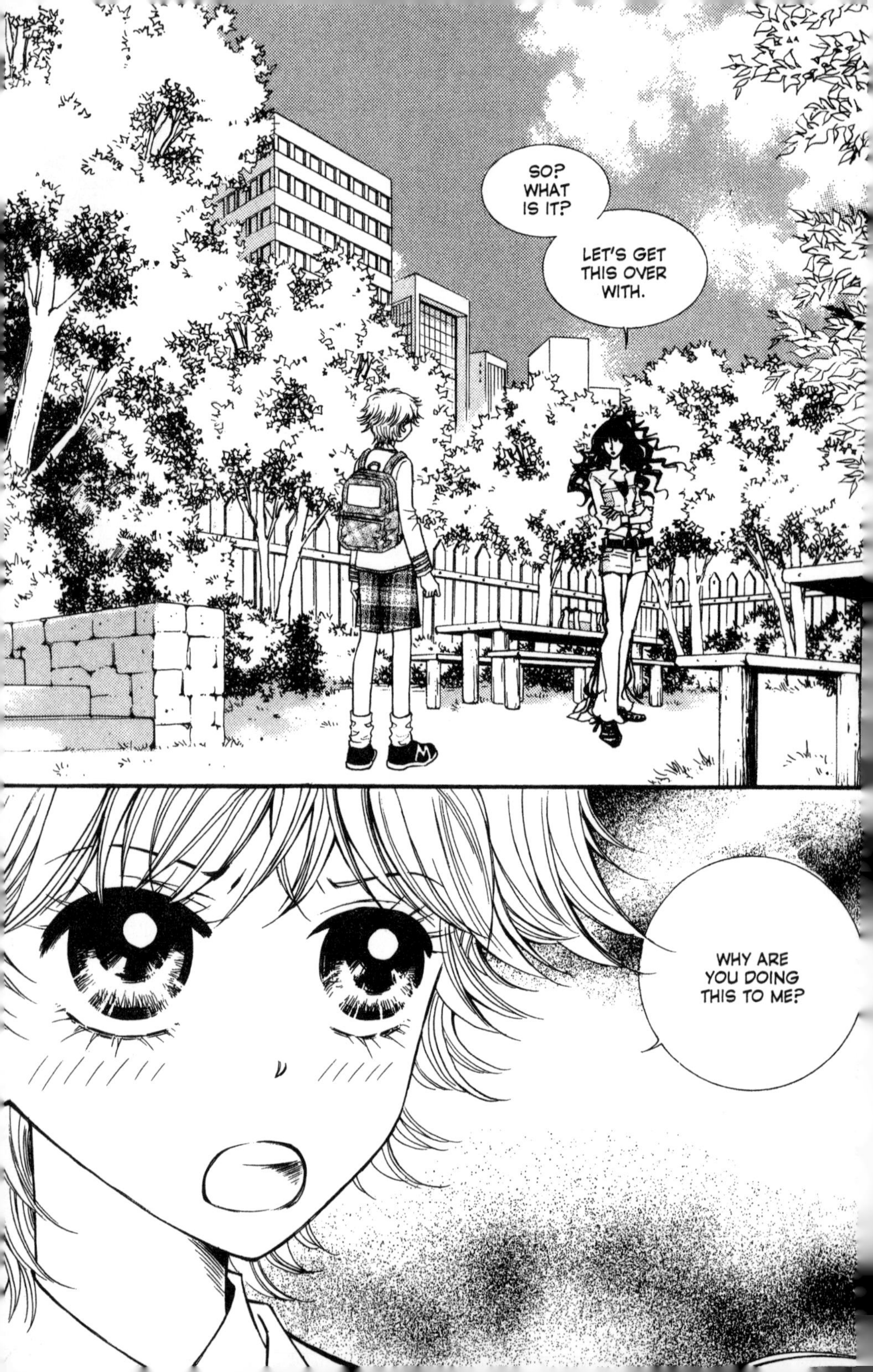
SO? WHAT IS IT?
LET'S GET THIS OVER WITH.
WHY ARE YOU DOING THIS TO ME?

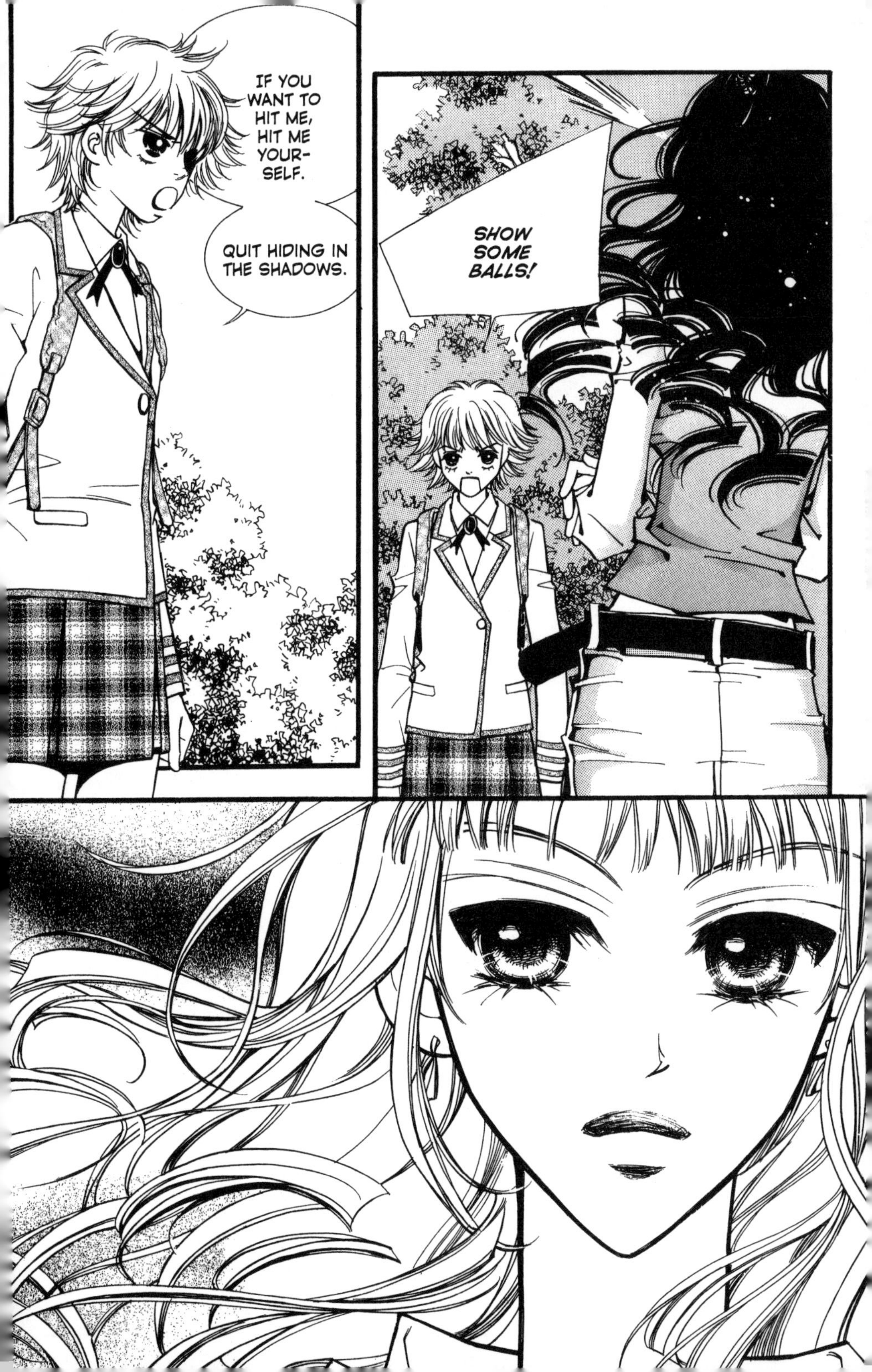
IF YOU WANT TO HIT ME, HIT ME YOURSELF.
QUIT HIDING IN THE SHADOWS.
SHOW SOME BALLS!

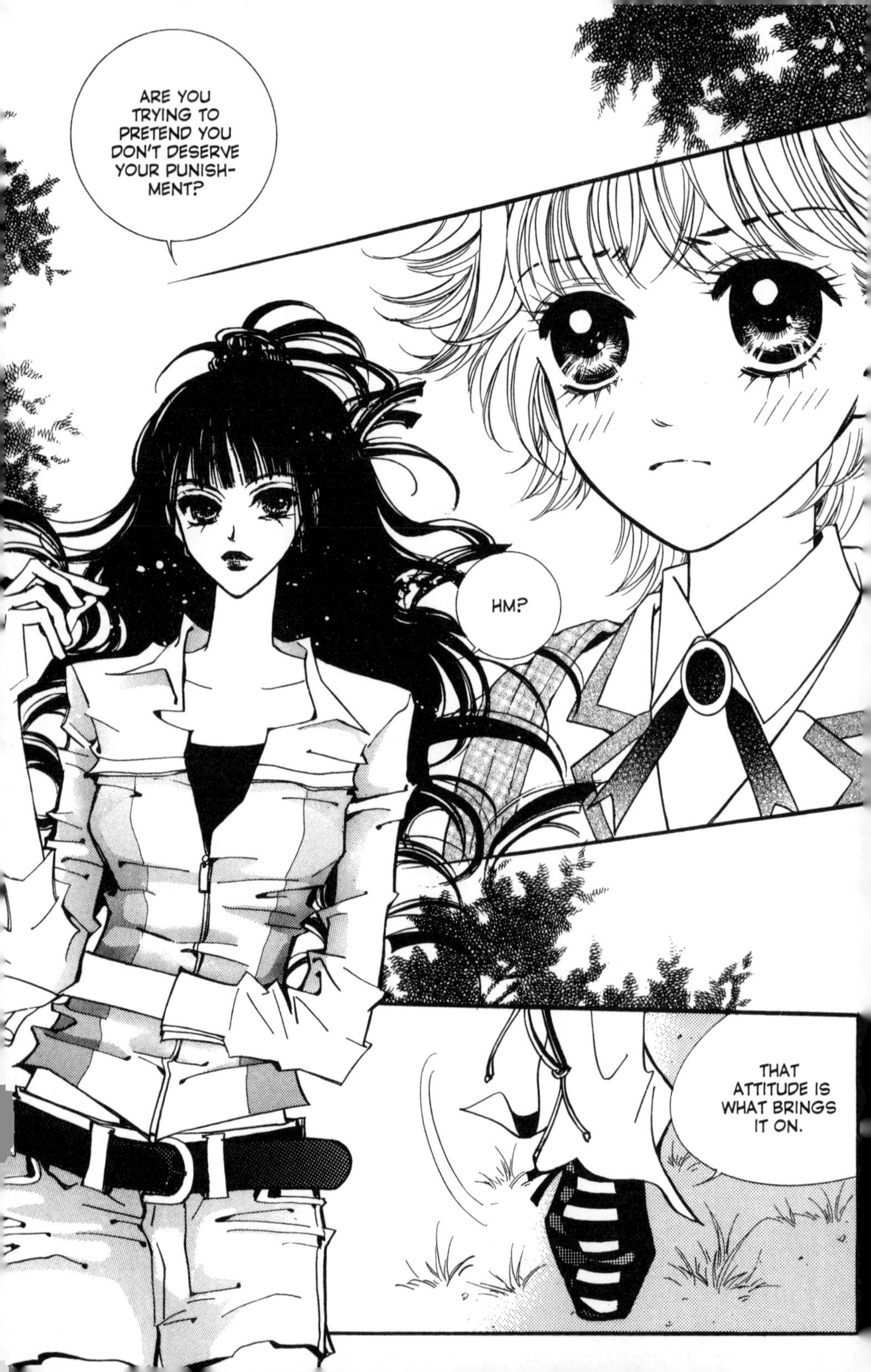
ARE YOU TRYING TO PRETEND YOU DON'T DESERVE YOUR PUNISH-MENT?
HM?
THAT ATTITUDE IS WHAT BRINGS IT ON.

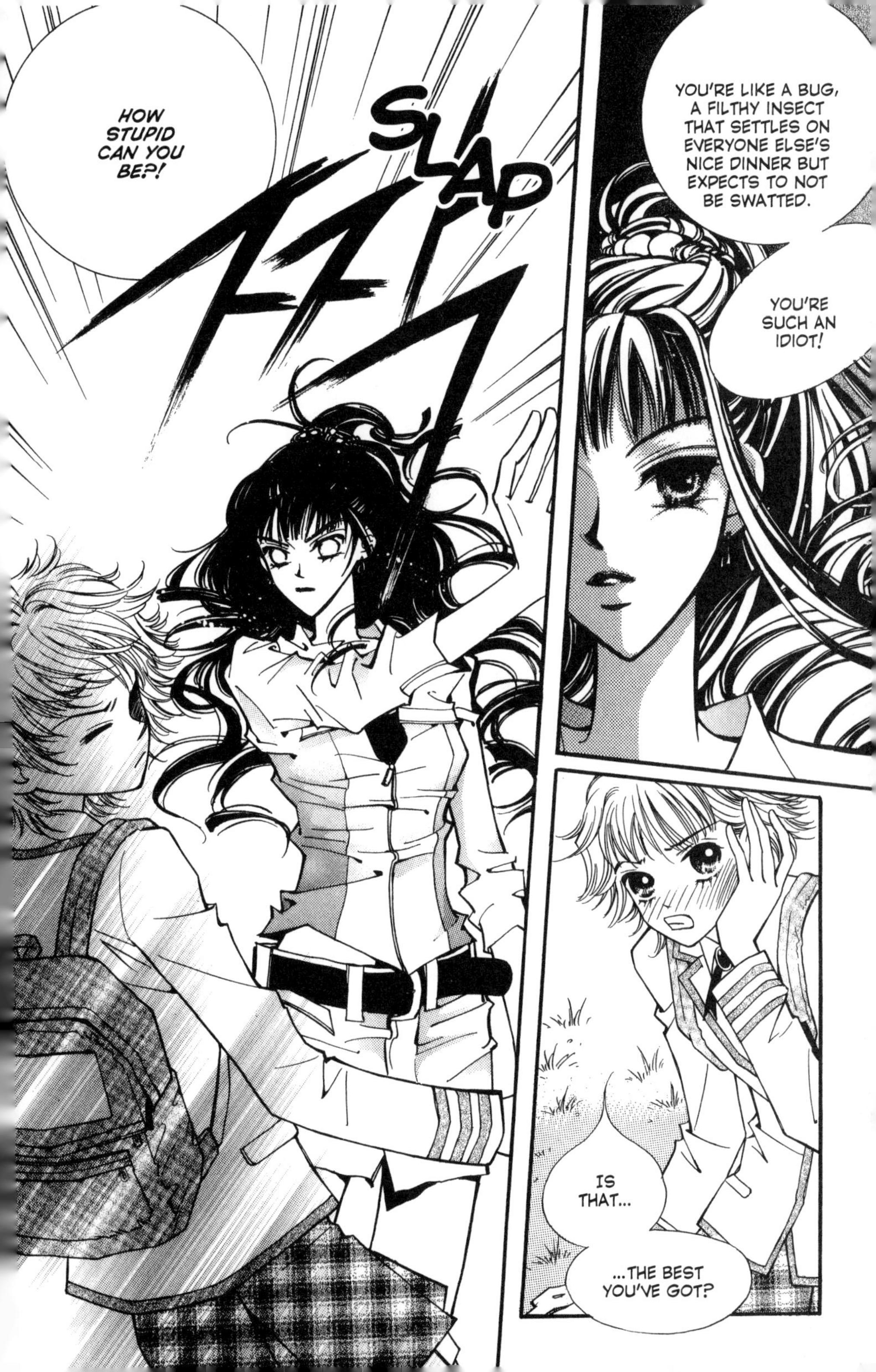
HOW STUPID CAN YOU BE?!
SLAP
YOU'RE LIKE A BUG, A FILTHY INSECT THAT SETTLES ON EVERYONE ELSE'S NICE DINNER BUT EXPECTS TO NOT BE SWATTED.
YOU'RE SUCH AN IDIOT!
IS THAT...
...THE BEST YOU'VE GOT?

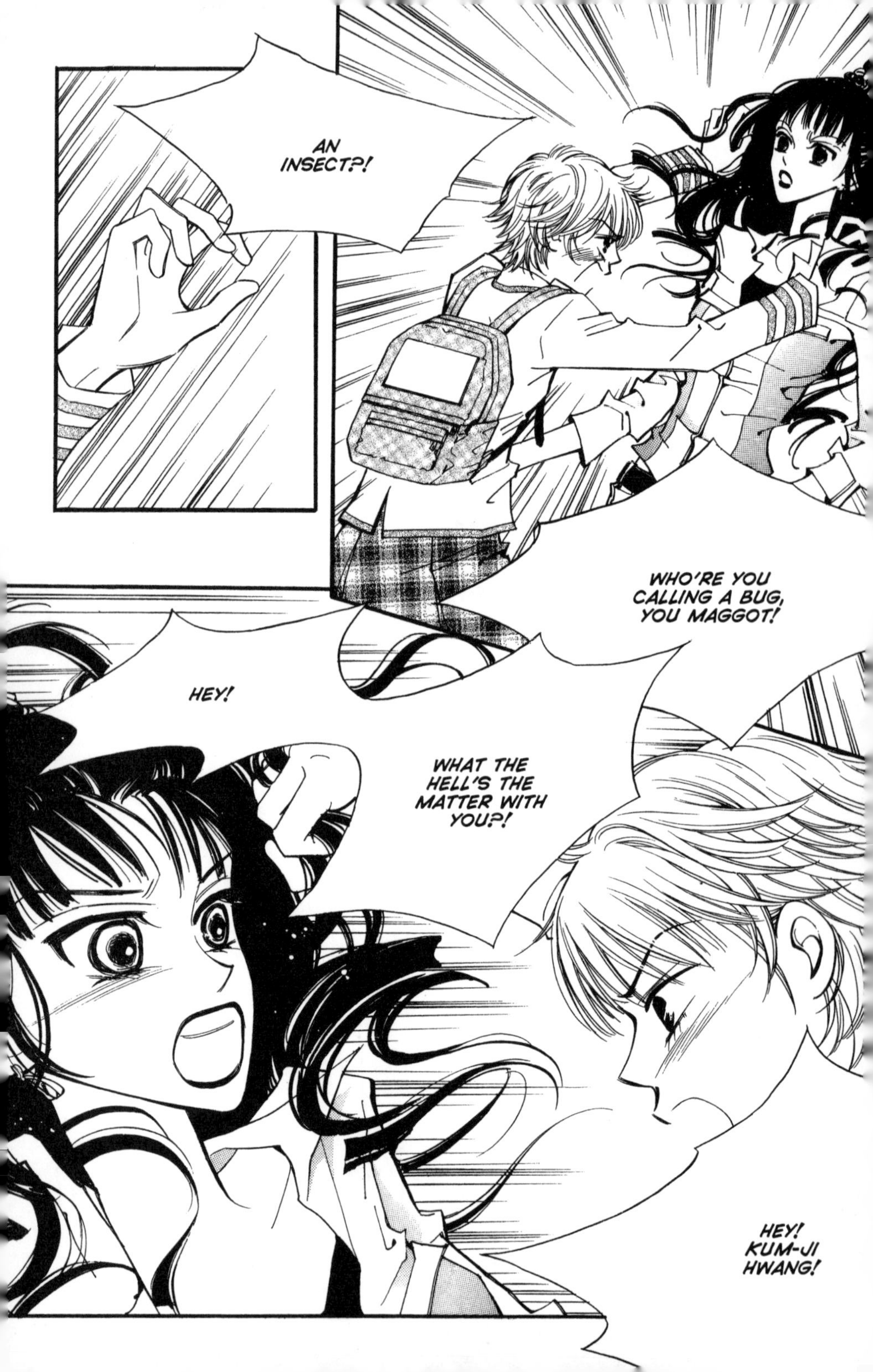
AN INSECT?!
WHO'RE YOU CALLING A BUG, YOU MAGGOT!
HEY!
WHAT THE HELL'S THE MATTER WITH YOU?!
HEY! KUM-JI HWANG!

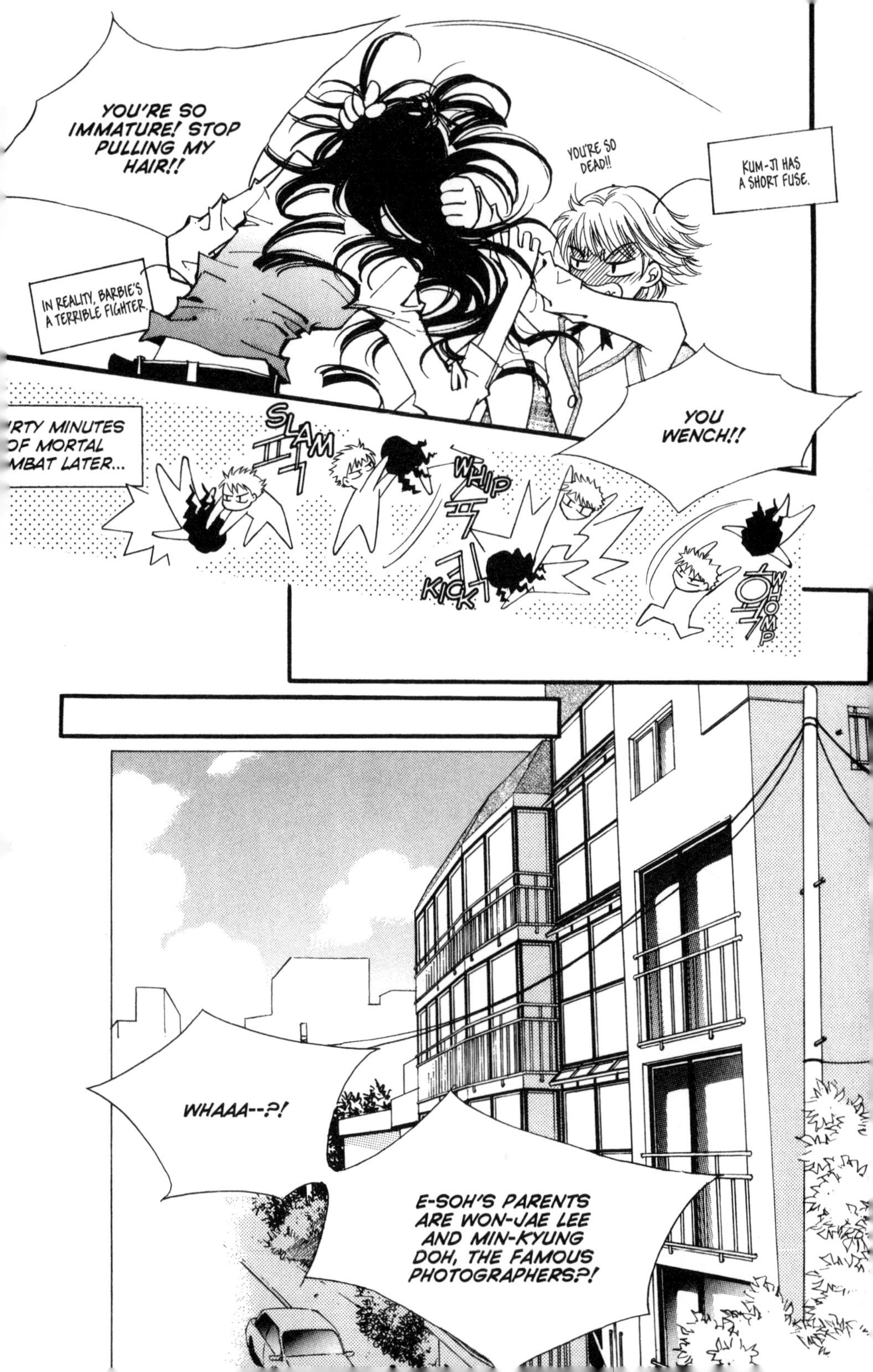
YOU'RE SO IMMATURE! STOP PULLING MY HAIR!!
YOU'RE SO DEAD!!
KUM-JI HAS A SHORT FUSE.
IN REALITY, BARBIE'S A TERRIBLE FIGHTER.
RTY MINUTES OF MORTAL MBAT LATER...
YOU WENCH!!
SLAM
WHIP
KICK
WHOMP
WHAAA--?!
E-SOH'S PARENTS ARE WON-JAE LEE AND MIN-KYUNG DOH, THE FAMOUS PHOTOGRAPHERS?!

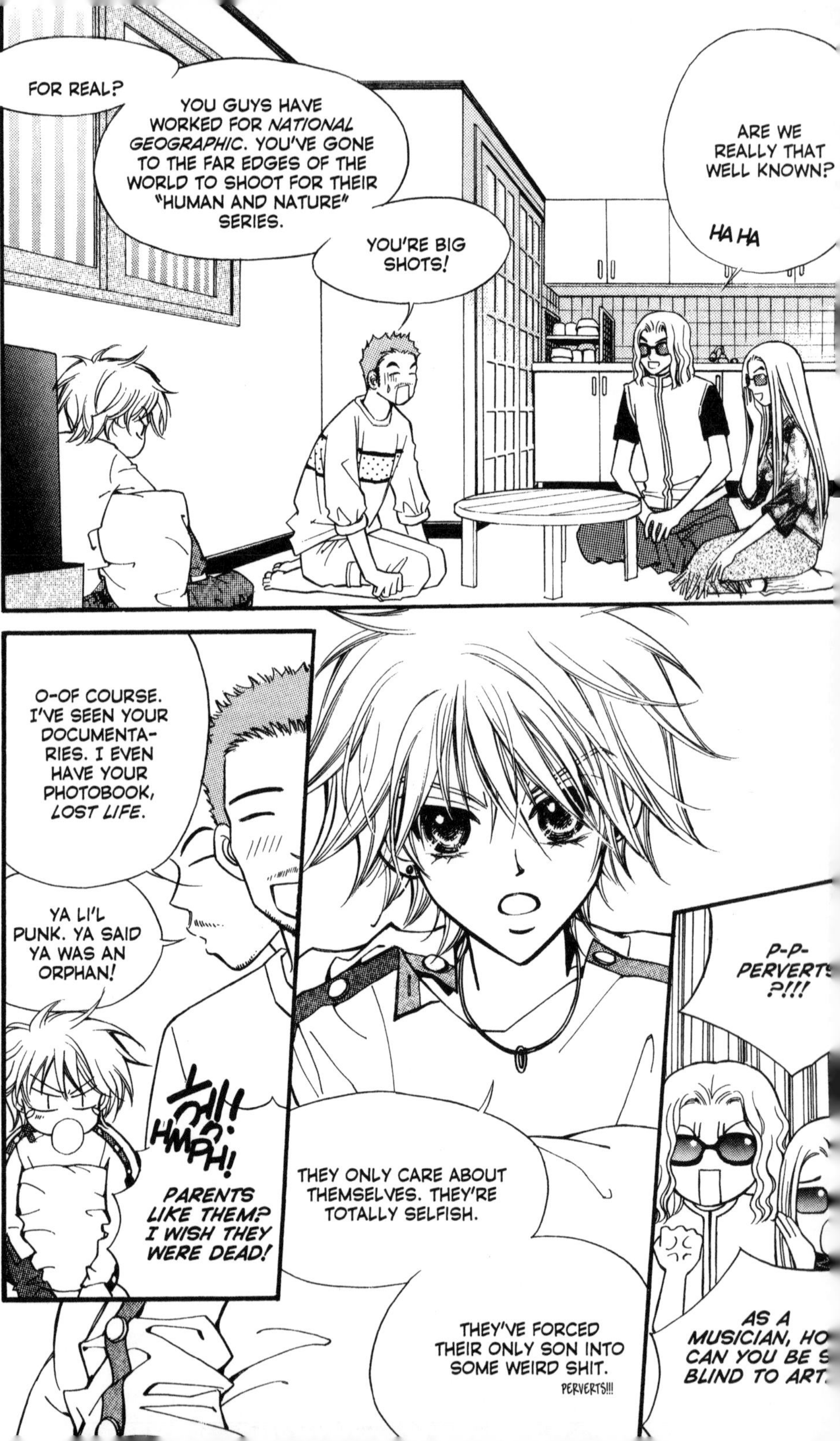

FOR REAL?
YOU GUYS HAVE WORKED FOR *NATIONAL GEOGRAPHIC*. YOU'VE GONE TO THE FAR EDGES OF THE WORLD TO SHOOT FOR THEIR "HUMAN AND NATURE" SERIES.
YOU'RE BIG SHOTS!
ARE WE REALLY THAT WELL KNOWN?
HA HA
O-OF COURSE. I'VE SEEN YOUR DOCUMENTARIES. I EVEN HAVE YOUR PHOTOBOOK, *LOST LIFE*.
YA LI'L PUNK. YA SAID YA WAS AN ORPHAN!
YAH! HMPH!
PARENTS LIKE THEM? I WISH THEY WERE DEAD!
THEY ONLY CARE ABOUT THEMSELVES. THEY'RE TOTALLY SELFISH.
THEY'VE FORCED THEIR ONLY SON INTO SOME WEIRD SHIT.
PERVERTS!!!
P-P-PERVERTS?!!!
AS A MUSICIAN, HO CAN YOU BE S BLIND TO ART.

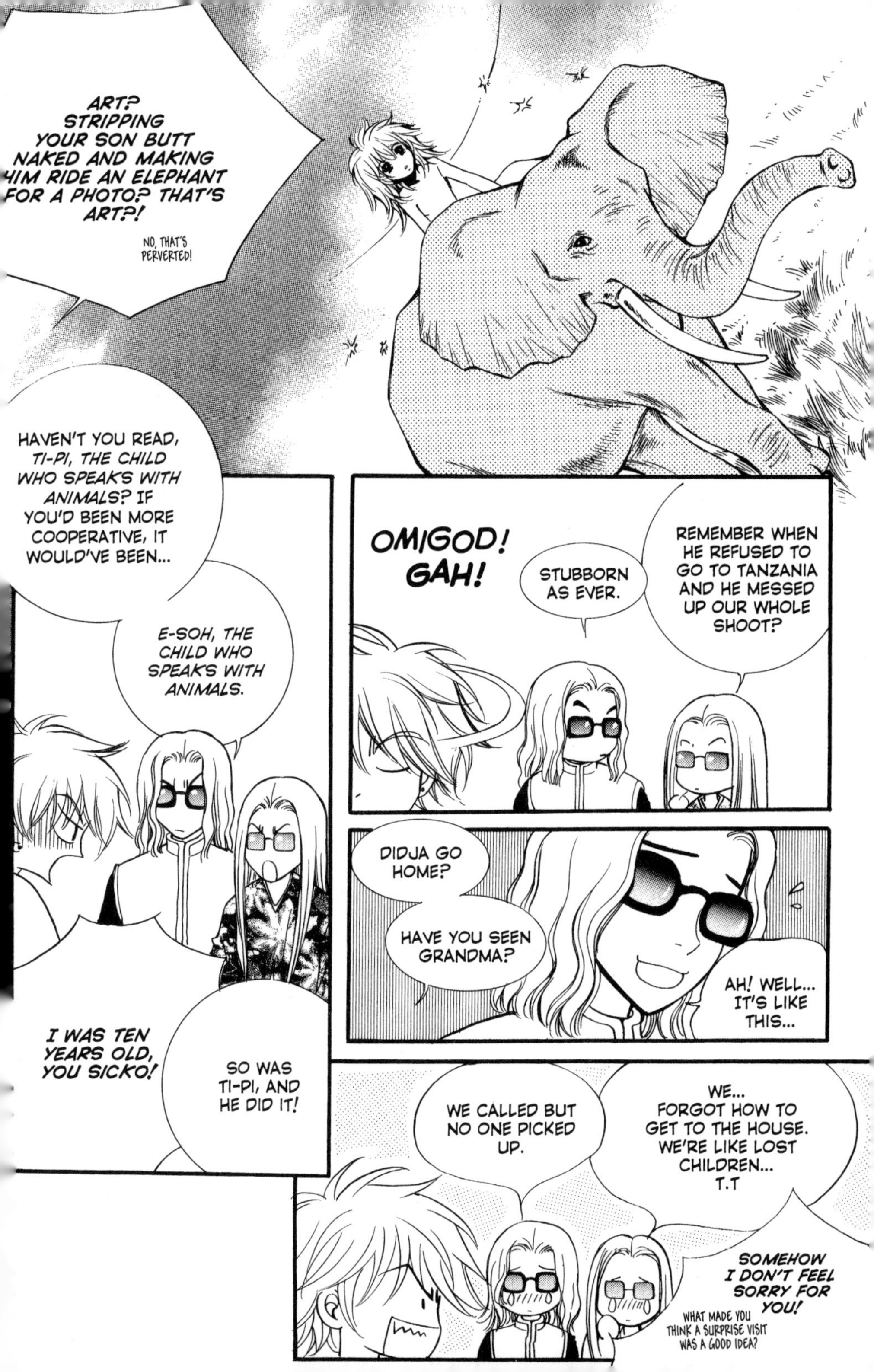
ART? STRIPPING YOUR SON BUTT NAKED AND MAKING HIM RIDE AN ELEPHANT FOR A PHOTO? THAT'S ART?!
NO, THAT'S PERVERTED!
HAVEN'T YOU READ, TI-PI, THE CHILD WHO SPEAKS WITH ANIMALS? IF YOU'D BEEN MORE COOPERATIVE, IT WOULD'VE BEEN...
E-SOH, THE CHILD WHO SPEAKS WITH ANIMALS.
I WAS TEN YEARS OLD, YOU SICKO!
SO WAS TI-PI, AND HE DID IT!
OMIGOD! GAH!
STUBBORN AS EVER.
REMEMBER WHEN HE REFUSED TO GO TO TANZANIA AND HE MESSED UP OUR WHOLE SHOOT?
DIDJA GO HOME?
HAVE YOU SEEN GRANDMA?
AH! WELL... IT'S LIKE THIS...
WE CALLED BUT NO ONE PICKED UP.
WE... FORGOT HOW TO GET TO THE HOUSE. WE'RE LIKE LOST CHILDREN... T.T
SOMEHOW I DON'T FEEL SORRY FOR YOU!
WHAT MADE YOU THINK A SURPRISE VISIT WAS A GOOD IDEA?

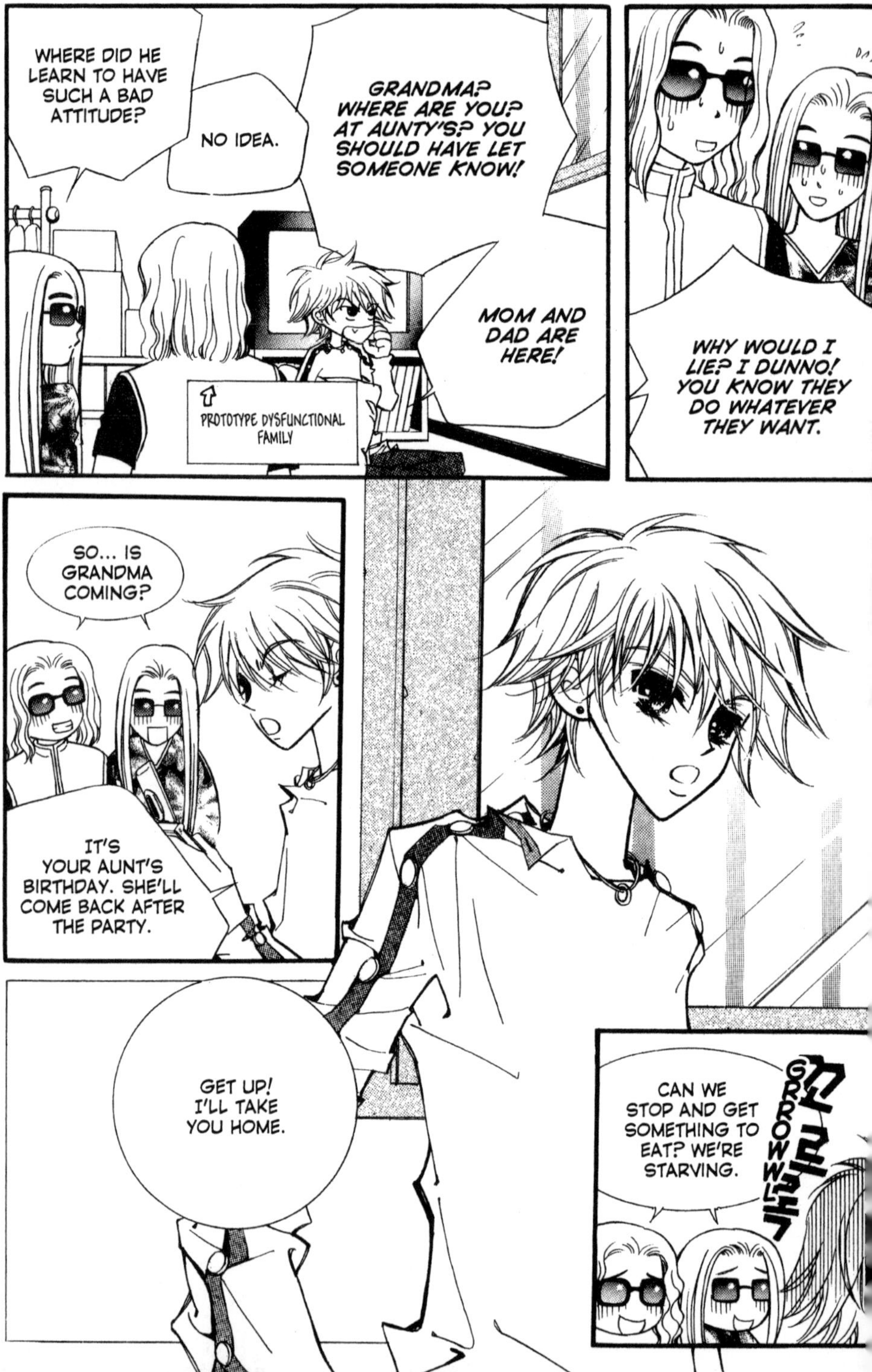
WHERE DID HE LEARN TO HAVE SUCH A BAD ATTITUDE?
NO IDEA.
GRANDMA? WHERE ARE YOU? AT AUNTY'S? YOU SHOULD HAVE LET SOMEONE KNOW!
MOM AND DAD ARE HERE!
PROTOTYPE DYSFUNCTIONAL FAMILY
WHY WOULD I LIE? I DUNNO! YOU KNOW THEY DO WHATEVER THEY WANT.
SO... IS GRANDMA COMING?
IT'S YOUR AUNT'S BIRTHDAY. SHE'LL COME BACK AFTER THE PARTY.
GET UP! I'LL TAKE YOU HOME.
CAN WE STOP AND GET SOMETHING TO EAT? WE'RE STARVING.
GRROWWL

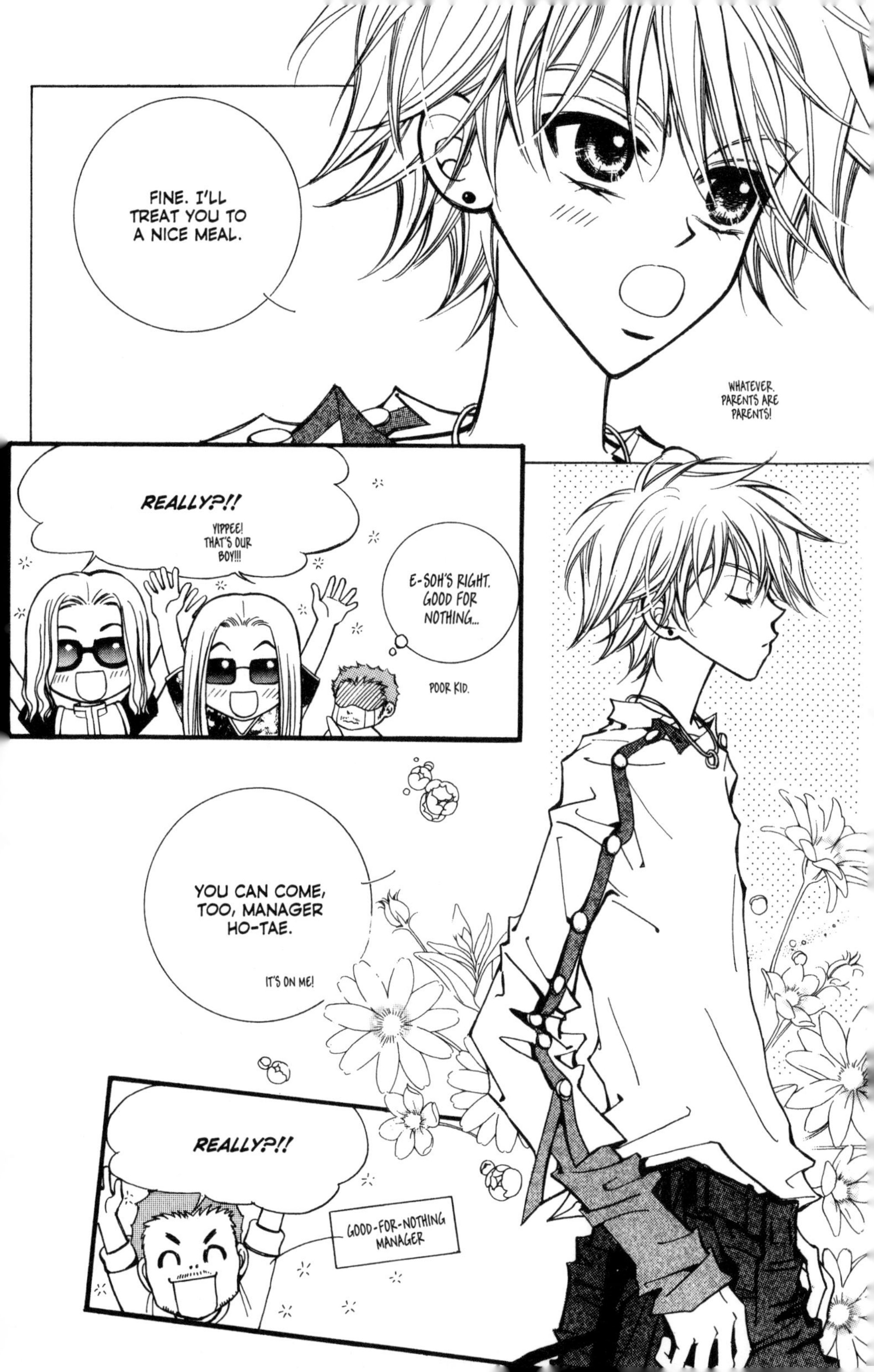
FINE. I'LL TREAT YOU TO A NICE MEAL.
REALLY?!!
YIPPEE! THAT'S OUR BOY!!!
E-SOH'S RIGHT. GOOD FOR NOTHING...
POOR KID.
WHATEVER. PARENTS ARE PARENTS!
YOU CAN COME, TOO, MANAGER HO-TAE.
IT'S ON ME!
REALLY?!!
GOOD-FOR-NOTHING MANAGER

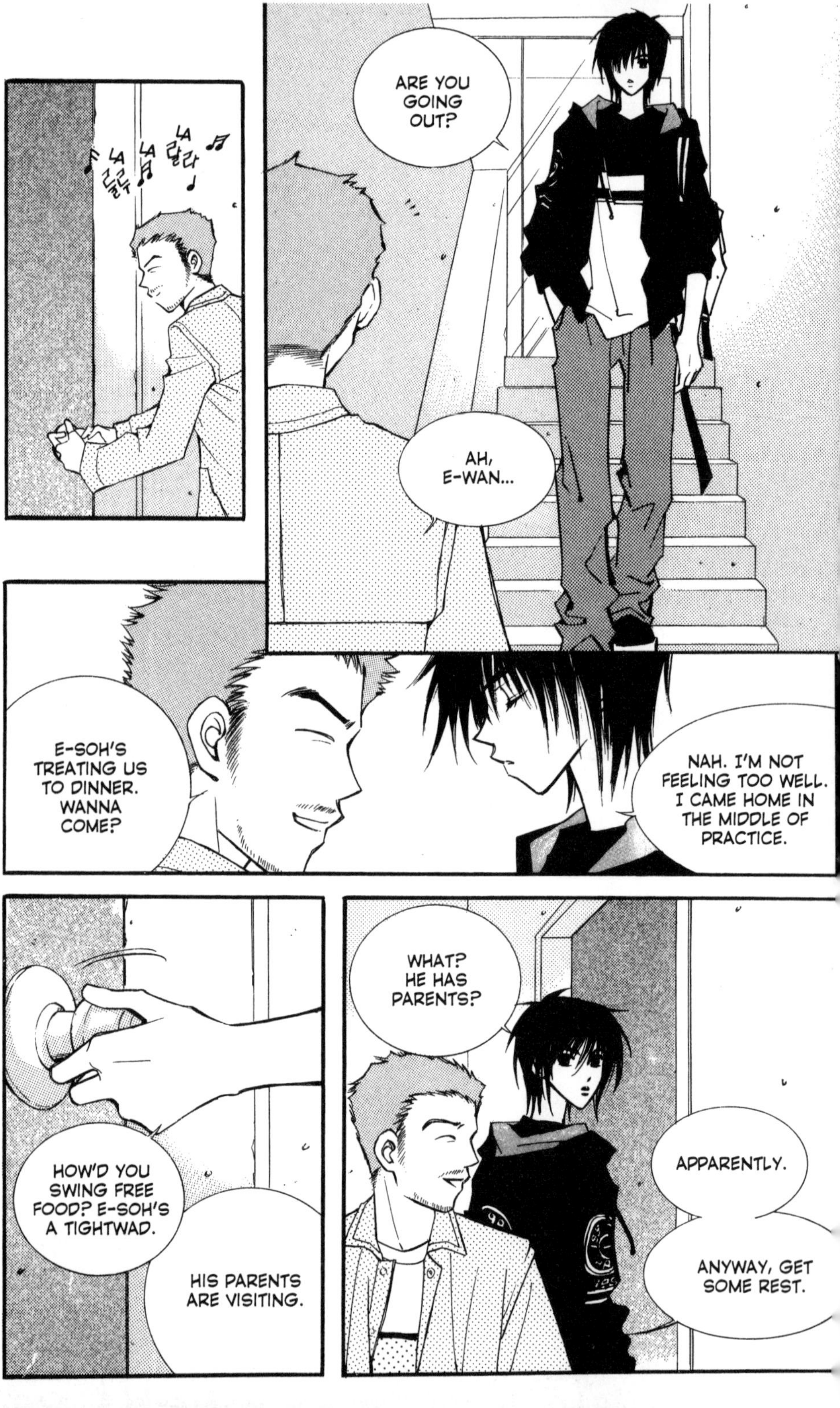
LA 룰루 LA LA 랄라
ARE YOU GOING OUT?
AH, E-WAN...
E-SOH'S TREATING US TO DINNER. WANNA COME?
NAH. I'M NOT FEELING TOO WELL. I CAME HOME IN THE MIDDLE OF PRACTICE.
HOW'D YOU SWING FREE FOOD? E-SOH'S A TIGHTWAD.
HIS PARENTS ARE VISITING.
WHAT? HE HAS PARENTS?
APPARENTLY.
ANYWAY, GET SOME REST.

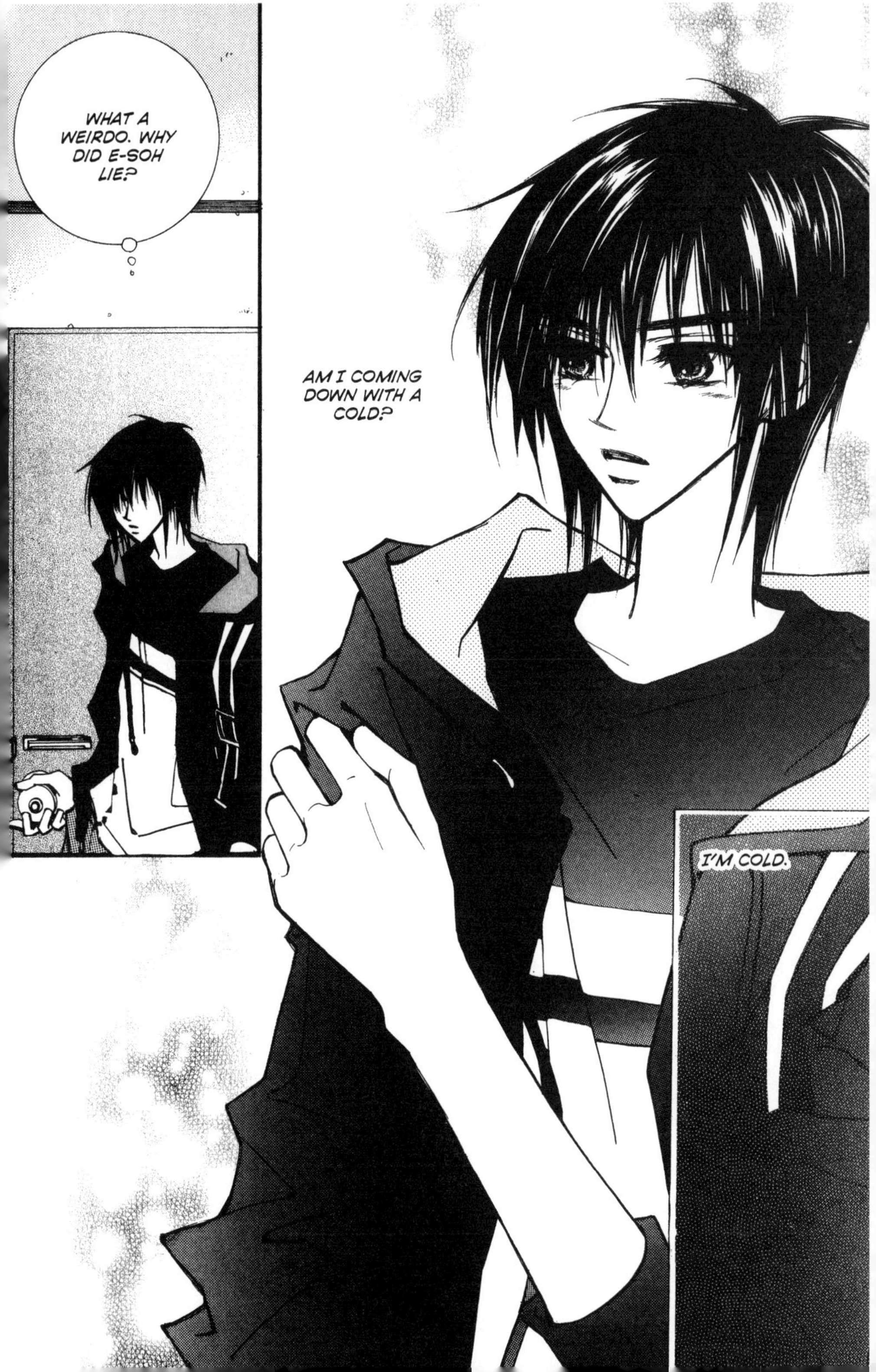
WHAT A WEIRDO. WHY DID E-SOH LIE?
AM I COMING DOWN WITH A COLD?
I'M COLD.

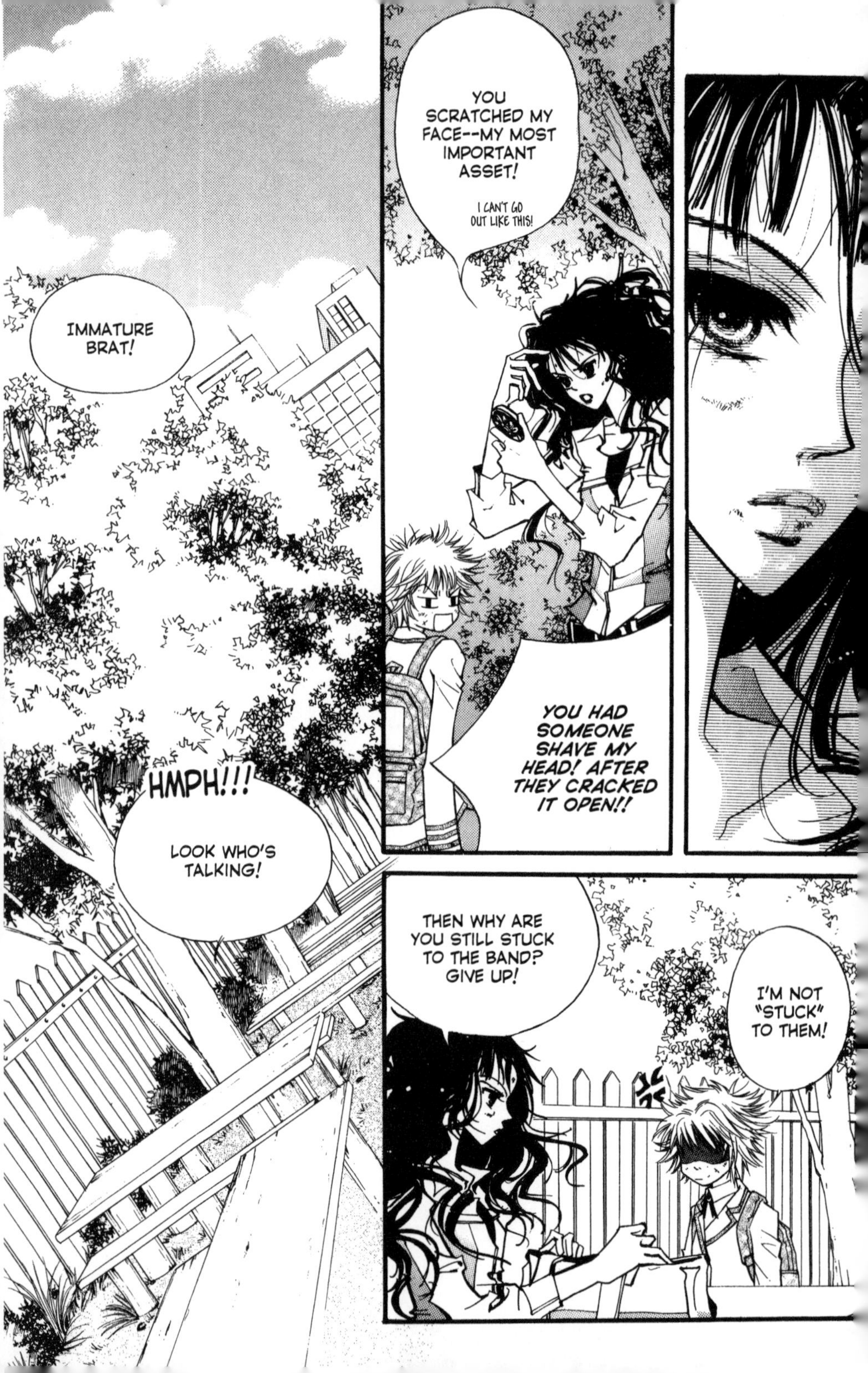
IMMATURE BRAT!
HMPH!!!
LOOK WHO'S TALKING!
YOU SCRATCHED MY FACE--MY MOST IMPORTANT ASSET!
I CAN'T GO OUT LIKE THIS!
YOU HAD SOMEONE SHAVE MY HEAD! AFTER THEY CRACKED IT OPEN!!
THEN WHY ARE YOU STILL STUCK TO THE BAND? GIVE UP!
I'M NOT "STUCK" TO THEM!

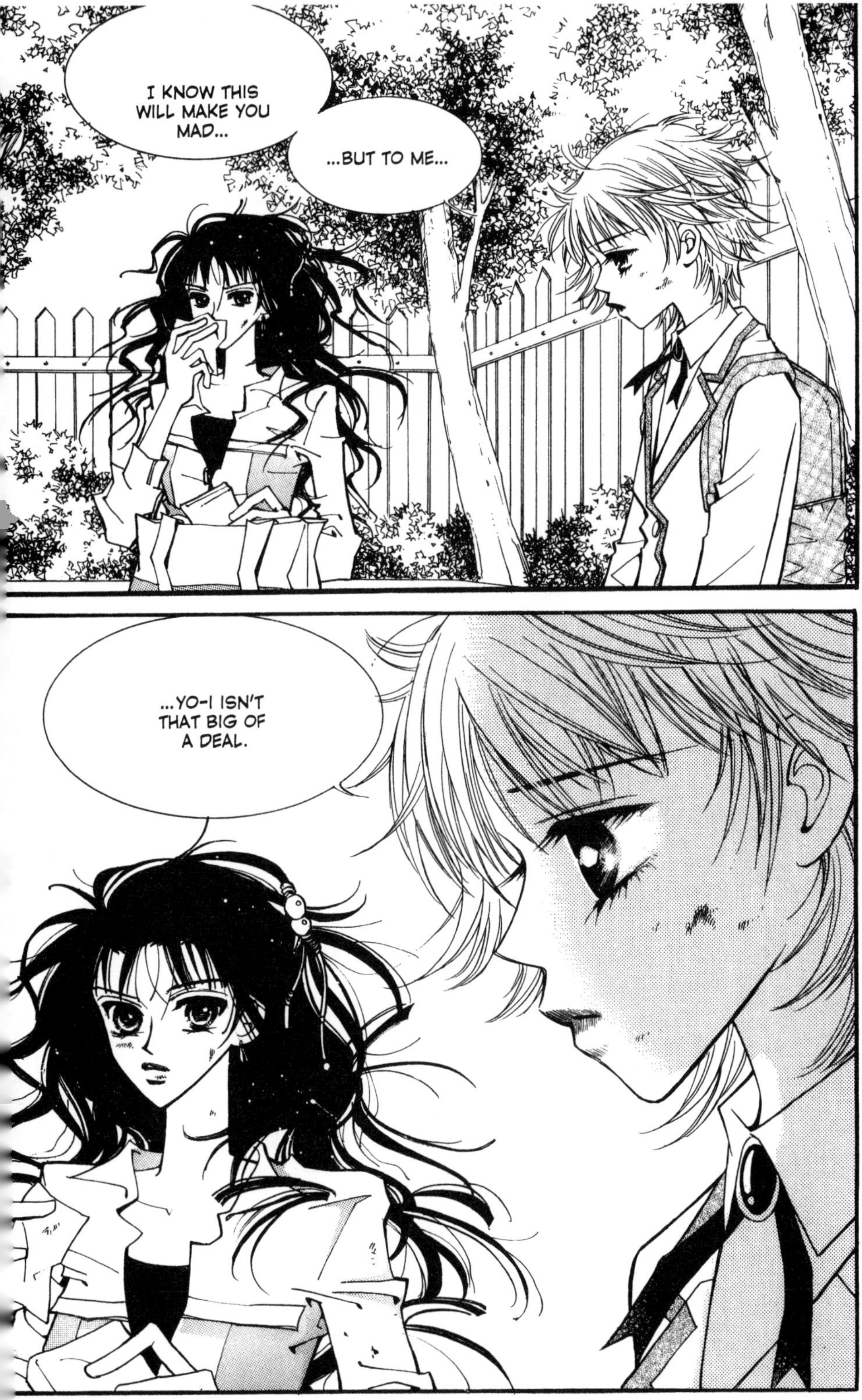
I KNOW THIS WILL MAKE YOU MAD...
...BUT TO ME...
...YO-I ISN'T THAT BIG OF A DEAL.

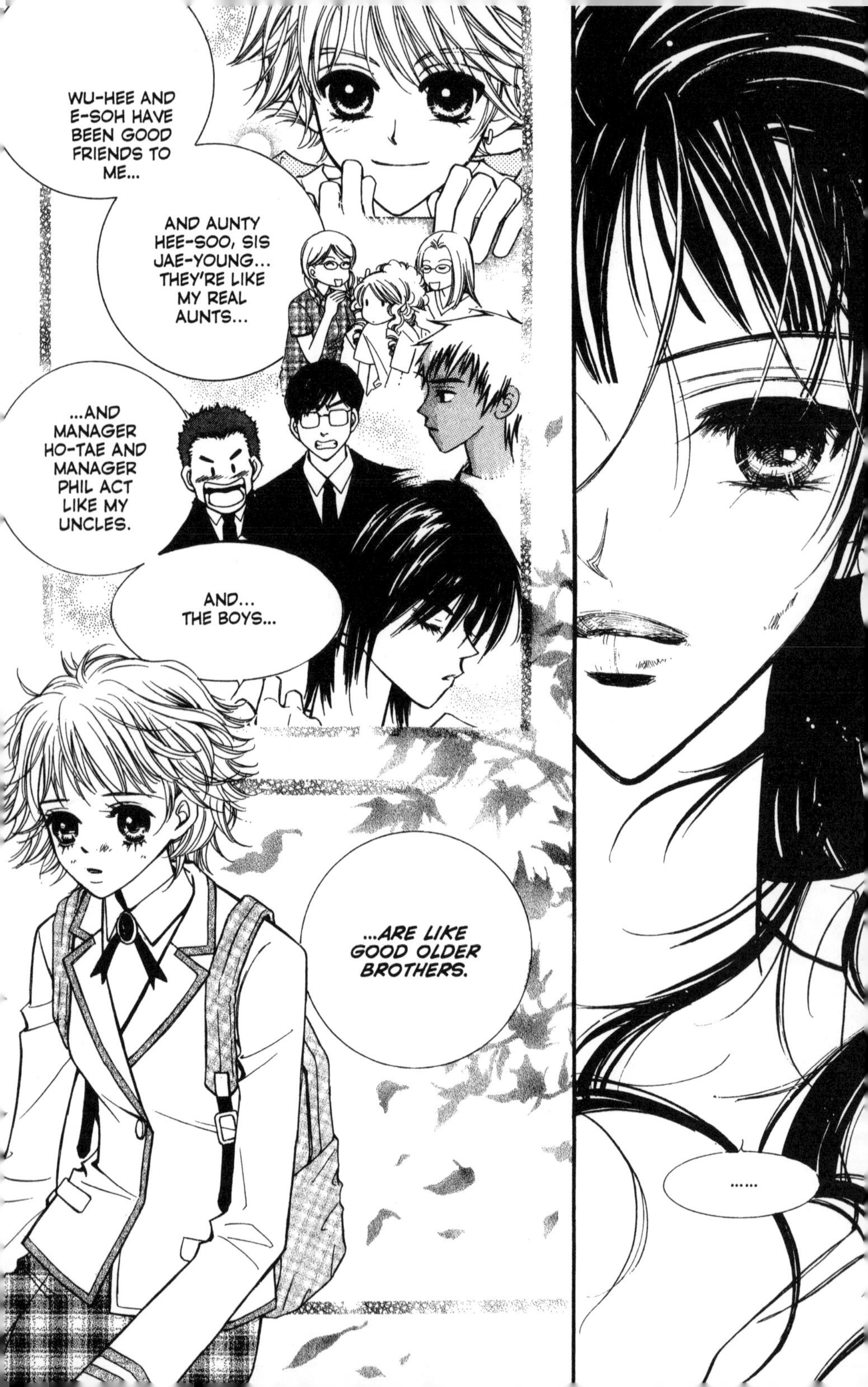
WU-HEE AND E-SOH HAVE BEEN GOOD FRIENDS TO ME...
AND AUNTY HEE-SOO, SIS JAE-YOUNG... THEY'RE LIKE MY REAL AUNTS...
...AND MANAGER HO-TAE AND MANAGER PHIL ACT LIKE MY UNCLES.
AND... THE BOYS...
...ARE LIKE GOOD OLDER BROTHERS.
......

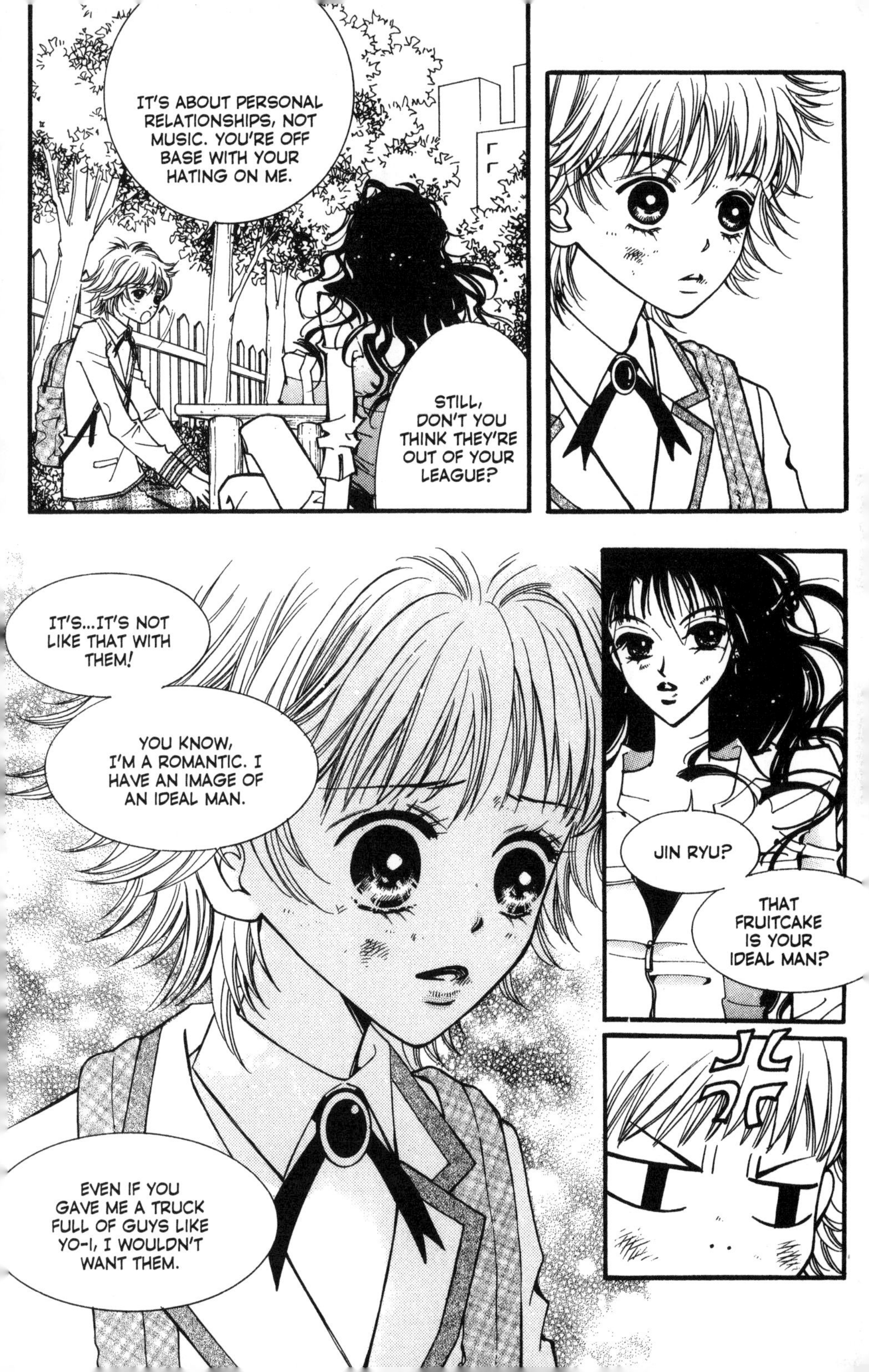
IT'S ABOUT PERSONAL RELATIONSHIPS, NOT MUSIC. YOU'RE OFF BASE WITH YOUR HATING ON ME.
STILL, DON'T YOU THINK THEY'RE OUT OF YOUR LEAGUE?
IT'S...IT'S NOT LIKE THAT WITH THEM!
YOU KNOW, I'M A ROMANTIC. I HAVE AN IMAGE OF AN IDEAL MAN.
EVEN IF YOU GAVE ME A TRUCK FULL OF GUYS LIKE YO-I, I WOULDN'T WANT THEM.
JIN RYU?
THAT FRUITCAKE IS YOUR IDEAL MAN?

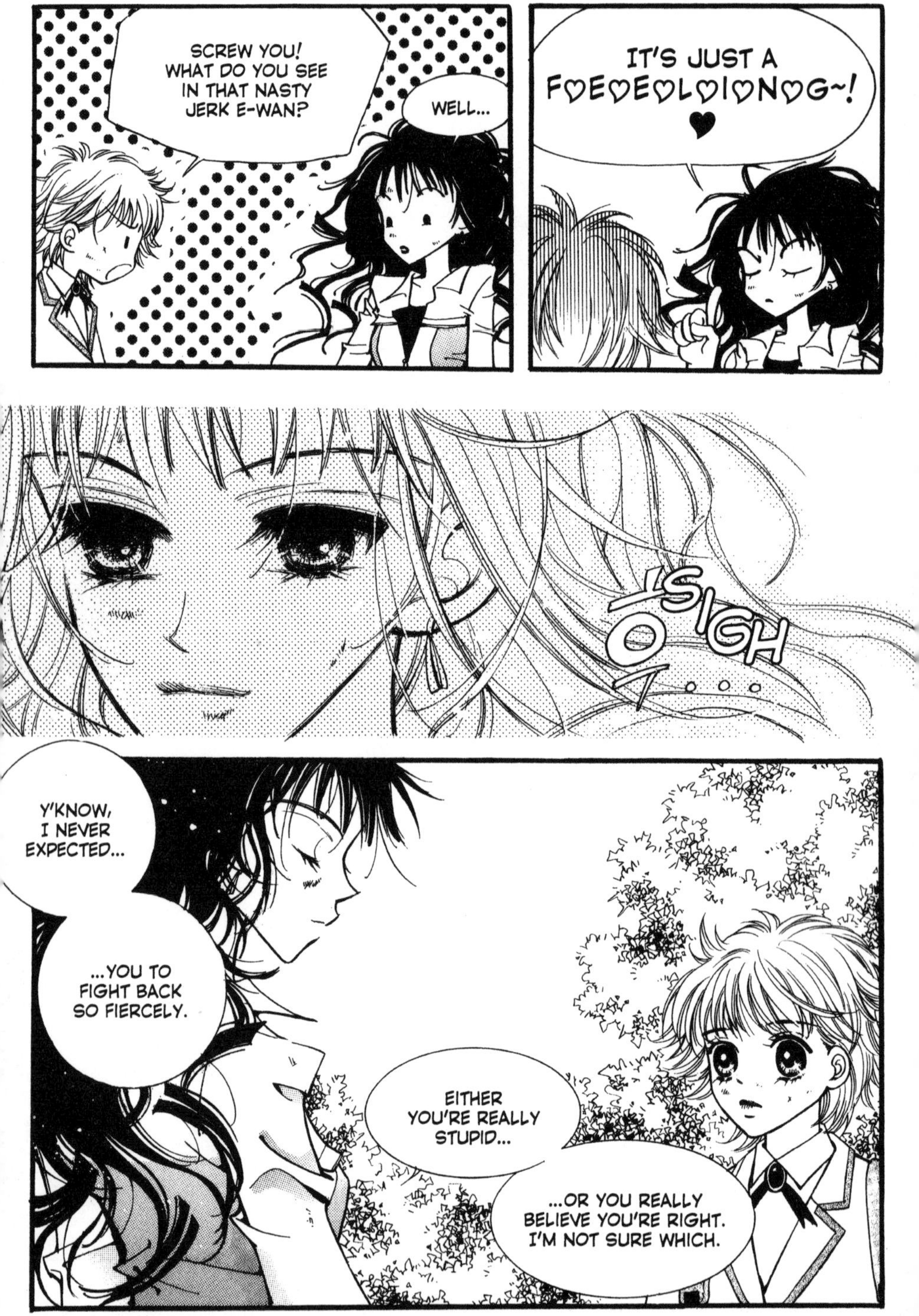
SCREW YOU! WHAT DO YOU SEE IN THAT NASTY JERK E-WAN?
WELL...
IT'S JUST A F♡E♡E♡L♡I♡N♡G~! ♥
SIGH
Y'KNOW, I NEVER EXPECTED...
...YOU TO FIGHT BACK SO FIERCELY.
EITHER YOU'RE REALLY STUPID...
...OR YOU REALLY BELIEVE YOU'RE RIGHT. I'M NOT SURE WHICH.

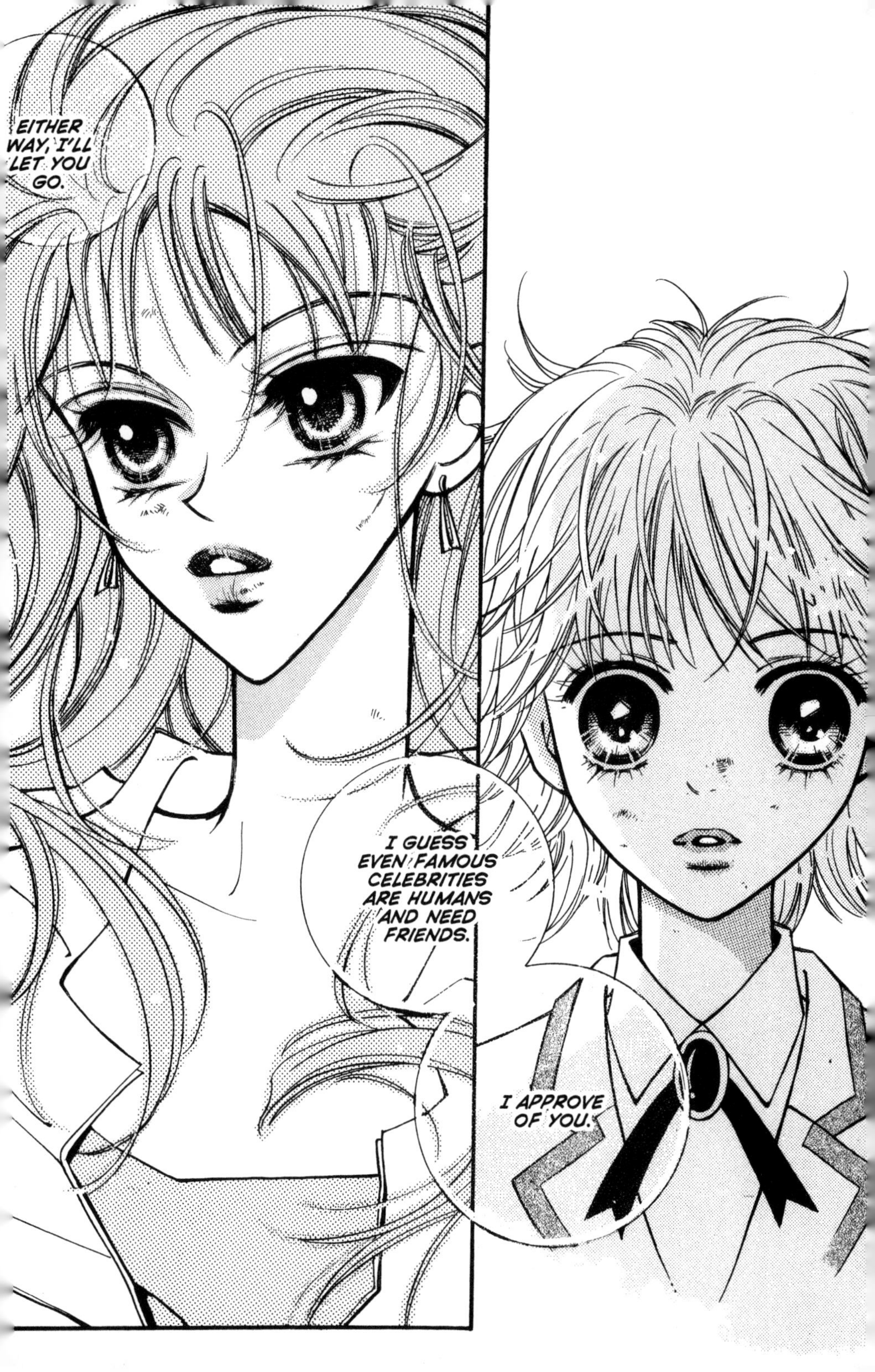
EITHER WAY, I'LL LET YOU GO.
I GUESS EVEN FAMOUS CELEBRITIES ARE HUMANS AND NEED FRIENDS.
I APPROVE OF YOU.

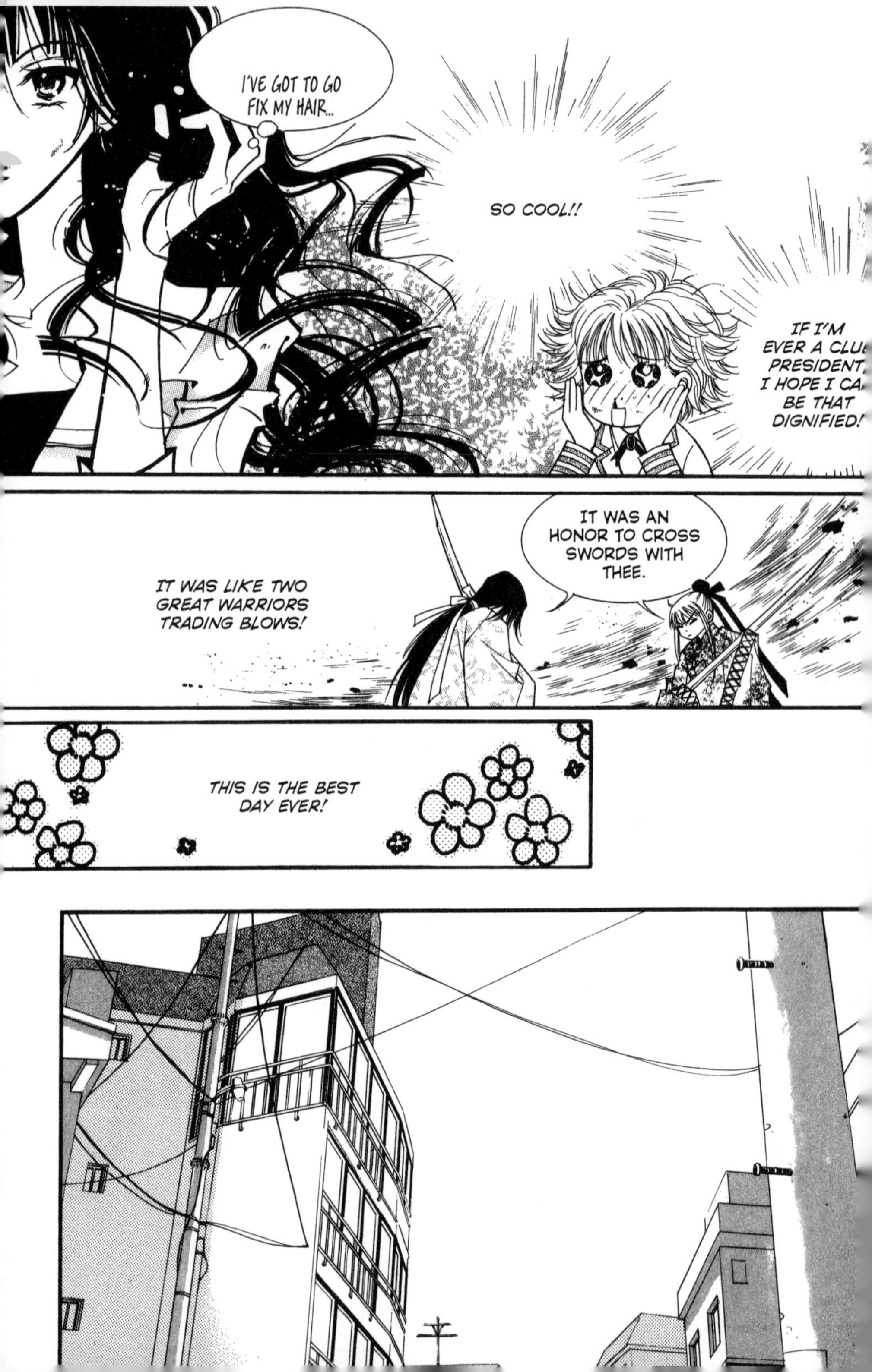
I'VE GOT TO GO FIX MY HAIR...
SO COOL!!
IF I'M EVER A CLU PRESIDENT I HOPE I CA BE THAT DIGNIFIED!
IT WAS LIKE TWO GREAT WARRIORS TRADING BLOWS!
IT WAS AN HONOR TO CROSS SWORDS WITH THEE.
THIS IS THE BEST DAY EVER!

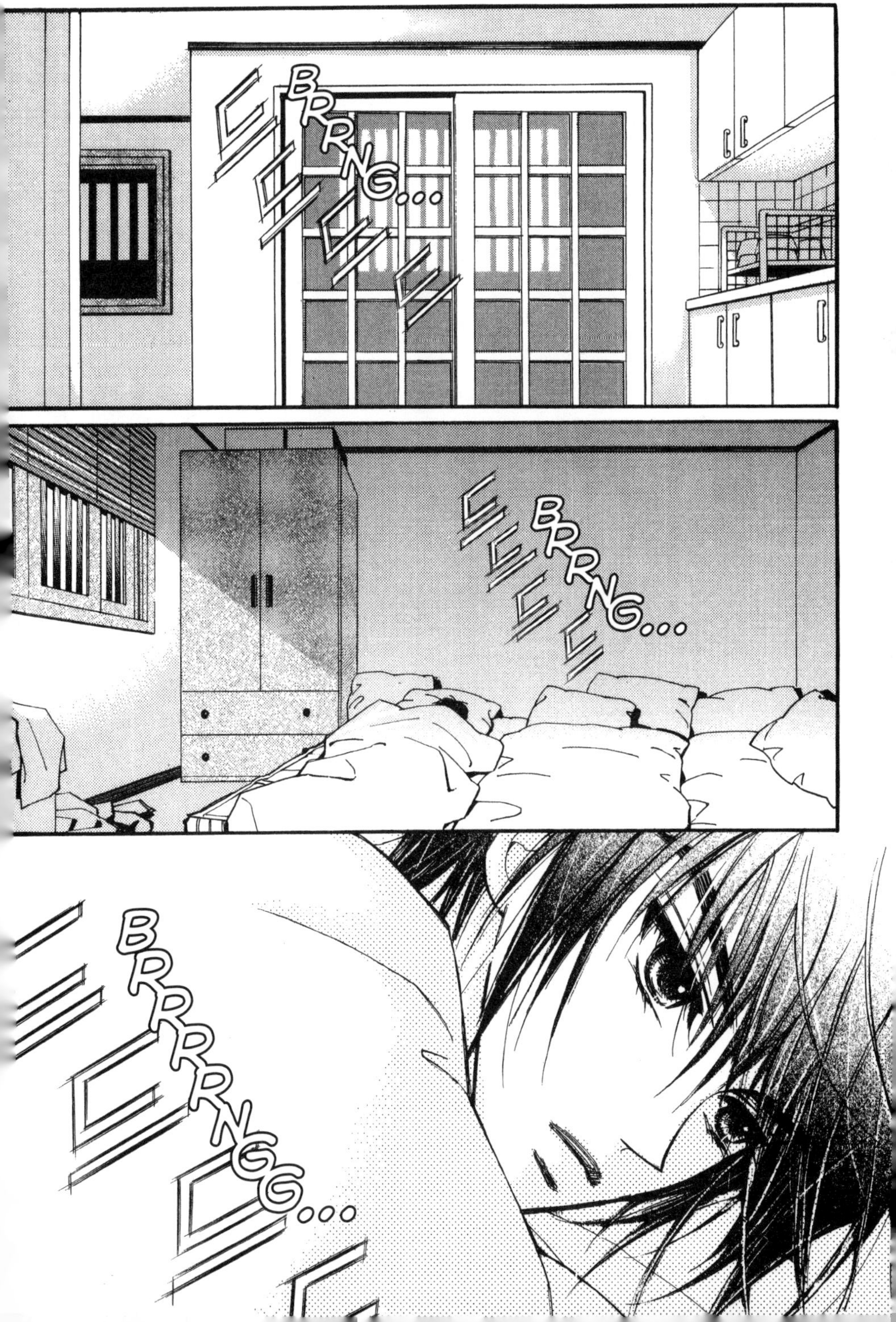
BRRNG...
BRRNG...
BRRRRNGG...

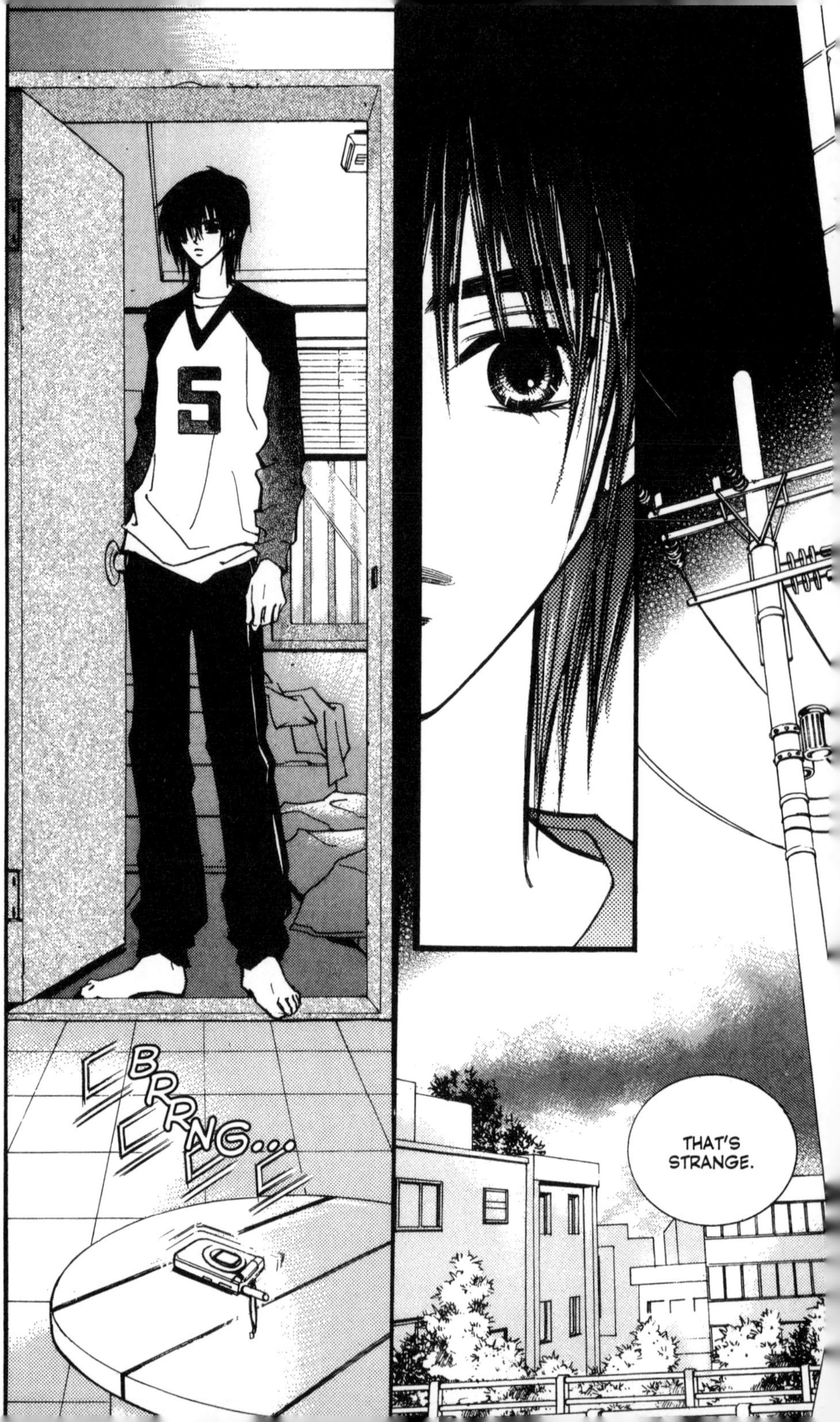
BRRRNG...
THAT'S STRANGE.

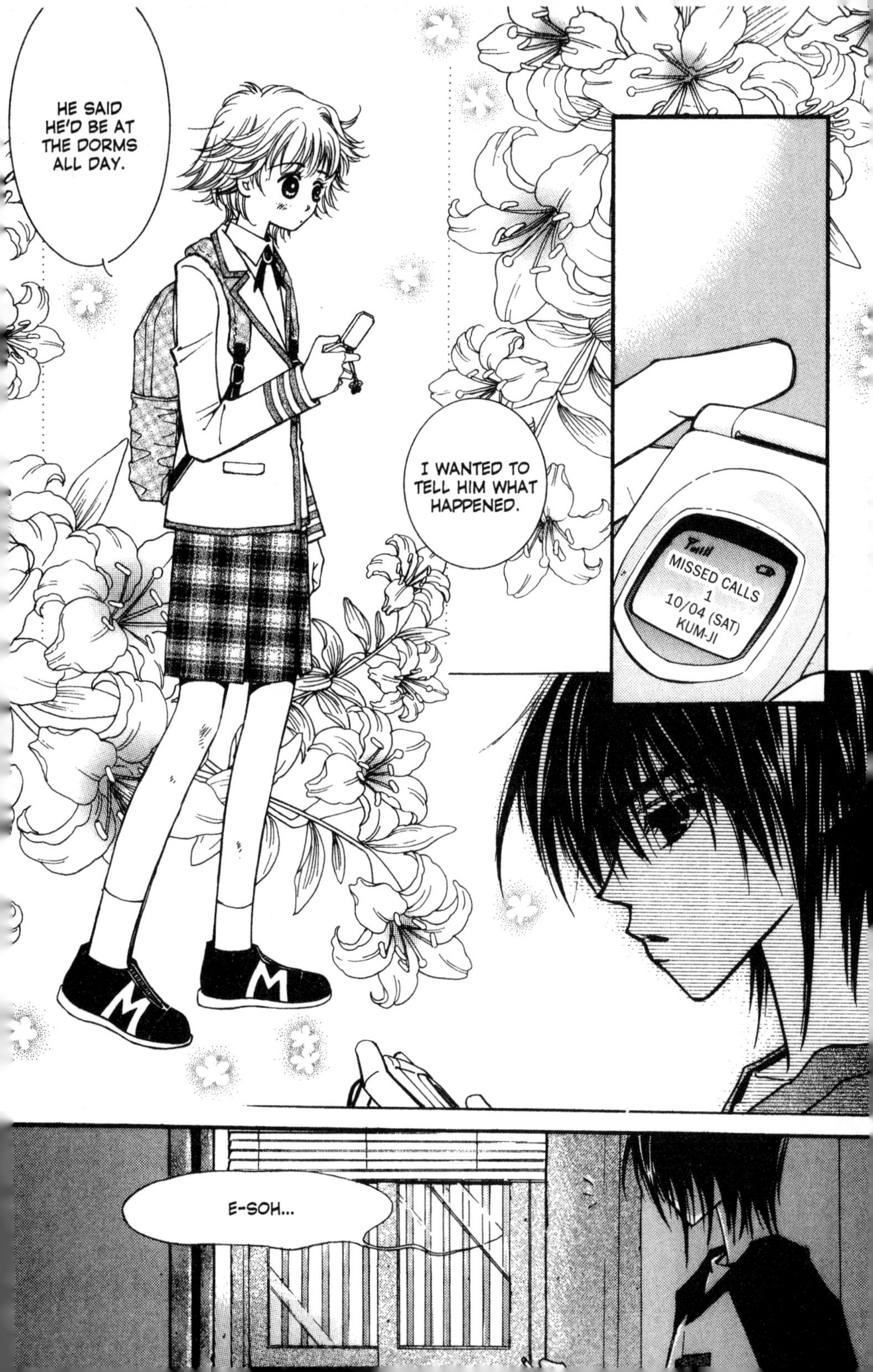
HE SAID HE'D BE AT THE DORMS ALL DAY.
I WANTED TO TELL HIM WHAT HAPPENED.
MISSED CALLS
1
10/04 (SAT)
KUM-JI
E-SOH...

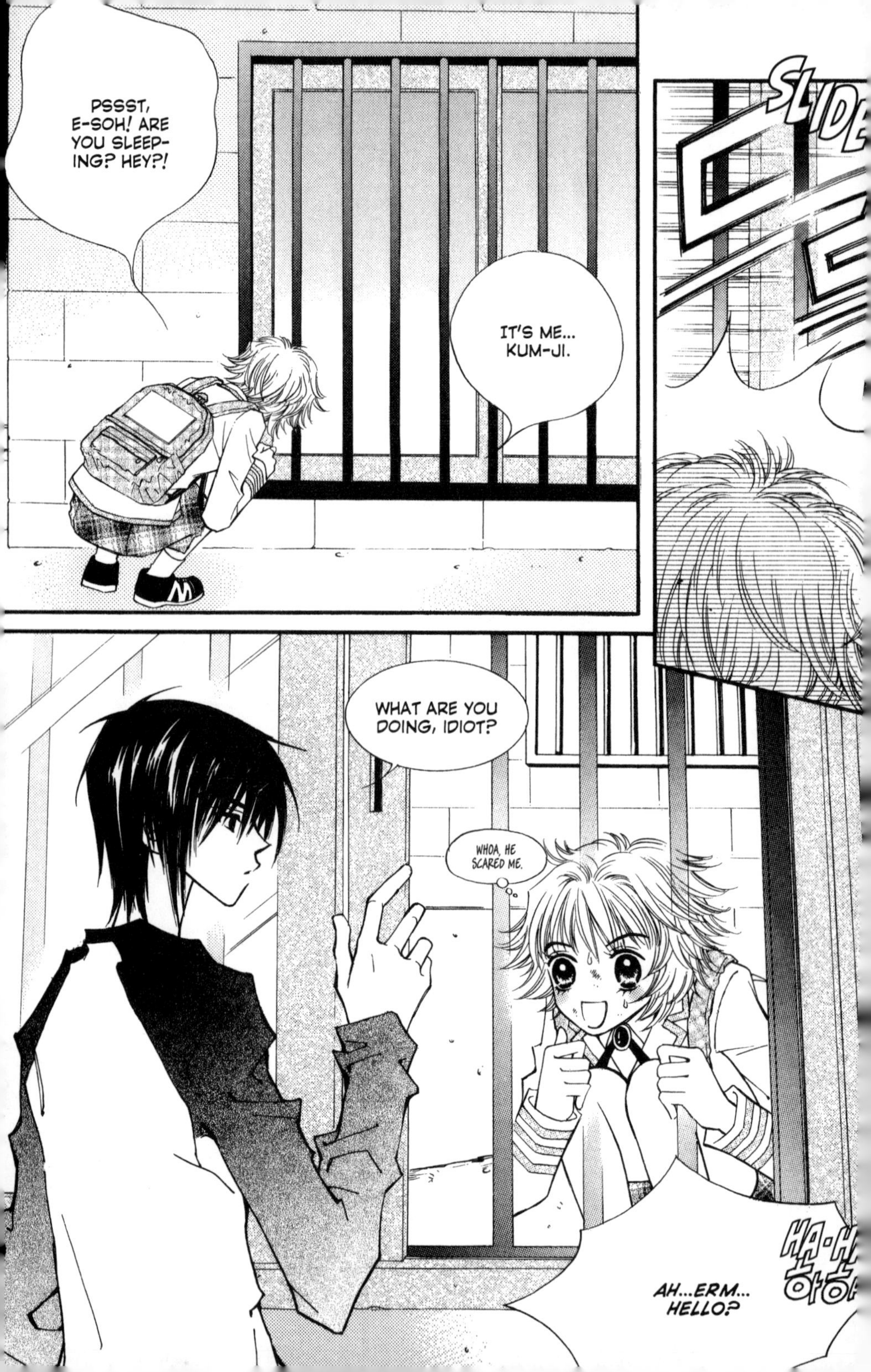
PSSST, E-SOH! ARE YOU SLEEPING? HEY?!
IT'S ME... KUM-JI.
SLIDE
WHAT ARE YOU DOING, IDIOT?
WHOA, HE SCARED ME.
HA-H
AH...ERM... HELLO?

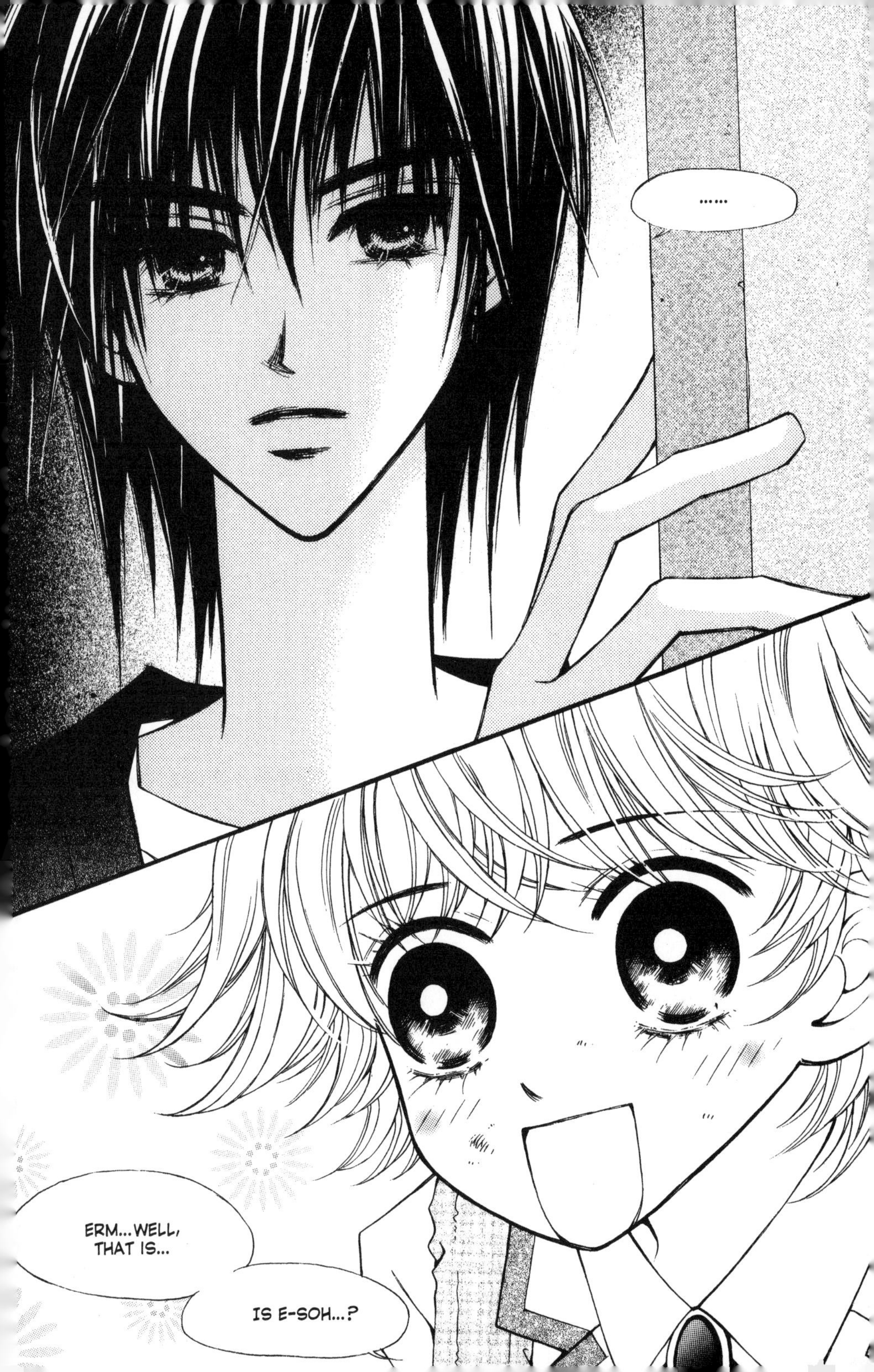
......
ERM...WELL, THAT IS...
IS E-SOH...?

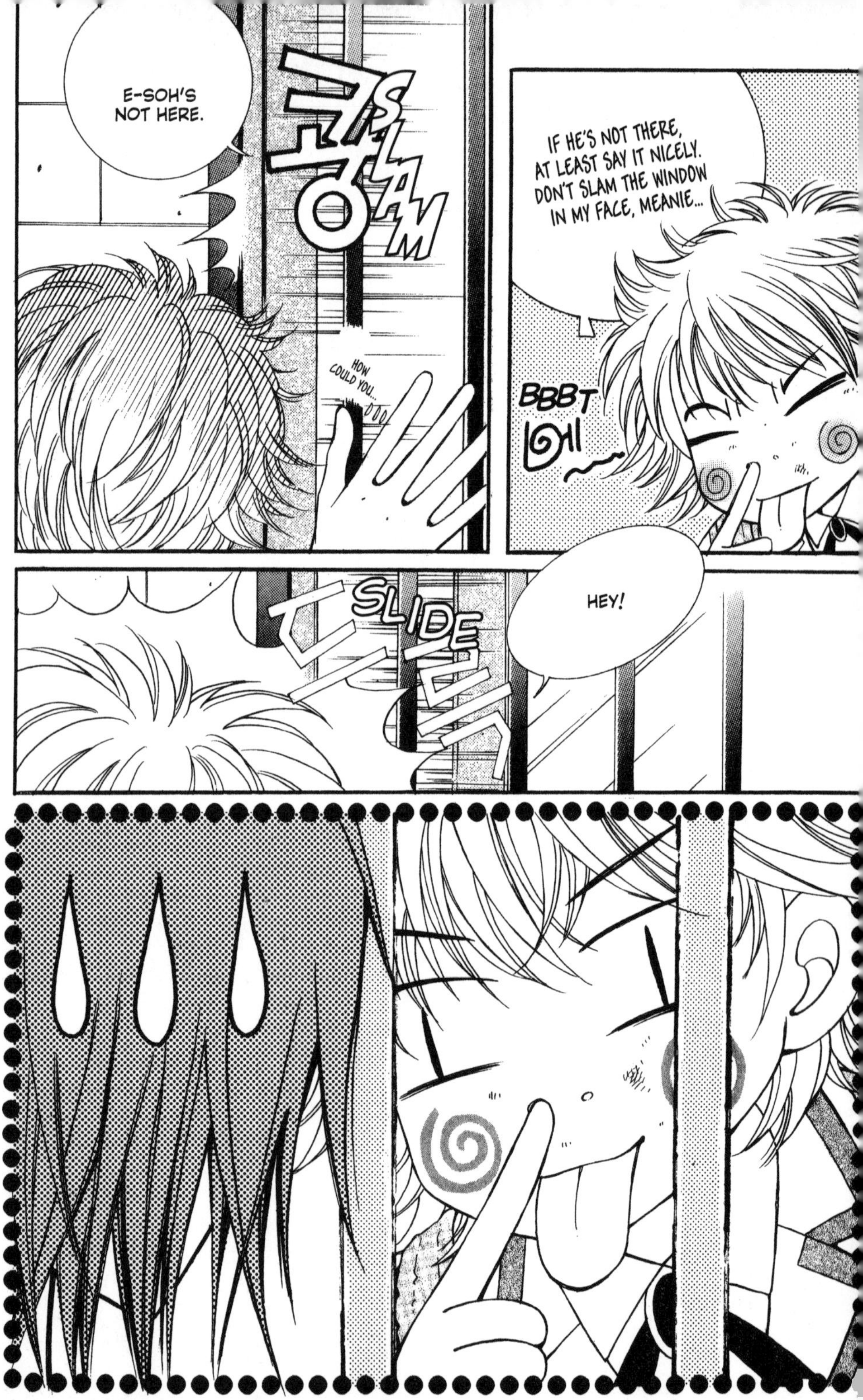
E-SOH'S NOT HERE.
SLAM
HOW COULD YOU...
IF HE'S NOT THERE, AT LEAST SAY IT NICELY. DON'T SLAM THE WINDOW IN MY FACE, MEANIE...
BBBT
SLIDE
HEY!

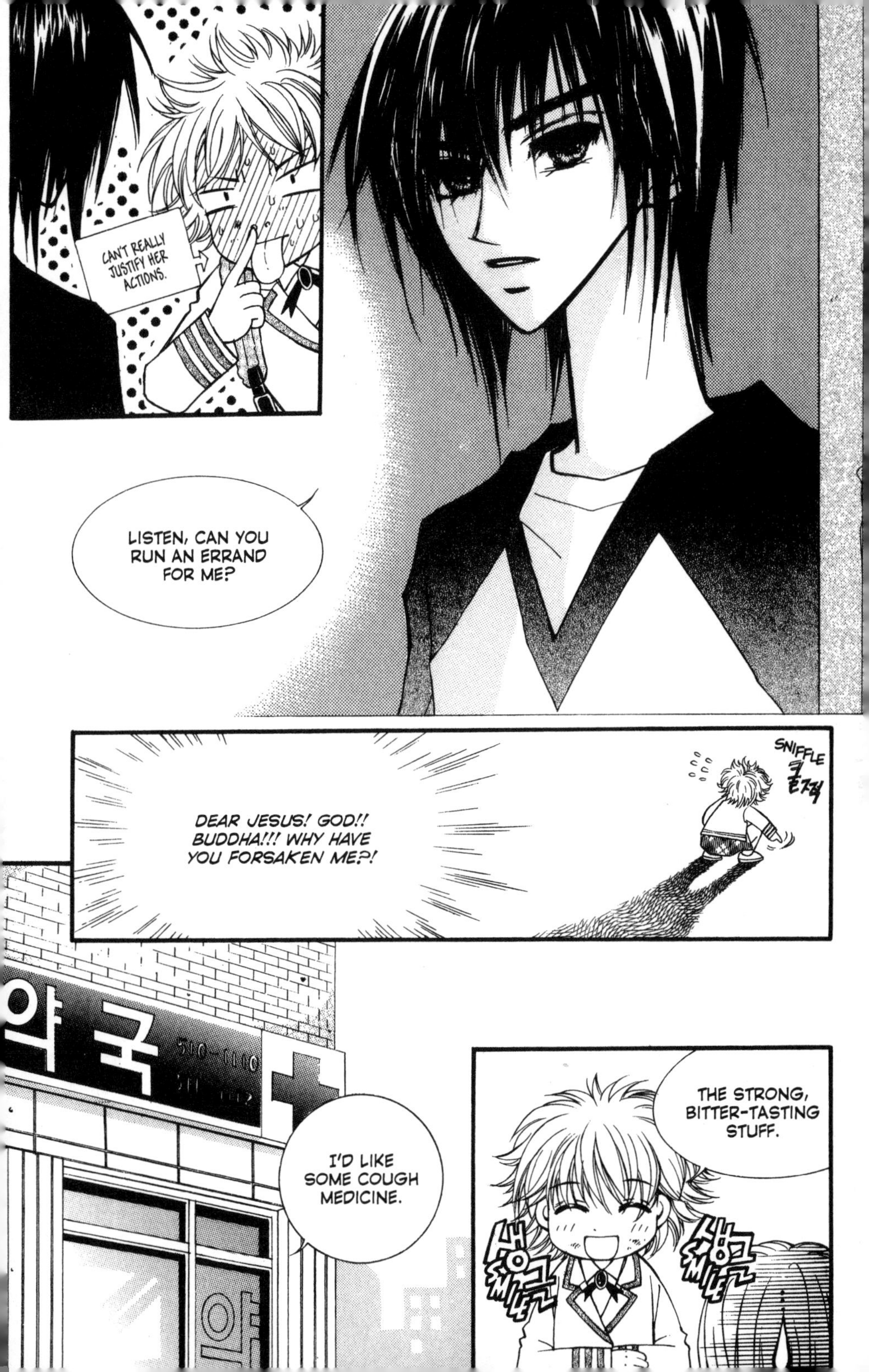
CAN'T REALLY JUSTIFY HER ACTIONS.
LISTEN, CAN YOU RUN AN ERRAND FOR ME?
DEAR JESUS! GOD!! BUDDHA!!! WHY HAVE YOU FORSAKEN ME?!
SNIFFLE
약국
I'D LIKE SOME COUGH MEDICINE.
THE STRONG, BITTER-TASTING STUFF.
방긋
SMILE
생긋
SMILE

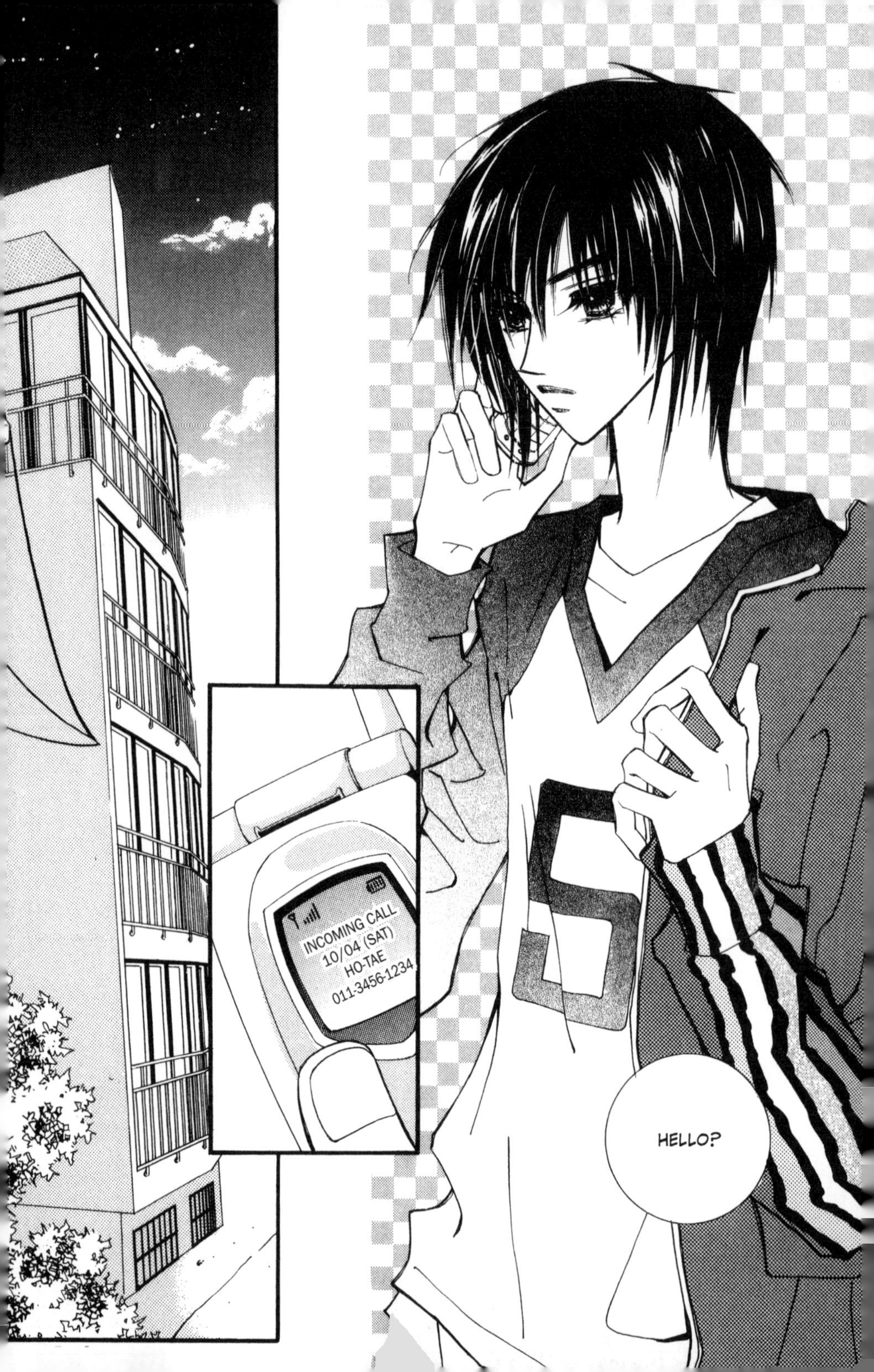
INCOMING CALL
10/04 (SAT)
HO-TAE
011-3456-1234
HELLO?

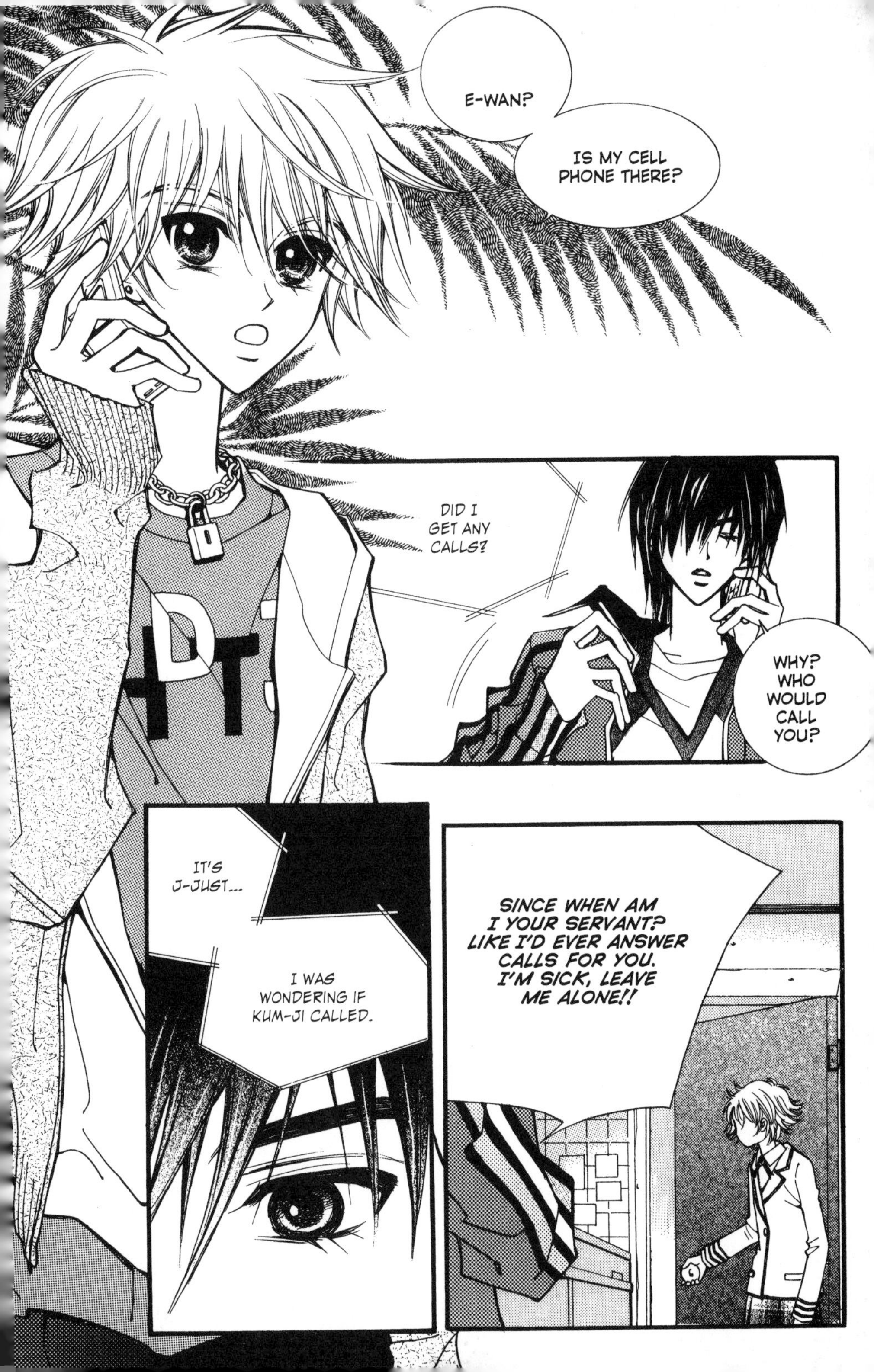
E-WAN?
IS MY CELL PHONE THERE?
DID I GET ANY CALLS?
WHY? WHO WOULD CALL YOU?
IT'S J-JUST...
I WAS WONDERING IF KUM-JI CALLED.
SINCE WHEN AM I YOUR SERVANT? LIKE I'D EVER ANSWER CALLS FOR YOU. I'M SICK, LEAVE ME ALONE!!

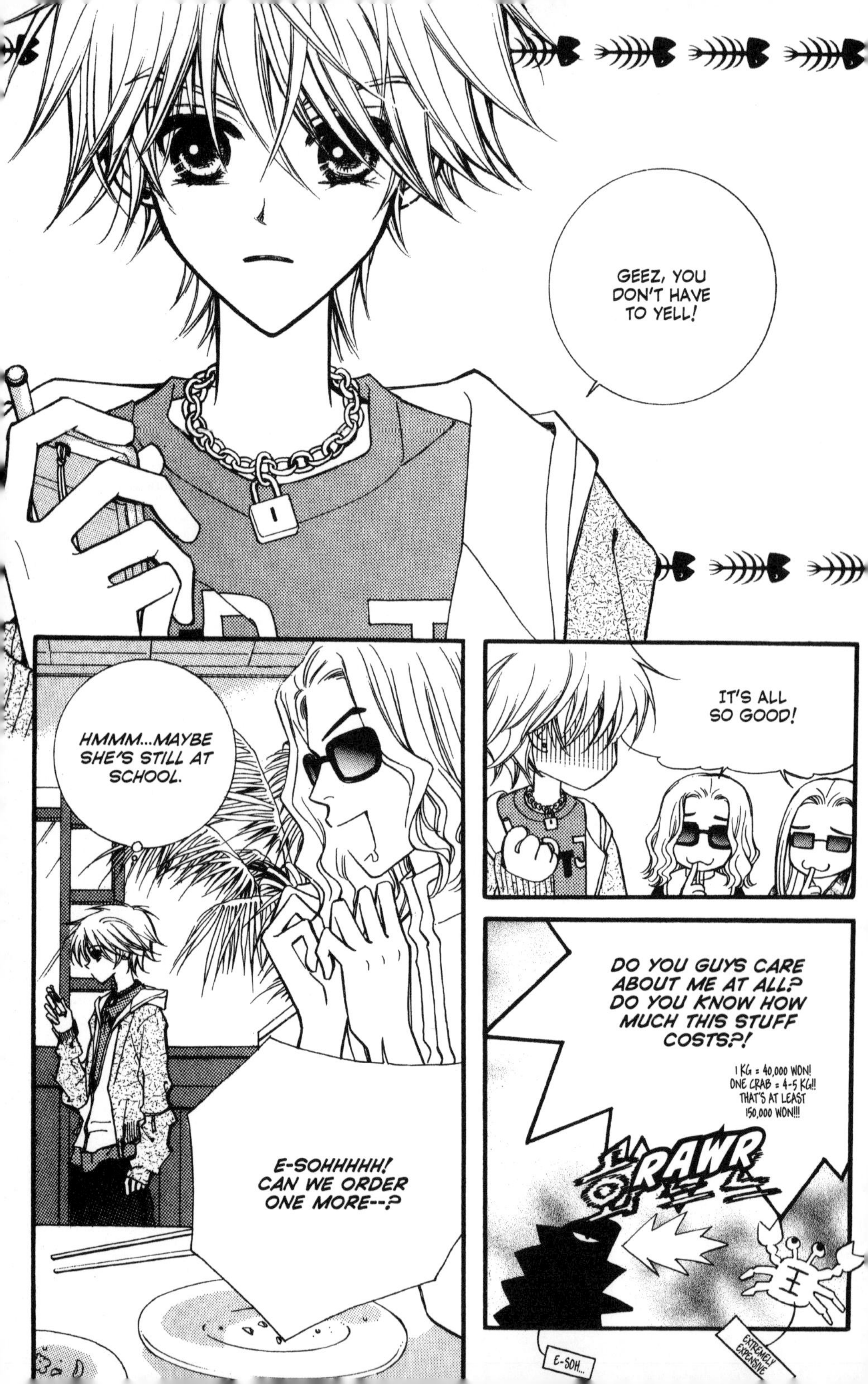
GEEZ, YOU DON'T HAVE TO YELL!
HMMM...MAYBE SHE'S STILL AT SCHOOL.
E-SOHHHHH! CAN WE ORDER ONE MORE--?
IT'S ALL SO GOOD!
DO YOU GUYS CARE ABOUT ME AT ALL? DO YOU KNOW HOW MUCH THIS STUFF COSTS?!
1 KG = 40,000 WON! ONE CRAB = 4-5 KG!! THAT'S AT LEAST 150,000 WON!!!
RAWR
E-SOH...
EXTREMELY EXPENSIVE

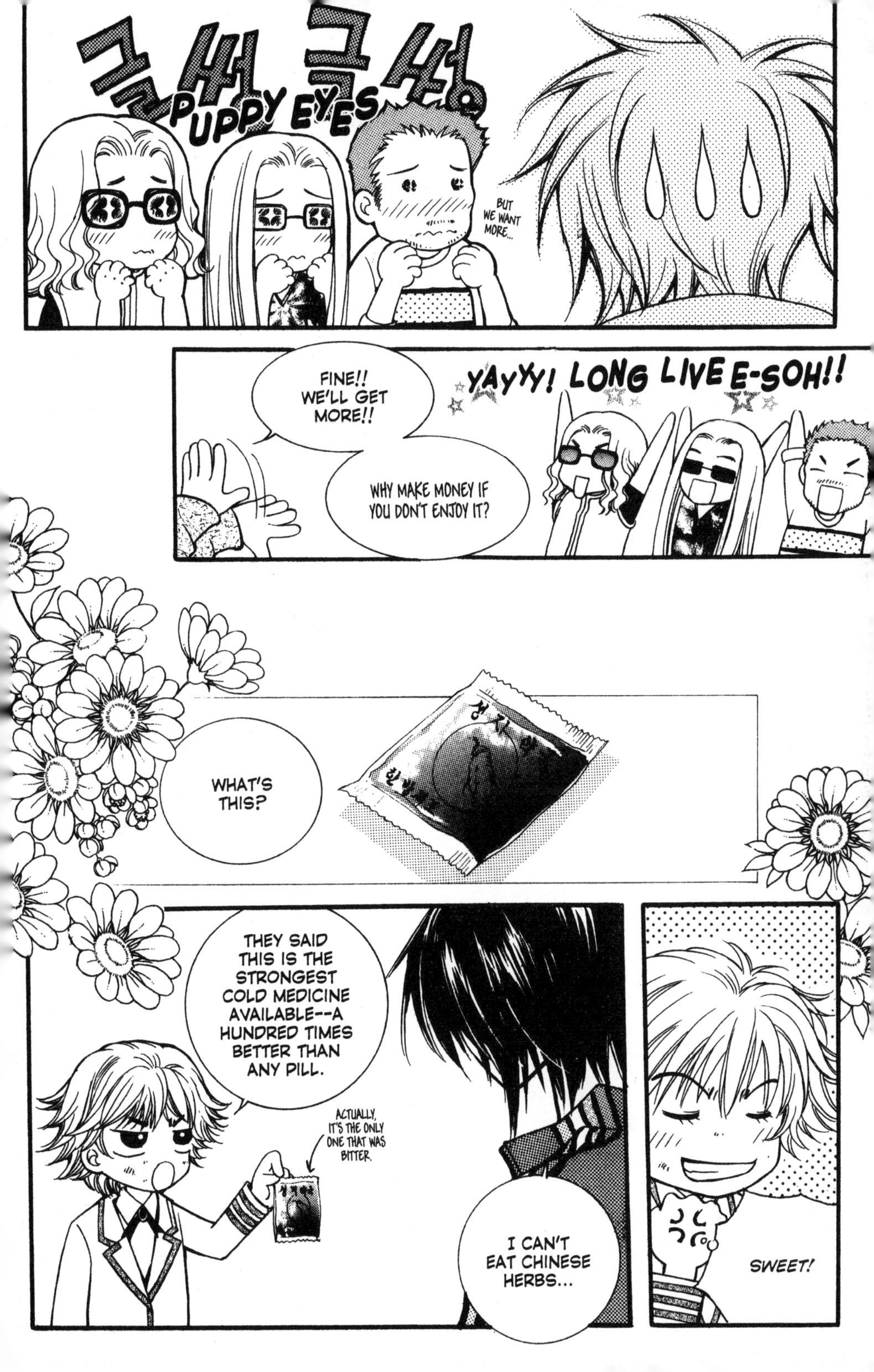

PUPPY EYES
BUT WE WANT MORE...
FINE!! WE'LL GET MORE!!
WHY MAKE MONEY IF YOU DON'T ENJOY IT?
YAYYY! LONG LIVE E-SOH!!
WHAT'S THIS?
THEY SAID THIS IS THE STRONGEST COLD MEDICINE AVAILABLE--A HUNDRED TIMES BETTER THAN ANY PILL.
ACTUALLY, IT'S THE ONLY ONE THAT WAS BITTER.
I CAN'T EAT CHINESE HERBS...
SWEET!

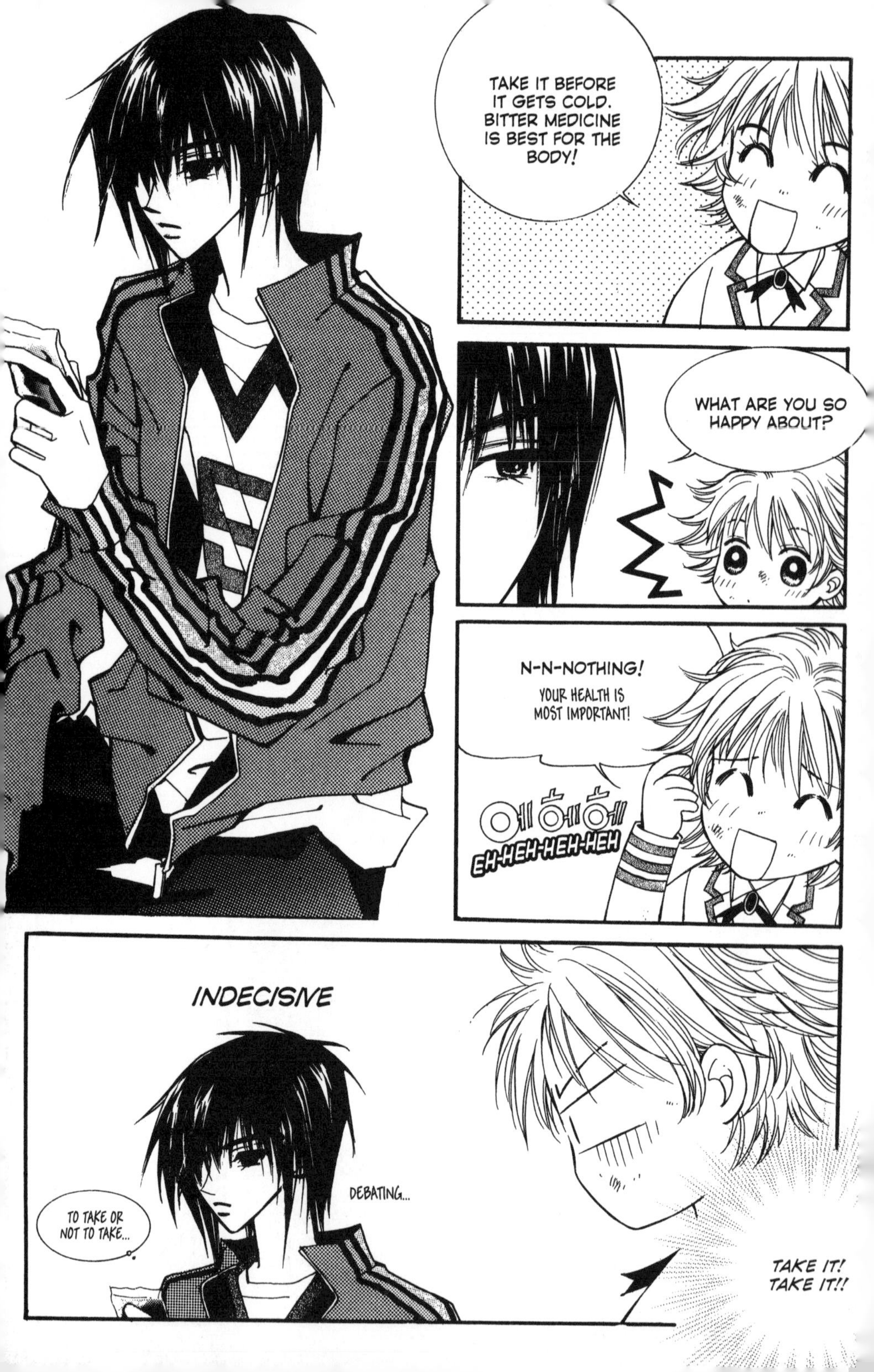
TAKE IT BEFORE IT GETS COLD. BITTER MEDICINE IS BEST FOR THE BODY!
WHAT ARE YOU SO HAPPY ABOUT?
N-N-NOTHING!
YOUR HEALTH IS MOST IMPORTANT!
에헤헤
EH-HEH-HEH-HEH
INDECISIVE
TO TAKE OR NOT TO TAKE...
DEBATING...
TAKE IT! TAKE IT!!

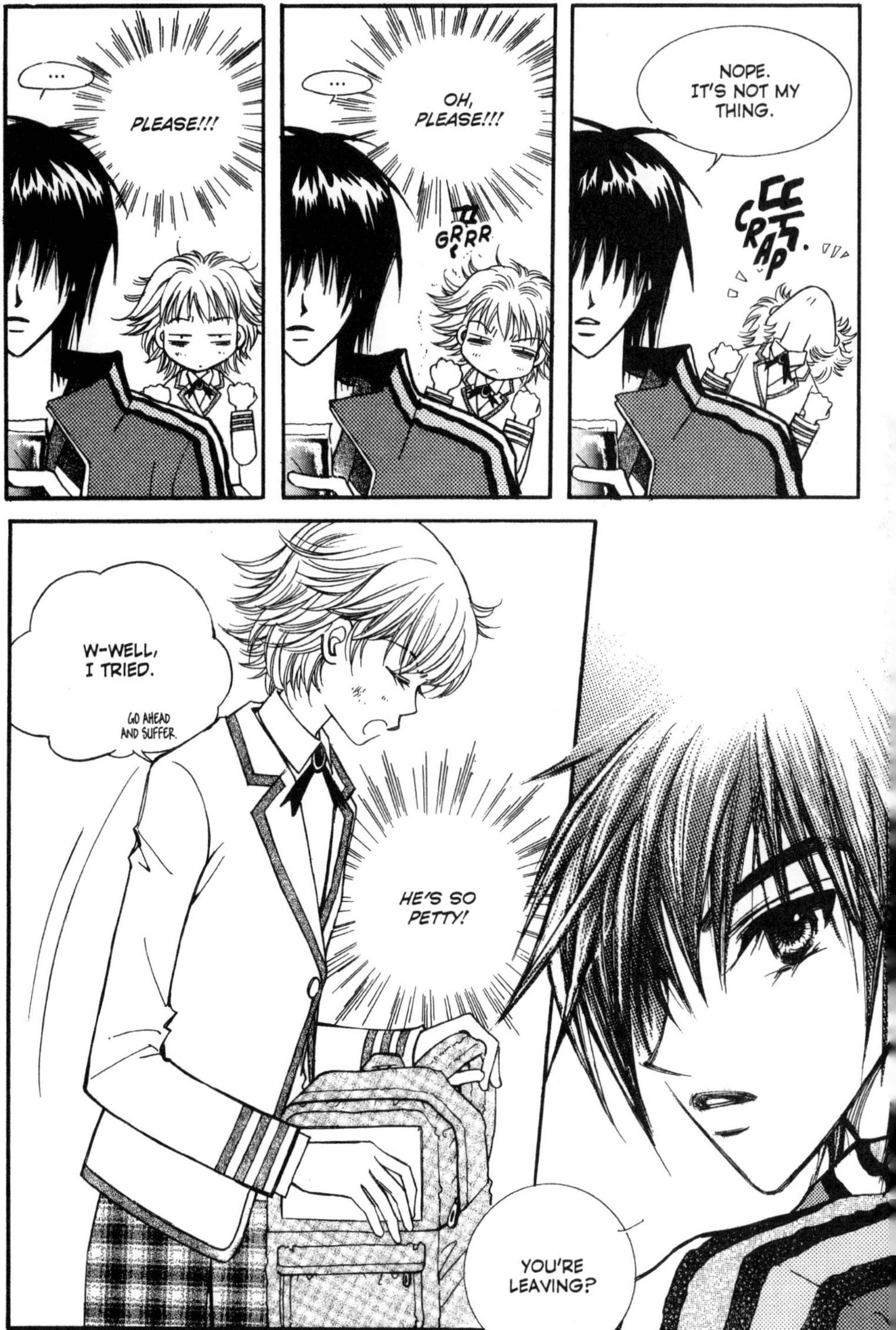
...
PLEASE!!!
...
OH, PLEASE!!!
GRRR
NOPE. IT'S NOT MY THING.
CCCRAP.
W-WELL, I TRIED.
GO AHEAD AND SUFFER.
HE'S SO PETTY!
YOU'RE LEAVING?

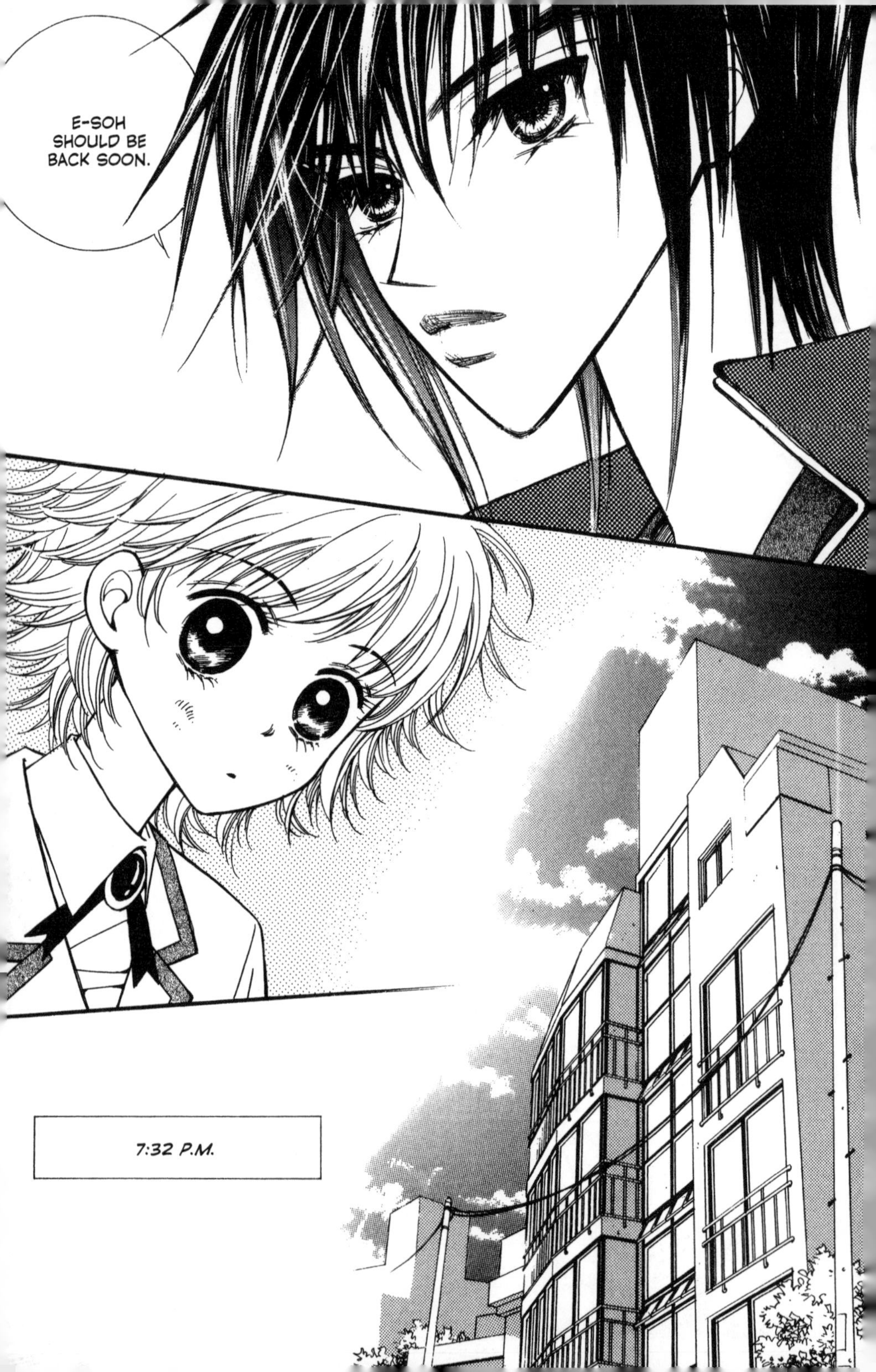
E-SOH SHOULD BE BACK SOON.
7:32 P.M.

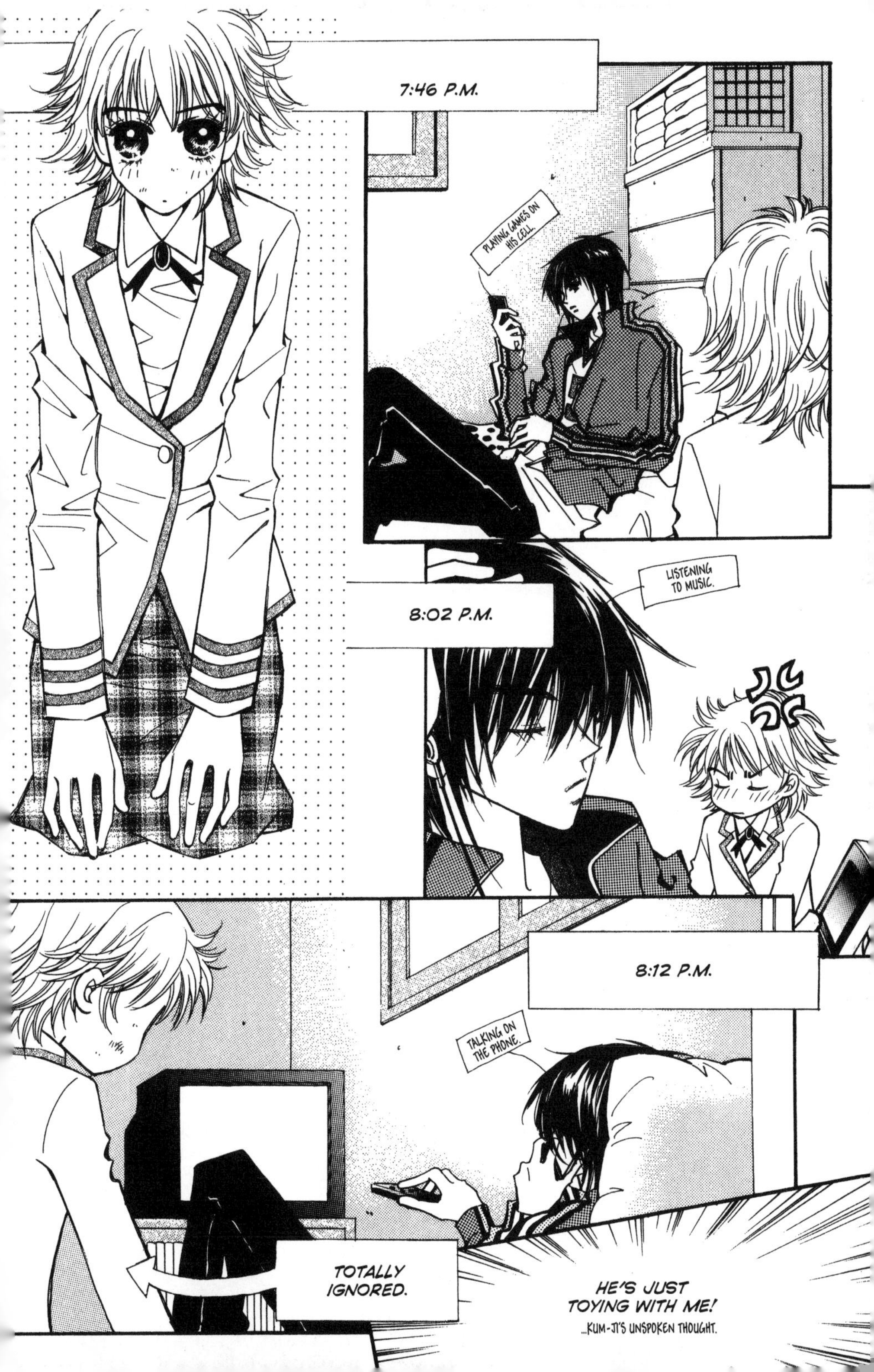
7:46 P.M.
PLAYING GAMES ON HIS CELL.
LISTENING TO MUSIC.
8:02 P.M.
8:12 P.M.
TALKING ON THE PHONE.
TOTALLY IGNORED.
HE'S JUST TOYING WITH ME!
...KUM-JI'S UNSPOKEN THOUGHT.

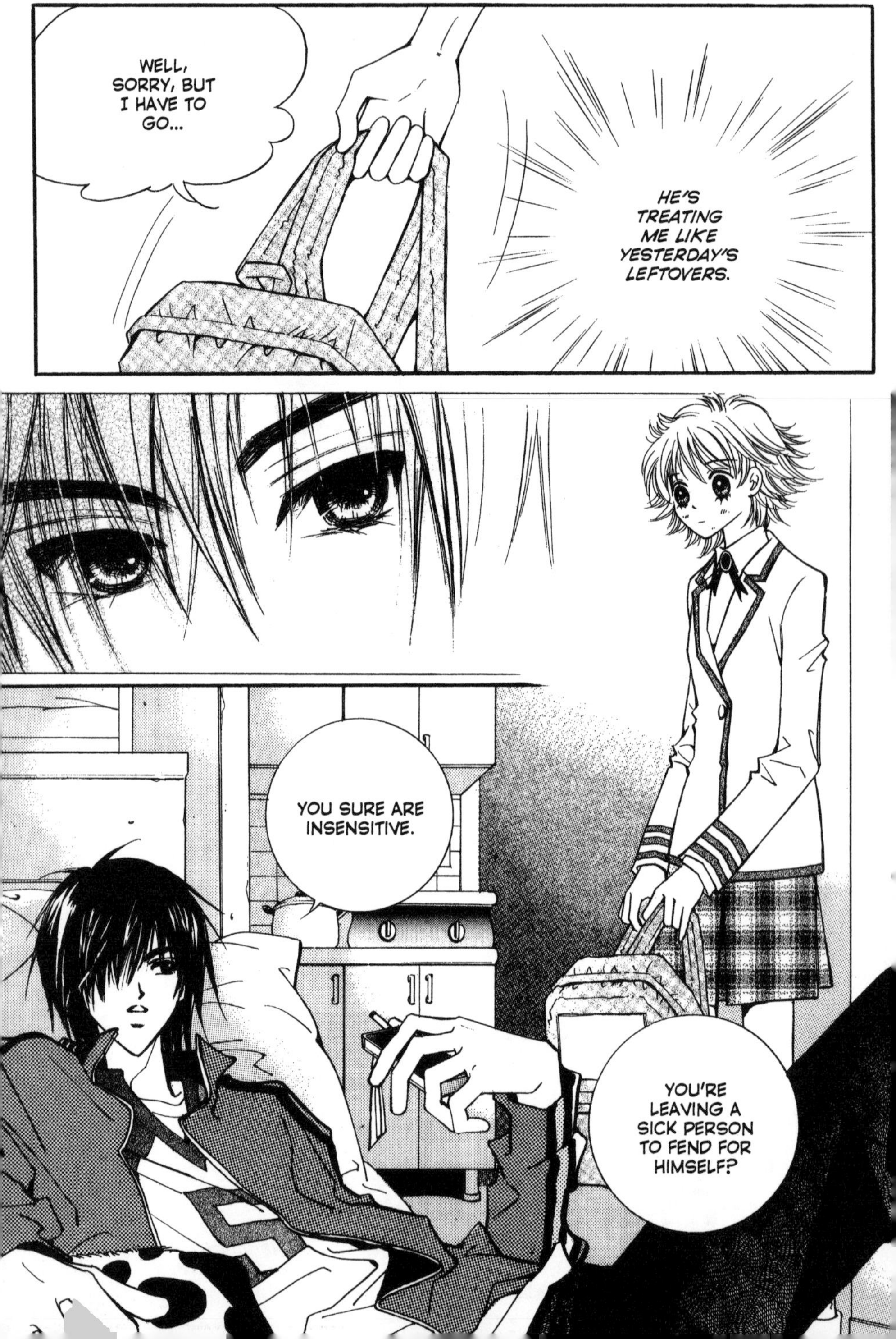
WELL, SORRY, BUT I HAVE TO GO...
HE'S TREATING ME LIKE YESTERDAY'S LEFTOVERS.
YOU SURE ARE INSENSITIVE.
YOU'RE LEAVING A SICK PERSON TO FEND FOR HIMSELF?

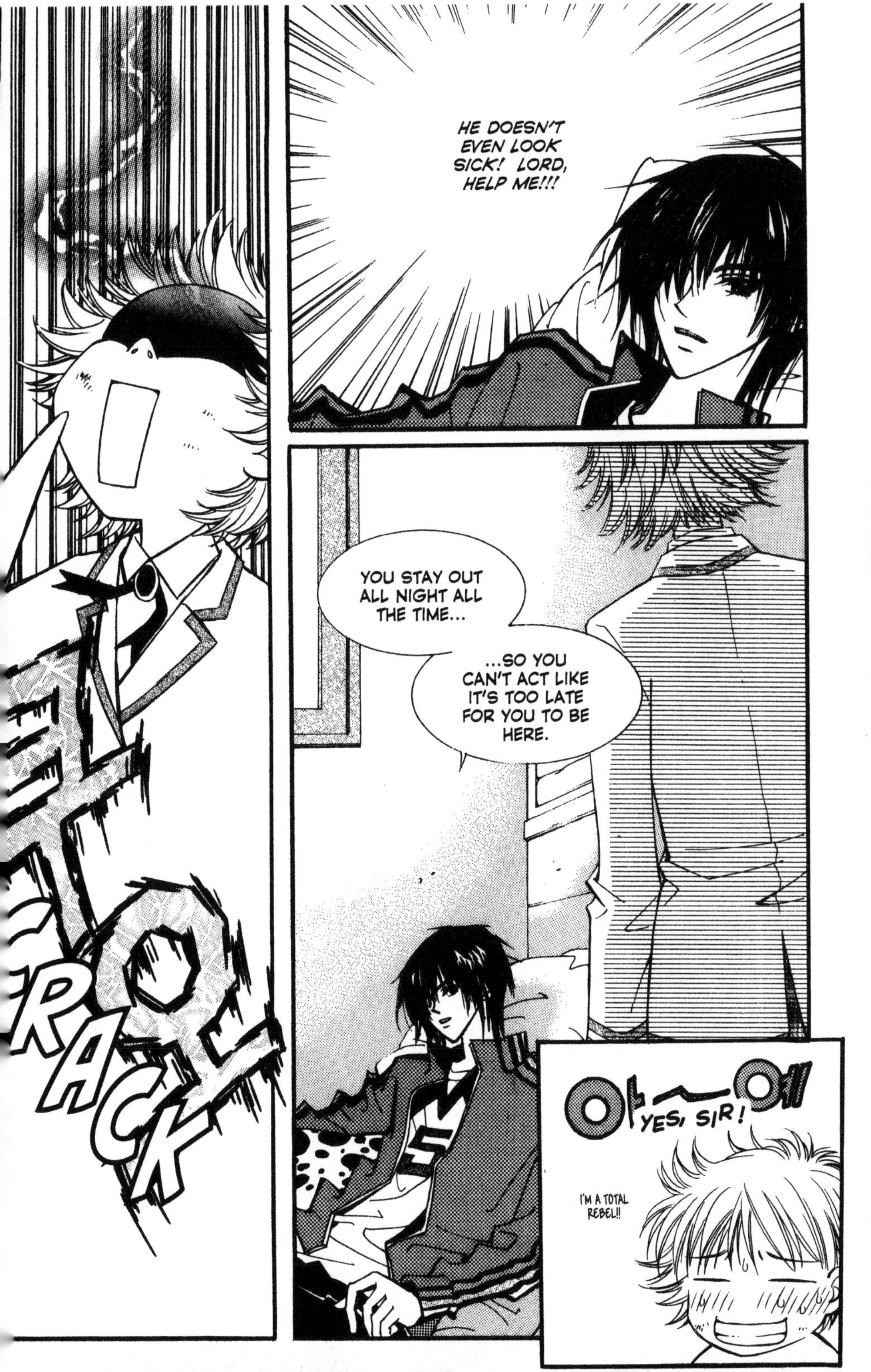
CRACK
HE DOESN'T EVEN LOOK SICK! LORD, HELP ME!!!
YOU STAY OUT ALL NIGHT ALL THE TIME...
...SO YOU CAN'T ACT LIKE IT'S TOO LATE FOR YOU TO BE HERE.
YES, SIR!
I'M A TOTAL REBEL!!

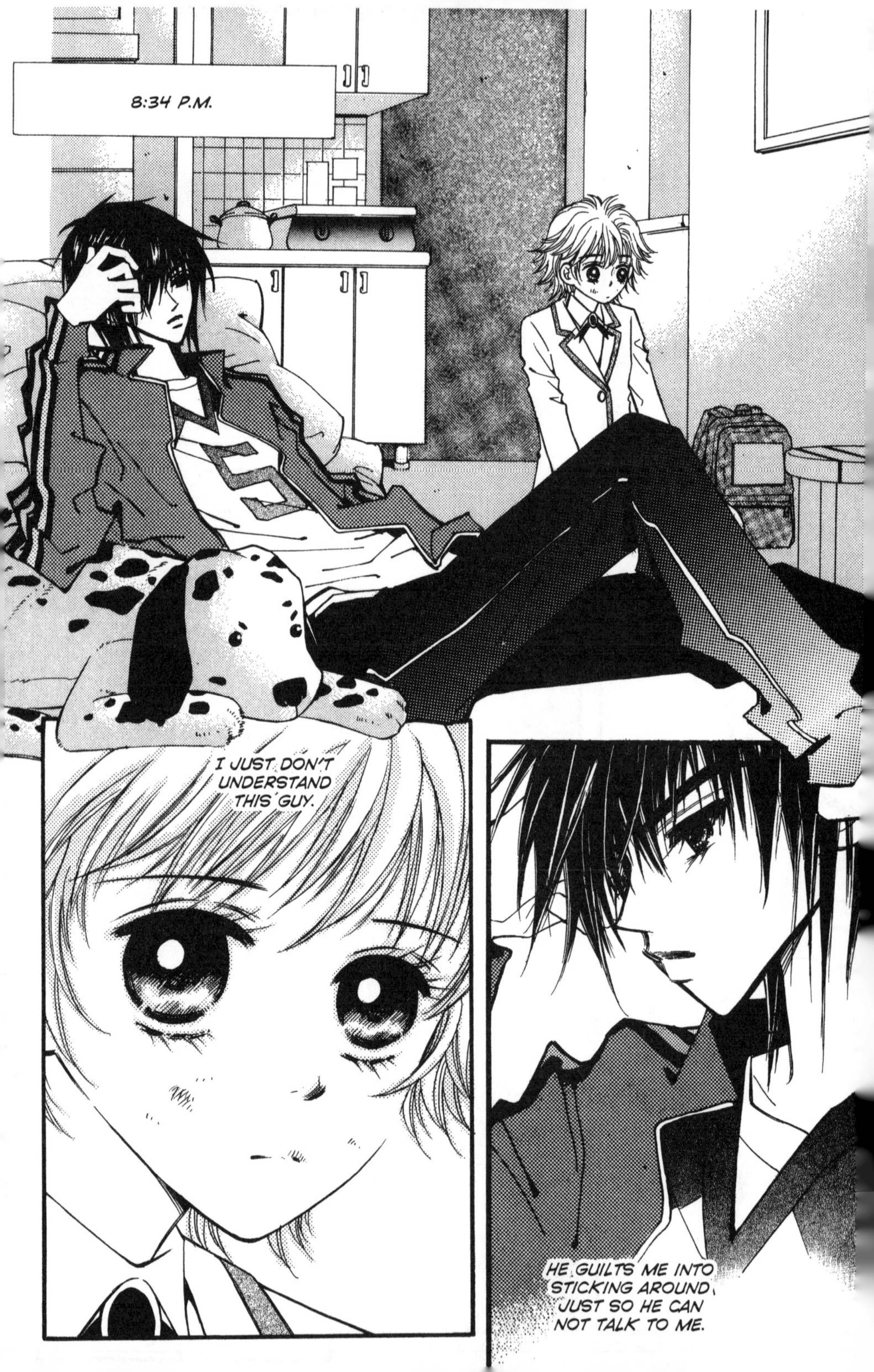
8:34 P.M.
I JUST DON'T UNDERSTAND THIS GUY.
HE GUILTS ME INTO STICKING AROUND JUST SO HE CAN NOT TALK TO ME.

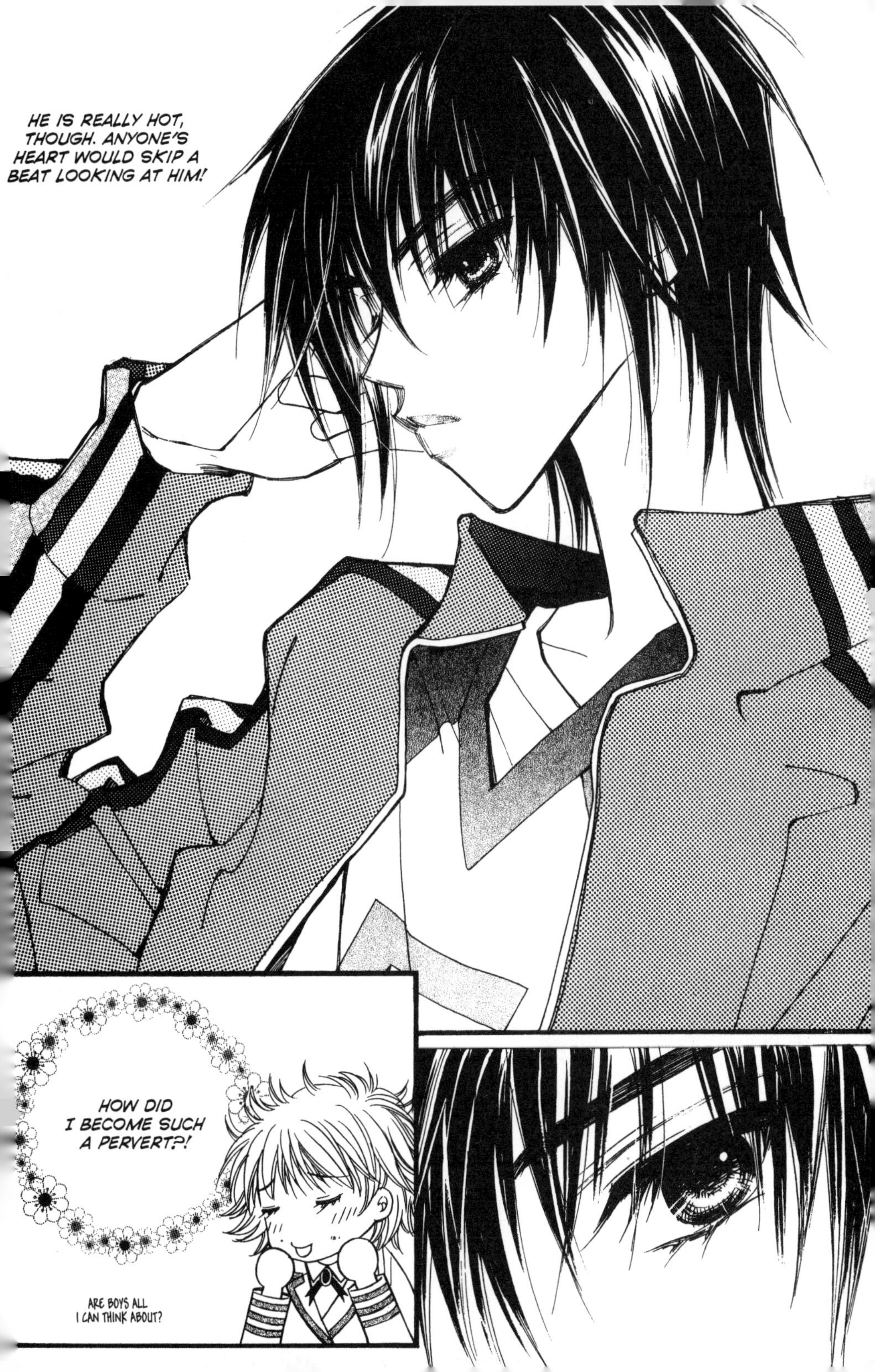
HE IS REALLY HOT, THOUGH. ANYONE'S HEART WOULD SKIP A BEAT LOOKING AT HIM!
HOW DID I BECOME SUCH A PERVERT?!
ARE BOYS ALL I CAN THINK ABOUT?

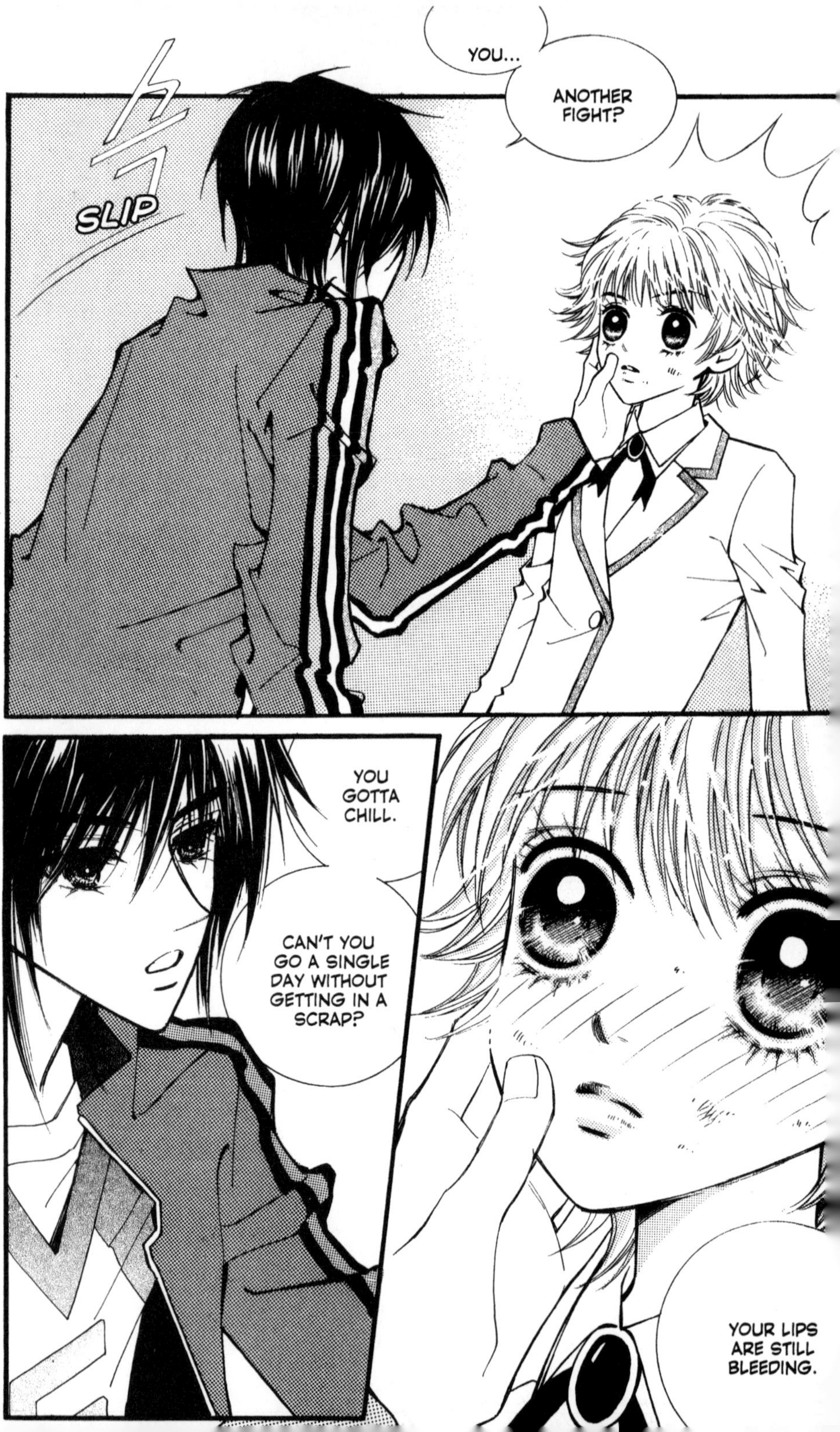

SLIP
YOU...
ANOTHER FIGHT?
YOU GOTTA CHILL.
CAN'T YOU GO A SINGLE DAY WITHOUT GETTING IN A SCRAP?
YOUR LIPS ARE STILL BLEEDING.

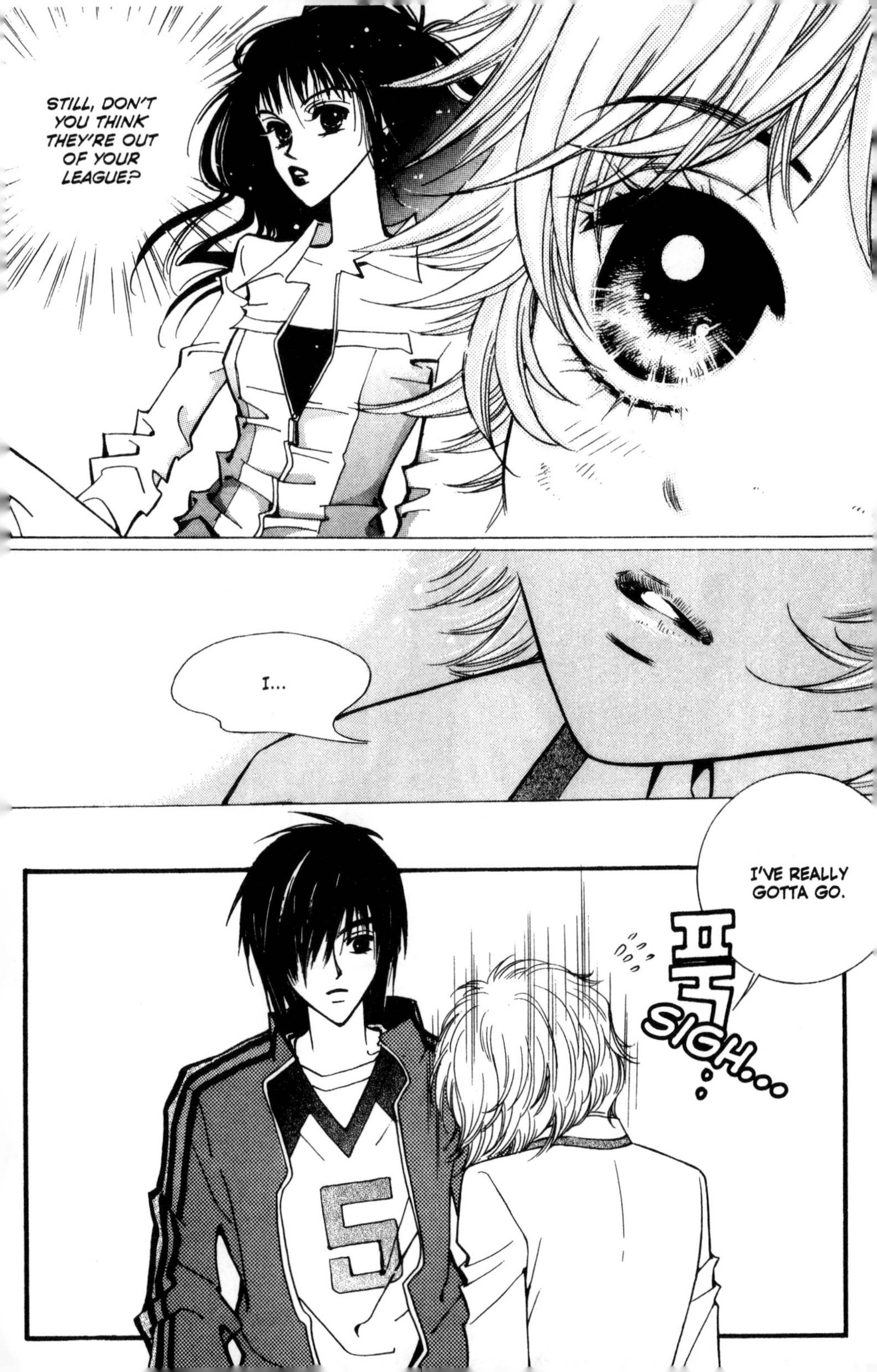
STILL, DON'T YOU THINK THEY'RE OUT OF YOUR LEAGUE?
I...
I'VE REALLY GOTTA GO.
하
SIGH...

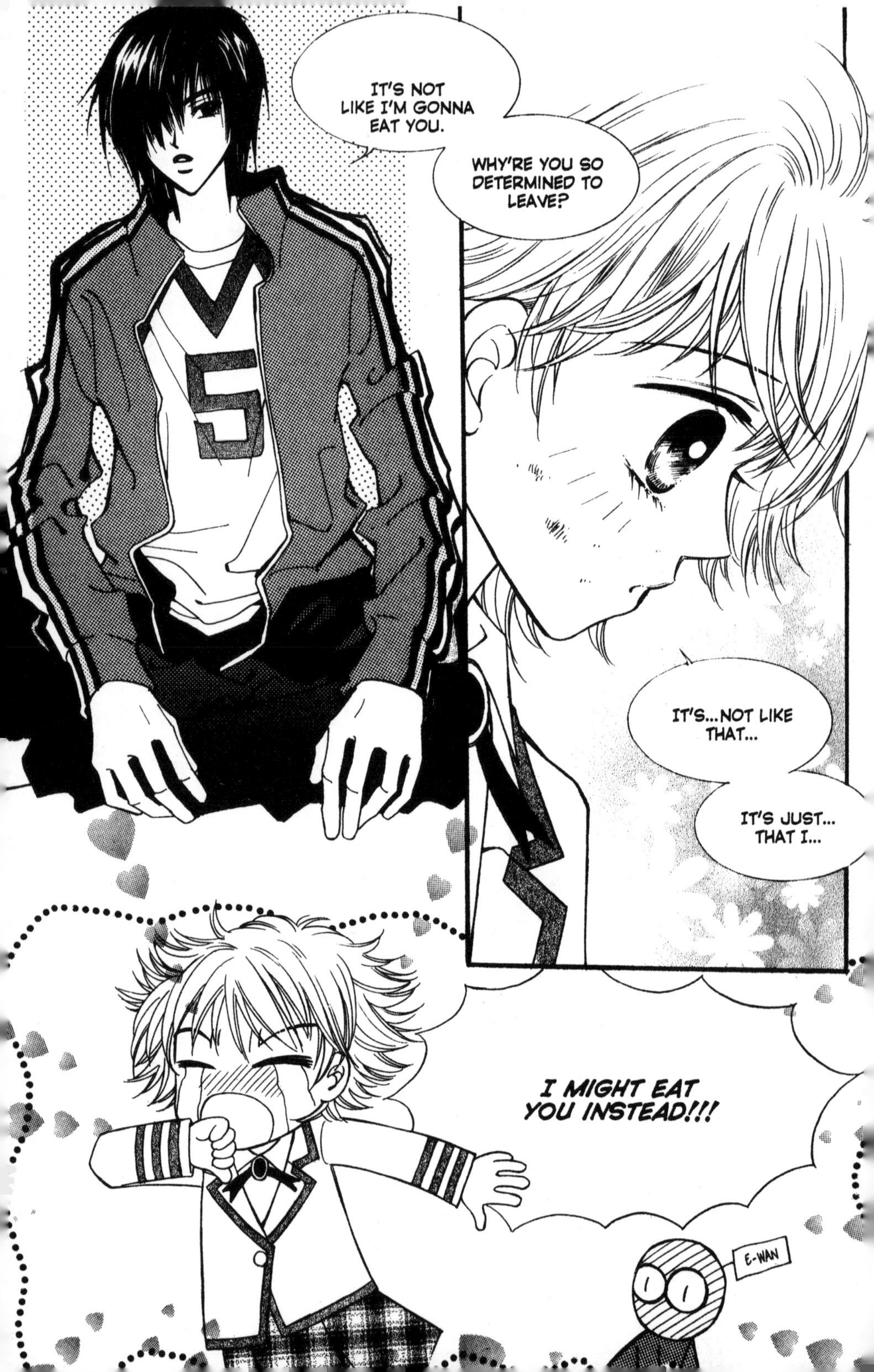
IT'S NOT LIKE I'M GONNA EAT YOU.
WHY'RE YOU SO DETERMINED TO LEAVE?
IT'S...NOT LIKE THAT...
IT'S JUST... THAT I...
I MIGHT EAT YOU INSTEAD!!!
E-WAN

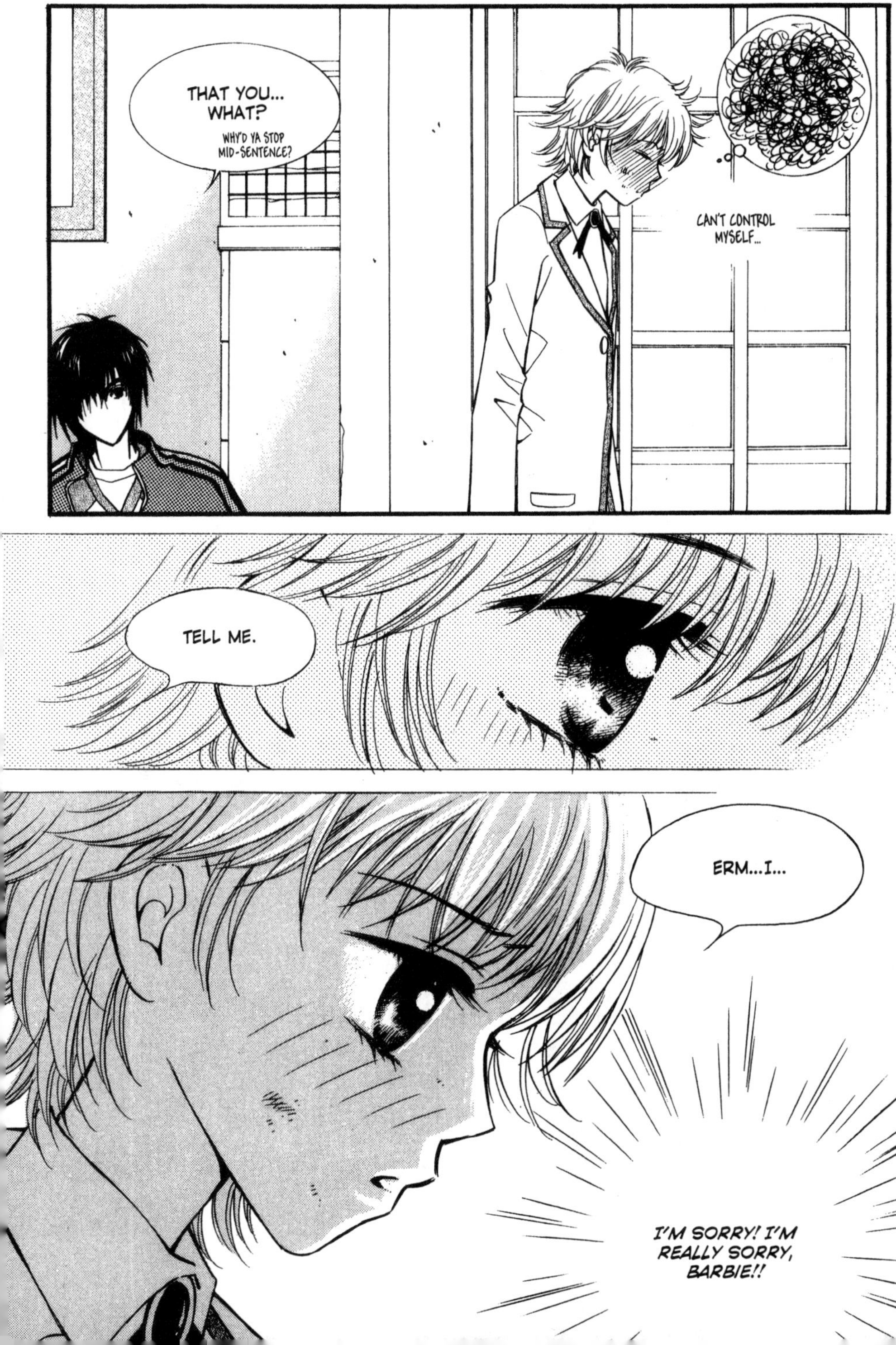

THAT YOU... WHAT?
WHY'D YA STOP MID-SENTENCE?
CAN'T CONTROL MYSELF...
TELL ME.
ERM...I...
I'M SORRY! I'M REALLY SORRY, BARBIE!!

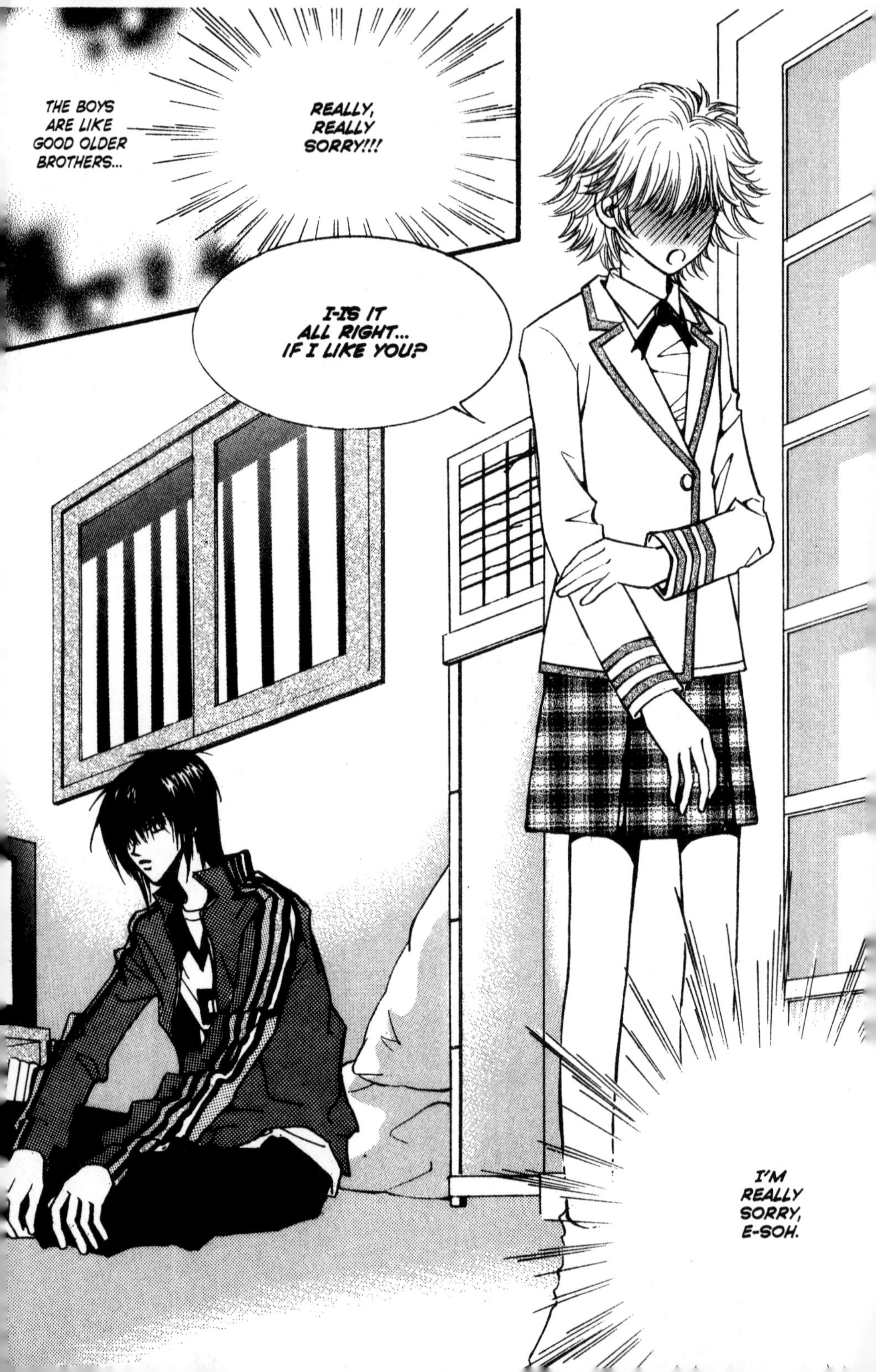
THE BOYS ARE LIKE GOOD OLDER BROTHERS...
REALLY, REALLY SORRY!!!
I-IS IT ALL RIGHT... IF I LIKE YOU?
I'M REALLY SORRY, E-SOH.

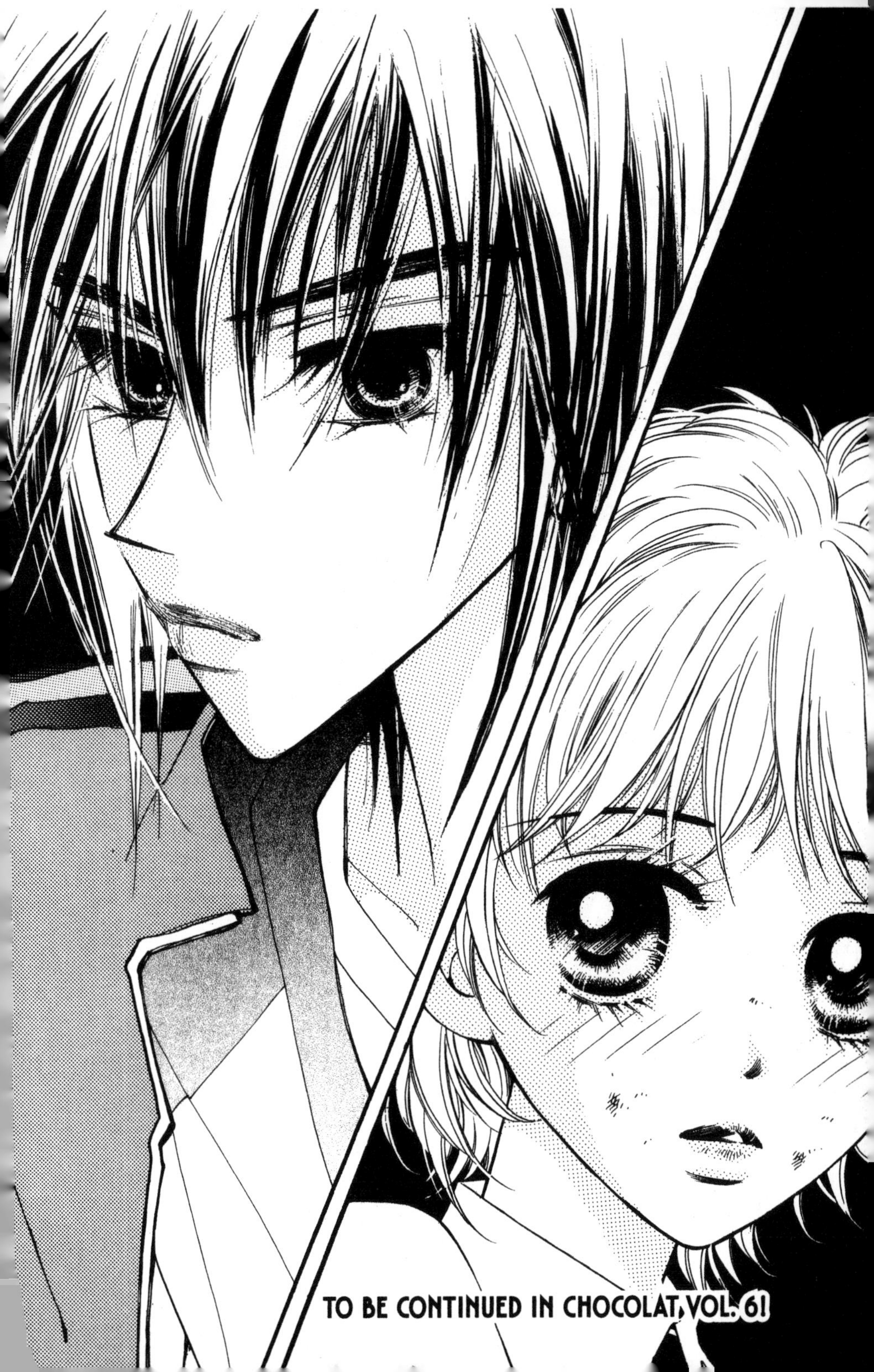
TO BE CONTINUED IN CHOCOLAT, VOL. 6!

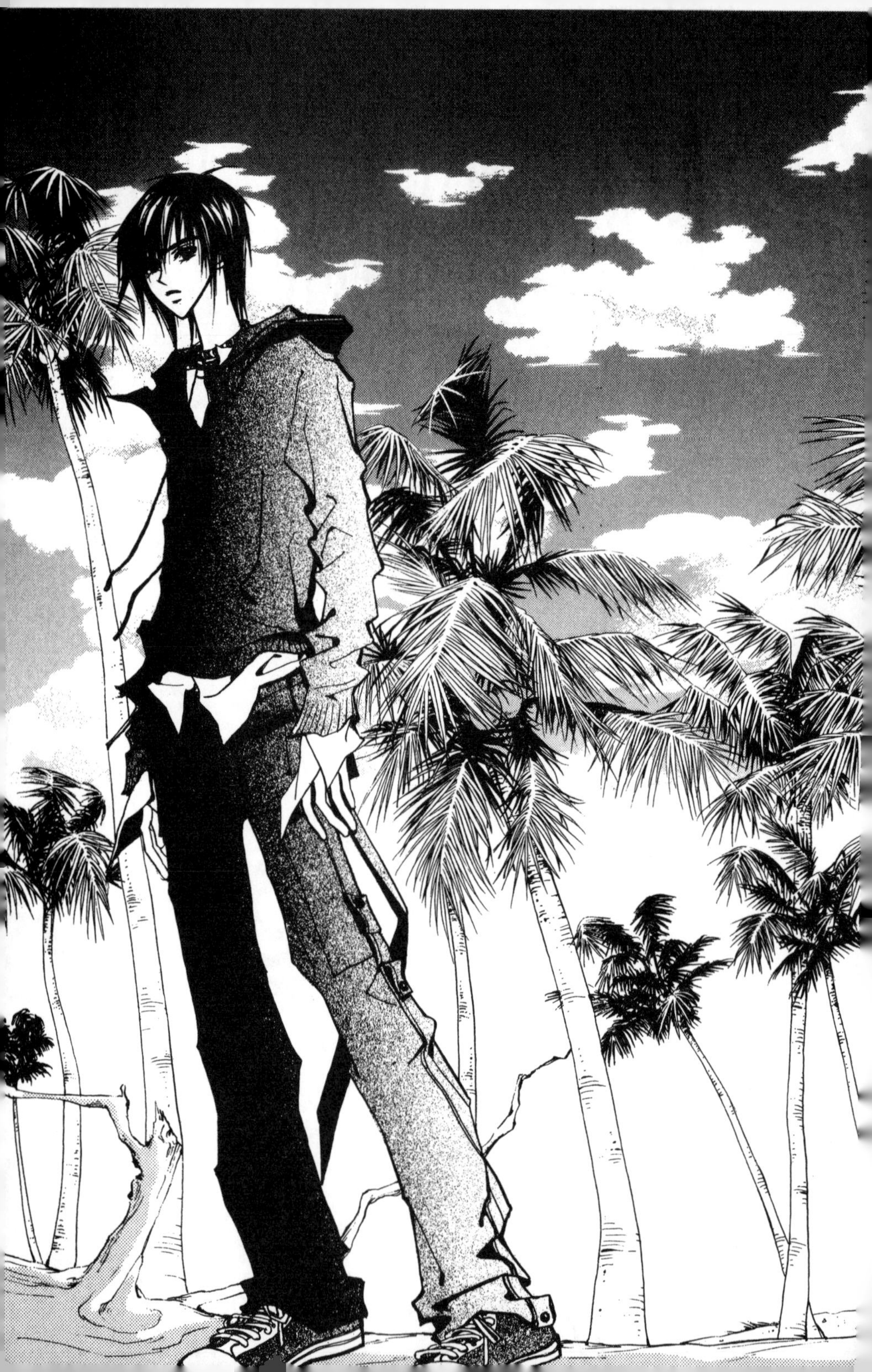

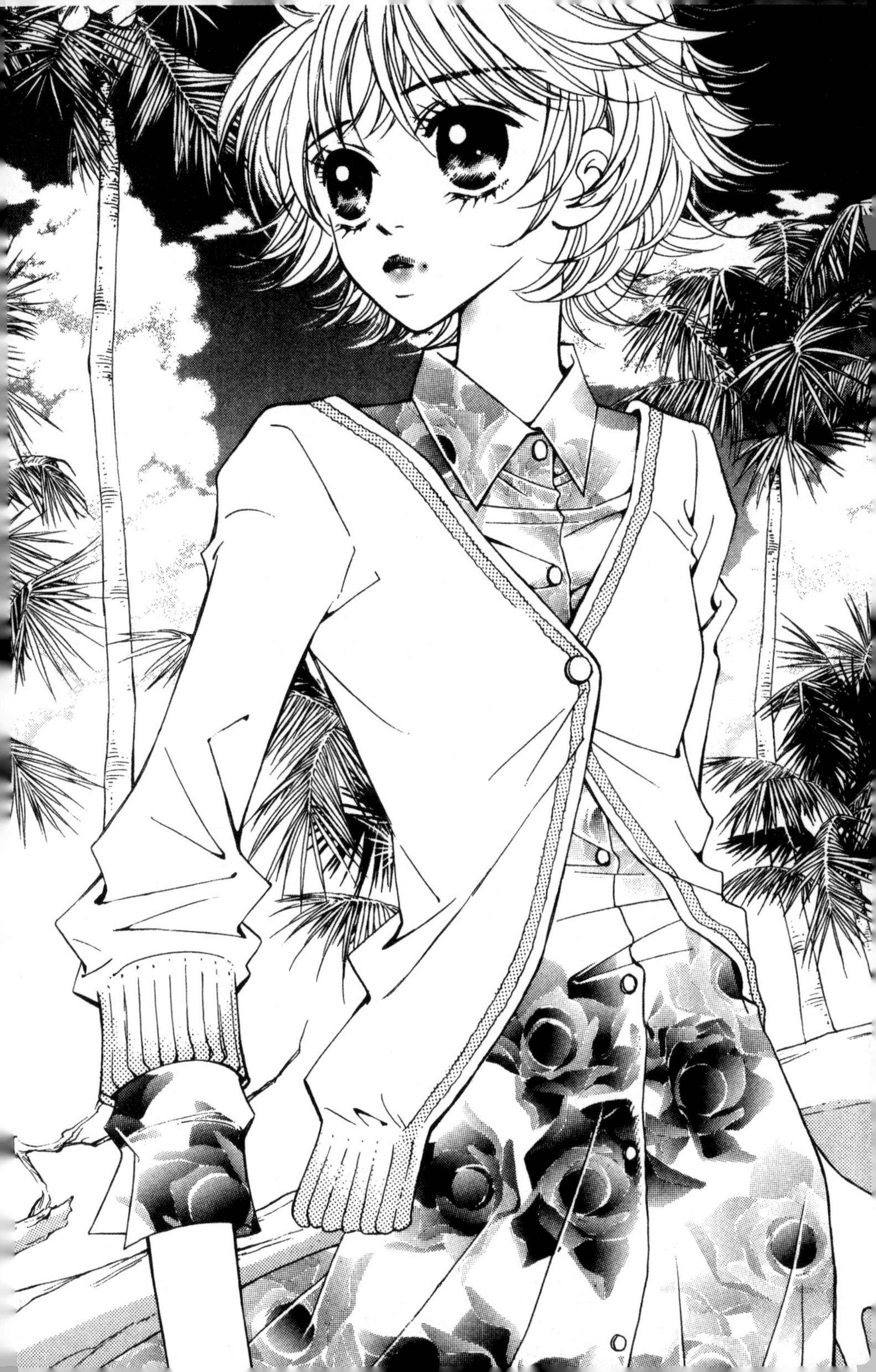

Chocolat vol. 5

Story and art by JiSang Shin · Geo

Translation: Jackie Oh
English Adaptation: Jamie S. Rich
Lettering: Terri Delgado · Marshall Dillon

Yen Press
Hachette Book Group USA
237 Park Avenue, New York, NY 10017

Visit our Web sites at www.HachetteBookGroupUSA.com and www.YenPress.com.

Yen Press is an imprint of Hachette Book Group USA, Inc. The Yen Press name and logo are trademarks of Hachette Book Group USA, Inc.

First Yen Press Edition: June 2008

ISBN-10: 0-7595-2907-8
ISBN-13: 978-0-7595-2907-6

10 9 8 7 6 5 4 3 2 1

BVG

Printed in the United States of America